"When Israel Nwachukwu first shared the vision of this book with me several years ago, I knew the Holy Spirit was about to do something extraordinary through him. What you now hold in your hands is not merely another theology book—it is a burning love letter from the heart of God to the heart of man. Brother Israel writes with the fire of a prophet, the precision of a theologian, and the tenderness of a son who has been overwhelmed by the love of the Father. In an age where the Gospel is often reduced to formulas and programs, this work boldly returns us to the blazing center: God's eternal romance with humanity—a romance that cost him everything on the cross of Calvary. I have watched this young man grow from a passionate university student into one of the most gifted biblical communicators of his generation. I have seen him weep over souls, fast for days seeking God's face, and labor over every sentence of this manuscript as an act of worship. The result is a masterpiece that will ignite fresh love for Jesus in every reader—scholar and layperson alike. May the same Spirit that moved over the face of the waters move afresh over every heart that reads these pages. May the Redeemer-King who left heaven to pursue you capture you anew. And may you, like the author, never recover from the wonder that the God of the universe is irrevocably, passionately, and eternally in love with you. To God alone be the glory!"

—PRINCE KINGSLEY UGBODU, Pastor, Kings Church Swansea, United Kingdom

"It is with profound joy and deep spiritual conviction that I wholeheartedly endorse the book *Redemptive Love Story* written by my long-time friend and brother in Christ, Pastor Israel E. Nwanchukwu. Pastor Israel is not only a seasoned minister of the Gospel but also a thoughtful theologian with a burning passion for unveiling the depth of God's love to humanity. Over the years, we have shared moments of spiritual discourse, scriptural engagement, and kingdom-driven reflections. I have personally witnessed his hunger for truth and his commitment to sound biblical doctrine. In this powerful piece, Pastor Israel masterfully unveils the eternal love narrative between God and man—revealing redemption not merely as a theological concept, but as a divine romance initiated by God himself. The book carefully explores the sacrificial dimensions of God's love, the mystery of grace, and the believer's responsive intimacy with Christ. This work is both doctrinally rich and spiritually refreshing. It does not only inform the mind but ignites the heart. It presents redemption as the ultimate expression of divine love—echoing the truth of Scripture that 'God so loved the world . . .' (John 3:16). Readers will discover afresh that salvation is more than deliverance from sin; it is an invitation into covenant love with the Father. I strongly recommend this book to pastors, leaders, students of theology, and every believer who desires to deepen their understanding of the love of God and its transforming power. This book will bless you, stir your devotion, and strengthen your walk with God."

—Ejobomhensele Odia Samson, Resident Pastor, Living Faith Church Worldwide, Nigeria

“I was granted the glorious privilege of reading my spiritual father and pastor’s book, *The Redemptive Love Story* by Israel E. Nwachukwu. And as I read, I beheld the unmistakable leading of the Holy Spirit in every line and every truth set forth throughout its pages. Having personally enjoyed the privilege of journeying for many years in close fellowship with Pastor Israel—praying together, searching the Scriptures together—I have seen the redemptive love of God poured out in his life and ministry. As a minister of the gospel under his spiritual mentorship, I testify that the depth of insight, the unction, and the anointing upon this work are the fruit of prolonged prayer, fasting, life experience, and abiding communion with the Spirit of truth. The Bible says that ‘With God all things are possible,’ and it is clear that his enabling grace has made this work possible. This book carries the unmistakable inspiration and understanding that comes from the Holy One: ‘But ye have an unction from the Holy One, and ye know all things’ (1 John 2:20). It will bring profound enlightenment to the soul and open the reader’s eyes to the immeasurable depth of God’s love for all people. Thank you, Pastor Israel, for shining as a faithful light for Jesus in this generation, imparting divine understanding that redounds to the glory of God. To all who will read this book, I declare that enlightenment awaits on every page. *The Redemptive Love Story* ranks as one of the most profoundly enlightening books I have ever read—second only to the Holy Bible itself. Love is the greatest, and Jesus is the only way to God.”

—Sister Lisa Pamela, A woman of God and Minister of the Gospel

"Having spent years in pastoral ministry studying, teaching, and preaching on the subject of God's love and redemption, I do not make commendations lightly. However, after carefully reading *The Redemptive Love Story*, I can confidently say that this is one of the most profound and illuminating expositions on the love story between God and his Son—and by extension, humanity—that I have ever encountered. Written by my long-time friend and brother in Christ, Pastor Israel E. Nwanchukwu, this book is a remarkable theological and spiritual work. Pastor Israel is not only a seasoned minister of the Gospel but a passionate revealer of divine truth. His insight into Scripture and his ability to present deep spiritual realities in a clear and compelling manner are evident throughout this book. *The Redemptive Love Story* unveils the grand narrative of redemption as a divine-human romance initiated by God himself. With theological depth and spiritual sensitivity, Pastor Israel articulates the eternal counsel of God, the sacrificial love revealed through Christ, and the intimate fellowship God desires with humanity. This work goes beyond intellectual theology; it invites the reader into an experiential understanding of divine love. In my years of pastoring and engaging with numerous theological writings on redemption and the love of God, few have captured the beauty, intentionality, and covenantal nature of this love as profoundly as this book. It is both doctrinally sound and spiritually enriching. It speaks to the scholar and the everyday believer alike. I strongly and without reservation recommend this book for publication and wide circulation. I am persuaded that it will deepen the faith of believers, inspire ministers, and draw many into a richer understanding of the redemptive love of God."

—Fredrick Obaroghedo, Pastor, Frederick Osasere Ministries

The Redemptive Love Story

The Redemptive Love Story

The Theology of Love: Divine-Human Romance

ISRAEL E. NWACHUKWU

RESOURCE *Publications* • Eugene, Oregon

THE REDEMPTIVE LOVE STORY
The Theology of Love: Divine-Human Romance

Resource Publications
An Imprint of Wipf and Stock Publishers
199 W. 8th Ave., Suite 3
Eugene, OR 97401

www.wipfandstock.com

PAPERBACK ISBN: 979-8-3852-6944-0
HARDCOVER ISBN: 979-8-3852-6945-7
EBOOK ISBN: 979-8-3852-6946-4

VERSION NUMBER 03/12/26

To the Triune God—Father, Son, and Holy Spirit—the Beginning and the End of this eternal love story, to whom alone belong all glory, honor, and praise, now and forevermore. I am all that I have become because you love me.

And in loving memory of my beloved mother, Mrs. Augustina Nwachukwu (1962–2012).

Thank you for raising me in the way I should go, and now that I am grown, by God's grace and mercy, I have not departed from the Way—though I wandered for a season after gaining the independence of adulthood, yet His amazing grace brought me back to the Shepherd and Overseer of my soul.

You sacrificed everything so I could attend the finest private schools in town.

You gave me far more than education—you gave me wings, faith, and an unshakeable conviction that the love of God is the greatest story ever told.

This book is the fruit of your prayers, your tears, and your boundless love.

I know you are smiling from heaven. Sleep on in peace, sweet Mum, until we meet again at Jesus' feet.

Your son,

Israel

Contents

Preface

THIS BOOK FIRST STIRRED within the secret chambers of my heart many years ago as a gentle, insistent whisper: "*Tell them how much I love them.*" What commenced as solitary, intimate devotional reflections—quiet communions with the Spirit of Truth—soon swelled into an irrepressible deluge, a fervent, uncontainable passion to proclaim from the rooftops of life what the Cross has been thundering into my soul with unrelenting clarity: the most resounding and extravagantly costly love letter ever penned by the Almighty to the sons and daughters of Adam.

The Redemptive Love Story represents my humble, reverent endeavor to trace that resplendent golden thread of divine romance—an eternal filament of pursuing affection—that weaves its luminous path from the primordial whispers of Genesis to the triumphant crescendo of Revelation. It lays no claim to the rigor of systematic theology, nor to the exhaustive scope of biblical commentary, nor to the erudition of academic dissertation (though it drinks deeply from the wells of each). Rather, it unfolds as a heartfelt love song—an extended, ardent hymn of adoration and wonder composed by the God whose love proved fiercer than our rebellion, whose grasp remained unyielding when we wandered farthest astray.

Should even a single soul, through the grace-laden medium of these pages, awaken afresh to the unfathomable height and depth, the immeasurable length and breadth of Christ's all-surpassing love—should one heart be ravished anew by the relentless tenderness of the Divine Lover—then every vigil of sleepless nights, every tear shed in intercession, every whispered prayer ascending like incense will have been infinitely recompensed, crowned with eternal purpose.

To Him who sits enthroned in everlasting majesty, and to the Lamb who was slain yet lives forever, and to the Holy Spirit, my gracious and infallible Teacher of Truth—be ascribed all blessing and honor, all glory and dominion, throughout the endless ages of eternity. Amen and amen.

Israel E. Nwachukwu
November 2025

Acknowledgments

In truth, no book is ever truly written in isolation. I stand on the shoulders of giants and, above all, on the faithful prayers of the saints. First and foremost, to my Lord and Savior Jesus Christ: You pursued me when I was unlovely, rescued me when I was lost, and called me when I was utterly unworthy. This book belongs to You alone. To my late mother, Mrs. Augustina Nwachukwu: You believed in me when I could not believe in myself. Your tireless investment in my life is the reason I can read, write, and dream today. I miss you deeply every day. To my father, Mr. Nicholas Nwachukwu: Thank you for your ceaseless encouragement, your steadfast prayers, and your unshakeable confidence in this work. Your quiet strength speaks volumes. To Pastor Prince Kingsley Ugbodu—my surrogate spiritual father in the faith (Kings Church Swansea, UK): You saw potential in a confused young man years ago and have never ceased speaking life over me. Thank you for your spiritual covering and the wisdom you have poured into my life. To Sister Yvette Bissong (UK): You prayed, corrected, believed, and refused to let me settle for anything less than excellence. This book carries the imprint of your relentless encouragement. To Sister Lisa Pamela—my spiritual daughter and mentee (US): Your hunger for God, your honest feedback, and your countless all-night prayer vigils helped bring this work to birth. Thank you for walking this path with me. To my siblings—Ken, Victoria, Mercy, Christian, George, and Blessing Nwachukwu—who stood with me through every storm, to my extended family, and to the entire Israel His Glory Ministry family: Thank you for your love, your support, and your steadfastness. Finally, to every preacher, teacher, and author whose writings have shaped my thinking (many of whom appear in the bibliography): Thank you for kindling torches that guided me through the darkness. Soli Deo Gloria.

Abbreviations General and Bibliographic

AMP	Amplified Translation
AMPC	Amplified Classic Translation
AT	Author's translation
BCE	Before the Common Era
CE	Common Era
Cf.	Compare; compare to, compare with
chap(s).	chapter(s)
DMO	Divine Mission Objective
EE	Emmanuel Effect
ESV	English Standard Version
GW	God's Word Translation
KJV	King James Version
MO	Modus operandi
NASB	New American Standard Bible
NCBC	New Century Bible Commentary
NETS	A New English Translation of the Septuagint. Edited by Albert Pietersma
NHEB	New Heart English Bible
NIV	New International Version
NKJV	New King James Version

NLT	New Living Translation
NRSV	New Revised Standard Version
NT	New Testament
RE	Resurrection Effect
RSV	Revised Standard Version
TLB	The Living Bible
TPT	The Passion Translation

Introductory Essay

LET ME TELL YOU a redemptive love story, one that will help paint you a narrative picture of the prehistoric, long-drawn-out journey that eventually led up to the redemption of the lost souls of all mankind, forever forging an unbreakable bond of unspeakable love between the Creator and the created. Through this sacred fabula, kindled in the ancient flames of eternity's heart, the Creator-God, with boundless benevolence and ceaseless compassion, ordains a path from creation's genesis to consummation's crown—orchestrating a redemption that transcends time, securing the perpetuity of human existence, and breathing the divine spark of spiritual rebirth. Redemption's road, rugged yet radiant, protologically runs its course from the very first page of the Old Testament (OT) and eschatologically leads all the way down to the very last page of the New Testament (NT) of the Holy Bible—it chronologically spans from timeless history and spills into time—further stretching across times and seasons within redemptive history. Drawing upon both faith and reason, the story presents God's purposeful design for redemption. Each step along the way—from the earliest moments to the final restoration—reflects a loving design to lift humanity from the pits of moral fallenness and existential brokenness, offering a brand-new start tied to an everlasting future, all grounded in the age-enduring reality of God's infinite goodness. I speak of an extraordinary Biblical story that is so riveting it is guaranteed to pique your theological interest, so breathtakingly inspirational it promises to arouse your intellectual curiosity, and so spiritually enlivening it is bound to change your life for the better, even venturing so far as to foster the transformation of your entire human experience into something much more meaningful, purposeful, and gloriously beautiful. And guess what, the divine novelty of the whole story makes it just about sound like a sacred *billet-doux*—a sacred love letter—dittoed *ex animo*—straight-out from the heart of God, personally addressed to each human person ever born. For so universal and all-embracing is the scope of this story, it literally has everything to do with you and me—something so profoundly consequential to say to just about every one of us. After all, God's favorite story is the human story—all about humanity from start to finish—all centered about his ineffable love for these unique creatures of his image and likeness. The Gospel of Christ demands that we ultimately see the Bible as a veriloquent lovelore about the Creator and the creatures of his love and no less.

The greatest story ever told is not a tale spun from the limited imagination of human minds nor committed to writing by the faltering pen of mortal hands; it is the true story of humanity itself, authored by the God whose Word became flesh and dwelt among us—enacted in the theatre of time by God the Son, as sovereignly scripted from eternity by God the Father, and then infallibly recorded in sacred history by God the Holy Spirit, so that through its reading we might believe, and in believing, have life in His name. This is the divine narrative in which the Triune God himself is both Author and Actor, weaving the destiny of mankind into the very life, death, and resurrection of the eternal Word made flesh. There are some stories that write themselves—some stories that essentially tell their own tale. The redemptive love story is one of such rare stories—the story of God's love for man is one that has historically written itself, so much so that we cannot pretend to do any more narrative justice to this specific story than it has already done plotting, setting, and enacting its own tale through the ages—etched in the sands of time across a span of 4 kiloyears and then unfolding so perfectly throughout the pages of the Bible for well across a period of 1500 years that its inherent beauty and grace almost immediately render any attempt at retelling inadequate. To claim otherwise would be tantamount to the presumption that we could somehow manage to tell the story of God's love for man any better than God himself has done, exhausting a monumental mosaic of 66 books apiece, weaving a resounding tale of devotion that echoes through the ages. And as we trace the storied progression of the revelation of his love—stretching from the original human, Adam, to its triumphant height in Jesus, the Second Adam—we move from the peaceful, lush garden of Eden to the shadowy, anguished olive trees of Gethsemane. This path reminds us of the exacting care in the wise men's long, determined trip, guided by the bright shine of the Star of Bethlehem as they crossed endless, silent night deserts to reach the plain manger where

God made his stunning arrival on earth. More like the steadfast watch of ancient stargazers charting a comet's fiery trail across the midnight skies—heralding wonders yet to unfold—glad tidings yet untold, their journey uncovers one layer after another of deliberate purpose, revealing the smooth, connected rhythm of God's farsighted plan unfolding over all of history.

In this sacred discourse, we do not stop at surface-level talk on God's love; we press onward, venturing past the usual doctrinal talking points on the subject—plunging instead beyond the shallow streams of familiar theological discourse to unearth the ineffable depths of his love for man. Like mists dispersing before dawn, we demystify the primordial mysteries that have long veiled this sacred divine-human romance, akin to the Bridegroom's whisper piercing the veil of night. Hence, peeling back the veil of mystery, this story of redemption showcases the pulsating heart of the Creator's agape love for his fondest creatures, that all may behold, comprehend, and wholeheartedly embrace. In this moment of revelation, with unveiled faces, we perceive the Creator-God as the master planner of redemption—not as a spur-of-the-moment remedy, but as creation's ultimate destiny, where his foresight anticipates our fall and weaves grace into the very fabric of our existence. With a heart aflame with the unquenchable desire to see the creatures of his image and likeness redeemed from sin, restored to glory, and reconciled to fellowship, Creator-God has taken a series of historically unprecedented steps that most convincingly demonstrate his love and commitment to mankind. This is a love so primordial and all-encompassing that it birthed the stars, sculpted the mountains, and whispered immortal life into the vessels of mortal clay in humanity's protoancestors, now distilled into the singular, world-shattering act of the Son of God stepping from eternity's throne into the squalor of a Bethlehem stable, his divine mission not conquest or correction alone, but an extravagant outpouring of affection that propelled him through parables of mercy, miracles of restoration, and the agonizing crescendo of Calvary's Cross, where nails and thorns were forged into a quill pen, his blood flowing as the ink to pen heaven's love letter to a lost and wayward world. And so what this book endeavors to do for the most part is to exegetically identify, illuminate, and magnify those awe-inspiring, never-before-seen gestures as the substance as well as the summit of this unique story of divine romance. Come on, let us face it, calling balls and strikes: if the story of redemption were simply limited to the text of Scripture alone, without tangible historical acts substantiating it, it would simply be reduced to an empty tale, lacking any transformative power and devoid of any real-world impact. And when you think even more deeply about it, words alone, without corresponding actions, are bound to remain abstract and totally detached from reality, unable to bridge the gaping chasm between prophecy and fulfillment—theory and practice—ideas and experience—revelation and reality—orthodoxy and orthopraxis. Likewise, the words of Scripture, standing alone on their own, no matter how theopneustic and authoritative they might be, cannot bear on their shoulders the weight of God's redemptive promises.

Consequently, the story of God's redeeming love for man requires the flesh-and-blood reality of events such as the life, death, and resurrection of Christ to bring it to life—enacting its core meaning. In quite colloquial terms, God needed to have his skin in the game, and this is precisely what we see him do to ensure humanity's eternal salvation. For the power and efficacy of Biblical redemption lie not in its inspired narrative alone, but in its divine realization through God's intervention in human history: manifest in miracles that transcend the limits of nature, in covenants that irrevocably bind his promises to humanity, and ultimately, the Incarnation, where God embraced man's humanity in the personhood of Jesus the Christ—as the term *Heilsgeschichte* implies. The Incarnation, therefore, is not merely a theological claim but a historical event that literally demonstrates God's relentless commitment to humanity's restoration. The same goes with the resurrection of Christ and the empty tomb, none of which is merely symbolic or figurative but defining historical events that validate the hope of eternal life. Hence, with resounding clarity, we can now understand why the Apostle Paul would quickly arrive at the conclusion that "*But if there is no resurrection of the dead, then Christ is not risen. And if Christ is not risen, then our preaching is empty and your faith is also empty*" (I Corinthians 15:13–14 NKJV). These real-life events—witnessed, recorded, heralded, and debated through history—transformed the letters of the Bible into living testaments and turned the message of the Gospel into redemptive reality. Thereby demonstrating that God's words of prophecy and promise in the Scriptures have indeed been backed by his works—the work of redemption—and have not been left to suffer the fate of the lifeless ink of a quill pen left dried upon the dust-ridden pages of a scribe's scroll. Ensuring that redemption is not just some forlorn hope but a tangible truth already enacted within spatiotemporal reality. But without these redemptive acts, the Bible, give or take, would be no more than a collection of lofty religious ideas, abstract moral ideals, and perhaps a book of empty promises and unfulfilled prophecies, and not a record of divine intervention in human affairs. Besides them, the fatiloquent claims of Scripture would end up ringing hollow, like a script without actors to bring it to life—like a blueprint never built—like a song never sung. In effect, this interplay of words and works—promises made and promises kept—ensures that the story of redemption is not only heard but transformatively felt, offering a foundation for faith that rests firmly on what God has done to prove his love for mankind, not just what he had said or the promises he had made, anchoring hope in reality.

None of this was lost on the Son of God himself, as he too recognized the need to appeal to his works and not just his words as the basis and most compelling impetus for faith, saying to his audience on several occasions, "*If I do not do the works of My Father, do not believe Me; but if I do, though you do not believe Me, believe the works, that you may know and believe that the Father is in Me, and I in Him*" (John 10:37–38 NKJV) —and again—"*Believe Me that I am in the Father and the Father in Me, or else believe Me for the sake of the works themselves*" (John 14:11 NKJV). In the person of Christ, therefore, God's redemptive promises and their eschatological fulfillment eventually unite in holy matrimony—in him, divine revelation and cosmic reality finally embrace each other with a sacred kiss. For Christ came walking in the steps of prophetic fulfillment—fulfilling a conservative estimate of about 200 Messianic prophecies of Scripture all pertaining to man's redemption—demonstrating God's love and unwavering devotion toward mankind in just about every one of those prophecies written concerning him and the redemptive work he was here to accomplish for mankind. Which further led him to say to his epigones right after his resurrection—at the completion of his redemptive mission: "*These are the words which I spoke to you while I was still with you, that all things must be fulfilled which were written in the Law of Moses and the Prophets and the Psalms concerning Me . . . Thus it is written, and thus it was necessary for the Christ to suffer and to rise from the dead the third day*" (Luke 24:44, 46 NKJV). Clearly, the crux of the Gospel is not anchored on the fact that '*it is written,*' but that all that '*were written*' about the Messiah has been historically accomplished. In other words, the soteriological significance of the Christian message stands firm on the historical fact that the God-Messiah actually came, he saw, he suffered, he died, he rose, and he conquered all. But if the message of the Gospel had simply stopped at 'it is written' or was written, there could be no glory to it—there would be no good news to herald from the rooftops. It all boiled down to a matter of—no cross, no glory, and no gospel—no crown of thorns, no crown of glory, and no good news. At the Cross was where the glory lay waiting for the Christ, so he had to journey to Calvary to clinch the glory and have the Gospel of his eternal accomplishments preached afterward. And as God would have it, not only did Christ expend 33 years of his life fulfilling prophecies from cradle to the grave—matching the words of Scripture promising man's redemption with his actual works accomplishing redemption from A to Z—he did it so overwhelmingly that his works ended up exceeding anything that the authors of the Four Gospels were able to squeeze into their biographical records taken together. Having done all, ticking all the boxes, and ensuring that no redemptive stone was left unturned—Jesus confidently declared with a note of eternal finality—"*It is finished*" (John 19:30). So all-inclusive and all-conclusive were the works of Jesus that John, his beloved disciple, felt compelled to conclude his Gospel with the following addendum: "*This is the disciple who testifies of these things and wrote these things; and we know that his testimony is true. And there are also many other things that Jesus did, which, if they were written one by one, I suppose that even the world itself could not contain the books that would be written. Amen*" (John 21:24–25 NKJV). The Tetrevangelium, though inspired, yet could not exhaust his deeds, far exceeding anything the authors could possibly have had captured in their collective accounts.

So, for a fact, the Christian God did not just stay back up there—aloof in the heights of heaven, merely paying lip service to his love for us down here on earth—as though saying to each one of us on pen and paper alone: "*Yes, I have loved you with an everlasting love; Therefore with lovingkindness I have drawn you*" (Jer 31:3 NKJV); he instead ventured down here and became like one of us, taking a thousand and one steps in his descent into human history, ultimately to demonstrate what his love actually meant. He did all of this in his incarnate humanity for us to see—laying bare the concrete reality of His love, allowing the evidence to stand openly before us, so that the chips of our faith might fall where they will in response to what we have seen and touched. Love, we often say, is proven when tested. God's love for man was tested to the uttermost in the redemptive work of the Cross and was found to be genuinely palpable and pure. In these historic acts also, we witness God's eternal plan gloriously unfold before our very eyes, transforming our human story into a sacred tapestry woven with his redemptive love. For he came down here not minding the fact that we were all full of sin—tainted with moral filth cap-a-pie, unlike himself, who inherently had an impeccably clean moral *tabula rasa*—with no taint of actual sin. So yes, by all means, the very act of God becoming Man carries in itself an immensurable significance—a mystery of staggering, almost incomprehensible weight. Yet this Incarnation was but the beginning: by pressing still further along the same trajectory of redemptive sacrifice, descending even to die an atoning death on the Cross for the sins of all humanity, God revealed a degree of divine love and devotion without parallel in all eternity—never before witnessed, and never to be witnessed ever again. The historical reality that the Creator-God became Man—thereby demonstrating, once for all time in the course of human history, that He alone is mankind's true and perfect Lover—stands as the single greatest event to have transpired on earth since its very foundation: a wonder surpassing every other wonder since the dawn of creation itself. This ought to make for the greatest tidings ever proclaimed—the greatest news worth sharing, for there could be no news more worthy of being heralded from the rooftops of life than the gospel of God's love for man—there could be no cosmic occurrence more worthy of making the headlines of history than the Creator-God taking the form of his own creatures on cosmic soil. The story of this gospel is quite telling, by far, the most compelling story of Love's redemption ever told, not based on fiction but totally grounded in historical reality, and at the same time, anchored in verifiable facts. That God became man in Jesus Christ is nothing less than a love story inscribed in living flesh and blood: a theodrama enacted upon the stage of human history, one that beckons us, as image-bearers, to embrace the redemption accomplished by the very One who walked among us in our own likeness.

If the Bible had just one message to share with the world, it is above and beyond all else, the good news of *'God's love for man'*, everything else we may come to know about the Creator-God and his expansive work of creation is predicated on the fact that there is just some sort of intrinsic quality unique to man that exclusively makes him the single creature of God's vested interest—the sole object of his Divine love—the sovereign beneficiary of his manifold goodness throughout creation. So here, we narrow down our focus to the heart of the story of redemption—on what really matters, whilst leaving out the peripherals—those inconsequential details. Both exploring and unveiling the overarching significance of the redemptive act called the 'Incarnation'—the eternal weight of so great a sacrifice that purchased eternal redemption for all mankind, relying solely on the Scriptures—sola scriptura. For I reckon that the best we could ever hope to achieve is to allow the Bible speak for itself—resounding with its own Divine clarity—shaping and illuminating every conversation we dare to weave around this gloriously majestic subject. And on that note, it is safe to say that we are on good grounds and have started off on a good foot. As this ultimately allows us to narrow down our focus to what God has done, and not what man had done—viz—all that God has done in the Redemption to remedy all what man had done at the Fall. Also, by shining the spotlight on man's special place in the heart of creation, the Book endeavours to highlight the ultimate significance of our special place in the heart of the Creator-God himself. So may I please use the following chapters of this Volume in bearing out to you the heart of the All-loving God—a heart of Omnibenevolence, by the way, that has only man for its object. Not so often do we hear anyone speak for God, the only One who ceaselessly holds his breath in peace, rarely ever breaking his silence, perhaps because we are all too busy, way too preoccupied with the affairs of our own lives to even begin to grant him any audience whatsoever. Nevertheless, in order to do any literary justice in my noble effort to theologically describe for you all what I see in the heart of God's love, methinks I should first have to resign from my reclining position of intellectual solitude, as I momentarily take a break from my theological posture of prolonged silence, both pronouncing a death-sentence on my dead-silence and a life of relevance on my exurgent voice. Even venturing so far as to break through this atmospheric horizon so dense with the cacophonic dissonance of competing theological voices, whilst arising to the occasion with the promptitude of a ready-writer; one ever so willing to spill the much required ink on the writing tablets of your human hearts, in bearing out to you the truth—the whole truth and nothing but the truth.

And I am talking about the truth pertaining to the cruciform demonstration of God's love for the human race—exactly as enacted in history and inscribed on the cordiform pages of God's heart—the Holy Bible. Speaking to you from my heart is one thing, but speaking to you from the sacred letters of God's heart, that is, the Bible, is yet another thing altogether. For these are not lifeless letters " . . . *written with pen and ink,*" *by human hands, but living epistles inspired "by the Spirit of the living God; not one carved on stone, but in human hearts*" (2 Cor 3:3 TLB). Although I do not particularly claim to possess the literary proficiency of a literati nor the encyclopedic lore of a theologian, I can at least take some comfort in having the prophetic proficiency of a humble messenger of truth—even the teachable heart of an autodidactic theologue, lest I be found guilty of the charge: educated head but empty heart. Perhaps you may have to first consider me for acceptance in your good graces, only enough to lend me your ear of advertency, as I speak to you as no more than a Gospeller of the glorious gospel of God's love—no more than a Messenger of his liberating message of truth—no more than a Steward of the manifold mysteries of his grace. So permit me to speak graciously to you, if I may, from the epicenter of the heart of God's love, from where I can at least momentarily afford the rare privilege of prophetic grandiloquence in describing for you in fine-tooth comb detail all that I see—exactly as I see it all. Perchance, I should waste no further time in casting far away from me all pretenses of poetic breviloquence, as I outrightly admit to you from the onset that you may just have to pardon my prosaic pleniloquence. But because I also understand that time is of the essence, you have my promise that none of yours will be wasted in any pointless stultiloquence, as this entire story will definitely be worth every dime of your time spent poring over the pages of this book of written letters.

Bearing in mind that what we will be recounting here is not just one of those numerous cock-and-bull stories out there, nor is it some sort of old wives fable floating around, and certainly not some mumbo jumbo fairy tale, folklore, or Munchausenism, but the greatest love story ever told—the greatest lovelore ever written, one whose narrative perfectly captures and conveys in riveting detail how the greatest existential human needs in all of human history were most consequentially met by someone of the most august parsonage you could ever imagine. And if by any chance you were to think of this individual as a Divine Panjandrum, you would be no longshot away from the truth. Speak of a larger-than-life figure—this is him. After all, one does not get any more important and dignified a figure than the Supremely Relevant Being himself—the Sublime God. Quite a significant share of the adult population in this day and age, will almost certainly acquiesce to the notion that the epic blockbuster movie '*The Titanic*' is one of the greatest romantic love stories ever told on screenplay, most of us may even go so far as giving it an 'A' rating at the Box Office, even the success of the movie itself does particularly tell the tale of how far it went in capturing the heart of a generation, but wait until you hear told or perhaps retold, the story of God's redemptive love for man—wait until your heart is awakened or perhaps reawakened to the truth about the height, the depth, the length, and the breadth that

God was willing to go and did go with his love for you as an individual, as well as for the rest of the human population in general. For God was readily willing, as it were, to ascend to the highest heights—the empyreal heaven—and deign to the lowest depths—the abysmal hadal—and even go as far as stretching the elastic band of his love for mankind beyond its widest limits—both to the easternmost and the westernmost—even as he sought to judicially enisle the sins of all men "*As far as the east is from the west . . .* " (Ps 103:12 NKJV). There remains an abundance of scriptural evidence to show that man is unrivalled and unchallenged in his place of privileged position and status in the heart and mind of his Maker and that he is, in fact, the sole object of his Divine love and the personality of his sacred affection, a rare privilege that the grace of God exclusively and uniquely affords all mankind—yourself included.

As goes the colloquial expression, man does particularly seem to have a living space of abode in God's head—even a loving place of adoption in the Godhead. So let me be the first to admit here and now that as I stand on the vantage point of this breathtaking towering height—viewing things from atop the epicenter of the heart of God's love—all I had imagined to see is none of what I see, as I was actually hoping to behold the spectacle of a never-ending list of things as they currently exist in the vast universe of things, but lo and behold, I see nothing I had anticipated in God's heart; I see no materiality—no material entities—but all I can see is an object of one in the heart of God's love—nothing else and no one else but 'man'—a human-spiritual entity sitting unrivalled and unchallenged on the throne-seat of God's heart. Much like I had theologically pictured the Most High God himself seated on the throne-seat of the Ark (chest) of the Mosaic Covenant in His Shekinah glory, for a prophetic foretype and foreshadow of his sacred place in *'the ark'* (chest) of the human heart—viz., the archetypical *Sanctum Sanctorum* that is housed within the innermost chamber of the archetypical temple of God—the temple of the human body. Perhaps that has something to do with why we unwittingly ended up naming the thoracic region of the human body that houses the heart—chest. Hence, the succedent narrative represents an expository account of what I see written on the pages of God's cordiform heart, as I began to browse through, page after page—leaf after leaf. And littered across the pages of that Book, or rather the Book of books, is a life-transforming and destiny-altering gospel message, one so sacredly written in the calligraphic letters of God's love, so solemnly handwritten in the red-ink letters of the Savior's blood—eternally flowing like a fountain from the bleeding side of that guiltless Man who was pierced through with the Roman-made spear of man's wickedness—perpetually dripping like raindrops from the limbs of that Suffering Servant who was nailed to the Cross with the human-made spikes of man's heartlessness.

So you had better believe it when I say to you that this is very unlike any story that could ever be told by a raconteur—way beyond any yarn that could ever be spun by a yarn-spinner, it is therefore nothing like any bombshell story you ever heard, nothing like any blockbuster movie you ever saw, and certainly nothing like any bestseller novel you ever read. Moreover, this is not just me telling the story per se, because God already did by himself in the prophetic Scriptures, through redemptive history, as he went to great lengths in painting the most vividly compelling Cruciform Portrait of his love for man, not merely using words or letters but demonstrable acts—redemptive acts that I prefer to dub the Most Graphic Demonstration of Love ever witnessed since the foundation of the world, as manifestly revealed in no place else but on the Cross of Jesus Christ, his Beloved Son. For undoubtedly, divine love is the only reason strong and compelling enough to have warranted God's incarnate appearance to man on cosmic soil—the primary impetus behind his priceless redemptive sacrifice for all mankind. But in order for any one of us to even begin to deeply appreciate the overarching significance of the timeless redemptive transaction (viz., the buying back of the human soul) that went down at the Cross of Jesus Christ, we would have to first understand exactly what stakes were involved and how high the stakes really were. Ask yourself, why in the world would Jesus, the only morally perfect Man to have walked the face of the earth, be found hanging on Calvary's Cross—all criminalized like a common criminal? And I mean, the only Man who ever knew to " . . . *refuse the evil and choose the good*" one hundred percent of the time—who alone exhaustively embodied the literal meaning of the idiomatic expression "*as innocent as a lamb*"—the only leopard whose skin was found unspotted by the blemish of sin—given his unblemished righteousness and unassailable moral character (Isa 7:16). Exactly what must have been at stake in the heart and mind of God when he meticulously orchestrated such a redemptive plan that eventually saw his Beloved Son and Fellow Member of the Holy Trinity so gruesomely cruciated and crucified and then left hanging *'forsaken'*—left for dead on that Cruciate Stake—all in excruciating pain for six whooping hours—all abandoned to his own fate in the cold and bloody hands of death; if not for some priceless value he must have so graciously and gratuitously bestowed on frail and fallen creatures like ourselves. A truth so reminiscently captured in the lyrics of the most popular English hymn, as written by John Newton (1779), 'Amazing Grace,' particularly the first stanza, where it says:

Amazing grace! How sweet the sound
That saved a wretch like me!
I once was lost, but now am found;
Was blind, but now I see.

In Jesus, we witness God's amazing grace essentially reaching all out from heaven and reaching all the way down to the nethermost depths of the mire of man's wretchedness in the state of fallenness in order to lift him out of that miry clay of sin and moral filthiness, triumphantly lifting him further up to the highest altitude of Divine glory above and beyond—setting his feet upon the Rock of Eternal Salvation—on the peak of Christ the Solid Rock. Because again, ask yourself, why did God see it fit and deem it both necessary and sufficient to stake his own life in his human form to save frail and fallen men and women, boys and girls like ourselves, not minding our wretchedness in moral fallenness, not to even mention our existential brokenness? The stakes must have been really high for him to go as far as doing all that he did for mankind on the Cross of Jesus Christ, would you not agree? For example, would you dare stake out your life or give it up to save your pet's, venturing so far as consenting to become a cat so you could sacrificially donate your kidneys to your cat, if it were going to cost that much to save its life, meanwhile it gets to live at your expense or in your place? I think not, and I am one hundred percent convinced that none of us will be willing to go that far, no matter how fond of our pets we might be or how much of an ailurophile or a cataholic we are. Now you can only begin to imagine the depths, the heights, the length, and the breadth that the Creator-God must have had to stretch the elastic band of his love to secure the redemption of your soul and mine, and how much we must really mean to him. Amazingly enough, I happen not to be alone in conceiving of the Bible as a book containing the greatest redemptive love story there is, ever was, and ever will be; a lot more others are equally in acquiescence that "*the Bible is a storybook . . .* "—one which—" *. . . tells a true story, whose story line goes like this: creation—fall—redemption—consummation*" (Morgan W. C., et al., 2014). Bingo! Indeed, we are looking at a story so characteristically Divine and at the same time so passionately human, so marvelously supernal and nevertheless so realistically spatiotemporal, so deeply spiritual and yet so consummately natural.

As far as the storyline goes, divine love is what compelled Deity to become part of humanity—part and parcel of the human story—partaking in the human experiment by first-hand experience, and by the same token, transformatively rewriting the whole story with a great 'new' and glorious eschatological future in view—whilst fundamentally undermining the not-so-great *'old'* and inglorious protological history, all with the same stroke of the pen—the finished work of the Cross of Jesus Christ. Almost as if to say, "*Behold, I make all things new*" (Rev 21:5a NKJV). When captured in the inspired words of the now famous and widely celebrated Apostle Paul, the same truth would just about sound like this: " . . . *old things have passed away; behold, all things have become new*" (II Corinthians 5:17 NKJV). Indeed, the gospel of God's redemptive love for mankind makes all things transformatively new in the life of any man or woman who would dare to believe it, and that effectively makes it the only extant true love story that its telling and retelling (preaching) possesses within itself the power and potency to positively impact and forever transform the lives of its hearership. It is on that account that the selfsame Apostle could again be seen in the following verse of Scripture expressing so much faith and confidence in it, as he dithyrambically declared, "*For I am not ashamed of the gospel of Christ, for it is the power of God to salvation for everyone who believes, for the Jew first and also for the Greek*" (Rom 1:16 NKJV). The gospel of Christ is, in its final analysis, ultimately about the good news of God's love for mankind, for Christ is the Son of God's love—the very demonstration of the Father's love for man. Hence the reason I am all the more persuaded *sans doute* that as you spend time poring over the pages of this book, the light of the glorious gospel of God's love will be shining forth from the Zion of my heart, with the glory of his infallible word pouring forth from the Jerusalem gates of my lips (cf. Isa 2:3b), and will find a place of settlement in your heart and get to be a blessing of incalculable proportions in your life. Amen!

A good story deserves a good intro, and trust me, so does this one—even more so one this good. Followingly, in the light of the theological weight and historical significance of the subject in focus, with no small reverence for its delicate spiritual nature, I decided it was best to set aside the customary proem—the 'Introduction' or 'Preface' with which we are mostly familiar, opting rather for the good old-fashioned *'Introductory Essay,'* which I strongly believe will better serve our purpose. So come hence with me, fellow pilgrim, as we venture further afield upon this awe-inspiring and soul-stirring endless odyssey, tracing the thousand-mile trail—nay, pardon my slip—the boundless, myriad-mile journey of God's love for the Adamic race, as it jets off with a pre-creation first step—God's redemptive first-step act of slaying his 'Isaac' for man's salvation ever before there was even a man on cosmic soil—ever before there was even a cosmos to begin with. Far beyond faint foreshadowing, the sacrificial offering of this Isaac figure—prefiguring the Lamb of Passover—serves as a foundational transaction that supports the core of creation itself. For by establishing redemption's predestined pledge as prior to creation in the divine order of things, it declares, with unyielding decree, the fundamental priority of redemption over creation—soteriology's sovereign sway above cosmogony's cradle, whispering that the universe emerges according to the Cross's framework, where suffering and glory form essential, intertwined aspects of God's life extended to us. This journey unveils the profound mystery of a love that predates the stars, weaving through the fabric of time to embrace the frailty of our human story. This is a love that held a vivid image of you in view before you appeared anywhere in existence—a love that prepared for your arrival before time itself began—a love that yearned for your story before the foundations of the world were laid—a love that operated freely and generously, predating the dawn of time, and wove itself into the timeline to support our fragile human experience. Here, we begin with the early chapters of Genesis, those ancient whispers of the primordial scrolls of the world's beginning, examining and explaining the creationary displays of God's love for man. We then move forward to New Testament Gospels, shedding light on the climactic moments of that providential love, where timeless divine plans meet the realities of history, confirming the consistent purpose behind it all.

1

That God Loved Man Enough to Become a Man

The redemptive love is what compelled Deity to become part of humanity—part and parcel of the human story—partaking in the human experiment by first-hand experience

For once upon a time—for well across a prophetic timeline spanning nigh fifteen centuries of human history, a book of divine revelation was both composed and canonically compiled for the human race, as inspired through forty distinct voices—some of whom are prophets, priests, patriarchs, and kings; others apostles, evangelists, sages, and even saints—all of whom are revered as *'holy men of God.'* But lo and behold, what you might find particularly interesting and at the same time theologically significant about this sacred masterpiece called *'The Bible'* or *'The Holy Bible'* is that, despite containing a miscellanea of sixty-six disparate manuscripts, all of which enjoyed the theopneustic penmanship of the said authors who had lived during sundry times and diverse Biblical epochs, yet somehow, as if being engineered by some miraculous process or as though guided by the unseen hand of God, they all ended up fortuitously telling a single unified story—a veriloquent story of human redemption. From page to page—prelude to postlude—they altogether form a prophetic tapestry of God's redemptive love for mankind, woven with hermeneutical unity and doctrinal coherence—progressively unfolding from the cradle of creation to the climax of consummation in a rhythmic crescendo that captivates the mind, convicts the conscience, and awakens the deepest yearnings of the human heart.

THE PRELAPSARIAN BEGINNING OF THE HUMAN STORY: THE CREATION OF MAN IN GOD'S IMAGE

According to the genesis of the redemptive love story, as vividly captured in the Book most befittingly named Genesis—the first book of the Bible—the book that begets beginnings—the selfsame book ordained to herald the beginning of man's beginning, we are introduced to a prelapsarian scene where humanity's eternal story takes off in soaring flight, like a bird of prey vaulting upon aerial currents of providential grace. Gloriously unscrolling with a seminal text that has the *dramatis personae* in protatic focus—the Begetter and the begotten—and therein came the most consequential poietic decree ever uttered—echoing with the eternal purpose of a love that unites heaven's vision with earth's own destiny: "*Let Us make man in Our image, according to Our likeness; let them have dominion over the fish of the sea, over the birds of the air, and over the cattle, over all the earth and over every creeping thing that creeps on the earth." So God created man in His own image; in the image of God He created him; male and female He created them*" (Gen 1:26–27 NKJV). And with that sovereign declaration, man was born on the sixth day of creation—in the twenty-sixth verse of the opening chapter of Genesis, the opening chapter of the human story is unveiled—the origin of man's cosmic existence is inscribed in scroll—the genesis of man's cosmic journey scripted in Scripture. In that epoch-making moment, a first-of-its-kind and one-of-a-kind specimen bearing the divine imprint was wonderfully and fearfully made—in male and female embodiments, Adam and Eve (humanity's apical ancestors) were sacredly sculpted to reflect the Creator's divine attributes and mirror his glory. Fashioned in his image—his immortal likeness cast in vessels of mortal clay, they were endowed with the extraordinary perquisite of personhood—rationality, relationality, morality, and creativity. In the very same twenty-and-sixth verse of this foundational Genesis chapter one, we have chronicled for us this profoundly special day of creation that bore witness to the Builder's blueprint to build this majestic being beaming with his beatific beauty, predestined to bear rule—to reign with righteousness and govern with reason. Commissioned as noble vicegerents within the divine hierarchy and empowered with delegated authority from the Sovereign Throne, Adam and Eve were to leverage their primordial primacy over all of the Creator's copious creation—spanning the full spectrum from lifeless elements to vibrant plant life in its verdant array to teeming animal life in its wild diversity and all the way up to the celestial life of starry hosts and angelic orders (cf. Ps 8:3–9). Forsooth, the sixth day was no mere grand finale in the creation timeline but the grand unveiling of the supreme masterpiece of the Creator's craftsmanship—the creation of creation's own centerpiece—man.

For within the interwoven narrative of cosmogenesis and anthropogenesis as betold in this sacred account, the universe, in its vast entirety, was created from nothingness by the divine decree, *'Let there be'*—a unilateral act of will that brought creation into being—*creatio ex nihilo*. In contrast, when the Creator turned to fashion mankind on day six, the language shifted to *'Let us make'*—a trilateral invocation that resonates with the perichoretic communion of the Blessed Three who are One. This linguistic shift from *'decree'* to *'dialogue,'* apart from signifying that all prior endeavors were but abiogenetic emergences from the formless voids of nothingness, ultimately reveals that humanity is not merely formed but summoned from the depths of God's own being, endowed with a sacred kinship to his essence, sharing in the same everlasting communion and boundless love that exist in the Triune Godhead. With the previous five days of creation standing still in reverent pause—awaiting the climax of divine craftsmanship with bated breath—God's voice, imbued with sovereign power and purpose, was heard on the sixth, thundering the most defining and decisive creative words that would ever proceed forth from his mouth: "*Let Us make man in Our image, according to Our likeness; let them have dominion . . .* " (Gen 1:26 NKJV). Summoning Adam to come forth, not from without—as though from external matter—but from within—all from the internal recesses of the divine ousia (essential nature of God). In other words, man did not come from out of *'nothing,'* nor did man come from out of *'something'*; man came from out of *'Someone'*—God. A towering testament revealing man not merely as a creature made but as one uniquely marked as God's carbon copy, mandated to bear the divine onus of stewarding creation's manifold marvels—to bear the eternal purpose central to the Creator's cosmic vision—central to his cosmic design. Further underscoring the anthropological dignity inherent in bearing the *imago Dei*—where man's dominion mirrors the

Cosmocrator's sovereignty. On the grounds of which the Church Father, St. Augustine of Hippo, was led to conclude that the soul of man, as a mirror image of the Divine essence, is *capax Dei*—capable of God. So history does not remember the sixth day as just another day amongst the many days of creation week; it remembers it for being a day unlike any other—a Day of Days in God's creation timetable—a red-letter day on creation's own calendar. Etched in the annals of Biblical history as a day of divine significance—marking a divine milestone—the creation of the crowning glory of the Creator's handiwork. As the Psalmist so eloquently affirmed, even though God had been working diligently for five days in a row, it was not until the sixth day that he "... *crowned them* [mankind] *with glory and honor*" (Ps 8:5 NLT). For creation wore no crown and had no crown on which to wear a crown until, of course, man stepped forward on the scene on day six—as the head that the crown fits.

Likewise, the sixth day, which participated in man's creation and witnessed his genesis, proudly wears the crown for being the most creatively special and hallowed day amid the days of creation week—the most decisive and momentous day in the Creator's masterplan. For therein, the Builder's blueprint prudently dictated he reserve his best piece for last—his *pièce de résistance* for day six—his highest effect for this ultimate stage—man. Though man was produced last in the temporal order, on the sixth day, this does not imply that he comes last in the order of nature—it by no means relegates him to some inferior status; rather, he comes first in dignity, first in glory, first in divine endowment, first in divine empowerment, first in finesse, first in the chain of being—*scala naturae*, first in the ladder of perfection—*scala perfectionis*, and most importantly—first in the heart and mind of the Creator-God. In the ordered hierarchy of divine acts, as articulated in the Hexameron, this transcendent sixth day, far from being relegated to the last place in the ascending order of excellence, excels amongst the days of the creative week as first-rate and not sixth-rate, outshining all others as the first and foremost in the hierarchy of finality, in potency fulfilled, and in rank amongst secondary causes. Indeed, this hallowed day is not merely ultimate in chronological sequence but profoundly primary in ontological essence and eternal import; wearing the crown of eminence, it assumes an exalted throne as the preeminent and transformative epoch in the divine agenda of genesis, not merely as the final act but as the dawn of creation's true awakening—the moment when the cosmos awoke to its divinely ordained vocation. For the scene of creation was as if in the potency of night, during the antecedent days' productions—from one through five, until the sixth day actuated its dawn. For not until the dawn of this sixth sunrise that eclipsed the previous five dawns, the universe slept in the penumbra of unusefulness and unrealized potential—slumbering in the twilight zone of anticipation, its purpose veiled until the auroral advent of the being for whose sake all creation exists illuminated its *raison d'être*. Unveiling the divine intention: all prior acts of creation were but preparatory, awaiting the one who would give them teleological significance.

Thus, this day, bearer of humanity's exurgent genesis, is creation's true beginning—not its end, a sacred epoch distinguishing itself profoundly amid creation's septenary span, forever cherished in the Divine mind as a day impervious to the oblivion of forgetfulness. The Creator-God, in his unrelenting pursuit of his vision and purpose for creation, sought no rest after five days of work, rather reserving his Sabbath only after humanity's birth, until his eternal intentions crystallized on day six, marking it as the most excellent in the creational order—the sole day of supreme actuality. Especially given that the antecedent works of creation would lack their *per accidens* purposes without man's *per se* finality on the sixth. Hence, man's debut at the narrative's denouement, on day six, by no means relegates him to some secondary status. Simply put, day six is so special because man made it so—a special day that solemnly commemorates the originary birthday of the Creator's image-bearer, forever celebrated as the crowning festal occasion in creation's septenary ledger. For this is the day that the joy of creation was made full—the day that man was made, indelibly engraved upon the Creator's eternal memory and heart like a sacred scarlet tattoo, enshrined as the sole vermilion-marked milestone in the liturgical calendar of creation's grand narrative. Lo, the sanctity and peculiarity of the sixth day of creation derives from humanity's imprint upon it, being the day that the Creator did something he has never done before, one he would not be repeating ever again—never! For though the heavens and the earth shall someday suffer the eschatological fate of passing away—their created essence returning to the primal dust of nothingness from whence they came—it is not so with the human species, for they shall outlive all creation and shall abide forever, one way or the other—whether in glory or in perdition. By virtue of being the Creator's undying reflection, man's destiny transcends this fleeting creation, eternally woven into the fabric of the Creator's everlasting vision. In the grand chronicle of existence, there could be no two captains in the ship of creation's destiny—no two God-image-bearers in the creation story—no two cosmic emperors in the Creator's universe. The fact is, the sixth day was not merely the end of the hexameral narrative of creation; it rather marks the beginning of creation's own story, for if it were not for the creation of man on the sixth day, creation would have no story to tell at all. The human story is creation's only story—as well as the Creator's love story. In the story of man's cosmic existence, God's creation finds its voice for the first time, with God's heart revealing its enduring, relational intent. For so the Creator would have it and no other way. Perhaps rightly so, when you are done ticking all the boxes—dotting the i's and crossing the t's.

Well, apart from this special day that saw the creation of Adam and Eve, there are two other distinctively eventful days that would go on to determine the quality of their human experience, levy a toll on their destiny, and essentially seal their cosmic fate. First, we have the first dawn in Paradise—Adam's first day in the Garden of Eden, his first footfall on God's green earth. Secondly, there was the dawn of a new day outside Paradise—man's first day outside the boundaries of the blessed borders of Eden's privatopia. The difference between both days stands as stark as sunrise and nightfall, and let me illustrate. Adam's first day on God's green earth was a Sabbath day, a Sabbath of rest and roo—rooted in God's finished work, one where he was invited to reap full harvest from the garden planted by God's providence, wherein he had bestowed no labor. As Genesis 2:8 affirms, it was "*The LORD God [who] planted a garden eastward in Eden, and there He put the man whom He had formed*"—not man who planted. Unburdened by toil, Adam drank deeply and freely of the blessings of God's goodness in the garden of his finished work—the paradise of his rest. Furthermore, his first human contact with Earth was Eden, when his boots brushed the blooming beauty of the Garden, a feat in that *locus amoenus* (pleasant place) that had God's glory and goodness for haven. But long before Adam's feet found footing in the golden groves of Eden, his essence wholly existed as a spiritual being, mirroring the divine nature of the Creator, who is Spirit, as Scripture declares: "*God is Spirit, and those who worship Him must worship in spirit and truth*" (John 4:24 NKJV). In this celestial realm, where truth and being unite, man's primal existence was one of intimate communion with his Maker, unencumbered by the material frame later fashioned for him. That earthly vessel, the body of dust, was a later formation—a secondary and temporary composition to house the primary reality of his spiritual nature—the so-called *'the inward man'* or *'the hidden man of the heart'* (cf. 1 Pet 3:4; 2 Corinthians 4:16). A careful reading of Genesis Chapters 1 and 2 unveils this mystery with measured precision: even though man was already created in the first chapter, the second reveals his absence on the surface of the earth, lamenting that "*there was no man to till the ground*" (Gen 2:5). All the more puzzling when you consider that God had already conferred his blessing on man in Genesis 1:28: "*Then God blessed them, and God said to them, "Be fruitful and multiply; fill the earth and subdue it; have dominion over the fish of the sea, over the birds of the air, and over every living thing that moves on the earth.*" Thus prompting the question: where, then, was the newly created Adam to whom God had said these things? He lingered yet in the heavenly realm where time and matter hold no sway, a spirit basking in fellowship in the eternal presence of the Creator-God, untouched by the material world.

This initial absence from the earthly realm discloses a solemn and foundational truth: man's communion with the Creator both precedes and supersedes his engagement with creation. Ere Adam would relish the opportunity of interacting with creation down here on earth, he already shared premortal communion with his Maker up there in heaven, a singular privilege no other creature enjoyed. Hence, the spiritual dimension, eternal and preexistent, always takes precedence, shaping man's identity before his earthly sojourn began. The fact that man's spiritual existence came first, both ultimate and primary, also reveals a timeless Biblical principle—spiritual reality will always take precedence over natural reality. This divine sequence further unveils the very heart of human existence: man is first and foremost a citizen of heaven, called to mirror the Creator's glory, and only then a sojourner in the material world, tasked with its care. Adam, even though, was formed and placed within the world, he was never "*of the world*"—but of God, because he came forth from God (cf. John 17:14–16). His essential identity and eternal citizenship were both rooted in the heavenly kingdom, even as he fulfilled his earthly calling to tend and keep the creation God had placed under his care. This does not necessarily suggest that he initially existed as a spectral wraith floating around in the ether but as a spirit endowed with the capacity as well as a celestial body that enabled him to interact with that ethereal plane of existence. Scripture affirms this duality of human nature: "*There are also celestial bodies and terrestrial bodies; but the glory of the celestial is one, and the glory of the terrestrial is another . . . There is a natural body, and there is a spiritual body*" (1 Cor 15:40, 44). But it was not until the formation of his natural body in Genesis 2:7 that Adam became a living soul, physically animated by the breath of life in his lungs, capable of having meaningful interactions with material creation. As it is written, "*The first man Adam became a living being*" (I Corinthians 15:45 NKJV). The human soul, spiritual in substance, indivisible in essence, and immortal in duration, is endowed with the noble faculties of intellect, will, and emotion, through which it discerns, deliberates, and cultivates virtues that reflect God's own likeness. Man's essence, however, is not merely soul or body, but a spirit, drawn from the Spirit of spirits—the fount of beinghood, existing first in the celestial realm. There, he enjoyed the privilege of witnessing the Creator's act of planting the Garden of Eden on his behalf and shaping his own corporeal body from the fleeting dust of the earth. Man's initial act was agapeic communion with God, a participation in the divine likeness, not engagement with the creatures subject to him. Only later did he interact with the material world, subordinate to his dominion.

This enigmatic phenomenon is by no means peculiar to Adam, since Eve herself was also an eyewitness to the delicate process by which her feminine figure was derived from Adam's own, occurring under the direct gaze of God within the heavenly sphere. It is essential to note, nonetheless, that the extraction of Eve's body from Adam's did not constitute the moment of her original creation, for the human spirit invariably precedes the crafting of the human body and persists beyond its earthly tenure. This pattern, evident in the case of the primordial couple at the outset of history, extends analogously to the entirety of their descendants, each one of whom was summoned into existence concurrently with them on the sixth day of the creative week, partaking equally in this pre-incarnate communion with God, whilst lingering in a state of suspended readiness for their introduction into the created order through the sacred rite of human procreation. This understanding illuminates aspects of the Biblical declaration: "*Thus the heavens and the earth, and all the host of them, were finished*" (Gen 2:1 NKJV). The comprehensive phrase '*all the host of them*' logically incorporates the full spectrum of human existence—encompassing the whole kindred of Adam. It follows, then, that God is not engaged in an ongoing process of forming the unborn—the future generations of Adam's progeny up there in heaven; rather, his labor of creating them was accomplished wholly on that sixth day. In this light, the plantation and preparation of the Garden of Eden on the seventh day, together with the formation of their physical embodiments, need not be classified as '*work*'—or, more precisely, as a novel phase of creative activity. As with Adam and Eve of yestertime, all their offspring partake in that selfsame prenatal privilege with God in the invisible realms of heaven. Nowadays, we see this Biblical episode reenacted everywhere, day upon dawning day, serving as the cosmic backstory to every new baby's arrival—a vivid testament to this primordial mystery rooted in the origins.

In a striking typological parallel, the covenant community of Israel—serving as a macrocosmic embodiment of humanity's original state—was entrusted with the preparatory venture of spying out the Promised Land as witnesses, the Canaan of their inheritance, before its full embrace. This reconnaissance mission culminated in their jubilant report: "*The land we passed through to spy out is an exceedingly good land. If the Lord delights in us, then He will bring us into this land and give it to us, 'a land which flows with milk and honey*" (Num 14:7–8 NKJV). This prefigurative act, rich with spiritual significance, highlights the intermediate state betwixt the creation of Adam and the divine pronouncement of dominion-oriented blessing upon him in Genesis 1:28 as an antecedent to the Creator's deliberate transplantation of him into the Edenic sanctuary per Genesis 2:7–8, a motif that correlates systematically with the extrication of Israel through the exodic deliverance and the pronouncement of the covenant promises on them in the Siniatic wilderness of wandering, which similarly prefaced the ultimate divine act of planting them in the eschatological homeland—the Promised Land. Unveiling the Creator's intentional design woven into the pilgrim's journey: the assurance of divine promise invariably comes before the fulfillment of inheritance, serving as the very essence of grace—a gracious prelude and participatory invitation to taste in advance what lies ahead. These prenatal and protological glimpses reveal faith's adventure as one marked by graced *aperçu*, where historical reconnaissance converges with existential readiness, preparing the human soul for God to uproot and replant it in its true, native soil. From this proleptic perspective, the light of faith grants a genuine vision of heaven's joys breaking into earth—not as a mere cartography of facts, but as an intimate, shared foretaste of God's eternal purposes, equipping the heart for the demanding yet guaranteed pilgrimage toward deep oneness with the Lord. Thus, it underscores a Creator who equips the pilgrim with sensory and spiritual assurance amid the uncertainties of obedience. In this way, the individual believer, as a small-scale reflection of that ancient pilgrim people, receives a gift of spiritual preview: a foretaste of the paradise of unbroken fellowship with God, granted before the divine initiative finally relocates the soul into that eternal reality. It suggests that the genesis of each person's existence replays this holy exploration—a premortal reconnaissance anew, wherein the human spirit, sensitive to the call of the age to come, looks forward to God's entry into our time-bound lives, spanning the gap from the primal blueprint of creation's genesis to the final moments of consummation's destiny.

This profound observation holds true without variance for each and every scion in Adam's expansive family tree, including those yet-unborn souls ordained for entry into the theater of earthly existence. In the serene altitudes of heaven, preceding their venture into the dynamic flow of created history, each has indeed shared in the intimate discourse with the Creator, a fellowship that predates the boundaries of clock and calendar. This backdrop richly informs the biblical pronouncement, "*Children are a gift from the Lord; they are a reward from him*" (Ps 127:3 NLT), thereby anchoring the phenomenology of birth in the bedrock of transcendent filiation. From God, children emanate, not as abstract creations but as participants in a prior heavenly conversation, that foundational agapeic communion that defines the spiritual narrative prior to embodiment. The preposition '*from*' carries layers of implication, suggesting a story of established familiarity with God's presence in heaven's hallowed hemisphere, from which the soul of every unborn child is now entrusted to the stage of earthly pilgrimage, ensconced for earthly ensoulment in the elegant architecture of bodily existence—the '*cosmic suit*' that mediates the eternal spark within the temporal frame, a subtle reminder of their otherworldly provenance. In this profoundly insightful oracle of origins by the Psalmist, we hear the timbre of pre-cosmogonic divine intimacy, preceding the spark of life's inception: "*For You formed my inward parts; You covered me in my mother's womb. I will praise You, for I am fearfully and wonderfully made; Marvelous are Your works, And that my soul knows very well. My frame was not hidden from You, When I was made in secret, And skillfully wrought in the lowest parts of the earth. Your eyes saw my substance, being yet unformed. And in Your book they all were written, The days fashioned for me, When as yet there were none of them*" (Ps 139:13–16 NKJV). Echoing the sacred journey of their primigenial forebears, the soul ('substance') of every pilgrim yet unborn gets to behold the Almighty's handiwork—the biological formation of their terrestrial vessel—that cosmic garment of the human body, within the veiled mysteries of the earth's hidden cradle—described as the secret place '*in the lowest parts of the earth.*' Like Adam, they, too, stand witness to the Sovereign Potter shaping their fetus in the hushed alcove of their mother's womb, where God, in his unerring election, breathes form into fragility within the chosen womb of predestination, a prelude to eternity's boundless fellowship. This sacred act of formation is one that would remain a secret between the yet-unformed and the Supreme Threader who weaves the thread of their existence, breath by breath, in the profound mystery of maternal grace. Although every such primordial memory of their antenatal existence gets erased completely, leaving their minds a tabula rasa—a blank slate from the point of conception onward. Thus, this preordained *lapsus memoriae* upon entering the world, rather than a loss, becomes the gift of innocence, as the erasure of premortal reminiscence is what safeguards the purity of faith's leap, thus allowing the soul to rediscover its origins through the lens of faith and reason, transforming the mental blank canvas into a dynamic interface for ongoing revelation, wherein the singular history of the agent intellect concurs with the universal order of creation's exemplar causality.

Wherefore, the divine declaration resounds with timeless truth: "*Before I formed you in the womb I knew you; Before you were born I sanctified you; I ordained you . . .* " (Jer 1:5 NKJV). The words of Paul echo in perfect accord: "*For whom He foreknew, He also predestined . . .* " (Rom 8:29 NKJV). This deeply intimate foreknowledge of God belongs not to the prophet Jeremiah alone; it extends to every child of Adam, reaching back to Adam himself and to Eve, his wife. The Creator-God foreknew Adam and Eve through prenatal fellowship in the sacred courts of heaven, long before their physical forms took shape. In this Edenic unfolding of the sixth day of creation—woven inseparably into the story of every one of Adam's descendants—our spirits, bearing forever the divine image, are oriented toward an upward journey: a pilgrimage that ascends toward the ultimate joy of beholding the Father's face in its unveiled fullness. This is the same glory glimpsed in the heavenly realms before our earthly sojourn began, where every beginning converges in perfect, harmonious design. Consequently, in the beginning, humanity's well-being depended not on the abundance of creation but solely on the boundless grace of the Creator—the unfailing wellspring of all goodness. In this divine order, creation existed to serve man, while man existed to serve God alone, offering worship and fellowship to the Eternal One as both his essence and his ultimate end. This sacred arrangement, woven into the very fabric of existence, safeguarded the sanctity and harmony of the created world—contingent upon humanity's steadfast fidelity to its spiritual origin and its living communion with God, a bond that precedes and supersedes all earthly ties.

Furthermore, the very first experience Adam savored upon the soil of this cosmos was a heaven-on-earth reality—a foretaste of celestial glory brought down to terrestrial ground, a radiant reflection of the uncreated order mirrored within the created realm. Consider the profound, multilayered preparation that God invested across the first five days of creation, each stage poised in hushed, breathless anticipation for the arrival of the Adamic race. Every layer stands as an eloquent witness to divine anticipatory zeal, trembling with pulsating suspense until the climactic unveiling of the sixth day. Herein lies the fathomless depth of godly foresight, woven indelibly into the very texture of human existence—the lavish outpouring of providential investment, poured forth in eager prelude to the appearance of those who bear God's own image. This mirrors the tender, sacred rituals of an expectant mother and the ardent vigil of soon-to-be parents: with hearts overflowing in forward-looking devotion, they fashion an entire world of wonder for their yet-unborn child—a world lovingly prepared in advance, even while the child remains hidden in the mystery of the unseen. Picture them in the quiet hush of anticipation, carefully assembling a sanctuary stocked with every essential: onesies crafted from the softest fibers to gently cradle delicate newborn bodies, a sturdy crib meticulously assembled and dressed in plush, inviting bedding, baby carriages poised and ready, stacks of tiny clothing folded with care, feeding bottles designed for effortless, natural suckling, and countless other thoughtful items—all standing watch like faithful sentinels within the warm, loving embrace of the nursery. They stock pantries with nourishing provisions to complement the mother's gift of breast milk, and gather every essential for hygiene and tender care—drawers filled with neatly folded diapers, corners kept pristine and ready for gentle wiping, walls bathed in soft, ethereal murals where artistic scenes dance like whispered dreams. Every possible need is anticipated, every detail thoughtfully enshrined, leaving nothing overlooked. What, then, is the deeper significance of such devoted preparation? At its heart, these parents become midwives to a custom-made universe: they are deliberately shaping and enveloping the world that will first receive their child. With unstinting generosity, they draw from the full reservoir of their mortal resources to lavish every conceivable necessity upon this awaiting space—offering it all in a spirit of pure, preemptive welcome. This labor of love is undertaken not after the baby's arrival, but in the radiant interval before the infant's dawn—long before the first cry pierces the silence—often stretching across many months of expectant gestation.

Weeks before the due date, the nursery stands ready, a testament to their parental anticipation. You can imagine the couples standing in the doorway, hands clasped like intertwining vines in an ancient garden, united in gesture and gaze, marveling at the space they have lovingly prepared. The room is far more than a place for sleep; it is a sanctuary reminiscent of the Garden of Eden, meticulously crafted for their child's earliest days, shaped by love long before the baby's first step. Yet behold the Divine Parent, who is never constrained by lack or limitation: in five majestic days, the Almighty creates not merely a room, but an entire universe—a vast, star-filled cradle for those made in his image and likeness. Those opening five epochs—light summoned from formless chaos, the firmament stretched as an enduring canopy, seas teeming with living creatures, land bursting forth in lush abundance, and the chorus of land animals—form the magnificent prelude, the richly woven foundation upon which the crowning achievement of the sixth day rises. Humanity, imaged in the very likeness of the Creator, surpasses in glory and holiness all the magnificent works of those earlier dawns. Though brought forth in the quiet whisper of a single day, we stand as the crowning achievement—the priceless jewels that complete the divine masterpiece and shine with incomparable value in the eyes of God. Indeed, the Genesis narrative unfolds as the supreme expression of parental foresight—the very pinnacle of anticipatory grace. God, the ultimate Expectant Parent, does not merely improvise or prepare a simple cradle for humanity; he designs and constructs an entire cosmos to serve as its nursery—a vast, galactic nursery. The first five days—light breaking through formless chaos, the heavens arched as a sheltering canopy, seas swarming with vibrant life, land erupting in verdant abundance and teeming creatures—are no mere preliminaries or afterthoughts. They constitute the intentional, meticulously crafted scaffolding upon which the climactic sixth day rests, when the image-bearers of God finally step into being.

With such profound preparation in view, we may rightly liken Adam to one of the honored guests in the Parable of the Wedding Feast recorded in Matthew 22:1–4. There, a gracious king, in an outpouring of sovereign hospitality, summons his beloved invitees to a lavish banquet prepared for his son, declaring, "*Look, I have prepared my dinner; my oxen and fattened calves are butchered and everything is ready; come to the wedding feast*" (Matthew 22:4 AMP). Apparently, everything was done and dusted—all necessary preparation for the wedding feast was complete. All the guests were asked to do was come feast—*bon appétit*, and felicitate with the celebrant and be merry whilst reflecting on the king's royal generosity. In the same way, the work of creation—accomplished and perfected before humanity's arrival—stands as an enduring monument to divine generosity. Neither Adam nor his wife contributed even a single effort toward planting the Garden of Eden or shaping the wider universe; God alone had fashioned and finished every aspect. As Scripture affirms, " . . . *the works were finished from the foundation of the world*" (Hebrews 4:3 NKJV). All that remained was for humanity to enter into God's Sabbath rest, to repose in it, and to feast upon the overflowing bounty of his goodness and benevolence. It is almost as though God spoke directly to Adam and Eve the words echoed later in Scripture: "*Come . . . inherit the kingdom prepared for you from the foundation of the world*" (Matthew 25:34)—a kingdom " . . . *prepared as a bride adorned for her husband*" (Rev 21:2 NKJV). This was a clarion invitation to behold, delight in, and inherit the primordial kingdom—the ultimate destination of humanity's cosmic journey—crafted in advance by the Creator's loving hand. In this light, the scene recalls the tender imagery of Psalm 23: the Lord, our Good Shepherd, in his inexhaustible beneficence, has spread a festal table before the first couple. In the verdant pastures of his Edenic courts, he has prepared every provision, inviting them to recline, rest, and find refreshment. Within the garden of his finished work, he has set a table laden with his goodness, where weary hearts—warmed by his astonishing grace—discover abiding repose in the eternal orchard of his covenant love (Ps 23:1, 5).

In essence, Adam's first day in Eden's Xanadu was a day blessed with a glorious dawn: he awoke enveloped in divine light, immersed in divine delight, his existence blossoming in the radiant presence of God himself. The goodness of that moment was so profound that one can almost hear the faint, primordial resonance of his voice carried forward into the Psalmist's exultant cry: "*This is the day the LORD has made; we will rejoice and be glad in it*" (Ps 118:24 NLT). Beyond bearing eloquent witness to God's tender, providential care for our first parents, this splendid Edenic scene unveils a breathtaking panorama of the Creator's love for the whole human family. It is a living portrait—more eloquent than a thousand words—where every brushstroke of the divine hand proclaims an eternal truth: the boundless, personal love of God for each and every human person. This primordial manifestation of God's goodness in creation stands as an age-enduring testament of his love for man. He would not be doing any of what he did in scenes of creation if it had not been for the fact that man uniquely holds a special place in his heart. No one would so lavishly bestow such extravagant and boundless providential care where genuine love is absent. For God only bacares the beloved—the creature of his semblance and similitude.

Something else this Genesis mythos does so impressively well is to accurately inform us about *'what'* man essentially is—his true identity as seen through the sovereign eyes of his Maker. And just as the foregoing protological analysis have endeavored to lay out in order, man is not narrowly the *'rational animal'* Aristotelians have taxonomically labelled him, nor is he merely the banal *"wise man"—homo sapien*—others anthropologically conceived him to be, nor is he simply that ever-evolving Neanderthal the Darwinian bioscientists arrogantly asserted he was. In fundamental exactitude, man transcends all these passing, superficial descriptions; he is nothing less than what the Creator-God declares him to be—his *imago Dei* incarnate, the embodied reflection of divine likeness. In the shadow of fleeting human wisdoms, where philosophies flicker like shadows at night, we stand as bearers of the Immortal Designer's seal—forever marked with the radiant imprint of his divine simulacrum, just as the sacred record of Genesis declares with unwavering voice. Behold, the intricate grandeur of our genetic code—our DNA's vast tapestry of three-billion-letter hallowed nucleotides that contemporary scientists have hailed as the very fingerprint of the Almighty himself, a breathtaking masterpiece that weaves together the pinnacle of moral freedom and self-conscious dominion, intertwining our ancient lineage with the living echo of God's delegated stewardship over creation. Within this divine script lies a quiet whisper of heavenly ingenuity: the singular, grace-bestowed anomaly of the ADSL gene—an outlier etched in the holy blueprint of humanity—conferring upon our desert-forged resilience the sharp, heaven-given clarity of mind. A playful echo of God's raw handiwork in nature, a witty revelation crowning our story of origins, singing of our Eden-rooted heritage in pure, poetic grace, and rhyming the wonder of our blessed ascent toward the divine.

For among the myriad wonders woven into the fabric of the creation story, none shines with greater brilliance than the revelation of humanity's exalted identity—the glorious gospel of our generative grandeur, apprehended through the unerring perspective of the Creator-God himself—proclaiming our preeminent pedigree in the pristine paradise of eternal Eden. This divine revelation ultimately provides a profound and thoughtful answer to the ancient wonder of the shepherd-king David: "*What is man?*" (Ps 8:4). In other words, what is this frail mortal that the Immortal God should take notice of him with such attentive regard, or the child of dust that the Lord should visit him with such tender care? Gathering together the strands of biblical insight and contemplative inquiry, the scriptural narrative presents us not as random products of cosmic chance or insignificant specks lost in an immense universe, but as deliberate centers of a purposeful creation—where scientific wonder at intricate complexity encounters theological awe at purposeful design, showing humanity as the meeting place of matter and meaning, crowned with glory yet anchored in humble origin, summoned into a relational communion that reflects the very inner life of God himself.

The weight of this truth settles upon the soul like an everlasting anchor: to truly apprehend and inwardly possess the boundless dimensions of God's love for humanity—its fathomless depths plunging into the abyss of our brokenness, its towering heights surpassing the heavens, its all-embracing width enfolding every tribe and tongue, and its unending length stretching from creation's first dawn to eternity's farthest horizon—we, wanderers of wonder, are first summoned to discern the true nature of our fragile yet dignified souls: an echo of Eden's evening, cradled in the mystery of our original nakedness, born from the womb of nonexistence into a noble nativity more exalted than the noblest of all created things. It is precisely in that exalted instant of intellectual and spiritual awakening—much like the luminous dawn of insight in the patristic meditation on divine mysteries—when the veil is gently lifted and the ultimate "why" behind such unfathomable love suddenly stands revealed: a love precisely proportioned to the sublime dignity of the human person: it unites the transient, material dimension of created existence with the imperishable splendor of the divine image imprinted within us. This love thus spans both the visible terrain of embodied life and the boundless reaches of the eternal, transforming what could seem an overwhelming outpouring of grace into the harmonious climax of the entire cosmic story.

Although the golden word *'love'* (âhab in Hebrew) rarely graces the ancient leaves of Genesis when describing the covenantal relationship and rapport between God and man, leaving these faint whispers of divine affection standing in sharp contrast to how it is woven throughout the Epistles of John as a core theme, where it echoes like a resounding anthem compared to mere footnote. Nevertheless, this reticence in verbal expression does not necessarily imply the absence of God›s love in the creation narrative—rather, his divine affection shines forth luminously through his deeds of creation, surpassing the bounds of mere proclamation. Upon careful reading and introspective reflection, the enlightened beholder perceives that God›s love was powerfully and effectively present within the mechanics of creation itself, pervading the foundational workings of his sovereign handiwork. For every act of his man-centered creation stands as a timeless testament of his devotion to humanity. At heart, his actions spoke profoundly louder than his words could ever do—his craftsmanship roared with such profound depth and volume where lips held silence, with those creative gestures of love drowning out unvoiced affection. This reinforces the heartfelt exhortation from John, the beloved apostle: "*My little children, let us not love in word or in tongue, but in deed and in truth*" (I John 3:18 NKJV).

To rephrase for clarity, right from that primal dawn of the human story, the Creator-God was practically exemplifying his love for humankind without explicitly uttering the familiar words "*I love you*" anywhere within the Pentateuch's inaugural scroll. Creating us in his own semblance and similitude stands as undeniable proof of that unspoken love; designing a world that revolves around our existence further deepens the assurance; welcoming us to feast *a piacere* on Eden's banquet of abundance right after the completion of creation's labor further compounds the mounting evidence; and electing us to exclusively share premortal communion with him in the heavenly courts before our entry into mortal life? That, too, was divine love in active motion, although not yet in full swing. All these instances underscore the supremacy of tangible works over trifling words in God's mode of revelation—where deeds outshine doctrines as the sun the moon—with right practice (orthopraxy) wielding greater revelatory force over right precept (orthodoxy) in ultimately unveiling the truth about God's ineffable love for mankind. Yet it belongs to thoughtful reflection to also recognize that these early sparks—these foundational outpourings of his deep and unrelenting love for the Adamic race—unfolded long before the dreadful hour when that love would stand confronted by the ultimate crucible of its supreme test, compelled to stretch beyond the farthest boundaries of its own nature and summoned to pour itself out in extravagant abundance across the unfolding chapters of the human story.

THE POSTLAPSARIAN HISTORY OF THE HUMAN STORY: THE FALL OF MAN

All things considered, life in Eden's early era was, for the newlyweds, altogether very good, glorious, and blissful. As their new world is what you would rightly call the dawn of a 'perfect world,' where everything went according to God's perfect will, his original plan, and his eternal purpose. At the heart of the paradisiacal order, there was absolutely nothing missing and nothing broken—no fracture whatsoever; every element, every facet of creation, reposed in its immaculate, unblemished condition of sublime perfection—a state organically pluperfect, where harmony pulsed through the very veins of existence like an eternal, unbroken symphony. This Genesis portrait of man's blessed beginning shows us a humanity on a rise—soaring, not one on a decline—falling into desolation. Adam, Eden's soaring sovereign, imparadised in God's rarefied presence, graciously flew in sacred summits and flourished in a flawless firmament, pure and perfect. Until, of course, his heart was lifted in pride above the height of his God-ordained flight—his ambitions towering beyond the towers of his own Babel—then came his fall—the Fall of mankind—a fall so catastrophic man will never be able to rise out of the depths of perpetual descent and decline without the intervention of the Divine. Adam, in his bid to transcend his created role, was enticed by the allure of forbidden knowledge and willfully succumbed to the temptation of the forbidden fruit, against God's express command: "*Of every tree of the garden you may freely eat; but of the tree of the knowledge of good and evil you shall not eat, for in the day that you eat of it you shall surely die*" (Gen 2:16–17 NKJV). Alas, in that fatal bite, he fell from flight to fright (Gen 3:9–10), leaving his lofty height in blithe loss to a lasting blight. Fundamentally disrupting the perfect harmony of God's creation, introducing—chaos for order—ashes for beauty—death for life—darkness for light, and so forth. His willful disobedience to his superior—the Creator-God—also meant that none of his inferiors—God's creation—would be obeying him going forward. Not even Adam's inferior nature, his body, would stay subject to him anymore; it rather would go on to assert dominion over him, getting him and his descendants to go against their own will, and even worse, the will of God.

Acknowledging the reality of this fallen condition, the Apostle Paul pens down the following thoughts: "*For what I am doing, I do not understand. For what I will to do, that I do not practice; but what I hate, that I do . . . For I know that in me (that is, in my flesh) nothing good dwells; for to will is present with me, but how to perform what is good I do not find. For the good that I will to do, I do not do; but the evil I will not to do, that I practice*" (Rom 7:15, 18–19 NKJV). This inner conflict did not escape the notice of ancient philosophers, who discerned two contrary motions within the human soul: one, stirred by grace, ascends toward the divine source of its being, yearning for union with the Creator; the other, weighed down by sin, is cast below its created dignity—chained to sensual appetites and epicurean desires. These sages acknowledged that humanity exists in an intermediate state of tension, poised between the celestial glory of its divine origin and the base instincts of its fallen nature—its rational soul reflecting the light of God's truth, its sensory inclinations bound to the frailty of earthly existence. Man, therefore, stands as a creature of paradox, sharing in the intellectual likeness of angels yet tethered to the sensual passions of beasts: his mind, radiant with majestic purpose, ascends to peerless virtue, molded in the image of divine glory, shining with celestial light; yet his senses, swayed by sordid impulses, sinking into fleeting shadows, and shackled to ephemeral desires, remain tethered to the beastly. Virtues, rooted in the soul, moderate these opposing impulses, and love, as the preeminent virtue, orders and tempers all others—not only because it serves as the archetype and measure for all virtues, but because God, having created man to bear his image, wills that all human acts, as in himself, be governed by love and directed toward love's eternal end.

As it turns out, in that fate-sealing moment when Adam took that eternally lamentable second bite—trailing ominously in the wake of his wife's first bite—a secondary dawn arose over the horizon of Paradise. Alas, the fateful second bite has just ushered in a second dawn, not in glory's gleaming gown but in the enveloping shroud of gloom's grieving garment, culminating in their anguished eviction from Eden's hallowed embrace in the devastating aftermath of the Fall. Indeed, this secondary dawn, so tragically inaugurated by the second bite, emerges as a dayrise eclipsed by the encroaching darkfall of doom and gloom—a mournful morning cast under the heavy veil of spiritual darkness and existential terror. Signaling a grievous genesis, they would grieve evermore, wishing that woeful day had never dawned over the azure skies of Eden—a moment in time that should never have happened in time—a time that should never have had the time of day, upending the time of their lives in Paradise. Envision it in the mind's luminous theater: the gates slam shut, a thunderclap of thorns, what wailing of worlds welcomes Adam—what a chorus of cosmic grief attends the banishment of this wayward wanderer, who now finds himself driven out into the wild wasteland of the uncharted world, wayworn yet ever wistful for Eden's walled wonderland. Consider also the archetypal tale of Eve's fateful chat in the verdant paradise of Eden, seduced by the serpent's sly reframing of divine command as mere suggestion—beguiled by his whispers that promised enlightenment but delivered exile and anguish. For not only did she rob herself of paradise—shortchange her shot at harmony—but she also ended up dragging her closest companion into exile, turning a shared bliss into mutual ruin. Her story serves as an eternal cautionary emblem: deception does not confine its venom to the victim alone.

In yielding to its allure, she did not merely forfeit her innocence and harmony; she set in motion waves of sorrow that rippled outward, touching every life bound to hers and turning a garden of abundance into a wilderness of regret. So too with us in the modern thicket of misinformation, manipulative narratives, and subtle distortions—whether propagated by others or self-imposed through denial. Beyond the personal toll of diminished potential and squandered opportunities, deception exacts a collateral devastation upon those we hold most dear: our families, our confidants, and our communities. We might extend a hand in love, offer counsel born of pure-hearted concern, or build bridges of support with the noblest of fibers—yet if those gestures are woven from threads of falsehood, they fray and fail, inflicting unintended wounds that scar deeper than any overt malice. Eve, being deceived, had paved the perfect runway for her husband's highfalutin pride to run swiftly ahead of him, with his downfall trailing them the whole time, only to soon catch up with these two who had become one in holy matrimony. Adam's onward ascent from glory to glory, undone by unchecked ambition, turned the glory of Eden's Paradise to peril, penalized by his own presumptuous sin of pride. Picture the Divine hand lifting Adam from the slimy depths of the miry clay of dust, where shadows feast on forgotten echoes, and planting his faltering feet firmly upon the ivory summit of the rock of glory and honor—yet behold the folly: Adam, enticed by the whisper of forbidden ambition and fueled by hubris to ascend beyond the stars of self-crowned sovereignty, slumped down into the abyssal shadows of utter debasement, a bottomless pit where echoes of glory mock the silence of his fall.

From soaring in the glorious heights of divine delight to stumbling in the inglorious depths of sin's shadow, his fall, a fatal flaw, forged a fractured fate, leaving all mankind languishing below, unable to leap back to the heights of Eden's lost luster. Alas, Paradise was lost—lost to pride—lost to that pride that went before the Adamic Fall, banishing bliss and birthing bitter brokenness in man's world. For so costly is the price of Adam's disobedience, generations of his descendants after him would have to spend their days in the futility of footing the bill. By simply mismanaging the token of free choice, with which God had uniquely endowed him, he chose the very path God explicitly cautioned him against, thereby sinking the ship of the blissful human experience that God—the Primum Mobile—had set in motion from the cradle of human existence. This pivotal act in Eden, aside from turning Adam's life upside down, also marked a tragic turning point in the formative years of the human story, radically transforming the story from one of divine communion to one of alienation and moral decline. Incurring the stain of the original sin fundamentally besmirched the *imago Dei*—the Divine likeness that set humanity apart as God's image-bearers, ushering in the unchecked reign of sin and unleashing the unfettered dominion of death, not just on Adam and his wife alone, but on his posterity (cf. Gen 2:16–17). Sin became an inescapable reality, weaving itself into the fabric of human nature and society, as Romans 5:12 attests: " . . . *through one man sin entered the world, and death through sin, and thus death spread to all men, because all sinned.*"

By allowing the serpent access into the sacred garden of his heart, Adam equally granted him unfettered access into the broader garden of his life and, by extension, threw wide open the gates of man's world to the malevolent influence of that same demonic force. With the serpent's sting of sedition came sin—with sin's sting of disobedience came death. Speaking of unwelcome guests, one can scarcely conceive of more egregious exemplars, since no intruder could possibly be deemed more abhorrent within the realm of human experience than Satan, sin, and death—Satan the adversary himself, along with the blight of sin and the shadow of death. Consequently, it became imperative for Cain, a primordial heir in Adam's genealogical succession, to be duly forewarned in the nascent stages of history, after succumbing to the temptation of that selfsame serpent and perpetrating the cold-blooded murder of his blood brother, Abel, with premeditated malice: " . . . *sin crouches at your door; its desire is for you [to overpower you], but you must master it*" (Gen 4:7 AMP). Nevertheless, given that sin maintains a dominant grip over humanity in its degraded condition following the primordial lapse, achieving mastery over such a formidable foe would unquestionably necessitate external intervention from beyond the human sphere, thereby underscoring the indispensable role of God's grace in the life of any descendant of Adam aspiring to moral virtue.

For although the Immortal Creator had fashioned them, His image-bearers, in the beginning—His immortal image majestically cast upon frail vessels of mortal clay—calling them "*gods*" and "*sons of the Most High*" God (Ps 82:6–7)—yet, through the grievous Fall, Adam and his descendants are destined to fall the fall of death—doomed to die the death of mere mortals. Their blessed semblance, once radiant with the sacred spark of divine essence, now dimmed by sin's sorrowful sting—their celestial crown of glory cast down to corruption's cruel conquest—their exalted origin humbled within mortality's unyielding grasp—their mortal frame, fated to crumble from dust to dust whence it came, yet ever yearning for salvation's eternal embrace. For by eating freely from the forbidden fruit, poisoned with the venom of rebellion, they fell headlong into sin—cast down from the empyrean heights of divine communion into the shadowed valley of sin's dominion. For by defying the commandment of the Righteous Lawgiver, they fell by the beguiling counsel of the crafty serpent. Sadly, falling into sin equally meant falling into death—for to turn from the eternal Source of Life is to embrace the stark privation of life. Alas, Adam barely even lived before he died—scarcely tasted the savory sweetness of divine life before the wretchedness of death's grim shadow fell upon him. He barely even walked before he fell—hardly ever walked in God's beatific blessing of immortality—before stumbling headlong into the chilling embrace of the serpent's cruel curse of mortality. He had barely even mastered his strides before racing swiftly into sin's treacherous snare—his faltering feet, yet to find their steady pace in the paths of righteousness, were woefully quick to run amok into the perilous pitfall of unrighteousness—echoing the wisdom of the Wise Preacher: "*A heart that devises wicked plans, feet that are swift in running to evil*" (Prov 6:18). Adam's heart, far too tender to discern the good from the evil, and feet, way too feeble and frail to stand steadfast in innocence, sprinted toward nocence, as if drawn by some fatal allure to forsake Divine grace. Oh, what a mournful misstep, venturing into vice's vile vortex! Revealing the reckless haste of humanity's first rebellion, mirroring the soul's perilous inclination to trade eternal glory for momentary guilt in a moment's reckless choice, ever prone to stray before we stand, ever eager to embrace our own unrighteousness before we fathom the heights of God's righteousness. Man, made brute, now a shadow of the man he once was, merely murmuring his Maker's memory. Oh, what a wretched man he became! Who will deliver him from this miserable life lived under the savage dominion of sin and death? (cf. Rom 7:24–25). (Prose Poem by Israel Nwachukwu: The Reckless Haste of Man's First Rebellion — abridged version).

Blaise Pascal paints quite a gripping imagery of this when he said:

> *"I [the God] . . . who formed you, and who alone can teach you what you are. But you are now no longer in the state in which I formed you. I created man holy, innocent, perfect. I filled him with light and intelligence. I communicated to him my glory and my wonders. The eye of man saw then the majesty of God. He was not then in the darkness which blinds him, nor subject to mortality and the woes which afflict him. But he has not been able to sustain so great glory without falling into pride. He wanted to make himself his own centre and independent of my help. He withdrew himself from my rule; and, on his making himself equal to me by the desire of finding his happiness in himself, I abandoned him to himself. And setting in revolt the creatures that were subject to him, I made them his enemies; so that man is now become like the brutes and so estranged from me that there scarce remains to him a dim vision of his Author."*

He goes so far as to point out that Adam, although had organically been created in the pristine state of immortality and incorruptibility, where no darkness dimmed his gaze—no decay dragged him down—no distress disturbed his delight—no shackle of suffering seized him. Yet, hurled himself into the mire of mortality and the chains of corruption. Indeed, man was "*not then in the darkness which [now] blinds him, nor subject to mortality and the woes which [now] afflict him.*" All the more true when you consider the Divine appraisal that was given at the concluding verses of Genesis chapter 1, declaring all God's creation *'very good'* in their primordial harmony, untouched by such corruption. Adam had everything he needed, furnished with all necessities required for the idyllic life that God had envisioned for both himself and all humanity. Per II Peter 1:3, we could say rightly that God, by his divine power and providence, had furnished the proto-couple with " . . . *all things that pertain to life and godliness* . . . " (II Pet 1:3 NKJV). So much so that God's blessings and boon, for them, did not necessarily come in the form of distant promises or prophecies they were to hope for or wait for, nor some prayer requests they were meant to believe for, but were readily manifest—made readily available within their immediate grasp. More like apples—ripe for reaping and freshly fetched off an apple tree at one's behest, this divine largesse, manifest and accessible, required no supplication, only reception.

So much so that you could not ask Adam and Eve to pray in this manner: "*Our Father in heaven, Hallowed be Your name. Your kingdom come. Your will be done On earth as it is in heaven. Give us this day our daily bread*" (Matt 6:9–11 NKJV)—without winding up preaching to the choir. The reason that would be pointless is, first, because God's kingdom had already come—his Edenic kingdom, its heavenly realities readily manifest down here on earth—in the paradisiacal garden, and his perfect will for their lives was already done or at least set in motion on earth exactly as it is in heaven. Besides, *'Our Father in heaven'* was more or less down here on earth below with them—his divine presence localized in the Garden of Eden. Such that they need not say in their hearts, 'Who will ascend to heaven?'—that is, to bring God's presence down from above, or 'Who will descend the earth below?'—that is, to bring his glory up from the abyss (compare and contrast with Romans 10:6–7). Intimate communion—that sacred, unmediated bond and boundless closeness with the Almighty God—was an exalted, irrevocable privilege the proto-couple lavishly enjoyed in Eden, ever basking uninterruptedly in the life-giving sunshine of his unveiled glory—that shekinah radiance of holiness and delight that enveloped their every moment and movement. So for them, in that idyllic paradise unmarred by the shadow of shame, the case was rather one of inescapable intimacy and ubiquity, reechoing the Psalmist's soul-stirring cry: "*Where could I go from your Spirit? Where could I run and hide from your face? . . . It's impossible to disappear from you or to ask the darkness to hide me, for your presence is everywhere, bringing light into my night*" (Ps 139:7–11 TPT). This verse bears witness to the Creator's all-pervading nearness, a stark reality Adam soon discovered with agonizing clarity when he got caught frantically stitching fig leaves to shield his shame and camouflage himself from the divine presence in the aftermath of his catastrophic fall into sin, only to realize with crushing inevitability that he could not really hide from or evade Omnipresence, not especially when so acutely localized within the four walls of Eden's wonderland, where each rustling of the leaves and sighing of the winds whispered the Creator's unwavering gaze (see Genesis 3:9–10).

What is more, in that pristine cosmic paradise, there would have been no need whatsoever to beseech God with such fervent supplications as *'Give us this day our daily bread,'* because all the bread of sustenance they needed and were ever going to need was already provided for, laid up in advance by the Creator's hand. Until, of course, man's hubris fractured this idyllic state, severing his rational soul from its unfettered communion with the Divine Source and compelling it henceforth to plead for the very good he once possessed without asking. Perforce, Adam's descendants will now have to ask to receive, seek in order to find, and even go doorknocking on heaven's gate to be granted the privilege of enjoying the same heaven's holy haven that God's grace once freely granted in galore. In essence, you should ask to receive, or shall we rather say, ask to reclaim what was originally given at creation; seek to recover what was previously granted but lost in the Fall; and knock to have the gates of God's Edenic kingdom reopened to us because we were locked out in the wake of Adam's disobedience (cf. John 3:3–5). Consequently, in your prayers you are not asking for anything new or seeking anything beyond what God originally bestowed upon your protoancestors in Eden. From the very genesis of humanity, he generously supplied every necessity required for a life of perfect existence. Consider, for instance, that in the garden—where neither sickness nor any debilitating force of nature held sway—Adam had no occasion to offer pleading supplications for life or health. The tree of life, which God himself had planted in the midst of the garden, stood perpetually available, ensuring the continual possibility of divine wellness and enduring longevity. It promised to renew their youth like the eagle's—preserving them in perpetual vigor and youthfulness, with no genuine threat ever endangering their physical well-being. All this remained theirs for as long as humanity desired precisely what God himself desired for them. Thus, communion with the Creator-God was not driven by any sense of lack—for every good was supplied in overflowing abundance—but from an ever-deepening desire to know and cherish him as the eternal Fountain of all goodness. This fellowship, grounded in growing intimacy with God, was purposed to draw Adam progressively nearer to the divine nature, binding man to his Maker in a relationship of ordered love—perfect in its eternal harmony—and so fulfilling the supreme mandate of love expressed in the Shema: "*Hear, O Israel: The LORD our God, the LORD is one! You shall love the LORD your God with all your heart, with all your soul, and with all your strength*" (Deuteronomy 6:4–5). Yet Adam, in his own choosing, preferred otherwise. In his attempt to break free from dependence on God—the very Source of all goodness—and to ascend instead to the summit of self-sufficiency, he plunged himself into a far deeper and more chronic dependency: not upon the good God, but upon himself and upon creatures lesser than himself. The Fall fundamentally remade humanity into beings defined by ceaseless need and disordered craving, their nature reshaped into one of perpetual reliance upon the external creation inferior to them. From the first man and woman onward, through countless generations of their far-flung heirs, all inherit this legacy of want, their souls bearing the weight of disordered desire, ever seeking the immutable Good from which they have become estranged by their own willful turning away.

The far-reaching consequences of Adam's rebellious act have rippled through every generation, manifesting in the moral and physical decay that marks the human condition when severed from divine grace. This mystery of the Fall—profound, sobering, and deeply unsettling—continues to baffle and rattle successive ages, laying bare the extent of humanity's fallenness while underscoring the urgent necessity of divine redemption. Yet even in this broken state, the human soul, though marred and wounded, still bears faint yet enduring traces of the divine image. Beneath the scars, it persists in a restless yearning for restoration, quietly reflecting God's original purpose despite the rupture of the Fall. Thus, the postlapsarian history of the human story—spanning the long centuries before the first Christmas—lingers in tragedy: a chronicle inundated with cycles of rise and fall, repeated moral failures, and unrestrained corruption. Across the vast expanse of history, man's restless yearning to reclaim the transcendental heights of Eden's lost luster persisted—an unquenchable cry etched deep within the soul of civilizations. From the majestic ziggurats of Babylon (circa 2000 B.C.) to the imperial grandeur of Rome, this enduring thirst for transcendent purpose has spanned millennia. Ancient rites—such as the sorrow-laden laments of the Sumerians (circa 2000 B.C.) and the sacred Vedic chants of ancient India (circa 1500–1000 B.C.)—gave voice to a timeless longing to restore the fractured bond between the Creator-God and his errant creation. In Babylon, priests climbed the terraced heights of their temple towers—the renowned ziggurats—performing solemn rituals and studying the movements of the heavens in order to discern the divine will, interpret the cosmic order, and align earthly affairs with the purposes of their gods.

Meanwhile, in Athens—the celebrated intellectual center of the ancient world around 500 B.C.—thinkers such as Socrates, Plato, and later the Stoics and Epicureans engaged in searching philosophical dialogues and rigorous debate, probing the nature of the Divine, wrestling with questions of existence and morality, and pondering the origin and structure of the cosmos. Even as late as the closing decades of the first century A.D., the Athenians and their visitors remained renowned for their insatiable hunger to explore and discuss novel ideas. The Book of

Acts 17:16–34 particularly recounts the Apostle Paul's encounter with precisely such thinkers in Athens. With verse 21 capturing their characteristic spirit: "*Now all the Athenians and the foreigners living there spent their time in nothing else than telling or hearing some new thing*" (Acts 17:21 TPT). This passage underscores their insatiable appetite for the latest ideas and philosophies, a pursuit that drew them continually to public gathering places such as the Areopagus. There, they eagerly debated the teachings of the Stoics and Epicureans, engaging in lively intellectual exchange. Yet, like the ritualistic inquiries of the Babylonians before them, their searching remained firmly anchored in the realm of human speculation—frequently overintellectualized, abstract, and ultimately detached from lived reality. Despite their sincere and earnest efforts, both groups fell short, unable to bridge the vast, untraversable chasm that separates fallen humanity from the eternal God. The Babylonians' elaborate rituals, rooted in polytheism, and the Greeks' sophisticated philosophical inquiries—though intellectually impressive—both fell short of the divine revelation needed to truly know the invisible Creator. In his address at the Areopagus, the Apostle Paul directly confronted this deficiency. He met the Athenians precisely where their restless search for truth had led them, then unveiled the one true God who dwells beyond human temples and surpasses every human conception. For, as Paul boldly proclaimed, it is only through God's gracious self-disclosure that humanity can discover the way to eternity—a path that remained hidden from both the ritualistic Babylonians and the speculative Greeks, despite all their sincere and diligent striving. The fateful fracture of the Fall—severing humanity's intimate communion with God—cast a creeping, pervasive shadow of moral corruption and idolatry across the long arc of history, leaving civilizations perpetually haunted by an existential hunger for transcendent meaning. This truth finds especially poignant expression in pagan societies, where the rise and fall of mighty empires vividly illustrate the ephemeral nature of human glory and the inherent vanity and fragility of all earthly power. Consider the successive collapses: Babylon, vanquished by Persian conquest in 539 B.C. (as foretold in Daniel 5), its legendary Hanging Gardens eventually swallowed by time; Alexander's sprawling empire, which disintegrated into warring fragments immediately following his death in 323 B.C.; Rome's long trajectory from republic (509 B.C.) through the decisive defeat of Carthage (146 B.C.) to its eventual dissolution; and Byzantium, the enduring eastern heir of Rome, finally yielding to Ottoman forces in 1453 A.D. Each downfall—whether through military overthrow, internal disintegration, or overreaching ambition—unveils a recurring cycle of ascent, hubris, overextension, and inevitable ruin.

This enduring lesson is inscribed indelibly across the pages of human history, standing firm and unshaken through every age: man, though created as an imperfect free moral agent and entrusted with the sacred gift of free choice, can neither establish nor sustain a perfect world apart from the perfect Moral Maker—God himself. Free moral agency, while a noble divine endowment, demands divine guidance if it is to fulfill its eternal purpose; without it, the inherent tendency toward chaos or self-destruction proves perilously strong. God has endeavoured to demonstrated this truth repeatedly throughout time. He first did so by placing Adam in the pristine paradise of Eden at the dawn of creation, entrusting him with the solemn responsibility of preserving that newly fashioned world in its default state of divine perfection. As Genesis 2:15 bears witness, "*Then the Lord God took the man and put him in the garden of Eden to tend and keep it.*" But of course we all now know that Adam failed woefully in that responsibility. While Eden symbolizes the original state of perfection, where humanity lived in harmony with the Creator-God, creation, and itself. Adam's moral failure in Eden underscores the fact that man's inherent imperfection will always stand as a hindrance, undercutting divine perfection. God sought once more to establish this same truth by leading the descendants of the patriarch Abraham—the Jewish people—into the Promised Land, a place flowing with milk and honey. Yet their history of repeated unfaithfulness—marked by idolatry, rebellion, and eventual exile—served only to confirm what Eden had already shown: human effort alone, however earnest, cannot sustain or preserve the divine vision of a perfect world. Both instances—Eden and the Promised Land—serve as foretypes, prophetic foreshadows that anticipate the eternal kingdom of God. Eden stands as the archetype of the lost ideal, the pristine harmony once enjoyed and then forfeited; the Promised Land represents a partial, historical realization of God's covenant promises, a foretaste of fulfillment granted within the bounds of time. Together they stir and awaken within the human heart a profound longing for transcendence—a yearning for a perfect world that lies beyond the reach of temporal decay. By the same movement, they direct humanity toward the eschatological hope of full restoration: a return to paradise can be accomplished not by human striving but through the redemptive work of God himself. This vision finds its eloquent expression in Augustine's magisterial work, *The City of God*, where he declares that true perfection is eschatological in nature—attainable only in the eternal kingdom of God, when every shadow gives way to the unending light of divine consummation.

It goes without saying that at the very core of the fallen human condition lies the word—pride—or, as Scripture so piercingly phrased it, "*the pride of life*" (1 John 2:16). This deep-seated vice did not perish with Adam when he died at the age of nine hundred and thirty; rather, it has persisted with undiminished force in the hearts of his descendants across countless millennia. Its manifestations infiltrate every sphere of human society one might examine—from the towering monuments of ancient ambition to the gleaming citadels of modern self-sufficiency. From the architectonic audacity of Babel, where humanity sought to reach the heavens by its own hand, to the hegemonic hubris of Babylon, the ancient serpent continues to offer the same primordial temptation: to dethrone God entirely or erase Him altogether—whether by expelling Him from the hidden chambers of the human heart or by banishing Him from the external structures and institutions that shape man's world. Thus the same primordial temptation reappears across the centuries, repackaged in ever-changing guises: "*Then the serpent said to the woman, 'You will not surely die. For God knows that in the day you eat of it your eyes will be opened, and you will be like God, knowing good and evil'*" (Genesis 3:4–5 NKJV). The insidious seed of doubting God's reality or His revealed truth—planted as the very hallmark of pride—continues to be carefully nurtured in human hearts to this day. Pride and doubt walk hand in hand as inseparable twin forces. From this poisoned root springs atheism as a bitter harvest, alongside authoritarianism, the collectivist constructs of Communism, the socioeconomic syntheses of Socialism, the delusion of self-divinization, and the persistent human aspiration toward apotheosis. Each of these ideologies, in its own way, seeks to supplant the Creator's sovereignty, to deny or at least diminish his very existence (his Dasein), to question or subvert his disclosed revelations, or to usurp his rightful governance over all things—leaving the soul adrift in the desolate void of self-proclaimed existential autonomy.

Satan had sold Adam his own treacherous obsession and bombastic delusion: not merely to "*become like*" God in similitude, but to "*become*" God himself—to transcend the boundary of likeness and seize divine essence outright. Tragically, Adam embraced this lie with unrestrained zeal, buying into it hook, line, and sinker, and thereby became a willing participant in the most audacious act of treachery ever conceived—against the Almighty himself. To aspire beyond one's created and ordained essence is already a grave fault; yet to conspire toward incarnating the Creator, to usurp his throne, represents an incomparably darker abomination. For true Godhood would demand either the subjugation of divine sovereignty—reducing God to captivity—or His complete eradication, since no cosmos can endure two supreme beings, nor can the order of being sustain two ultimate authorities. Yet God harbors no jealousy, no insecurity, concerning humanity's longing to reflect him; on the contrary, he himself invites and delights in such pursuit. He created mankind precisely as bearers and ambassadors of his image, and in his written Word he repeatedly summons mortals to press toward divine perfection: "*Therefore you shall be perfect, just as your Father in heaven is perfect*" (Matthew 5:48 NKJV). The Almighty takes joy in his image-bearers striving to embody his communicable attributes and perfections. This truth lays bare the real nature of the primordial transgression: the sin of the first man did not consist in desiring likeness to God, nor in pursuing divine similitude, but in fomenting a coup against the Creator—seeking to unseat him, to seize his authority, to overthrow his rule, and to claim for himself those incommunicable attributes that belong to God alone.

From that fateful Edenic moment onward, humanity has clung with stubborn tenacity to this disordered craving—the seditious impulse to become its own god. This satanic preoccupation has assumed countless historical disguises, infiltrating both individual hearts and the very structures of society in myriad forms. For example, individuals frequently seek to elevate themselves as pseudo-deities over their fellow human beings, giving rise to authoritarianism and despotism in every age. To carry out these ambitions effectively, however, such perpetrators almost invariably resort to the outright rejection—or at least the radical displacement—of the One True God. This pattern becomes especially pronounced in ideologies such as communism and socialism, where the state arrogates to itself the divine prerogatives once reserved for God alone: the ultimate provider, protector, and sovereign arbiter of human existence and national life. In this way, these systems mirror the unified defiance at Babel, where humanity, bound together by a single language, shared purpose, and collective ambition, sought to expel God from their cosmic domain and thereby claim divinity for themselves. But, of course, the rebellion proved so grave that God himself was compelled to intervene: he disrupted their conspiratorial ambition by scattering the builders across the earth and confounding their unified language into a multitude of tongues. Yet this unyielding desire to usurp divine authority—first ignited in the Fall within Eden—continues to beat as a restless, persistent pulse in the hearts of Adam's descendants. Though God's righteous judgment shattered Babel's collective, disordered ambition by diversifying their speech, the deep-seated inclination to ascend to divine status or dethrone the Creator has never been extinguished; it endures to this day. Far more than a mere echo of the fateful transgression in the Garden of Eden, this impulse mirrors the very vainglorious obsession of Satan himself, who was the first creature of God ever to declare in his heart: "*I will ascend into heaven, I will exalt my throne above the stars of God; I will also sit on the mount of the congregation on the farthest sides of the north; I will ascend above the heights of the clouds, I will be like the Most High*" (Isaiah 14:13–14 NKJV).

Do not be deceived when Satan veils his sinister ambition behind the seemingly modest declaration, "*I will be like the Most High.*" What he truly intends is nothing less than the usurpation of God's sovereignty—to exalt his own throne above the Almighty's. This very phrase exposes the heart of his seditious conspiracy: the determination to place himself in supreme authority over the Creator. It was precisely this rebellion, conceived in the adversary's heart long before humanity's creation, that planted the seed of the cosmic conspiracy which fallen humanity, in its weakness, eagerly embraced when it heard the serpent's whisper: "*You will be like God.*" To exalt his throne above God's and to sit enthroned there could only mean one of two outcomes: either God must somehow cease to exist, or he must be forcibly dethroned and displaced. This ancient plot, born of profound discontent with the station of being made in God's image—content merely to be "*like God*" rather than to become God himself—reveals the adversary's refusal to accept the boundary between creature and Creator, a refusal that has echoed through every age in humanity's own restless pursuit of self-deification. Born not from human ingenuity but from diabolical design, not of mortal origin but conceived in the adversary's prelapsarian rebellion, this impulse drives men relentlessly to exalt themselves—either crowning themselves as gods or subjugating their fellow creatures under a false scepter of authority. It mirrors the celestial fall itself, when Lucifer, drawing a third of heaven's angels in his wake, plummeted from radiant glory into the consuming craving to occupy God's rightful place. Atheism, therefore, is far more than a mere posture of intellectual skepticism or a dispassionate, disinterested denial of God's existence. It stands instead as a full-orbed philosophical manifesto of self-deification: by rejecting the Creator, humanity anoints itself as the sole architect and sovereign of its destiny. Yet across every age, this aspiration to divine heights has invariably collapsed beneath its own unsustainable weight. As every act of self-exaltation or domination reverberates as an echo of this primal sin—a futile, ever-repeated rebellion against the unchangeable eternal order. Across every age, humanity rewrites the same tragic narrative of hubris: a restless refusal to embrace the humble, ordained place assigned to us as creatures fashioned by God. In denying the Creator, man attempts to become the sole author of his own existence, yet this illusion of grandeur serves only to sever the soul from its true purpose and destiny. Left adrift, it wanders in the dim shadow of the unassailable Divine—whose throne stands forever secure, untouched and unshaken by all such striving. Though fashioned in the very likeness of God, man rebels against the creaturely limits inherent to his being—yearning not merely to mirror the Creator but to master Him. Like clay that rises in defiance against the potter's patient and skillful hand, humanity spurns the sovereign touch that formed it, aspiring instead to seize the sovereign role that belongs to its Maker alone. In this delusion, men dream of divinity itself, convinced that self-sovereignty would crown and perfect their existence.

Imagine a pot, swollen with presumption, that in its bloated bid to become its own potter would exhaust every means to avoid confessing the humbling truth: "*But now, O Lord, You are our Father; We are the clay, and You our Potter; And all we are the work of Your hand*" (Isaiah 64:8 NKJV). In this disordered craving to transcend its created nature, humanity spurns the humility of remaining God's handiwork and inverts the divine order entirely—elevating the pot above its Potter, as though the creature could ever usurp the Creator's sovereign prerogative. Isaiah 45:9–10 pronounces a solemn woe upon such subversive pride, where the thing formed dares to contend with its Former, questioning His wisdom or even denying His very existence: "*Woe to him who strives with his Maker! Let the potsherd strive with the potsherds of the earth! Shall the clay say to him who forms it, 'What are you making?' Or shall your handiwork say, 'He has no hands'? Woe to him who says to his father, 'What are you begetting?' Or to the woman, 'What have you brought forth?'*" (NKJV). God, through the same prophet, further condemns this inversion: "*Surely you have things turned around! Shall the potter be esteemed as the clay; For shall the thing made say of him who made it, 'He did not make me'? Or shall the thing formed say of him who formed it, 'He has no understanding'?"* (Isa 29:16 NKJV). In contemporary thought, this rebellion manifests in secular scholarship, where celebrated authors publish brash books with sensationalist titles, denying or undermining God's existence with scientific or academic certainty, enthroning human intellect as supreme. Such intellectual hubris does not only circulate within the academic landscape or the so-called ivory towers; it permeates cultural currents, polluting the Overton window, corrupting the spiritus mundi, leaving the vision of human destiny warped, while alienating the rational soul from its divine origin. This delusion of autonomy, rooted in a refusal to submit to the Creator's design, further estranges the soul from its true purpose. Yet the clay cannot become the Potter, nor can its rebellion undo the Potter's artistry, for its very form testifies to his eternal sovereignty, an unassailable truth no rebellion can overturn. For if any formed creature from the clay of the earth or the firmament above should rise in rebellion to disclaim the Creator-God who breathed life into its nostrils, lo, that rebellion is begotten of the serpent's subtlety; yea, if any fallen one, bearing the mark of Adam's curse, should nurse enmity against the promised Seed who crushes the head of the ancient foe, behold, that enmity abides in the snare of the Evil One—for he, the father of lies from the garden's dawn, has indeed cast a veil over their hearts, lest the light of the glorious gospel of truth should shine upon them.

In their ambition to transcend the boundaries of mortal existence, ancient rulers and prominent historical figures have, in the same vein, wielded their authority and leveraged ad captandum in claiming divine status, seeking the adulation of men to overcome the limits of their earthly existence. This phenomenon, although reflecting a universal human longing to transcend mortality and reclaim a lost dominion over creation, yet remains an aspiration twisted into prideful self-exaltation. Strikingly exemplified by the emperors of ancient Rome and other notable Mediterranean figures, who pursued deification with relentless zeal. Their efforts—often marked by grandiose displays of self-aggrandizement—betray a deep-rooted impulse to rise above the human condition—perhaps to recapture the *imago Dei* which was lost in the Fall. The Caesarean dynasty, with its calculated ambition craving for celestial crowns, epitomized this proud pursuit. Julius Caesar, a towering figure in Roman history, was officially deified as *Divi Iulius* ('the Divine Julius') by the Roman Senate in 42 B.C., following his assassination. This act of deification was not merely posthumous reverence but a calculated political maneuver to cement his legacy and authority. For Caesar himself had laid the groundwork for this divine status during his lifetime. Between 47 and 46 B.C., he minted the silver denarius, a coin that celebrated his illustrious ancestry, with the obverse bearing the image of the goddess Venus, from whom Caesar claimed descent, while the reverse depicted the mythological founder Aeneas carrying his father, Anchises, from the burning ruins of Troy—a potent symbol of Caesar's divine lineage and heroic stature. After being declared *dictator perpetuo* (dictator for life) in 44 B.C., Caesar further emblazoned his new title on another series of silver denarii, this time featuring a wreathed portrait of himself. This imagery, unprecedented for a living Roman, served as an emblem of his self-proclaimed deific status and despotic authority, imposing his godlike image on the Roman world. Caesar's successor, Augustus, another titan of ambition, continued this tradition of divine self-fashioning. Known as *Divi filius*—'Son of the Divine One', Augustus capitalized on his adoptive father's deified status to legitimize his own rule. His reign marked the consolidation of the Julio-Claudian dynasty's divine pretensions, as temples, statues, and inscriptions were erected to celebrate his divine sonship, honoring him as a living god.

Following lockstep in the footsteps of their primigenous forebears, the sons of men have historically never been content with remaining just human; they have always aspired to become more—to ascend to the status of Godhood by whatever means possible. Perhaps this drive reflects a distorted desire to regain the divine status lost in the original fall. However, this obsession with deification was not confined to Rome but echoed across the Mediterranean, where other rulers and charlatans similarly sought to ascend to divine heights. Among these figures was the Syrian king Antiochus IV Epiphanes, who boldly styled himself Antiochus Theos Epiphanes ('Antiochus God-Manifest'). This soi-disant divinity demanded that his subjects address him as a god, reflecting his ambition to transcend mortal limitations. Biblical accounts further highlight this pattern of hubris among rulers. King Nebuchadnezzar of Babylon, as described in the Book of Daniel 4, declared himself a god of the earth, erecting a golden statue to be worshipped by his subjects. His arrogance, however, was met with swift divine humbling: God reduced him to a beast-like state to remind him of his mortality. As verse 17 affirms, he did this "*In order that the living may know That the Most High rules in the kingdom of men, Gives it to whomever He will, And sets over it the lowest of men*" (Dan 4:15–17 NKJV). Similarly, King Herod Agrippa I, grandson of Herod the Great, reveled in the divine adulation of the masses. As recorded in Acts 12:21–23, Herod, seated on his throne, accepted the crowd's proclamation that his voice was that of '*a god and not a man.*' An act of blasphemy that provoked swift divine judgment: "*Immediately an angel of the Lord struck him, because he did not give glory to God. And he was eaten by worms and died*" (Acts 12:23, NKJV). Simon Magus, a first-century thaumaturgist also mentioned in the Book of Acts, captivated the people of Samaria with his magical feats and Svengalian influence. Proclaiming himself "*the Great Power of God,*" he held the Samaritans spellbound, convincing them of his divine authority through illusion and spectacle. These divine interventions recorded in Scripture—whether humbling Nebuchadnezzar, striking Herod, or exposing the falsehoods of figures like Simon Magus—underscore a timeless truth: no human can usurp the place of the Creator.

In Augustinian terms, these rulers succumbed to the *libido dominandi*, the lust for domination that seeks to supplant God's sovereignty. Created to love God above all, the soul, disordered by sin, turns inward, seeking its own glory. The historical quest for apotheosis—whether pursued through the scepter of political might, the adulation of cultural acclaim, or the pretense of otherworldly power—inevitably crumbles beneath the weight of human imperfection and God's sovereign dominion. In their pursuit of godlike status or a God complex, these rulers and charlatans reveal a tragic irony: in seeking to become more than human, they lost sight of the true dignity of their created nature—losing their essential humanity in their wrongheaded quest to become more than human outside God's redemptive program. Yet reflecting humanity's deep-seated desire to reclaim the divine likeness bestowed at creation, lost through rebellion, yet twisted into self-exaltation. The *imago Dei,* though tarnished, was never meant to be a stepping stone to self-deification but a call to reflect God's glory through obedience and stewardship. The quest for apotheosis, though born of a longing for transcendence, invariably collapses into the trap of towering pride, as God alone restores the soul to its intended purpose, not through self-deification but through humble submission to his eternal order, where God alone reigns supreme—as the Divine Thearch. As Troy burned under the weight of its own towering pride and the wrath of their fabled gods, so too did mankind stagger through the wreckage of its ambitions, each empire a new Ilium razed by its own pride. The Greeks, in their triumph, sought *kleos*—immortal glory—yet found only fleeting laurels, their victories dissolving like mist before the eternal. Homer chronicled tales of human conflict, but the heart of man, as the Psalmist declares, cries out for an eternal civitas—a celestial city not built by human hands—the New Jerusalem where the disconsolate soul may eventually find rest: "*For here we have no lasting city, but we seek the city that is to come*" (Heb 13:14, ESV). The ash heap of Ilium whispers of Paradise Lost, yet the divine purpose beckons—a redemption not won by sword or stratagem, but by grace that restores the wanderer to the garden of God's presence.

In the shadow of Augustus' golden age, Rome stretched its arms to embrace the world, its aqueducts and legions forging fleeting harmony from chaos, a transient reflection of divine harmony. Yet, as the Wise Preacher laments, all mortal works and their fleeting glory invariably come down to "*Vanity of vanities, says the Preacher, vanity of vanities! All is vanity*" (Ecclesiastes 1:2, ESV). The *Pax Romana* crumbled, as all earthly reigns must, under the weight of corruption and time's relentless march, for no mortal order endures without God's love and his righteous influence. The Stoics urged *apatheia*, detachment from the ephemeral, but the soul's deeper longing, as Augustine knew, was not for Rome's temporal peace but for the eternal Sabbath of God's kingdom come down here on earth. The Colosseum's roars fade into silence, but the promise of a city where the One True God reigns endures, calling humanity back to its primal innocence, to a Paradise where God's will is the eternal law. Athens, radiant with the light of reason, crowned itself with the Parthenon's glory, believing wisdom could conquer fate. Yet, as Sophocles warned, pride begets nemesis; the Peloponnesian War shattered the polis, exposing the fragility of human striving. Plato glimpsed the eternal in the Forms, but his Republic could not silence the soul's ache for something greater—a redemption beyond the cave's shadows. The Athenian agora lies silent, its stones a testament to vanished dreams, but the divine telos endures, pointing humanity toward an Eden restored, where the tree of life blooms anew.

Accordingly, the Scriptures exhort that we "*. . . seek first the kingdom of God and his righteousness . . .* " (Matt 6:33 NKJV), but in the recalcitrant spirit of mankind, it eschews the noble quest for that supernal kingdom and would rather incline toward the abdication of heavenly aspirations altogether, channeling their fervor into forging surrogate sovereignties—ephemeral enclaves of egotism, wherein righteousness recedes before the advance of self-interest—holiness hazarded for hegemony, where God's kingdom's blueprint is supplanted by blueprints of Babel—with temporal power mocking the eternal order. Within the template of prayer handed down to the community of faith in the Synoptic Gospels, the initial focus rests on exalting God as King over and above the kingdom—hallowing his hallowed holiness before beseeching the blessings of his kingdom. With the address "*Our Father who art in the heavens, hallowed be Thy Name*" *taking precedence over the plea "Thy kingdom come,"* it establishes the God-centered axis—a prelude of pure praise unto the King before the plea for his paradisiacal kingdom (Matt 6:9–10 KJV). As the concluding doxology of this petition further confirms, the Ever-Reigning Thearch, who alone possesses perpetual kingship—to whom kingdom, power, and glory pertain without end—surpasses and subsumes all such endowments. As Scripture attests, "*For Yours is the kingdom and the power and the glory forever. Amen*" (Matt 6:13 NKJV). Yet, the annals of humankind bear the scars of repeated endeavors to erect an earthly kingdom without its genuine Proprietor—the Eternal King—chasing shadows of power and glory whilst rejecting his overlordship. From this springs the prosecution of unjust wars—the needless maiming of bodies, the termination of countless souls, and the greedy plundering of resources, which reverse the consecrated scale and beckon a barrenness of the inner life. Hence, the prayer's pattern of praise preceding pleas functions as a ritual rampart, redirecting the petition toward Godward reverence, guaranteeing that requests for temporal sustenance arise from the fountainhead of heavenly ascription. Lest the soul succumb to the dualistic temptation of self-deifying veneration, forever pursuing the illusion of self-sufficient glory while ignoring the origin of genuine bliss. For Your prayer of prayers, O Lord of lords, acts as a gentle framework, lifting the groveling gaze from base desires to the beatific vision of your glory, that we might echo the angels' hymn, hallowing You in heavenly melodies before the murmurs of earth entwine.

Subject to man's miserable failure to maintain that pristine Paradise, which had God for its foundation and cornerstone, every ensuing effort—every eager endeavor to erect an equivalent Eden without God—has always fallen facefirst. Similarly, every attempt—every ambition to build up some version of Babel and to possess an experience of heaven-on-earth without the Creator of heaven and earth—has been accomplished only with grave expense and has nonetheless dissolved into utter desolation. Like fleeting mirages in a desert of dreams, these illusions of autonomy dissolve under the weight of their own imperfections, for all such systems and structures, divorced from their origin, are ordained to frailty and fall. Highlighting the inescapable dependency of creation upon its Creator for enduring order and purpose. No kingdom endures without God as its foundation and keystone; the only kingdom guaranteed to withstand time's erosion is that which stems from God, illuminated by his truth, radiant as the sun by day and the moon by night. The call for the Apostles to pray *'Thy kingdom come'* points to a profound relational dynamic: it is an invitation for God and humans to harmoniously share an eternal space of unbroken fellowship, like it was at the beginning of creation, much like a family reunited after long division. From the very foundations of creation, it has never really been God's idea to create a partitioned existence—where man is domiciled down here on earth and himself up there in some distant heaven. Rather, his dateless and changeless purpose has always been to foster a divine-human symbiosis within the context of his eternal kingdom—where his eternal kingdom comes down to be with men and for him to forever dwell with them as their God and loving Father, while they become his cherished people and beloved children (as vividly portrayed in Revelation 21:1–4). By meticulously stitching together the threads of scriptural revelation, we can establish further that the God who created heaven and earth in Genesis 1:1 never really intended for man to have an earth without a heaven—he did not envision a scenario where countless souls would claim a terrestrial domain divorced from its celestial counterpart—a desolate terrestrial wasteland robbed of the transcendent glory and ecstatic delight that the upper spheres of heaven bestow. This is what the calculated act of planting the Garden of Eden on the hallowed Sabbath day of rest essentially signified: the spatial merger of ethereal heaven and corporeal earth, representing the fusion of supernal and sublunary realities in a shared existence between the Creator-God and the creatures of his likeness. In its deepest sense, God did not segregate the exalted heights of heaven solely for his solitary delight nor the lowly plains of earth for humanity's collective estrangement—far from it! Rather, mankind constitutes the foundational cause for the creation of heaven and earth at time's inception—the very catalyst that prompted the Eternal God to interrupt the seamless expanse of eternal timelessness and institute a beginning. Eden came into being after the toil of six days of creative work, not merely as an appendage but as a profound integration of heaven and earth already formed during those days. In this theological framework, it served as an archetypal and adumbrative emblem of the

New Creation of God—distinct from the hexameral works of creation. Here, in this sanctified expanse, God and humanity were invited to an abiding partnership of love and uninterrupted relational depth. Consider the recurring Biblical epithet *'God of heaven and earth,'* set against the near absence of *'God of heaven'* in isolation—a subtle reminder of the Creator's intent for an undivided sphere of existence. Again, by purposefully ensuring that Adam's first day in the terrestrial demesne unfolded on the Sabbath, God, with supreme intentionality, revealed the ageless truth that his original design was a perpetual Sabbath, a timeless state of rest and intimacy with him that was never meant to end. This narrative arc also explains the Scriptures' silence on any succeeding day beyond the seventh, as the chronicle halts its day-counting markers—omitting any reference of an eighth dawn, alongside its chronological ambiguity concerning the formation of the woman's body from the man's (Gen 2:21–22) Adam's stewardship in naming the animals (Gen 2:20), to mention but a few. Thereby attesting that these happenings transpired within the timeless embrace of God's presence—a hallowed duration divinely intended to endure eternally, untouched by the shadow of finitude.

This heavenly vision is allegorically mirrored in the parable of the prodigal son, where the father shows absolutely no concern over his senior son's protracted domicile in the paternal estate, even as the younger sibling severs ties with the family, declaring prodigal independence, claiming his inheritance, and embarking on a path of self-exile. In everyday human terms, an adult child's indefinite cohabitation under the parental roof is bound to become a subject of great concern to the parents at some point and may even become a focal point for fervent intercessory prayers toward autonomy and maturation. Yet, this is hardly ever the case with God—the archetypal Paterfamilias, as it stands in stark philosophical contrast to the divine paradigm of his kingdom, where he, as the Everlasting Father, has the ultimate goal of bringing forth everlasting sons who will dwell with him in his everlasting kingdom in perpetuity. In substantiating this parallel as correlating with God's beatific vision for the heirs of his kingdom, the father of the prodigal son goes on to state plainly, "*Son, you are always with me, and all that I have is yours*" (Luke 15:12–32 NKJV). Always—indefinitely! Hence, we have the Scriptures also affirming that "*Now a slave does not remain in a household permanently (forever); the son [of the house] does remain forever*" (John 8:35 AMPC). Slaves may come and go, but sons abide with God the Father forever—not as "*. . . strangers and foreigners, but fellow citizens* *with the saints and members of the household of God*" (Eph 2:19 NKJV). This has always been God's greatest dream for mankind—his beatific vision for his eternal family. The prodigal son's departure symbolizes a rupture from filial obedience, much like Adam, who wanted to keep his Edenic largesse without God appearing anywhere in the photo album of his life. This enduring moral teaching remains firm: in the absence of God's presence and his righteous influence, every kingdom inevitably disintegrates into oblivion—each sovereignty unfailingly dissolves into insignificance. Just as the prodigal son failed to hold onto his familial inheritance in the absence of his father in the portrait of his life, similarly, no individual among humanity can sustain the divine bestowals absent of the Bestower—God.

This enduring principle unfolds on a micro-scale in the Garden of Eden, where Adam failed to keep that beatific Edenic estate with which God had blessed him, and on a macro-scale where the Israelites after him altogether proved yet again that no government of men, whether personal or communal, will ever be able to guarantee the self-preservation of any earthly kingdom or polity for so long without God himself in the center. Only the eternal empire built upon the Eternal God, graced by his truth as its sunlit pathfinder by day and moonlit steersman by night, stands firm through all ages. Everything else that can be shaken will definitely undergo some form of shaking and will not withstand the shaking but shall fall down flat like the towering walls of Jericho—once putatively considered impregnable. The philosophical principle that everything that has a beginning, perforce, has a destined end governs the transient kingdoms of this world but falters before the kingdom of God. For only two created entities, divinely originated and eternally enduring—birthed yet unending—transcend the universal law of finitude: the kingdom of God and the sons of the kingdom. These mirror the ark of salvation in the Diluvian flood, where solely the ark and its inhabitants had what it took to endure the cataclysm. The vessel foreshadowed the eternal kingdom of God, while its occupants embodied the heirs of the kingdom destined for eternal redemption. This sacred duality, rooted in divine intent, reveals a profound mystery: creation's temporal bounds yield to the eternal purpose of the divine order. The vessel's endurance and salvific triumph over the flood signify the kingdom's unassailable eternity and the unyielding nature of God's sovereign governance, while its dwellers reflect the eternal vocation of those chosen for redemption, standing as testaments to God's promise to uphold an elect remnant amidst the fleeting currents of the world. Through God's sovereign act of election and protection, the sacred genealogy of the righteous—Noah's kin, shielded from tempests of deluge and decay—from the ravages of time and tribulation, thus preserved, becomes the ur-church—transformed into the archetypal ecclesia—a floating Zion adrift upon the turbulent deluge of primordial chaos, damp with chaotic waters of cosmic anarchy yet dry-shod upon the rock of redemptive assurance, awaiting the radiant genesis at the empty tomb's dawn, where timeless daybreak shatters the shadows of mortality forever.

It is also significant that in John's Apocalypse, the eschatological kingdom—the New Jerusalem—was said to have been seen protruding from the Eternal God himself. It reads, "*Then I, John, saw the holy city, New Jerusalem, coming down out of heaven from God, prepared as a bride adorned for her husband*" (Rev 21:2 NKJV). Additionally stating that, "*And I saw no temple in the city, for its temple is the Lord God the Almighty and the Lamb. And the city has no need of sun or moon to shine upon it, for the glory of God is its light, and its lamp is the Lamb*" (Rev 21:22–23 RSV). Clearly, both the celestial city and the holy temple within it, having proceeded from God, thus part and parcel of his eternal essence, have a beginning or an originating point, yet no end in sight. Very much like the sons of the kingdom who are *'of God,'* the kingdom and everything within it are endowed with an eternal shelf life. For the Eternal God is the only entity in the seen and unseen world who has no beginning of days nor end of life—the First Cause who causes all to come into being. In principle, everything he causes to be has a beginning and naturally has an end, except those that emanate from him and remain fused into him. Like the first heaven and earth that were created from out of the primal dust of nothingness, everything else that begins to exist is destined for some terminus ad quem—save those that are grafted into the Everlasting, Immortal God, who alone grants escape from the cycle of creation and cessation—in whom alone the mortal dons immortality in a redemptive dance with the infinite. God's eternal kingdom alone, immutable and impervious to corruption, stands as an impregnable citadel—far beyond the reach of time's erosion and decay's corrosion; all else, forged in time, crumbles back into the dust of nothingness—ascending from obscurity only to plunge back into its embrace. Centuries before John, the Prophet Isaiah had himself caught a revelatory glimpse of this eschatological reality—the consummation of all things, where the current heaven and earth fade out of existence, yet the new heaven and earth (representing the kingdom of God—the New Jerusalem) and her denizens remain before God forever. He articulates this vision in two successive oracles, saying, "*For behold, I create new heavens and a new earth; And the former shall not be remembered or come to mind. But be glad and rejoice forever in what I create; For behold, I create Jerusalem as a rejoicing, And her people a joy. I will rejoice in Jerusalem, And joy in My people; The voice of weeping shall no longer be heard in her, Nor the voice of crying*" (Isa 65:17–19 NKJV). And then he adds in the subsequent chapter, "*For as the new heavens and the new earth Which I will make shall remain before Me," says the Lord, "So shall your descendants and your name remain*" (Isa 66:22 NKJV). In interpretation, this everlasting kingdom of God (the New Jerusalem) shall 'remain' before the Everlasting God forever, and the everlasting sons of God (her people) shall dwell therein with him throughout the futurity of eternity. Thus, the eternal kingdom reflects God's unchanging nature—divine aseity extended to creation, where its inhabitants share in his immutability and immortality, abiding forever in his presence.

Bereft of God's essence and influence, however, no sovereignty will persist—the exclusive sovereignty fated to endure temporal trials is that which relies on the Almighty as its wellspring and bedrock. For though kingdoms kindle and kingdoms quench—empires rise and dissolve into emptiness, but the glory of God's kingdom glows and grows ever so grander. Consequently, every mortal life, born in time, succumbs to death and decay, barring those who amalgamate with the Timeless Sire—the Almighty God. The wisdom of King Solomon echoes: "*For everything there is a season, a time for every activity under heaven. A time to be born and a time to die. A time to plant and a time to harvest. A time to kill and a time to heal. A time to tear down and a time to build up*" (Ecclesiastes 3:1–3 NLT). By joining with God, who never fades out of existence, we escape the end that awaits all else and find the perpetuity of existence in him. The Almighty, as the divine Ipsum Esse Subsistens (Self-subsistent Being himself), grounds all beings, rendering human endeavors ephemeral without this anchorage. This echoes ancient wisdom on causality, where finite chains require an infinite sustainer to avoid absurdity. This approach bridges ancient Biblical texts with modern existential concerns, highlighting God's grace and love as the mechanism for transcending mortality's grip. Philosophically, it subverts the *Heraclitean flux* of incessant change, affirming a Parmenidean permanence that endures exclusively within the celestial sphere. The Solomonian citation illuminates a teleological perspective on time, where profane activities revolve in cycles of vanity, yet a sacred union with the Everlasting God shatters this futility, bestowing profound eschatological hope rooted in eternal redemption. The parable of the Prodigal Son vividly illustrates ontological dependence, demonstrating that estrangement from God—the Prime Reality—plunges the soul into existential nullity and destitution, whereas reconciliation and return bestow eternal substantiality and true being. This portrayal resonates profoundly with Neoplatonic emanation, wherein all reality flows from and remains contingent upon the transcendent One, yet it remains firmly anchored in Biblical truth, emphasizing relational restoration through divine grace rather than impersonal necessity.

In the foundational narrative of biblical redemption, the Tower of Babel emerges as a profound symbol of the adversary's overarching scheme—a conspiracy echoing the ancient serpent's primordial rebellion, aimed at uniting humanity in a supreme defiance against divine authority. As depicted in Genesis 11, this episode arises in the aftermath of the flood, where a cohesive human society, sharing a single language and a common aspiration, endeavors to construct a monolithic edifice reaching toward the heavens, embodying their quest for autonomy and self-glorification. Far beyond a simple historical anecdote, this event unveils the cunning blueprint of Satan's end-times vision: a conspiracy to forge the varied strands of human existence into a counterfeit unity, igniting a global uprising that undermines God's covenantal sovereignty and derides the Creator's mandate for humble dispersal across the earth. From a philosophical perspective, Babel compels us to contemplate the delicate equilibrium between oneness and diversity; its deceptive wholeness, tainted by the enduring mark of original sin, perverts our intrinsic bond with the Creator-God, channeling innate potential into a defiant overreach that diminishes personal identity and breeds profound alienation. Consequently, what begins as collaborative endeavor sours into tyrannical narcissism—a motif that echoes ominously in Hegel's philosophy of the all-encompassing state and Nietzsche's exaltation of the *übermensch*, both of which spurn the self-sacrificial humility that God requires of humanity. In eschatological terms, Babel prefigures the corrupt alliances portrayed in the book of Revelation, where a superficial worldwide unity, veiled beneath golden symbols, conceals an entrenched hostility toward God, repudiating the primordial divine summons to varied humility as the authentic bedrock of genuine relationships. Yet, in luminous opposition, the biblical ideal of Zion arises as the radiant blueprint of God's redemptive purpose: a divine invitation to assemble humanity not in insurrection, but in exultant submission to his sovereign overlordship. God yearns to unite his creation, not under the atheistic canopy of Babylon's empire, but beneath his own sovereignty—Zion. Celebrated in the Psalms as the impregnable seat of heavenly governance and envisioned in Isaiah's prophecies as the epicenter of redemptive restoration, Zion summons the Divine Architect to gather the scattered peoples from every nation, tongue, tribe, and group into a symphony of harmonious worship. Here, the shattered tapestry of human existence—rent by sin's divisions and Babel's judgment—is not coerced into unity through force or hatred, but mended through grace into a covenant of profound harmony. Jews and Gentiles alike, as pilgrims from distant horizons, converge not as adversaries but as the family of the redeemed, ascending to the Lamb's radiant banquet in a chorus of eternal praise. Beneath the scepter of the King of kings, their manifold voices intertwine in doxology, forging an indissoluble fellowship that banishes the shadows of ancient division and inaugurates the era of enduring peace—shalom—a kingdom where true unity thrives, extending an open invitation to the feast of heavenly hospitality.

In summary, this primordial transgression, as inscribed in the sacred chronicles of divine-human relations, had set in motion a cyclical drama of hubristic aspiration and dissolution, relentlessly rooted in the ruinous rebellion of humanity's primal fall, each society a transient shadow of a once-glorious harmony now lost to man but ever found in God—a pristine state now shrouded in the mists of time's passage. Rise, ruin, rinse, repeat—societies surge, stumble, shatter—rising and falling like tides under the weight of their own pride—each epoch echoing Eden's exile, their ruins recurrently whispering of a paradise forsaken yet ever sought. For within the heart of humanity burns an unquenchable desire for a purpose that transcends the ephemeral glories of earthly dominion. This existential hunger, etched in the deepest recesses of the human soul, points to a divine teleology—an eternal end that beckons beyond the ruins of temporal kingdoms. However, the persistent failures of human striving lay bare a stark reality: no mortal power can heal the breach wrought by the first act of rebellion—no human effort, however noble, would suffice in an attempt to hoist fallen humanity from the wreckage of its fallenness. In effect, this realization lays the groundwork for understanding sin's disruption and the necessity of grace's restoration in the grand narrative of divine providence. This aligns with natural law, where divine order restores human disorder through grace. For only through transformative intervention of God's grace could hope arise for humanity's fractured purpose to be restored and its destiny realigned with his original plan and eternal purpose for creation. For only the healing balm of his love can heal man's existential wounds, and only through providential intervention can the shattered fragments of creation be gathered, its sacred design renewed. Without redemption, our existence—earnest, eager, endless in effort—ends in emptiness. This origin story sets the stage for a redemptive drama, where God's love, undeterred by human frailty, pursues humanity through the ages, culminating in a prophetic crescendo that unveils the eternal restoration of all things and reconciliation with God.

THE INCARNATION: THE REDEMPTION OF FALLEN MAN

From there—the pristine Garden of Eden—to here—the shadowed Garden of Gethsemane: the narrative journeys from the primal dawn of Eden's early error through endless eras where men, bewitched by the profane ambition to seize divine authority for themselves, have sought to erect a heavenly kingdom on earth apart from God, only to crown themselves as gods in the process, falling ever deeper—until, in a breathtaking reversal of destiny, the story arrives at the moonlit, olive-shaded groves of Gethsemane in the first-century Greco-Roman world. In that singular, history-altering moment, redemption's unquenchable hope breaks forth to rewrite the entire human story forever. In a glorious reversal ordained by heavenly grace and divine mandate, the sacred story turns from the creative acts of God's love to the redemptive acts of that same love—from the majestic formation of Man, fashioned in God's holy image—through the tragic shattering of the Fall, broken by sin's enticing whisper—to arrive triumphantly at this climactic chapter: the Redemption of Man. Unfolding as a postlapsarian genesis in the second half of the Bible's eternal scroll—a glorious rebirth that dawns over the human experiment as the Second Act of Scripture's Holy Testament. Yet another related book, the Gospel of John—mirroring the Genesis primal creation narrative—reveals in medias res that the selfsame God who had created man in his image and likeness in the very beginning "*became a man* [named Jesus the Christ] *and lived among us!*" (John 1:14 TPT, the words in parenthesis are added). Kindly take a momentary pause and *Selah* on the profound significance of that statement for a second, and I mean, the slightest chance that the God who had created human beings in his Divine image and likeness, *da capo*, historically became a human being himself and lived among humans is just about as staggering a revelation as it gets. Because, if what we had with creation at the beginning was anything near God's deification of the human species—having " . . . *made them only a little lower than God and crowned them with glory and honor*," then what we had transpire in this 'Incarnation' was nothing short of God's humanification of himself—having " . . . *made Himself of no reputation, taking the form of a bondservant, and coming in the likeness of men. And being found in appearance as a man* . . . " (Ps 8:5 NLT; Philippians 2:7–8 NKJV). The Creator-God, in other words, having made man like unto himself in his work of creation—theomorphism—goes on to make himself like unto man in his work of redemption—theanthropism.

The moment we begin to take into critical cognizance the fact that most, if not all, of the mysterious poltergeistic Divine appearances that humans have generally encountered throughout the OT times could very well be summed up under the theological labels of theophanic, christophanic, angelophanic, and even hierophanic representations and adumbrations of the Creator-God, then his unprecedented incarnate self-disclosure in the 1st century A.D. suddenly begins to take on a whole new theological meaning and a lot more historical significance altogether. In Jesus of Nazareth, therefore, humanity was graced with the rare privilege of beholding face-to-face for the very first time since time began the Pantocrator and Creator of the heavens and the earth representing himself down here on earth and speaking up for himself in person—without any human intermediaries or angelic plenipotentiaries—without any oracular mediums or adumbrative eidolons or sacred simulacra. Precisely what the writer of the Letter to the Hebrews was alluding to in his prophetic reflection that the selfsame "*God, who in ancient days spoke to our forefathers in many distinct messages and by various methods through the prophets, has at the end of these days spoken to us through a Son, who is the pre-destined Lord of the universe, and through whom He made the ages. He brightly reflects God's glory and is the exact representation of His being* . . . " (Heb 1:1–3 Weymouth's Translation).

But then, of course, to secure the full legitimacy and authenticity of his incarnate entry into man's world, it became fundamentally imperative that he pass through the very genealogical red tape of human childbirth itself. The eternal Son could not simply appear arbitrarily; he had to navigate the ordinary, earthly procedures of conception and birth, entering our story through the same biological and legal channels as every other human being, thereby grounding his divine mission in genuine human descent and fulfilling every promise of the covenant. Because—"*Since we, God's children, are human beings—made of flesh and blood—he became flesh and blood too by being born in human form; for only as a human being could he die and in dying break the power of the devil who had the power of death . . . And it was necessary for Jesus to be like us . . .*" (Heb 2:14, 17 TLB). We hence have the Scriptures confirming exactly as foretold by the Prophets of old that the God incarnate was indeed " . . . *born of a woman, born as a Jew*"—to a Jewish woman named Mary, the mother of Jesus, who so happens to be the Christ (Gal 4:4 TLB).

In this sovereign act of divine humility, the eternal Son entered human history through the very lineage and people he had chosen, fulfilling every prophetic promise and anchoring redemption in the concrete reality of Jewish motherhood and messianic expectation. Noteworthily, the manner of his conception was utterly unique to himself alone, standing forever as a radical departure from the ordinary birth of the sons of men—a truly *sui generis* occurrence, one-of-a-kind in the fullest sense. For he assumed full humanity not through the usual union of human parents, but by the miraculous means of parthenogenesis: a sovereign, divine act that transcended and defied every known marker of natural conception, marking his entry into the world as an unparalleled wonder of God's power and grace. This is precisely why the Synoptic Gospels remain consistent in their witness: "*This is how Jesus the Messiah was born. His mother, Mary, was engaged to be married to Joseph. But before the marriage took place, while she was still a virgin, she became pregnant through the power of the Holy Spirit*" (Matt 1:18 NLT). Within the socio-religious framework of first-century Jewish society, according to Deuteronomic Law (Deut 23:2) and the prevailing cultural norms of the time, Joseph—Mary's betrothed—would have been entirely within his legal rights to regard the child Jesus as a *mamzer* (ממזר), that is, an illegitimate child born out of wedlock or due to suspected infidelity during betrothal—a bastard in the strict legal sense. On those grounds alone, he would have been fully justified if he had mistrysted Mary, rejected the child, and moved on with his life.

But whilst all of this imbroglio was yet brewing under the surface in his mind, just as Joseph weighed his options so carefully, holding his cards to his chest, there was a momentary Divine intervention, which here is what we are told happened next as a result: "*Then Joseph, her fiancé, being a man of stern principle, decided to break the engagement but to do it quietly, as he didn't want to publicly disgrace her. As he lay awake considering this, he fell into a dream and saw an angel standing beside him. "Joseph, son of David," the angel said, "don't hesitate to take Mary as your wife! For the child within her has been conceived by the Holy Spirit. And she will have a Son, and you shall name him Jesus (meaning 'Savior'), for he will save his people from their sins"* (Matt 1:19–21 TLB). In the stillness of his sleepless night, God sent an angel to speak peace and purpose, transforming Joseph's hesitation into holy resolve—his righteous uncertainty into courageous embrace of the miraculous. And guess what, none of these extraordinary occurrences was by any chance spawning out of happenchance or mere accident—they were all unfolding precisely according to God's preordained plan for man's redemption, all coming together nicely in fulfillment of the Prophet Isaiah's centuries-old prophecy, which declared: "*Therefore the Lord Himself will give you a sign: Behold, the virgin shall conceive and bear a Son, and shall call His name Immanuel*" (Isa 7:14 NKJV). What appeared miraculous and unforeseen to human eyes was, in divine reality, the long-prepared climax of God's eternal purpose to dwell with his people.

It was not long before certain faithful witnesses—those who had closely followed the unfolding events of Jesus' life and ministry—began to ponder deeply the deeper meaning and ultimate significance of his birth. The more they preoccupied themselves with the task of poring over the Hebrew Scriptures and piecing together the fragmented pictures of the prophetic puzzle pertaining to the Messianic figure, the more they were compelled by the mounting, agglomerative evidence to draw the obvious conclusion that none of the surrounding circumstances pertaining to the events of Jesus's life—His birth to a virgin in Bethlehem—were accidental or coincidental, but rather divinely orchestrated fulfillment of ancient Messianic prophecies. Moved by this realization, the author of the Gospel attributed to Matthew penned down the following thought: "*So all this was done that it might be fulfilled which was spoken by the Lord through the prophet, saying, "Behold, the virgin shall be with child, and bear a Son, and they shall call His name Immanuel," which is translated, "God with us*" (Matt 1:22–23 NKJV). As a Jewish scribe familiar with the hopes of Israel, he suddenly could see clearly that these ancient prophecies were more like signposts pointing to the long-awaited Messiah. With each layer of prophetic revelation deepening his recognition that Jesus was indeed the embodiment of Isaiah's prophecy. For the name Immanuel, which by his very own interpretation meant *'God with us,'* established with prophetic certainty that the Messianic figure is God made flesh, and by extension, the One to enact Yahweh's redemptive plan that the Scriptures long envisaged. Further confirming that Jesus's incarnate birth marked the beginning of his mission to bring salvation to the sons of men, fulfilling the Scriptures with divine precision and purpose, an age-enduring testament to God's faithfulness to his promises.

As it turned out, these prophets and apostles—scribes and saints—were not alone in bearing witness to this historically significant moment of God's arrival into man's world, as God's holy angels from heaven-on-high were themselves not left out of the equation, for as though sounding off a heraldic fanfare in full trumpet's blast, they too lent their angelic voices in testifying to the sons of men about the birth of the Savior-King: "*Do not be afraid, for behold, I bring you good tidings of great joy which will be to all people. For there is born to you this day in the city of David a Savior, who is Christ the Lord. And this will be the sign to you: You will find a Babe wrapped in swaddling cloths, lying in a manger.*" "*Glory to God in the highest, And on earth peace, goodwill toward men!*" (Luke 2:10-12, 14 NKJV). The Creator has just become a creature, the Infinite clothed in the swaddling clothes of finitude, born in Bethlehem's lowly manger—cradled in straw. Recall, if you will, from our earlier reflection, the same Creator-God who, rather than hastily fashioning a simple cradle for humankind, meticulously designed the vast expanse of the universe and the lush Garden of Eden to serve as their natal nursery in the beginning. Yet, in the sublime paradox of his descent—when he chose to enter his own creation in human form, he did not secure even a modest comfort for his birthplace; instead, he reclined in the rough-hewn austerity of a stable's manger. Such a spectacle, if nothing else, enshrines an indelible witness to the self-emptying lowliness of the Godhead. Indeed, it surges past the confines of that which we term 'humility,' defying encapsulation by any lexicon in our language or the collective patois of the sons of men—a mystery far too profound for utterance, an abyss of condescension.

Throughout this unparalleled abnegation, he evinced not the slightest tremor of self-doubt or fragility. Let that truth resound in the chambers of your soul. Picture it this way—a cosmic curtain parts open, and the God who shaped humanity and fashioned all creation steps onto the stage of history as Jesus the Christ. This is the Incarnation—the mystery of mysteries! Furthermore, not even the Gentile nations were by any means excluded from participating in this all-embracing mirth—the '*good tidings of great joy*' that greeted the Savior's birth, as their inclusion was symbolically marked by the august visitation of the Magi, the three mystic wanderers who had journeyed all the way from the East—far beyond Israel's borders, down to Jerusalem, where they had come solely on a mission to pay homage to the newly *'born King of the Jews.'* With their caravan, laden with treasures—gold for a king, frankincense for a priest, and myrrh for a sacrifice—all wrapped as precious gifts for the God-baby, they clairvoyantly inquired of King Herod and the Jewish leaders, "*saying, "Where is He who has been born King of the Jews? For we have seen His star in the East and have come to worship Him*" (Matt 2:2 NKJV). Taking their leave of Herod not too long thereafter, they still had the same lodestar they had been tailing from the East continue to serve as their satnav, leading them all the way down to the precise location where Baby Jesus was being nursed in a manger, and straight away—" . . . *they rejoiced with exceedingly great joy*" (Matt 2:10 NKJV).

Since the foundation of the world, never for once has there ever been such a cosmic alliance between humans, constellations, and celestial beings—as the stars, angels, and the 'multitude of the heavenly host' that guided the Magi and shepherds to Bethlehem's manger to bear witness to the Virgin Birth marked a Divine convergence, unprecedented in its significance (cf. Luke 2:13). For the Creator's grand entrance into the world, such a cosmic moment was demanded—the first time heaven and earth sang in unison—uniting humanity and the stars in awe of the Savior's arrival. This is the first Christmas, and as you can imagine, for every good reason in the book, the joy in the air is infectiously palpable. For how gloriously hallowed a 'Christmas Day' it must have been the day that Christ was born in Bethlehem of Judaea. And still continues to be for billions of Christians around the world circa 2000 years later. For the joy, jouissance, and jubilance of Christmastide have in no way, shape, or form been restricted to the first Christmas but have continued unabated, kept alive and ablaze in the hearts and souls of all who are named after the Christ—Christians. A Day of Days it was—the day Jesus was born—so much so that the renowned Prince of Preachers, Charles Spurgeon, deeply felt the need to have it yclept *'the Great Birthday'*—a special birthday unlike any other it was indeed—one that forever changed history as we know it (Spurgeon, 1876, pp. 709–710). For so historically significant is God's Date of Birth (DOB) that it warranted the universal designation of the current date era of each passing year on the Gregorian Calendar as *'In the year of our Lord'—Anno Domini* (A.D.).

And as things currently stand, Christmas Day just so happens to have menologically emerged—through the providential ordering of history—as one of the two supreme red-letter days upon the Gregorian calendar, standing in peerless dignity with none other but its sister—Easter. Because the miracle of the Incarnation has caused the Lord Jesus Christ to reign sovereignly over our reckoning of time, every annual revolution in the *Anno Domini* era may now be regarded as an *annus mirabilis*—a miraculously good year—indeed, a veritable Dominical Sabbatical Year, a banner year renewed perpetually with each circling of the sun. For Christ is Himself "*the Lord of the Sabbath*," the One in whom the ancient Sabbath finds its antitypical and perfect fulfillment. Yet, what is even more gospel a news to our hearts—more music a sound to our ears—is this: Christ has essentially made every single day of the calendar year '*the day of salvation*' for all mankind (see. 2 Cor 6:2). Among those who grasped this mystery was Saint Augustine of Hippo, who saw the eternal Sabbath as already begun within the heart that reposes in Christ—where his lordship over time converts every ordinary day into a living opportunity for redemption, the promised "today" of Hebrews already present and active in the Person of the incarnate Lord. Thus, this Sabbath is no mere future expectation or some distant hope; it is rather a realized participation in redemptive rest, whereby the believer, united to the incarnate Word—who is both Lord of the Sabbath and its consummate fulfillment—already enters into the eternal repose. If there ever was a baby who deserved to have the luminous crown of nimbus encircling his pate at birth, it is the Baby in the Nativity—Jesus, whose birth is the very essence of Christmas. For the miracle of Christmas is ultimately centered about the miracle Baby himself, from whom springs the miracle of salvation for all humanity. For the birth of Christ is that good news that never stops making news—that Gospel message that never gets old, all because God's gift of a Savior to the world has remained that gift that keeps on giving and never runs out—that wellspring of salvation that keeps on welling up and never runs dry. No object of wonder, then, hear the angels of the Lord sound so begladdened to announce that the Savior's birth ultimately signalled the glad tidings of salvation 'to all people' and not some people—goodwill toward all mankind and not some privileged few.

And here is how John's Gospel so beautifully summarizes the glorious birth of the God incarnate in KJV language, or Early Modern English, if you will: "*In the beginning was the Word, and the Word was with God, and the Word was God. The same was in the beginning with God. All things were made by him; and without him was not any thing made that was made . . . And the Word was made flesh, and dwelt among us, (and we beheld his glory, the glory as of the only begotten of the Father,) full of grace and truth*" (John 1:1–3, 14 KJV). Although Jesus is clearly the personification of 'the Word' who was 'born' into the spatiotemporal world through the agency of the Virgin Mother—thus 'the Seed of the woman' who was first mentioned in the Protevangelium (Gen 3:15), he was nonetheless begotten of God the Father in dateless eternity's past, the sense in which he is said to be 'the only begotten of the Father'—the same who 'was with God' before the world was and was himself God—" . . . *whose origins are of old, from the days of eternity*" (Mic 5:2b BSB)—consubstantial, coequal, coexistent, and coeternal with the Father. This view of the Incarnation is one that was commonly held by the Church Fathers, the likes of St. Athanasius (c. 296–373 A.D.), and has since been magisterially codified into the Catholic Faith, maintaining that "*The right faith therefore is that we believe and confess that our Lord Jesus Christ, the Son of God, is God and Man. He is God of the substance of the Father begotten before the worlds, and He is man of the substance of His mother born in the world; perfect God, perfect man subsisting of a reasoning soul and human flesh; equal to the Father as touching His Godhead, inferior to the Father as touching His Manhood*" (Athanasian Creed).

The Apostle Paul chimes in to add his apostolic voice to the series of prophetic confirmations we have littered across the NT Bible, stating pointedly that ". . . *God was [indeed] manifested in the flesh . . .* " (I Timothy 3:16 NKJV). Absolutely no surprise then to also hear the writer of the Letter to the Hebrews echo the following words directly from the horse's mouth (Jesus) in hindsight: " . . . *a body You have prepared for Me*" (Heb 10:5 NKJV). Because in reality, all God ever needed to become part and parcel of man's humanity and to legitimize his brief but perennially significant stay in man's world was a human body or flesh. Quite evidently, Jesus is not some random man who, somehow, managed to attain the status of a god; he is the Creator-God who became a man. That is all the more true when you consider that what humanity actually needed for its redemption was not a god, nor was it a demigod nor an admixture of half-god and half-man, for not even an angel would have sufficed, save a man—a full-blooded man, and that is precisely what God became—a Man—100% a Man. Besides, a god or anything else will not qualify for a worthy substitute to take the place of sinful humanity and die the vicarious death of a Paschal Lamb on the Cross; only a man would—a sinless man, for that matter. For a man (Adam) it was who got humanity into the whole fatesome predicament in the first place, and a man it was going to take to get humanity out in the clear (see Romans 5:14–19). Where no morally perfect or sinless man exists anywhere in man's universe, for all of Adam's progenies were conceived and born in sin and have all sinned and fallen short of the glory of God's image in which they were aboriginally created, the only viable option left in the universe was for God to become a man, and that is only if he wanted to see humanity rescued from the brink of eternal damnation. Thus, God, for no other compelling reason but his love for man, decidedly became the Man we all needed—the sacrificial lamb humanity so desperately needed for a ransom, thereby seeing to it that the redemptive transaction went through successfully. Simply put, God loved man enough to become a man to save all mankind, for he became our Knight in shining armor—the Savior of men.

Against that backdrop, it then becomes readily obvious to us today in retrospect that those Jews who had accused Jesus of blasphemy at the time, on the grounds of the charge that " . . . *You, being a Man, make Yourself God,*" were themselves greatly mistaken if only they had realized that just the opposite was actually the case, in that You, being God, made Yourself a Man (John 10:33 NKJV). Especially owing to the fact that the individual they were addressing was in reality their God—'the God of Israel' who self-effacingly decided to become a Man and not some self-seeking egomaniac attempting to apotheosize himself. Interestingly, what the Lycaonians had said of Paul in the Book of Acts 14:11 turns out to be approximately true of Jesus: "*The gods have come down to us in the likeness of men!*" That makes for a fairly accurate characterization of God's incarnate appearance to man, except, of course, to clarify that it was specifically God the Son (the Second Person of the Trinity) who, in this case, came *'down to us in the likeness of men'* sometime in human history, not the so-called 'gods' or, more precisely, some pagan deity like they had imagined. Jesus, even though he was born of a woman, nevertheless did not shy from affirming his divine origin, stating plainly, "*For I have come down from heaven, not to do My own will, but the will of Him who sent Me*" (John 6:38 NKJV). He came into the world 'through' Mary by birth but not 'from' Mary, as his divine identity and existence originate from the eternal Godhead, not from humanity.

And just like the songwriters of the now famous Christmas carol 'Hark! The Herald Angels Sing' aptly put it in their lyrics: not only did he come down from heaven to earth in the likeness of a Man, he was also *'Pleased as Man with man to dwell'* (Charles Wesley and George Whitfield). In other words, he took great pleasure and pride in living up to his prophetic name Immanuel—God dwelling with men on earth—not as

'God' per se but as a fellow Man—not in the capacity of his divinity but in the capacity of man's humanity—abandoning his glorified empyrean estate for man's fallen cosmic estate—divesting himself of all divine privileges only to embrace the lowly state of a 'Suffering Servant'. Perfectly capturing the core meaning of the theological term *'kenosis.'* But just in case you are one of those who might have found themselves tempted to believe that Jesus must have had a human body different from ours—a celestial body of some kind—the Bible immediately steps in to set the record straight, specifying further that he literally took upon himself " . . . *the likeness of sinful flesh to be a sin offering. And so he condemned sin in the flesh*" (Rom 8:3 NIV). What that also tells us is that, even though he was a Man in every way possible—by every yardstick of the measurement—he yet was not tainted with human sin (neither Adam's original sin nor any actual sin of his own), as he forever stands as the only Man who ever had the moral fiber to deny himself a bite from that primordial apple tree of sin from which all men have eaten in disobedience and was therefore not bitten by that notorious venomous serpent of temptation who had misled all humanity down the garden path—further downhill the path of moral degeneracy.

From the fateful fissure of the first Fall—that archetypal tumble in Eden's shadowed grove, where frail flesh faltered from Father's flawless form—fading fervently in Eden's emerald echo, resounding through timeless twilight; ah, man has never stopped falling ever since he fell at the Fall—he has never stopped falling short of everything else since he fell short of the glory of God's image and likeness in the Garden of Eden. Falling from grace and bound by sin's gravity ever since—fallen man is ever destined to keep on falling until he experiences the againrising and ascension of the Christ. For Christ, the heavenly Man, is the only Man who never fell—the last Man standing in the midst of all fallen men who fell at the Fall of Adam's disobedience into sin. For the primordial apple did not fall very far from the tree after Adam and Eve had allowed God's commandment to fall on deaf ears, eating off the tree of the knowledge of good and evil in the beginning of time, and leaving their descendants the bitter legacy of the fateful Fall that fractured Eden's sanctity, defiled human innocence and severed man's relationship with his Maker (Gen 3:1–7). Alack and alas, Adam, once a highflier, having dug a pit by his own transgression, now finds himself fallen headlong into it, utterly cast down, yea, downcast and doomed downward—grounded and grovelling in a warped world of woe, leaving his descendants doomed to drink down the dregs of his defiance. His kin, rooted in his sin, cannot uproot their cursed condition inflicted by the Fall, forever fallen from his former heights in Eden—sinners encumbered by sin's heavy yoke—prodigal sons estranged yet ever-called homeward. Only Christ, the unfallen and infallible Second Adam, graciously takes the fall for all fallen and fallible descendants of the First Adam—transplanting the fallen to grace—breaking the agelong vicious cycle of unending fall into moral degeneracy and spiritual darkness in the fractured lives of all fallen men—halting mankind's perpetual descent, and yes, decline into sin's existential void by the shed blood of His cross—raising an ever-falling race trapped in death's fathomless abyss to the empyrean height of everlasting life and glory's radiant light by His triumphant resurrection and ascension. Hark! Yet behold! Christ the Redeemer, in His gracious vigil, "*upholds all who fall, And raises up all who are bowed down*"—For though we all falter and fall—in our shared frailty, where faltering begets falter—falling spirals to fall, we yet shall not be utterly forsaken—for no utter desolation consumes us. For though our path be strewn with stumbles and twilight triumphs of defeat, yet, Christus Victor, in His merciful guardianship, shall cradle the stumbling soul and lift the crestfallen spirit from its lowly bend—upholding us with the right hand of His righteousness. And on the third day, He shall raise us up in His glory—On that radiant dawn, He hymns us heavenward, ever-skyward, haloed in holiness, That we may live in the glorious sight of His presence forever—Beholding, with unveiled faces, yea, face to face, the ever-increasing glory of His countenance—Basking beatified in the eternal splendor of the Beatific Vision—that felicitous facet of *visio Dei*. Alleluia! (Ps 145:14, 37:24; Hos 6:2) — (Prose Poem Title: Fallen Man—an Ever-falling Race).

Lo and behold, as the morning star, by its light, pierces the dark veil of the night, so the wondrous birth of the Redeemer rent asunder the bleak bondage of humanity's unending night, birthing the dawn of a new beginning for a race languishing in the shadows of its fall, heralding a holy hope marking the consummate commencement of God's redemptive plan. This grand genesis of the Gospel of redemption, Scripture proclaims to be "*The beginning of the gospel of Jesus Christ, the Son of God*" (Mark 1:1 NKJV). Before the blessed breaking of this prophetic day of Christ, also designated "*the day of salvation,*" man's days were drear, draped in darkness deep, each dawn heavily shrouded in recurrent oppressive twilight—darkened by the dominion of sin's sorrowful sting. The coming of the Messiah unveiled a luminous horizon, a salvific dawn for a race estranged from divine light. And for the first time since Eden's fall, "*The people who sat in darkness have seen a great light, and upon those who dwelt in the region and shadow of death, light has dawned*" (Matt 4:16 NKJV). This divine sunrise, radiant with the glory of the Son of God—whom Scripture hails as 'the Sun of Righteousness' (Mal 4:2)—ushers humanity into an era of divine illumination, where souls are no longer bound by the tyranny of obsidian night. Before Christ, each sunrise merely prolonged the dominion of darkness over man's world, deepening the dismal condition of the sons of men trapped in the malaise of spiritual desolation. Yet, with his coming, a new reality emerged, fulfilling the prophetic promise of the Jubilee, wherein captives are set at liberty, the brokenhearted are healed, and the oppressed are delivered, their souls transfigured by the ineffable light of God's redemptive love, leading them to live forever in the light of the Savior's deliverances (cf. Luke 4:18–19).

However, despite his divine origins, 'the Son of Man' (as Jesus preferred to call himself) hardly ever saw the need to portray himself as a godlike figure, and so he barely ever came across to anyone as some distant and unapproachable divine persona, but as a man who laughed with friends, wept over suffering, and broke bread with outcasts. He humbly humanized himself so much that Lazaruses and lepers were considered welcome to have a seat at his table, for so down-to-earth a man was he that little kids had no trouble accessing him—often making his guestlist. Mark's Gospel, in fact, tells us that on a certain occasion, he went as far as rebuking his disciples for merely attempting to keep the kiddies back from coming to him: "*Then they brought little children to Him, that He might touch them; but the disciples rebuked those who brought them. But when Jesus saw it, He was greatly displeased and said to them, "Let the little children come to Me, and do not forbid them; for of such is the kingdom of God. Assuredly, I say to you, whoever does not receive the kingdom of God as a little child will by no means enter it*" (Mark 10:13–15 NKJV). This Man taught in synagogues, healed the sick, and dined with sinners, revealing God's heart in tangible human form. And if you would believe it, he even touched a leper, as Matthew records that "*And behold, a leper came and worshiped Him, saying, "Lord, if You are willing, You can make me clean." Then Jesus put out His hand and touched him, saying, "I am willing; be cleansed." Immediately his leprosy was cleansed*" (Matt 8:2–3 NKJV). That is something not so many of us would dare to do, especially not in today's world.

Within the context of Second Temple Judaism, leprosy was not merely a physical ailment but a social and religious death sentence, as the

Jews were, by strict religious observances, disbarred from making any human contact with lepers, given that the Mosaic Law (Lev 13–14) had declared it outrightly verboten. And Jesus understood exactly this, yet it did not stop him from making real, meaningful, and compassionate contact with this socioreligious pariah. Not only did he subvert the Levitical prohibitions that rendered lepers outcasts, but he also drastically redefined the concept of purity through compassionate action. An act that ended up not only healing the leper but also restoring and reintegrating him back into the communal fold of wider society. For his touch is no ordinary touch at all; it is the touch of God's love for man—the touch of a love that transcends rules—the gracious touch of God's healing power brought to bear in man's humanity. One way or the other, everyone who genuinely encountered this God in human form felt his loving, healing, and transformative touch. Even those he did not come close enough to touch, who, notwithstandingly, came behind and touched him, were themselves healed of their affliction all the same (see. Mark 5:25–34). All of which stands in sharp contrast to the conduct of the religious elites of his day, particularly those priggish and sanctimoniously overbearing Pharisees, who, in their effort to wear the veneer of moral grandiosity and compel sacerdotal deference from the laity, would, for a custom, " . . . *make their phylacteries broad and enlarge the borders of their garments . . . to be called by men, 'Rabbi, Rabbi'*" (Matt 23:5–7 NKJV). Very unlike the pattern we typically witness in most men, wherein authority often manifests through dominance or exalted dignity, it was Jesus's gracious and good-natured humanity that proved his greatest attraction—his most captivating appeal—not the aura of his commanding charisma, not the radiant manifestation of his divine glory, not even the astonishing miracles, wondrous signs or displays of supernatural power that marked his ministry. His presence carried such quiet, unassuming grace that being near him made you feel deeply accepted, warmly welcomed, and—above all—personally loved and truly cared for. In him, those burdened by weariness, marginalized as outcasts, or broken in spirit encountered not harsh judgment or remote detachment, but the gentle, all-embracing compassion of a Savior who drew intimately close, bearing a deep empathetic understanding and a heartfelt cherishing of every single human person. His humility ran so deep and complete that he rarely—if ever—felt any need to claim, flaunt, or even remind others of the privileges belonging to his divine nature. His exemplary humanity simply made everyone feel at home with divinity, not estranged from it.

By this admirable model of his incarnate life, he showed us a version of our humanity we never knew existed until he came among us to embody it. In essence, the Creator, who had sculpted humanity in his likeness, now bore the shining example of that likeness himself par excellence, as his life forever stands as a living parable of what it actually means to be God's perfect image-bearer, fulfilling humanity's original mandate.

Undoubtedly, this Incarnation stands towering tall as the ultimate revelation of God's image, thus underscoring what theologians have termed the 'hypostatic union'—Christ as fully God and fully man—bridging the infinite gulf between the Creator and his creatures. By uniting divinity and humanity, Christ bridged the long-standing rift of separation between God and man—linking the ethereal essence of heaven with the tangible presence of earth. In effect, transforming a tale of tragic alienation and redirecting man's destiny toward genuine reconciliation and intimate fellowship with God, while profoundly shaping the spiritual convictions of millions across countless generations. Moreover, by assuming the role of God's flawless and unerring image-bearer, Christ archetypally realizes the full potential that humanity was originally designed to achieve—a destiny unfulfilled in the first man, Adam, due to inherent shortcomings. It took the God incarnate stepping into man's fractured world to provide all the divine answers to humanity's inconsolable cry. Through His sacrificial and redemptive journey, Christ crosses the vast existential chasm carved by the Fall, painstakingly mending the shattered core of human meaning and vocation. In His limitless grace He effects the reconciliation of all creation with its rightful Sovereign Creator, rekindling the divine image within the human soul and bringing to full realization the original mandate to reflect God's glory across the whole expanse of existence. In the Person of Christ, the eternal purpose that forever escaped the reach of the mightiest empires, the deepest philosophies, and the wisest sages at last finds its perfect fulfillment—calling humanity to faithful stewardship over creation in harmonious conformity to God's unchanging design. The crippling inheritance of the Fall, which doomed generation after generation to endless longing amid the ruins of their own endeavors, meets its decisive and ultimate reversal in the redemptive triumph of Christ, granting a hope that rises above every temporal collapse and restores the created order to its appointed destiny: humanity once more bearing God's majesty in unending fellowship with Him. Truly, the anguished narrative of human history—marred and fractured by the consequences of the primal transgression—has reached its decisive turning point in the mystery of the Incarnation—marking a pivotal theological and historical turning point in the trajectory of the human story. One where God, by his gracious intervention in human affairs, diverted the doomed direction of human history—weaving a brand new genesis into the fabric of the human story. This divine act established a covenant rooted in grace, designed to overcome the devastation wrought by the Fall—rewriting the splintered storyline of downfall into a splendid story of salvation, thereby converting profound adversity into enduring triumph.

CONCLUSION

Upon the bedrock of the foregoing exposition, the radiant clarity intensifies manifold: since the primordial forging of humanity in God's image and likeness at creation's exurgent dawn—one of the most sublime Divine acts the cosmos has ever beheld, or perchance the most pivotal, far-reaching decision ever decreed in the eternal councils—is God's sovereign descent into manhood, the Incarnation itself. Assuredly, the redemptive love is what compelled Deity to become part of humanity—part and parcel of the human story—partaking in the human experiment by first-hand experience. The Creator-God's meticulously calibrated resolve to assume the form of his own cherished creatures and dwell amidst them as one of their own for the unadulterated span of temporal sojourn stands as such a profoundly sobering spectacle that our frail, finite minds can scarcely hope to fathom the boundless infinitude of the love that birthed this unparalleled, unprecedented act of sacrificial kenosis. For every subsequent feat God would enact or consummate in his incarnate humanity—every oblation he would tender as a Man—must inexorably cascade from that Brobdingnagian decision he rendered beyond the confines of the spatiotemporal veil, venturing into the flux of time expressly to become a Man. The audacious decision to become a Man—undertaken by God the Son in his transcendent Divine capacity—this theocentric act the sacred Scriptures expressly ascribe to Divine love; yet the resolute determination to proceed with the redemptive plan, culminating in a vicarious death for all mankind upon Calvary's Cross—salvation's holy grail—he was compelled to forge as a Man (within the ken of his incarnate humanity)—this theandric act the Bible ascribes with precision to Divine grace. In the pleromatic fullness of time, Grace (Christ) redeemed him (man), whom Love (God) had masterfully sculpted in his image and likeness at time's inaugural genesis. The Apostle Paul, in the resonant valediction concluding his Second Epistle to the Corinthian assembly, enshrines this eternal harmony, distinctly apportioning love to the Person of God the Father, grace to God the Son, and fellowship to God the Holy Spirit, proclaiming, "*The grace of the Lord Jesus Christ, and the love of God, and the communion of the Holy Spirit be with you all. Amen*" (II Corinthians 13:14 NKJV). In essence, if divine love sufficed to summon God the Son from celestial throne to earthly cradle as a Man, then divine grace alone empowered that Man to ascend the jagged slopes of Calvary's Cross as the spotless sacrificial lamb. Bear in mind, the crucifixion of Christ would have remained an impossibility absent God's antecedent act of becoming a Man, nor could the resurrection of Christ have dawned except upon the foundational miracle of the Incarnation to inaugurate it all.

The historical starting point of '*The Redemptive Love Story*,' therefore, is—according to my reckoning—the Incarnation—the point from which God historically took the form of a man—that Man who became the embodied expression of his love for all mankind. Just as it unfolded in the primordial genesis of creation at the very outset, wherein the nascent cosmos lay entombed in the penumbra of unusefulness and unrealized potential—slumbering languidly within the twilight zone of anticipation, suspended in silent vigil and stationed in quiet readiness for the advent of the First Adam—so too can we draw a parallel inference concerning the climactic Advent of the Last Adam, as though the beleaguered, fallen creation had endured in protracted repose amid the potency of night, its redemptive purpose shrouded in veils of obscurity until the auroral advent of the Incarnation of Christ pierced the gloom, rousing it to the resplendent awakening of its destined dawn. For he stands as the preeminent light of the world, descending to irradiate and dispel the enveloping darkness that had ensnared the fallen world throughout the antecedent four thousand years since the cataclysmic Fall, heralding an effulgent renewal from the shadows of antiquity. For had God not become Jesus, the promise of redemption would have remained just that—a promise—a promise left unfulfilled. If he did not become a Man, there hardly would be any substance to the story of redemption at all, because by then, the whole thing would have been reduced to all talk and no action—just empty promises and unfulfilled prophecies of a manqué Redeemer, with no tangible historical acts to have them grounded in reality. Even we ourselves are generally in agreement that actions speak louder than words, a maxim that, quite obviously, is not lost on God himself.

Thankfully, history, with its own two eyes and ears, bore witness to an extraordinary event that no eye had ever seen and no ear heard—the annals of history, with its own quill pen and parchment, chronicled for us the tale of this earthshaking wonder that was both seen and heard for the first time since the world began: that the God of creation entered into creation grounds around 4–6 B.C. and walked the face of the earth in the form of His own creatures for some 33 years.

This Incarnation transcends the boundaries of abstract theological abstraction, manifesting instead as a verifiable historical event, corroborated by the testimony of eyewitnesses and meticulously chronicled within the sacred annals of the New Testament. Jesus, humbly birthed in the humble cradle of Bethlehem, nurtured through the humble environs of Nazareth, and ultimately crucified beneath the Roman aegis of Pontius Pilate, incarnated the Divine image with unblemished perfection while sojourning amid the frailties of humanity. For want of a better term, this extraordinary, epochal feat is one I have ventured to call—the adventurism of Divine love, a bold, audacious venture into the human odyssey. For not only did the Creator-God traverse the fleeting sands of time enshrined in vulnerable flesh and blood, but he also etched indelibly upon the temporal canvas the footprints of His redeeming love for mankind—the unmistakable footmarks of his saving grace extended to the wayward sinner. God, in sovereign condescension, simply became a Man precisely to accomplish for all humanity that which no solitary man could ever achieve for himself, let alone extend in sacrificial solidarity to his fellow sojourner. This grand narrative—arcing majestically from the primordial dawn of creation to the luminous fulcrum of the Incarnation—compels us to behold ourselves afresh, with renewed wonder and purpose. Far from being capricious accidents adrift in the flux of chance, we emerge as intentional masterpieces of divine artistry, bearers of God's image destined to mirror and magnify his eternal glory. That the transcendent Creator deigned to become one of us unveils a love that defies all human comprehension—a God who not only authored our existence from the dust of eternity but intimately joined our pilgrimage to illuminate our intrinsic, inestimable worth within the gaze of his unchanging eyes and to deliver us from the self-imposed shackles of our rebellion. The intertwined stories of Genesis and John are, in profound essence, our own sacred chronicle, summoning us to embody our calling as image-bearers in a fractured world where God once walked purposefully in the steps of redemption's blueprint.

2

God's Love for Man

MOST CERTAINLY, THE FULL scope of all we have just covered becomes all the more intriguing the moment you begin to realize that the whole story is just as man-centered (anthropocentric) as it is God-centered (theocentric), with both the anthropocentric and theocentric elements gloriously amalgamating in the person of Christ—thus Christocentric. After all, the story is chiefly concerned with God's historical dealings with mankind through the ages, through a series of sundry relationships that eventually paved the way for his incarnate appearance in the personhood of the God-Man whom we all now know to be 'Jesus the Christ.' Beginning from the hexameral account of creation in the Book of Genesis down to the Tetrevangelium account of the Incarnation and Redemption, the gist of the entire story is centered on man and his unfolding relationship with his Maker—God. Not surprisingly, the weightiest and most profoundly significant word you are ever going to encounter resounding through the vast corridors of the English Bible is none other than 'God'—that majestic appellation, *Elohim* in Hebrew, *Theos* in the classical eloquence of Greek, and right next to it is yet another three-letter word, 'man'—*âdâm* in Hebrew—*anthrōpos* in Greek, and then in-between both entities reigns the magnanimous word 'love'—the fervent *'ahab* in Hebrew's passionate cry, the self-sacrificial *agapē* in Greek's exalted virtue. In essence, *'God's love for man'* stands as the most profoundly consequential statement of fact in the entire Bible, a divine axiom that eclipses all others in its transformative majesty and inexhaustible depth. It accounts for the greatest doctrine of faith and ethics that could ever be drawn or pedagogically deduced from the unified message of all sixty-six books taken together. And then, of course, it represents a single bullet point summary of the whole Biblical narrative rendered in a few short words. So much so that if you studied the Bible cover-to-cover and somehow ended up missing the all-important message about God's love for man, then it is safe to say that you have just missed the whole essence of the Scriptures altogether—you have misconstrued the very substance of the whole story—you have equally miskenned the main point that the Grand Author himself (God) was endeavoring to make all the time. What further depths of wonder may we draw from this sublime truth: that God, who exists as love in his very essence, has sovereignly appointed mankind as the supreme object of his inexhaustible affection? In his divine artistry, by crafting humanity to bear his beatific image and likeness, he has—through that very act—irrevocably designated them the exclusive recipient of his boundless love, a predestining election in which the Creator's heart discovers its most radiant reflection in the creature he so passionately cherishes.

Quite frankly, if it were not for the relentless love of God for wayward humanity, our theological musings here would almost immediately be reduced to pointless rambling—empty babbling—useless wrangling. Chasing vaporous nothings until the heart bleeds dry, all amounting to nothing short of the very *'vexation of spirit'* Solomon decried—all volume and void—startling the ear but starving the soul. Paul's oracle in 1 Corinthians nails it down with prophetic precision: "*If I were to speak with eloquence in earth's many languages and in the heavenly tongues of angels, yet I didn't express myself with love, my words would be reduced to the hollow sound of nothing more than a clanging cymbal*" (13:1 TPT). Thuswise, every word or deed—whether Godward or manward—crumbles to chaff without love's fire—essentially empty without love undergirding them. For though our words be so eloquently spoken—our books so euphuistically written—yet without love, they all end up sounding equally just as empty as they are noisy—mere husks, resounding yet rotten—" . . . *great swelling words of emptiness . . .* " Peter flayed (2 Pet 2:18 NKJV). Nobody truly enjoys the indistinct and discordant sounds of clanging cymbals; they are by no means music to our ears. If anything, they perturb our auditory sensibilities while vexing the tranquility of our human soul. Not even the Almighty himself, I am inclined to believe, would encounter any difficulty or hesitation thinking of the Holy Book as an empty book were his love removed from its sacred precincts, nor would its storied annals retain a whisper of narrative substance or redemptive depth absent the radiant enshrining of his love for man at the front and center of every chapter and verse—emblazoned indelibly as the front-burner issue on just about every page and folio you turn.

Dare I even venture so far as to suggest that without love, and I mean the God kind of love—agape—man's world as we know it could potentially become an empty, barren place—desolate void—an existential wasteland utterly stripped of meaning and light in only a matter of a few short seconds—just at the twinkling of an eye—even before the completion of the batting of an eyelid? After all, history has repeatedly shown us how much damage hate, when embedded in the hearts of men the likes of Hitler, can wreak within a reasonably short amount of time—how so quickly such darkness, when harbored in the hearts of our neighbors, can potentially put out every glimmer of light in our world. For except and unless the fire and fervor of God's love is kept ablaze and alive in the hearts of men, the raging fury of the infernal fires of hell is bound to raze man's world down to the dust of apocalypse in only a matter of time much shorter than we could say Jack. Even after the fall, the entire created order—every star in its orbit, every atom in its place—continues to cohere solely by the tenacious, providential grip of God's unrelenting love for mankind: that singular, redemptive force of goodness, the divine adhesive that holds the fractured cosmos in ordered beauty, all things aligned in purposeful teleology toward the ultimate flourishing and eternal good of humanity itself. But if you thought that the world, as we know it, is already twisted enough as it is right now, or, to invoke a more visceral idiom, insanely topsy-turvy in the bewildering disarray we presently endure, then brace yourself for the far more terrifying apocalyptic picture of a world utterly stripped bare of God's love for man—a dystopian nightmare where the very architecture of divine grace has collapsed into an irrevocable chasm of exclusion. Trust me, you would recoil in abject horror, retreat in righteous repugnance from even briefly dwelling in that utterly godforsaken and hopeless wasteland, wholly bereft and stripped bare of the sweet and sustaining embrace of the divine love or impoverished to the marrow of divine grace. No mortal mind among us could truly comprehend—much less willingly choose or long for—the overwhelming moral and spiritual chaos of such grace-deprived, love-forsaken void.

THE PRICELESS GIFT OF GOD'S LOVE: THE PINNACLE OF PROFOUND SELF-SACRIFICE

In truth without exaggeration, God has authored and handed down but a single volume, and this Holy Book has got one universal story to tell—viz, the love-inspired story of his ever-unfolding relationship with humankind, a tapestry woven from the threads of divine affection. Though sovereignly inspired by the breath of God, it remains indelibly the story of man—the profoundly human drama, forever bound to the redemptive love that the Creator has poured out toward every soul. This is the one gospel the Lord Himself delights to proclaim to whoever has ears to hear. In piercing contrast stands the heart of man—so profoundly deep, so impenetrably dense, and so shrouded in abyssal darkness—that even the Bible itself had to pose the timeless question, "*Who can know it?*" (Jer 17:9). I, too, have stood in wonder before that abyss, marveling at its hidden depths. But God's heart is never to be considered a closed book; rather, it lies open before us—an unveiled scroll of divine mysteries, a transparent diary overflowing with heavenly secrets, just about as open in transparency and accessible as the Bible lying right next to you at this very moment. Correspondingly, his love for man is neither to be considered a secret nor some indecipherable mystery, it stands revealed as a Polichinelle secret—an open secret. Never was a mystery so thoroughly demystified, a hidden truth so radiantly disclosed that it has nothing to hide. It has been inscribed forever upon the pages of history and blazoned upon the Cross like a blazing beacon, an unmistakable, luminous declaration for every eye to see and every heart to recognize: the eternal, passionate outpouring of divine love.

The Scriptures, when they speak of the profound depths of God's heart and the hidden mysteries once concealed within its most intimate chambers, declare with resounding assurance: "*But we know about these things because God has sent his Spirit to tell us, and his Spirit searches out and shows us all of God's deepest secrets*" (1 Cor. 2:10 TLB). Truly, every thread of enigma that formerly veiled God's love for mankind has been completely unraveled and laid bare through the revelation of His Son—every unspoken secret, every buried confidence once locked away in the sanctuary of divine affection toward the children of men, has been forever unsealed and heralded abroad by the victorious Gospel, that eternal trumpet of divine disclosure. The Almighty is in no way like a timid secret admirer; he encounters no barrier, no reluctance, in openly manifesting his benevolent purposes to humanity—he withholds nothing in making known the fullness of his divine love to its intended objects. With every concealing veil now gloriously removed, the radiant truth stands beyond all dispute: his heart holds nothing but love for man. This heart of undivided devotion acknowledges humanity alone as its sole and cherished object. Needless to say, God's supreme joy resides in the sons of men—his deepest longing is to commune intimately with them—his steadfast commitment is directed toward each one individually. And straight from the horse's mouth, we are told in the affirmative: "*Rejoicing in His inhabited world, And my delight was with the sons of men*" (Prov. 8:31 NKJV). Among all the Creator's manifold works, his delight rests not upon the myriad hosts of angels in the heavenly realms, nor upon any of the countless creatures that roam the earth; it rests exclusively upon the sons and daughters of men dispersed across the face of the globe. Therefore, God's love for humanity is no mere footnote in the pages of Scripture; it is the headline message of the entire Bible—the beating heart and central theme of the one true Gospel.

Consequently, it should come as no surprise to any of us that, in reality, the Bible verse that has historically risen to unparalleled popularity throughout the annals of divine lore—standing as the most treasured declaration indelibly inscribed upon the heart of Scripture—turned out to be none other than the amazing John 3:16, which reads, "*For God so loved the world that He gave His only begotten Son, that whoever believes in Him should not perish but have everlasting life*" (Christian Today, 2022). Invariably hailed as the golden text of the Bible, this verse is far more than a sublime utterance of divine oratory from the lips of Christ; it constitutes the prophetic script he himself enacted with passionate fidelity upon the stage of redemption, the covenantal pathway he walked across the darkened terrain of a fallen creation. Indeed, it is the very biography he lived—from the gentle cradle of Mary's womb at Bethlehem's first light to the solemn sepulcher that received his atoning body in the gathering shadows of Golgotha. With every breath infused by the Spirit, every redemptive trial endured, every Messianic oracle fulfilled, he bore living testimony to and incarnated the covenantal agape love that resounds as the unbroken theme through the whole canonical testimony. At its core, John 3:16 unveils with piercing clarity the portrait of the Creator's boundless agape for his beloved creatures, supremely manifested in the gift of his "only begotten Son"—the inestimable bestowal of his self-outpouring love. If love indeed reigns as the sovereign pinnacle of God's immutable nature, as the Scriptures thunderously attest (1 John 4:8, *"God is love"*), then the profound act of 'giving' emerges as the most exalted expression that can ever arise from the infinite wellspring of his nature of love. Beyond all contradiction, the ultimate proof of love is giving; scarcely any greater expression one could ascribe to love besides giving, positioning it as a witness that towers above all alternative displays of affection.

There are, however, varying levels in the noble practice of giving, all of which are ranked according to the intrinsic value and lasting significance of the gift so offered—a measure that elevates the act beyond mere transaction into realms of profound significance. While sacrificial giving occupies one of the loftiest positions in this hierarchy, selfless giving or genuine self-sacrifice stands alone at its supreme peak and thus represents the highest conceivable demonstration of love—the grandest and most sublime manifestation that love, in its infinite sacrificial beauty, can ever attain. Among the most illustrious exemplars of sacrificial giving enshrined within the sacred canon, if not the greatest thereof, stands vividly chronicled for our edification in the venerable Book of Genesis 22, wherein the Almighty sovereignly tested the faith of the patriarch Abraham by directing him to sacrifice as a burnt offering his dearly beloved *"only son,"* Isaac, the child he loved beyond measure and treasured above every earthly possession, surpassed only by himself. Yet, the single act of giving that towers above all others throughout the entire chronicle of world history—surpassing even Abraham's poignant, foreshadowing sacrifice of his dearly loved son Isaac—is none other than God's supreme and transcendent gift: the sacrifice of his own beloved Son, Jesus. While the story of Abraham highlights his extraordinary obedience, demonstrated in the willingness to sacrificially part away with someone who, even though precious to him, was distinct from himself, God, in the stark verity of redemptive reality, immeasurably outgave him by sacrificially offering Someone utterly indistinguishable from himself—a coeternal, consubstantial fellow member of the Trinity.

For the unparalleled gift of God to man is himself—'God'—God the Son, who assumed the form of a Man to consummate and supremely manifest God's eternal love for humankind in its fullest expression. And thus, in this rare and peculiar case, both the Giver and his Gift are essentially one and the same—the Redeemer and his Ransom in indivisible unity—the Father and his Son in profound relational harmony—the Triune God in perichoretic perfection. For, as enshrined in the Doctrine of the Trinity, the Persons of God the Father, God the Son, and God the

Holy Spirit subsist in one and the same indivisible substance, though distinctly individuated in their eternal relations, yet consubstantial in essence, coeternal in being, co-equal in majesty, and co-existent in boundless fellowship. Consequently, one cannot truthfully affirm possession of the Father exclusive of the Son, nor embrace the Son apart from the Spirit; such a fragmentation would rend the seamless tapestry of divine unity. In this light, we may discern with clarity a profound facet of what the Apostle Paul intended when he proclaimed, "*But you are not in the flesh but in the Spirit, if indeed the Spirit of God dwells in you. Now if anyone does not have the Spirit of Christ, he is not His*" (Rom 8:9 NKJV). Within the compass of this singular verse, he masterfully equates indwelling by '*the Spirit of God*' with indwelling by '*the Spirit of Christ,*' unveiling the profound consubstantiality wherein the Spirit's presence attests to the holistic embrace of the Triune indwelling, binding believer and God in unbreakable communion. For the selfsame rationale, the Scriptures are at times seen blurring the lines of distinction between God the Father and Jesus Christ the Son, particularly in those poignant passages where they allude with precision to the redemptive sacrifice of the Cross. Exemplified in such arresting declarations as " . . . *the church of God which He purchased with His own blood*" (Acts 20:28 NKJV), even as we unequivocally recognize that it was Jesus whose vital ichor was specifically poured forth upon the Cross as the sacrificial Pasch, the unblemished Lamb, for the comprehensive redemption of humankind. This sublime act of divine self-giving, wherein the Logos Incarnate emptied himself unto death, not only towers as the unrivaled demonstration of love—transcending all measures of affection—but also as the consummate revelation of purpose, wherein the telos of creation finds its crimson fulfillment in the Father's heart for the sons of men.

God, the fountain of fervent love and the source of all goodness, finds fullest joy in the act of self-communication—freely giving himself—graciously granting his glorious goodness to man, the elect recipient of his boundless generosity. Beyond the likeness of the imago Dei, a unique correspondence unites God and humanity for their mutual perfection, not because God lacks anything—for he is perfect in himself—but because the human soul, with its insatiable longing for fulfillment, is completed only through the abundant gift of divine grace. This grace flows like a mighty river, meeting the soul's deepest needs. God's nature, complete and unchanging, finds its truest expression in this act of giving, where his overflowing goodness pours into human nature. Humanity, with its profound capacity to receive, and God, with his infinite desire to bestow, form a sacred exchange: one has great want and capacity to receive good, and the other has overflowing abundance and the desire to graciously bestow it. Nothing so complements human need as divine abundance, nor divine abundance as human need, for the greater the abundance, the stronger its urge to pour forth and share itself, and the deeper the poverty, the more fervent its desire to receive, like a void yearning to be filled. The meeting of this boundless generosity with human indigence is so harmonious that one might question whether the divine joy in giving surpasses the human satisfaction in receiving, until, of course, the Son of God made clear that "*It is more blessed to give than to receive*" (Acts 20:35). Now, where there is more blessedness, there is equally more satisfaction—thus, the divine essence, perfect in its generosity, derives far greater satisfaction in distributing its riches to the necessities of the sons of men than we do in receiving. Like a nursing mother whose lactating breasts would often become so milk-laden that she must offer it to her child, although the infant receives it with a ravenous appetite, yet the nurse freely offers it with even more eagerness and relief. While the suckling infant is driven by its necessity to be fed, the mother is pressed by the need to discharge the overflowing abundance of her breast milk. Likewise, humanity's lack yearns for this divine fullness to fulfill its need, but God, moved by nothing else but his own overflowing goodness and boundless benevolence, pours forth to humanity's poverty, whilst yet having no need of our poverty, being perfect in and of himself and unbettered by bestowing, seeks no benefit from human want.

For God is never at the receiving end in the communication of his goodness or his likeness to man; on the contrary, he gives munificently, but our poverty, on the other hand, would languish in want and remain miserable if it were not enriched by the supply of God's abundance. God's plentiful provision—pulsing with potent presents, his plentiful provision—pouring pure profit, his plentiful provision—bursting to bestow blessings, longs to lavish; man's pressing poverty—hewn to hold divine gifts, our pressing poverty—hankering for higher good, our pressing poverty—hungry for holy grace, craves completion. All of that becomes even more significant in the light of Christ's redemptive gift of himself. For the greatest of love's gifts is the gift of self—the sacrifice of oneself for the sake of others. Jesus affirmed this to be the case when he said, "*Greater love has no one than this, than to lay down one's life for his friends*" (John 15:13 NKJV). The Passion Translation of the Bible renders it even more forcefully: "*For the greatest love of all is a love that sacrifices all. And this great love is demonstrated when a person sacrifices their life for his friends*" (John 15:13 TPT). Actually, one can neither give anything more treasured than himself nor part away with any gift more valuable to him than himself. For, at its foundational principle, no man can possibly treasure anything else in the world more than he treasures his own self. By the selfsame inexorable rationale, it holds that you cannot extend love to any other soul with an intensity surpassing the measure you lavish upon yourself. Hence, the Golden Commandment enshrined in Scripture deems it prudently sufficient that every man endeavor to love his neighbor with precisely the same ardor and depth as he loves himself. This further leads us to conclude that God held nothing back whatsoever when he offered up his Son, nor did he spare a single facet when he imparted his Spirit, inasmuch as yielding the Second and Third Persons of the Trinity constituted nothing less than the ultimate surrender of himself—his inmost core, undiminished and unreserved. And verily, when his Son, in the fullness of redemptive consummation, ultimately laid down his life upon the sacred altar of sacrificial oblation at Calvary—he, too, proffered the forfeiture of his most cherished possession: the transcendent, self-immolating sacrifice of himself, the eternal emblem of divine largesse. That agrees with the testimony of Scripture that " . . . *He has appeared to put away sin by the sacrifice of Himself*" (Heb 9:26 NKJV). For the God-Man could not conceivably have treasured anything more profoundly than he treasured his own sacred life, so by voluntarily laying down that precious life as the priceless ransom—a supreme oblation of inestimable worth—he surrendered his all, his utmost essence, for the eternal salvation of mankind, all enshrined as the radiant, irrefutable demonstration of the Father's boundless love extended to every soul within humanity's vast embrace.

Furthermore, the profound rationale underpinning God's descent into manhood transcends mere admiration for the contours of human frailty, nor was it a perfunctory display to flaunt the resplendent attributes of his Divinity through the frail vessel of man's humanity; nay, it resides unequivocally in the fathomless depths of his love for mankind—a love so vehement and unyielding that he willed to shoulder and discharge the exorbitant, incalculable price demanded for humanity's redemption, sealing the covenant of grace with the currency of divine self-sacrifice. Who, even in the most fervent depths of religious contemplation—whether across a millennium of yearning or the inconceivable stretch of a billion years—could ever have dared to imagine that the three weighty words "God," "man," and "love" might one day be fused together in perfect, harmonious concord within the compass of a single sentence? Yet behold it, shining forth with the clarity of noonday light: the holy, morally flawless Creator-God joined inseparably to sinful, morally broken creatures, with "love" standing as the adjoining word that binds the two in unbreakable union—miraculously bridging the otherwise unbridgeable gulf between divine purity and human wretchedness. Though such a union may sound profoundly paradoxical to the natural ear, Holy Scripture offers abundant and unequivocal testimony to the Creator's perennial longing to draw near to humanity in intimate communion, manifesting through innumerable forms and tokens a singular, affectionate attachment directed exclusively toward the sons of men—a divine tenderness, a heavenly "soft spot" of electing love and tender regard, as contemporary language might aptly express it. With such unquenchable earnestness did he crave this communion and associative bond with mankind that he forthwith coined for himself the eponymous theonym "*. . . the God of Abraham, the God of Isaac, and the God of Jacob . . .*" (Exod 4:5), a covenantal appellation resonant with eternal import. In its narrower ambit, this served as a deliberate memorial inscription, etching his eternal identity indelibly with these venerable patriarchs of faith who had traversed the pilgrim paths of intimacy with him to varying measures of fidelity and devotion; yet, in its more expansive sweep, it proclaimed his ultimate aspiration to be universally acclaimed as the all-loving God, eternally contextualized within the progressively unfolding tapestry of his redemptive relationship with humankind—the sole creature he sovereignly and purposefully singled out from the cosmic chorus, meticulously fashioned after the exquisite blueprint of his own Divine similitude.

That is quite a big deal because it shows us to what extent the Creator-God was willing to go in his effort to identify with the human species in particular, unlike anything ever seen with his angels or any other creatures for that matter. No sooner did he become a Man, consummately identifying with man's humanity in what is now theologically termed—the Incarnation of the Logos. Hence the grounds for my insistence that the prophetic revelations of God in the Scriptures are always posited in the context of his unprecedented and unparalleled relationship with humans, but hardly ever in relation to the angels, brutes, or any other impersonal creatures for that matter. There just seems to be some sort of intrinsic quality unique to man that naturally makes him the single creature of God's vested interest—the sole object of his divine love—and the sovereign beneficiary of his manifold goodness. And as far as we can tell, that unique existential quality appears to be something we could all liken to what the Frenchman has coined *je ne sais quoi*—a rare indefinable quality, as it were, or what the English churchman may himself prefer to call the spark of divinity in man's humanity.

FROM EDEN TO ETERNITY: THE BIBLE'S BOUNDLESS NARRATIVE OF GOD AND MAN

It may be worth reiterating here, even at the risk of belaboring the point, perhaps in the strongest possible terms this time around, that the Bible is a book written for man—ultimately about God's love for man, as inspired by God Himself—under the penmanship of holy men of God (see 2 Peter 1:19–21; 2 Timothy 3:16). So both the Old and New Testaments are better off being considered epistles of divine love. Needless to say, the Book is simply not a history book for teaching history lessons but a sacred book for ultimately teaching God's love for man, *inter alia*, the sanctity and value of human life. Inasmuch as the historically chronicled story of the life and public ministry of Jesus (as captured in the Four Gospels) befits the taxonomic classification that has it placed on the shelves of either the biographical or hagiographical genre, it is nonetheless very much our human story, as it is His divine-human story, about as much the anthropic story of man as it is the theanthropic story of the God-Man, simultaneously told side-by-side—one in relation to the other. Thus, the canonical Scriptures do not constitute a theological autobiography or a celestial self-portraiture centered upon the Divine subject; indeed, the thematic storyline offers but a marginal account of God in his own right, presenting instead the overarching narrative of human existence—the historical and existential record of humankind, acutely sensitive to the progressive dynamics of its covenantal relationship with the Creator and the broader created order that surrounds it. Had it been God's intention to make it all about himself, a sacred composition exclusively extolling his eternal essence and immutable edicts—the resultant text could plausibly resemble the Qur'an or other extant religious literatures, yet he ordained otherwise, embracing the human story within his grand design. He made it so much about man, weaving mankind so integrally into its exegetical framework, that he himself became a Man midway through the tale. This hypostatic union—the God incarnate—did not lay down his life upon the cruel stake for man's sake, only to then turn around and make the story of redemption all about himself. No—not the faintest whisper of self-aggrandizement—he rather constructs the salvific paradigm as quintessentially human in its path, interwoven from proctological themes to eschatological finale with an inexhaustible trove of divine love oriented ever toward our redemption.

The Creator, who crowned his creative act with man at its core and teleological summit, thereby rendering the aetiology of existence profoundly man-centered, is identical to the Redeemer, who mirrored that focus in his redemptive mission and its doctrinal elaboration—unwaveringly anthropocentric. His love for man is embedded in each intricate detail, for within the subtlest particulars dwell ceaseless traces of his tenderness for mankind, scattered like eternal invitations across the storyline's sweeping horizons. Which again, makes it all the more significant a realization that the first person ever to be mentioned in the whole Bible is God—the Creator, and next to him is man—the creature of his Divine love (see. Genesis 1:1 & 26–28). So much so that the storyline begins and ends with both entities concurrently making recurrent appearances in the picture—from the Books of Genesis all the way through Revelation. Noteworthy, the statistical witness from Strong's Hebrew and Greek Concordance only deepens the wonder: "God" resounds 4,444 times in 3,876 verses, with "man" trailing yet still commanding 2,615 appearances across 2,331 verses—vastly eclipsing such terms as "angel," which occurs a comparatively modest 201 times in 192 verses alone.

Predominantly reflecting the Divine-human ownership of the story in essence, because while that illustrates Divine prominence, it by the same token demonstrates the overarching significance of humanity's special place in the grand scheme of things. Albeit, this is besides the appearances of sacred deonyms and other pronouns used for God and the proper names and pronouns for individuals mentioned throughout the Scriptures. That would also explain why all other living creatures who had been organically created impersonal by nature and essence are often only mentioned in passing, whether they be brutes or angels, all of whom were essentially being featured as nonactors—assigned nonactive roles in the story more or less. Except, of course, until that serpent (Satan the devil) defiantly abrogated to himself an active role as a bad actor—the villain—and then, suddenly, the whole story began to take on a whole new twist for the worse—until for the better, spawning from a deep sense of tragedy and then climaxing in a heightened sense of Gospel. But despite all the twists and turns, the Scriptures, notwithstandingly, still manage to keep the central casts (God and man) as their central focus in sum and substance. We hence find that the canonized Bible substantively kicks off with the iconic 'sorry story' of the fallen man by whom sin and death came (Adam), but then it caps off with the most iconic 'success story' of the risen God-Man from whom righteousness and eternal life egressed (Christ Jesus).

INCARNATE ENIGMA: CHRIST AS GOD-MAN—BEYOND THE VEIL OF 'MAN OF GOD'

Percase, I should also be quick to point out from hereon that whenever the neologized compound 'God-Man' is employed in making any specific references to Jesus, it must not be mistaken for or equated with the seemingly cognate term 'man of God,' for there is a great difference between both. God-Man essentially refers to the unparalleled extramarriage of Godhood and manhood in the personhood of Jesus the Christ, the Incarnation of Deity in humanity, or more simply, God in human flesh. Exactly why Jesus was both called 'the Son of God'—connoting his Godhood or Divinity—and 'the Son of Man'—connoting his Manhood or Incarnate humanity. And given the fundamental distinction between both terms and the overarching implications that particularly followed from him becoming a Man, we can better understand why it is that those demonic entities whom he often encountered in his earthly ministry usually had no difficulty acknowledging that he was indeed the Son of God, saying often, "*What have we to do with You, Jesus, You Son of God? Have You come here to torment us before the time?*" (Matt 8:29 NKJV); or the Holy One of God—"*Let us alone! What have we to do with You, Jesus of Nazareth? Did You come to destroy us? I know who You are—the Holy One of God!*" (Mark 1:24 NKJV). But when it came down to admitting that he is 'the Son of Man'—who had come in the flesh—the Incarnate Word, they found this impossible an admission to make. And John, in his First Epistle, writes in this regard: "*By this you know the Spirit of God: Every spirit that confesses that Jesus Christ has come in the flesh is of God, and every spirit that does not confess that Jesus Christ has come in the flesh is not of God. And this is the spirit of the Antichrist, which you have heard was coming, and is now already in the world*" (I John 4:2–3 NKJV). From all indications, these malign spirits would have had no problem with the Son of God staying back up there where he was and remaining who he was—'*the only begotten of the Father*,' thus leaving humanity to its stygian fate. But venturing down here to become the Son of Man—the Christ and Savior of the world—is what turned them into the Antichrist spirits they became. Apparently, they understood very well that God the Son—the Second Person of the Trinity becoming a Man on cosmic soil—is what actually changed the course of human history and wrought such great salvation for the sons of men. Something that, by the way, homochronously turned out to be their worst nightmare—their greatest undoing.

And that much, they would not want to admit to be a historical fact; hence, they must deny that Jesus was ever here. That being said, it is worth pointing out that, although the term God-Man is more or less a fanciful term of the theologian's coining, intended to help emphasize the unity of divinity and humanity in the person (hypostasis) of Christ, it is yet one you would barely ever come across anywhere in the Scriptures. If anything at all, the Scriptures affirm Jesus to be precisely a man more than they do anything else, because that is precisely what God became down here on earth. Perhaps the only caution in using such nonce terms in describing Jesus is that there remains that tendency for it to be misunderstood by those who are not so theologically inclined, as it tends to suggest that Jesus simultaneously functioned as God and Man in carrying out his earthly ministry—thus exploiting a combination of the privileges of his divinity and humanity. Which is far from being the case, as he relied entirely on the agency of the Holy Spirit to accomplish the extraordinary feats we see him accomplish in his ministry. For even he himself did not shy from affirming repeatedly that "*I can of mine own self do nothing . . .* " (John 5:30 KJV), and again: "*Then answered Jesus and said unto them, Verily, verily, I say unto you, The Son can do nothing of himself, but what he seeth the Father do: for what things soever he doeth, these also doeth the Son likewise*" (John 5:19 KJV). He obviously had no self-reliance, having stripped himself of the privileges of his Divinity.

While the phrase 'man of God,' on the other hand, is traditionally used in describing certain men who have the call of God on their lives into preacherdom, or as is often said around Christian circles—those who are called to the Fivefold or Pulpit Ministry—whether in the capacity of an Apostle, a Prophet, an Evangelist, a Pastor, or more contemporary sacerdotal titles such as Vicar, Reverend, Preacherman, Clergyman, holy man, votary, and what have you. I suppose the best illustration to sort of help you understand that even better would be the John the Baptist and Jesus distinction; in that John was, on the one hand, a man of God or a man sent from God, while Jesus, on the other hand, is God in and of himself. To wit, the God who both called and sent John. Hence, the Bible tells us that "*God sent a man named John to be his messenger*" (John 1:6 GW). Partly what John himself was alluding to in his response to some Jewish delegates who were sent down from big-city Jerusalem to come inquire from him at the sylvan backcountry of Bethabara, somewhere beyond the Jordan, in whose streams he went about his baptismal business: "*Who are you, that we may give an answer to those who sent us? What do you say about yourself?" they asked, to which he responded, "I baptize with water, but there stands One among you whom you do not know. It is He who, coming after me, is preferred before me, whose sandal strap I am not worthy to loose*" (John 1:22; 26–27 NKJV). Alternatively stated, John was sent ahead as the harbinger who was to go prepare the way for the coming of his Lord—the God of Israel, whereas Jesus is the God of Israel himself—the 'coming' One or the soon-coming Messianic King at that time, whose sandal straps John considered himself unworthy to untie. But if for any reason whatsoever, John had kept silent or kept himself back from acknowledging who Jesus really was, I tell you the truth that even the very stones underneath his feet would have wasted no time crying out in protest, descrying him as their Omnificent Maker.

To his credit, however, he appears to have deeply imbibed the underlying principle captured in his Master's witty saying that " . . . *a servant is not greater than his master; nor is he who is sent greater than he who sent him*" (John 13:16 NKJV). For the same reason also, he would go on to testify concerning him in yet another place that "*He who comes from above is above all; he who is of the earth is earthly and speaks of the earth. He who comes from heaven is above all"—therefore—"He must increase, but I must decrease*" (John 3:30 & 31 NKJV). Even though Jesus did not necessarily need the light of John's ministry to glow dim in order for his to shine any brighter. But as it turned out, that final clause of John's statement there symbolically marked the end of his own ministry, both ushering in and giving way for the epic and revolutionary ministry of Jesus Christ. The whole theological significance of all that appears to have been further underscored by the fact that John was actually " . . . *not that Light, but was sent to bear witness of that Light*"—while Jesus forever stands as—" . . . *the true Light which gives light to every man coming into the world*" (John 1:8 & 9 NKJV). John could, in that sense, be considered 'the lesser light'—who, like the moon, was destined to rule by night, with Jesus being 'the greater light'—who, like the sun, was destined to rule by day—the Day of the Lord (cf. Gen 1:16; Psalms 136:7–9). And here is how Jesus summed up that entire relationship between himself and John the Baptist for his countrymen: "*You have sent messengers to John, and what he testified about me is true. I have no need to be validated by men, but I'm explaining these things so that you will believe and be saved. "John was a blazing, shining torch, and for a short time, you basked in his light with great joy. But I can provide more substantial proof of who I am that exceeds John's testimony—my miracles! These works, which the Father destined for me to complete—they prove that the Father has sent me! And my Father himself, who gave me this mission, has also testified that I am his Son. But you have never heard his voice nor seen his form*" (John 5:33–37 TPT). And as far as the story of redemption goes, and as was foretold by numerous OT prophecies, it is through the dazzling brightness—through the glorious radiance—through the shimmering incandescence of this Man's shine that all peoples who have long sat in darkness will finally get to see the light (cf. Matt 4:16).

It should already be obvious at this point that our human story effectively has God as part of it—God the Son as part and parcel of it all. God essentially has his skin in the game, as they say. With the Divine story consequently interwoven into the human story from the onset, the chances are just about everything we may come to know of God (the Creator) in all the Canonical Scriptures taken together, we would inadvertently and unavoidably find to be in relation to man (the creature of his love). Quite similar to the biblical narrative, where heaven is mentioned in relation to the earth more often than not. And not only does the above storyline and its narrative style represent an ironclad Biblical leitmotif, or shall we say, a unifying thematic thread that runs throughout the entire Bible, but it also happens to be one of the earliest narrative portraits that we are presented with just as soon as the curtains are drawn open on the very first page of the Bible, where we have the incipit text in The Book of Genesis, Chapter 1 and verse 1, informing us of how that "*In the beginning God created the heavens and the earth.*" Essentially setting the tone for all subsequent discussions pertaining to the confluent interrelation between heaven and earth, mirroring the vertical relationship between the God of heaven—the Creator—and the man of earth—the sole creature of his vested interest. Hardly a marvel, then, to see the God-Man begin his 3-year earthly ministry with a beckoning call to all Earthicans:

"*Keep turning away from your sins and come back to God, for heaven's kingdom realm is now accessible [on earth]*" (Matt 4:17 TPT—the words in parenthesis are added). This also serves to explain why he would every so often be seen throughout the Gospels using earthly human stories we could all relate to as narrative vehicles for conveying to us the understanding of his often acroamatic and otherwise subliminal messages about God and his heavenly kingdom. And for the same reason also, his messages were typically delivered in the form of parables—parables that were usually anecdotal and prescriptive by their very nature and scope.

In fact, the Greek word *parabolē* (parable) appears 48x in 46 verses in just the Synoptic Gospels alone, and that Biblical statistic is of some significance. Much of what we come across in the entire Bible is God speaking to us in purely human terms, often by employing the use of anthropomorphic language intended to help us come to grips with the complex realities of his divine nature and the often incomprehensible truths about his spiritual kingdom. For example, by saying something to the effect of, "*To what shall we liken the kingdom of God? Or with what parable shall we picture it?* (Mark 4:30–32 NKJV), the Son of God was simply endeavoring to use our everyday human stories to help get us *au fait* with metaphysical concepts and Divine truths. In effect, drawing strong correlations or striking parallels (whether by similitude or by contrast) between the ethereal realities of God's kingdom and the corporeal realities of man's world. Ultimately, with the goal of fostering the understanding, given how much he knew at the time, that "*No one has gone up into heaven, but there is One who came down from heaven, the Son of Man [Himself—whose home is in heaven]*" (John 3:13 AMP). That is to say, no man has ever been to and fro heaven enough to come down here to tell the rest of us what things are like up there or who and whatnot is up there, save himself alone, who had enjoyed the singular privilege of being sent down here from up there, partly for the purpose of establishing transdimensional foreign relations between heaven and earth, thus making possible a filial and familial relationship between God and man for the first time since creation and then the Fall of man and man's world, which soon followed in the Garden of Eden (the birthplace of the human story, or rather—the God-and-human story).

From all indications, however, the Creator-God appears to have systematically chronicled the whole redemption narrative to be just this way and would have it no other way, ultimately because his love for man is one unmistakable case he would consistently be making throughout the

Good Book, down to the very last page where he finally draws the narrative curtains closed with the Book of Revelation. So make no mistake about it, what we are looking at here, give or take, is a waterproof case for God's ineffable love for mankind—as ultimately embodied by no one else but his Divine Son—consummately demonstrated nowhere else but on the Cross of his Divine love. Seen in this light, the prophetic revelations of God in Scripture could hardly ever be considered a standalone, because it is ultimately by coming to know God in the Son of his love that we simultaneously come to know ourselves in truth; it is by studying that novel Book of Divine Revelations that we progressively come to better understand, in short, the long story behind our own existence—our human story told from origin to destiny. Blaise Pascal appears to have put it even better: "*Not only do we know God by Jesus Christ alone, but we know ourselves only by Jesus Christ. We know life and death only through Jesus Christ. Apart from Jesus Christ, we do not know what is our life, nor our death, nor God, nor ourselves*" (2010; pg. 581). Quite similar to King David the Psalmist testifying to the effect that "*The Lord is my light . . .* "—basically referring to him as " . . . *the light by which we see*" (Ps 27:1 NKJV; Psalms 36:9 NLT). No different from John the Evangelist calling the same Lord " . . . *the true Light which gives light to every man coming into the world*" (John 1:9 NKJV). Even the Church Father—Augustine viewed Christ as the interior light dispelling ignorance. That profound biblical reality would later become a foundational intellectual conviction among the founding members of one of the West's most renowned academic institutions, Oxford University, immortalized in Latin upon their coat of arms and motto—*Dominus illuminatio mea*—"The Lord is my light."

Borne out of their intellectual conviction that there could be no meaningful intellectual progress nor spiritual enlightenment without God and his Christ. All of that is simply just another way of maintaining that without God's light of revelation enlightening us and illuminating our lives by his Son, we would substantially remain in existential darkness—even the darkness of ignorance. Hence, the Divine knowledge reveals us like a mirror reveals a man, showing us the true reflection of our face—right down to the very true colors of our inner selves, thus helping us see and then to take cognizance of the extent to which we are shrunken from or *'fallen short of the glory'* of the Divine image and likeness in which we were aboriginally fashioned or how much of an exact replica we might yet remain, if at all. An age-enduring testament to the fact that we were indeed made in God's image and likeness at the genesis of our human story. Evidently, both the knowledge of God and that of man are so betwined together and complementary to one another that they could hardly ever be considered mutually exclusive nor distinctively conceptualised in all Scripture, because learning about one inevitably leads to the knowledge of the other. It is almost as though God is using the whole Biblical narrative to tell us what we really need to know about ourselves—in the light of our progressively unfolding relationship with him. Hence, when captured in sum and substance, the whole redemptive love story essentially has got everything to do with the Creator-God telling us about the long-drawn-out transmigratory journey of his love from heaven to earth; how far he himself has had to travel in pursuit of the object of his Divine love and how so meticulously he has had to sweep through the Cosmos, turning up every rock and uncovering every rug—searching through every nook and rummaging through every cranny for every last one of his lost silver coins (the lost souls of men).

THE MYSTERY OF DIVINITY BEFORE THE INCARNATION: HUMANITY'S QUEST FOR THE INVISIBLE CREATOR

Notably significant also is that Paul would later go on to use the adjectives *'invincible'* and *'immortal'* in describing the mystery shrouding the Divine identity of the Creator-God of the OT, perhaps as a way of helping us come to grips with the unknowableness or imperceptibleness of his Divine parsonage besides and before his incarnate self-disclosure in his Son (see 1 Timothy 1:17). All part of the point he was endeavoring to hammer home to heart in his dialogue with a number of Stoic and Epicurean philosophers he had encountered at Athens, stressing that:

> *"for as I was passing through and considering the objects of your worship, I even found an altar with this inscription: TO THE UNKNOWN GOD. Therefore, the One whom you worship without knowing, Him I proclaim to you: "God, who made the world and everything in it, since He is Lord of heaven and earth, does not dwell in temples made with hands. Nor is He worshiped with men's hands, as though He needed anything, since He gives to all life, breath, and all things. Therefore, since we are the offspring of God, we ought not to think that the Divine Nature is like gold or silver or stone, something shaped by art and man's devising. Truly, these times of ignorance God overlooked, but now commands all*

> *men everywhere to repent, because He has appointed a day on which He will judge the world in righteousness by the Man whom He has ordained. He has given assurance of this to all by raising Him from the dead*" (Acts 17:23–31 NKJV).

Theologically, the connection between Genesis and John is profound, in that the *imago Dei* in humanity finds its archetype in Christ—the visible image of the invisible God (Col 1:15). Because up until God made an incarnate self-disclosure—not until His Son personally showed up on the cosmic scene—there was really no frame of reference anywhere that any man could point to and say: Look here, this is what the God of heaven looks like, or see there, that is someone unto whom we shall liken Him, so he was to all men, more or less, '*THE UNKNOWN GOD*'. As we all were in substantial darkness of ignorance as to whom he really was or what his Divine image and likeness was actually like. And this, of course, has left so much room for misconceptions, errors of judgment, and a lot of religious guesstimations, philosophical assumptions, and all sorts of distorted views of his Divine personage. So, give or take, the true nature of divinity historically became a subject of anyone's guess. Which further gave rise to all sorts of idolatrous worship, mythical and superstitious beliefs, and religious fetishisms—videlicet, the erroneous ascription of molten, graven, or carved images tied to fiendish deities to the Divine image and likeness of the Creator-God. Even as far back as the OT times, the prophets have time and again found themselves grappling with such questions as, "*With whom, then, will you compare God? To what image will you liken him?*" (Isa 40:18 NIV). Again, the answer to that valid primordial question is that there had never at any time in the history of the world been any entity unto whom men could properly liken God's parsonage—no image accurately bearing His Divine resemblance whatsoever. The grounds for which the Prophet Isaiah felt inspired to press even further with the same line of questioning: "*Can he be compared to an idol formed in a mold, overlaid with gold, and decorated with silver chains? Or if people are too poor for that, they might at least choose wood that won't decay and a skilled craftsman to carve an image that won't fall down! Haven't you heard? Don't you understand? Are you deaf to the words of God—the words he gave before the world began? Are you so ignorant? God sits above the circle of the earth. The people below seem like grasshoppers to him! He spreads out the heavens like a curtain and makes his tent from them*" (Isa 40:19–22 NLT). Notice how he touches on the fact that '*God sits above the circle of the earth,*' meaning he is far out of reach—way beyond every man's ken. So much so that not even the monotheistic Jews, who boasted of having a covenant relationship with the One True God and of being the custodians of the divine revelations that had been handed down in the Scriptures, could really claim to be familiar with the image of His divine resemblance, much less know who he really is.

In fact, the Mosaic Law expressly forbade them from likening 'the LORD,' their God, to any image of any kind (whether of man or of beast)—as that would rise to the charge of idolatry—nor were they to liken him to the sun—heliolatry—nor the moon—selenolatry—nor the stars—astrolatry (see. Deuteronomy 4:15–19). The same could be said of all other religions of the world, none of which really knew the invisible God whom they professed to be the object of their worship. So religion, in relation to God, was, for most religionists, by and large, a matter of blind faith. We could again see why Paul would also go on to lump all the OT dispensation of man's religious quest for God into a basket he labelled *'the times of ignorance'* altogether. And rightly so. Because in reality, they had absolutely no mental frame of reference for God, for there was none among men, none among angels, and none in fallen creation whatsoever. And where there was no mental frame of reference for God or for that Divine image and likeness of God in which Adam and Eve were aboriginally created in the beginning extant anywhere in man's world, it became incumbent upon God to become the perfect frame of reference for his own Divinity, although not in the capacity of his Godhood per se, but in the capacity of man's humanity. If by any chance he remotely wanted mankind to behold his image and likeness in Adam, I think he would have had no difficulty painting us a narrative picture of what he and his wife actually looked like before the Fall in the Scriptures, none of which he did, only going so far as to mention that they were both found 'naked' in the aftermath of the Fall—which could also be understood as being stripped bare of the glory of his Divine similitude in which they were aboriginally fashioned. That is an important piece of evidence that further leads us to conclude that God never really considered Adam to be his perfect image bearer and never really wanted us to look up to him or see him as such. He instead would go on to leave us prophetic pointers littered across the OT, all endorsing His Son as the archetypical Adam who was to come—" . . . *the brightness of His glory and the express image of His person* . . . " (Heb 1:3 NKJV). Christ, in this sense, is the first Man to have had God's seal of approval as the Incarnate Bearer of the *imago Dei* and worthy ambassador of His moral likeness.

Which soon led John, the beloved disciple of Jesus, to pen down the following thoughts in the Gospel that now bears his name, saying, "*And the Word became flesh and dwelt among us, and we beheld His glory, the glory as of the only begotten of the Father, full of grace and truth*" (John 1:14 NKJV). The reason this is significant is that up until we 'beheld' the glory of God's image and likeness in His Son, there was literally no frame of reference extant anywhere in our world for Him. And like Paul himself had concluded, all men have already fallen short of that glory of that divine image in Adam. So not even the direct descendants of Adam, and I mean, the likes of Cain and Abel, were privileged to behold the glory of the image and likeness of God in which their parents had been organically created before the Fall. Given that the imago Dei of the invisible Creator-God in which they were aboriginally fashioned had been irredeemably and irreversibly besmirched by the original sin (*peccatum originis*) at the time they were born, which also meant they only grew up knowing the defaced humanity. That was the extent of man's religious quest for the invisible and unknown God of all creation—until, in the fullness of time, he decisively made an incarnate self-disclosure within human history. Hence we can understand why there needed to be a New Covenant, one that came with a Divine promise that essentially guaranteed that none of us—whether Jew or Gentile—would need to " . . . *teach his neighbor, and none his brother, saying, 'KNOW THE LORD,' for all shall know Me* [God], *from the least of them to the greatest of them*" (Heb 8:11 NKJV). Thankfully, in Christ Jesus, for the first time since the world began and at long last, the invisible God finally became visible—the immortal God eventually became mortal—the unknown God historically became known and thus knowable.

Yet take heed: the 'Invincible God' of whom we now speak is none other than the selfsame Deity whom John the Baptist had solemnly attested to his fellow Jewish countrymen during that epochal moment, affirming that no human being had ever seen in the annals of history until precisely then—the very same 'Immortal God' to whom the ancient Prophets had borne unwavering witness as utterly non-mortal until he condescended to assume mortality in the person of that Jesus who was born in Bethlehem and hailed from Nazareth (cf. John 1:18, Numbers 23:19). Thus, in the epochs preceding this divine advent, the perennial reality had always been a case of "*No man hath seen God at any time; [save] the only begotten Son, which is in the bosom of the Father . . .* "—and for precisely this cause as well: " . . . *no man knoweth the Son, but the Father; neither knoweth any man the Father, save the Son, and he to whomsoever the Son will reveal him*" (John 1:18; Matthew 11:27 KJV, the word in parentheses is added). However, immediately following God's incarnate self-disclosure in His Divine Son, the entrenched religious paradigm underwent a seismic transmutation, evolving forthwith into the revolutionary declaration: " . . . *He who has seen Me has seen the Father* . . . "—so much so that we could no longer say to the Son—"*Show us the Father*" (cf. John 14:9 NKJV). The mask of mystery has been forever removed—the veil of divine secrecy rent asunder, stripped away like a shroud from an ancient tomb, and we can now see God's face with unveiled clarity and intimate proximity—yea, beholding Him face-to-face in the unmediated glory of divine revelation, by steadily beholding the incarnate face of His beloved Son, Jesus Christ, that mirrors the Father's essence in perfect fidelity and unfading light.

Historically speaking, where man's religion had miserably failed to forge any possible pathway or establish some ladder of ascension leading him toward the immortal and invisible God enthroned up there in the empyrean heaven, that transcendent God proactively took it upon Himself to make His way down here to man in the personage of Jesus Christ, whom he sent from celestial realms to terrestrial soil as the ultimate attestation that he is, and that he eternally lives. Ideally, humanity should have been passionately devoted to an upward pilgrimage toward God—pursuing him with tireless zeal that far exceeds even Elon Musk's recent relentless drive to reach Mars through SpaceX missions. Yet, in an act of astonishing love, God flips the script entirely: rather than leaving us to exhaust ourselves climbing the unreachable heights of his holiness, he came down to us. In the Incarnation, he meets us in our weakness and wanderings, displaying boundless grace. This represents the ultimate reversal: instead of humanity—like the proverbial Muhammad—failing in its desperate and futile attempts to climb the mountain of God's transcendence, the Mountain itself (God) comes down to meet us where we stand lost and helpless. We, the unworthy descendants of Adam—should have been found lying prostrate in deepest humility before the golden gates of God's supernal kingdom, echoing the Roman centurion's heartfelt plea: "*Lord, do not trouble Yourself, for I am not worthy to have You come under my roof. That is why I did not consider myself worthy to come to You* . . . " (Luke 7:6–7). Yet, in a stunning reversal, the perfectly worthy God willingly descends from His empyreal glory to enter our fallen dwelling—the cursed home of a sinful race—running toward us with boundless compassion, just as the father in the Parable of the Prodigal Son rushed joyfully to embrace his returning, wayward son (Luke 15:20). This divine initiative powerfully confirms the historical truth of Isaiah's prophetic words, where God speaks through the prophet in the first person: "*I was found by those who did not seek me; I revealed myself to those who did not ask for me. To a nation that did not call on my name, I said, 'Here I am, here I am'*" (Isa 65:1 NIV)—an everlasting witness to God's persistent, uninvited pursuit of those who are indifferent or unaware.

THE PINNACLE OF DIVINE DISCLOSURE: CHRIST AS JEHOVAH-AGAPE, LOVE INCARNATE

Within the unfolding weave of progressive revelation, successive generations of the sons of men may have been graced with the privilege of witnessing fleeting displays of varying attributes of God's ineffable character, manifested through emblematic foreshadows and veiled intimations—affording them piecemeal apprehensions and incomplete unveilings, by which he became revered under a laundry list of hallowed deonyms and majestic titles, including: *Jehovah-Sabaoth*—the Omnipotent Lord of heaven's celestial legions; *Jehovah-Shalom*—the Bestower of transcendent peace; *Jehovah-Jireh*—the All-Sufficient Provider amid every exigency; *Jehovah-Rohi*—the Vigilant Shepherd tending the wanderings of the soul; *Jehovah-Nissi*—the Victorious Ensign over every conflict; *Jehovah-M'Kaddesh*—the Holy One who consecrates and purifies the chosen remnant, and myriad others besides. But lo, precisely at this summit of the prophetic calendar—the perfect culmination where ages coalesce into one—God burns with an unquenchable zeal, earnestly desiring that every individual across humanity come to a close, personal understanding of His essence, intimately apprehending Him through the clarifying facet of His only begotten Son, in whom he has been gloriously epitomized and exhaustively revealed as *Jehovah-Agape*—the eternal Incarnation of the Divine love.

Inasmuch as we are willingly ready to affirm the Divine Omneity of the Almighty—upholding with unswerving theological certitude that he indeed embodies Omnipotence, Omnipresence, Omniscience, Omnificence, Omnicompetence, Omniferousness, Omnifariousness, and every such all-encompassing attribute one might enumerate—yet, in that very same breath, we dare not falter or slack in our heartfelt declaration that he transcends and surmounts all these glories as Omnibenevolent: supremely all-loving—more profoundly affectionate than in any other facet of His boundless being. While his power is limitless—crafting mountains and galaxies with ease—his presence is eternal—filling every space and time with his glory—and his knowledge is complete—encompassing every thought, deed, and destiny—yet, it is his love that most profoundly defines who he is, who he was, and who he will forever be. Far from being a mere attribute or an action, God's omnibenevolence remains, by far, the most defining essence of his beinghood, seamlessly woven into the fabric of his greatness, holiness, and justice. That is to say, love is not merely one of God's many virtuous qualities but the very essence from which all his actions and attributes flow graciously—both the source and action of salvation. His love simply wears the crown of his greatness among all divine attributes. Theologically, to affirm God's love as preeminent is to confess that his every action is governed by a benevolent love that seeks our salvation and invites us into a covenantal relationship with him. We therefore must hold fast to the truth that God's all-encompassing love is the most defining expression of his nature—surpassing all other attributes in its depth and significance.

Consequently, no contemplation of God's greatness is ever really complete without due and repeated emphasis on the all-surpassing greatness of his love, as most profoundly revealed in Christ's self-emptying life of humility and sacrificial death—the ultimate revelation of Divine greatness. It is a commonplace observation amongst religious devotees and their erudite scholars across diverse world's religions that they would hardly encounter any difficulty acknowledging and even extolling the most exalted qualities and characteristics of the shadowed Sovereign they conceive to be the Creator-God, as filtered through the interpretive framework of their particular religious heritage; yet, when confronted with the profound exigency of truly apprehending him on an intimate, relational footing—a profound shift from mental assent to heart-deep acquaintance, forthwith they abruptly find themselves floundering and faltering—floundering in the foam of frail conjecture and faltering on the fractured ice of intellect's winter—clinging theologically to desperate straws in a sea of uncertainty. This stark, almost tragic shortfall, their incapacity to bridge the chasm, arises fundamentally from the cardinal truth that genuine communion with God's relational and covenantal love—that oath-bound compassion that animates His eternal purposes and invites humanity into participatory fellowship—remains an impossibility apart from the redemptive agency of His only begotten Son, Jesus Christ. He, it is, indeed, whom the Father has sovereignly commissioned into the theater of human history, and in whose earthly sojourn, veiled in flesh yet radiant with glory, the otherwise inscrutable Divine has condescended to manifest Himself, rendering the Invisible God visible, accessible, knowable, and intimately near to the sons and daughters of Adam.

The greatness of God finds its consummation in his love, as the greatest Divine acts in all Scriptures are, invariably, acts of Divine love—those unprecedented acts that demonstrate God's philostorgy for the human family far more than they do anything else. Insofar as it remains true that everything about God is great—every Divine quality speaks of His infinite greatness—it is also true that every atom of greatness in God remains inextricably rooted in his nature of love, with each Divine attribute reflecting his all-encompassing omnibenevolence more than any other trait. Because God is love itself, his words and deeds—from the dawn of Creation to the triumph of Redemption and the forging of covenants—manifest his relentless desire to pour out boundless love upon mankind. He acts perpetually in love precisely because he is love itself; he is ever found walking and speaking in love for the selfsame reason—because such is his very being. When we turn to human conduct, we rightly discern that any deed stripped of love or not impelled by love cannot trace its origin to God. The principle applies with equal force to the Almighty Himself: every volition and every act proceeding from him—untouched by malice, untouched by spite, untouched by any shadow of ill will—flows invariably from his essential nature as love and remains forever circumscribed within the boundless yet holy parameters of that love.

Christ's humility in becoming human and his exaltation in resurrection not only reveal the limitless depth of God's love but also the pinnacle of his divine greatness, outshining all Biblical wonders in the Scriptures—from the Books of Genesis to Revelation. For no other miracle in Scripture shines anywhere half as bright as this redemptive marvel, where Jesus, though co-equal with God, became a servant, died on the cross, and rose in glory. And God the Father, rarely ever swayed nor impressed by human actions, was so deeply moved by his Son's selfless humility and love that he exalted him—crowning him with unmatched greatness—conferring on him a peerless name, so every knee bows and every tongue confesses Jesus as Lord (see Philippians 2:5–11). Though

God's omnipotence can move mountains and shape the cosmos, it is his redemptive love, demonstrated in the work of the cross, that transformatively impacts us. For the same reason also, the Holy Spirit convicts sinners, not by the violence of God's might nor by coercion of his power, but by a strictly tenderhearted impression of his love, where the revelation of the atoning sacrifice of Christ reveals God's heart. This love, rooted in the Triune communion between Father, Son, and Spirit, is the foundation of God's gracious acts—seeking the sinner, offering mercy to the fallen, and extending grace to the undeserving. By the tenderhearted act of this simple conviction, the Holy Spirit gets the sinner to see his existential need for the Savior. No coercion applied, no violence employed, none required. For the Son of God is the One who eventually paved the only extant way for all mankind to now have and experience the most meaningful relationship with God—apart from religion—thus fundamentally undermining the core relevance of man's established religions. In essence, signifying also that man's religion had indeed outlived its usefulness with the Advent of Christ. Now you can better understand why Jesus would go so far as to stake out the audacious claim that he is in and of himself 'the Way'—viz., the single pathway that leads to God, besides Whom no man can come to this God whom he alone dared to call 'Father'—*Abba Patēr* (cf. John 14:6). Until date , it remains just about true that in the absence of Christ, the Son of God, no mortal man can yet claim to have beheld the divine substance of the immortal God.

Paul, in his letter to the believers, reaffirms that the God of the Christians—described as dwelling in unapproachable light—" . . . *whom no man has seen or can see* . . . " (1 Tim 6:16). Viz., he is still a transcendent Deity whom no human being has ever fully seen or could possibly see in His unmediated glory and undiluted essence. This profound invisibility underscores a key truth: no finite mortal, bound by the limitations of earthly existence, can yet gaze upon the complete essence of God's divine substance—his eternal immortality, infinite holiness, and boundless perfections—in their raw, undiluted, and overwhelming purity. Instead, humanity has only been granted glimpses of this divine reality through mediated revelations, most notably in the incarnate form of Jesus Christ, where God's majesty is *'humanified'* (made accessible through human flesh and frailty) for our comprehension and relationship. Jesus represents the relatable embodiment of the divine—the ultimate Man with whom every person, regardless of background or struggle, can connect on a deeply personal level. Before this historic act of incarnation, where eternity intersected with time, the invisible qualities of God's character—His wisdom, power, love, and moral perfection—could only be dimly discerned through indirect means. In the realm of Natural Theology, for instance, these attributes shine faintly through the wonders of the created universe, as Paul notes in Romans 1:20: "*For since the creation of the world His invisible attributes are clearly seen, being understood by the things that are made, even His eternal power and Godhead, so that they are without excuse." Similarly, the Psalms poetically celebrate this: "The heavens declare the glory of God; And the firmament shows His handiwork*" (Ps 19:1), portraying the sun's daily journey as a bridal procession symbolizing divine splendor (Ps 19:4–6). Yet even these revelations, while awe-inspiring, remain vague and impersonal, like shadows on a cave wall. At their best, God's attributes were more tangibly revealed within the intimate framework of His covenantal bonds with the people of Israel—through prophets, laws, and miraculous interventions—but even here, true personal intimacy with the Divine remained elusive. No one could claim to 'know' God in the depth of a filial or familial relationship; the encounters were filtered through symbols, sacrifices, and selected mediators like Moses, who glimpsed only a veiled glory (see Exod 33:18–23). This distance highlights a core human dilemma: our finitude clashes with God's infinity, leaving us yearning for a bridge.

Thus, one compelling reason for the immortal, eternal God to enter mortality—fully embracing human vulnerability, temptations, sufferings, and limitations (Heb 2:17–18; 4:15)—was to shatter this barrier. By identifying completely with our humanity, he rendered himself approachable, empathetic, and intimately knowable. No longer a distant thunder on the horizon, God becomes the carpenter from Nazareth, the teacher by the seashore, the friend who weeps at gravesides (John 11:35). This revelation is exclusive to Christ: " . . . *He who has seen Me has seen the Father; so how can you say, 'Show us the Father'?*" (John 14:9), and it is in Christ and Christ alone that the fullness of Deity dwells bodily (Col 2:9), making the abstract eternal personal and the unreachable reachable. In this light, the evocative title of Mary Wollstonecraft Shelley's poignant 1833 novella, The Mortal Immortal: A Tale, serves as a strikingly apt metaphor for the profound Christian mystery of Christ's dual nature—the seamless hypostatic union of undiminished divinity and authentic humanity in one person. Yet, to capture the theological priority more precisely, we might invert it to *'The Immortal Mortal,'* emphasizing the primary reality: the eternal Son of God, inherently immortal in His divine essence and preexistent glory (John 1:1–2, 14), voluntarily assumed mortality—what he eternally was not—for our sake. This divine condescension reaffirms where he " . . . *did not think of equality with God as something to cling to. Instead, he gave up his divine privileges; he took the humble position of a slave and was born as a human being. When he appeared in human form*" (Phil 2:6–8 NLT). Precisely because of this timeless-to-temporal descent, we must handle language with care when speaking of the Eternal One. The verb 'was'—the simple past tense of 'to be,' implying a fixed point in time—cannot aptly describe the God who transcends chronology until that pivotal moment when he stepped out of eternity and into time, as the hymn writer puts it. Prior to the incarnation, to say 'He was' would confine the I AM (Exod 3:14; John 8:58) to a mere historical footnote, diminishing His ever-present reality. Only then, in the manger's cry and the cross's agony, does the full triune declaration ring true: he 'is' (the unchanging Now), 'was' (the eternal Past), and 'is to come' (the unfolding Future)—the Alpha and Omega (Rev 1:8), now forever intertwined with our story through the God-Man.

As the inspired author of Hebrews so eloquently declares, drawing a line in the sand for faith's foundational posture: "*But without faith it is impossible to please Him, for he who comes to God must believe that He is [present tense, the eternal I AM], and that He is a rewarder of those who diligently seek Him*" (Heb 11:6, NKJV). Not a mere historical artifact relegated to the dusty annals of 'was'—a God frozen in the irretrievable past—but the vibrant, pulsating Reality who invades the now with undiminished vitality. Yet, in the radiant afterglow of Christ's Advent, this declaration swells into a triumphant crescendo, refracted through the prism of the empty tomb and the ascended throne. We can now proclaim with unbridled confidence that our God is none other than "*the Alpha and the Omega . . . who is and who was and who is to come, the Almighty*" (Rev 1:8, NKJV). He is the Living One, who once 'was dead' in the harrowing depths of Calvary's shadow, only to burst forth alive forevermore, the keys of Death and Hades dangling triumphantly from His pierced hand (Rev 1:18, NKJV). This is no abstract chronology; it is the heartbeat of redemption, where eternity's pulse syncs with history's fragile rhythm. Far be it from the Christian confession to peddle a diluted myth—that the divine essence merely masqueraded as Deity on earthly soil, strutting about in ethereal robes amid the muck of humanity, or that God somehow 'became God' in a redundant epiphany among mortals. No, the scandal of the Incarnation cuts deeper, rawer, and more revolutionary:

the transcendent Creator literally " . . . *became flesh and dwelt among us*" (John 1:14, NKJV), not as a lofty overlord but as one of us—a fully vested Man, bone of our bone and breath of our breath, threading the needle of divine immutability through the tattered fabric of human frailty. He pitched His eternal tent in the squalor of our stables, supped at our tables laden with Galilean fish and bread, and wept salt tears indistinguishable from our own. This is the God who, in the fullness of time, stooped to our level not with a detached wave but with callused hands that hammered nails and mended nets alike. With this seismic shift in view, we can pivot back to those venerable Old Testament prophets—those thunderous voices of antiquity who, under the Spirit's unerring dictation, hurled indictments against anthropomorphic idolatry: "*God is not a man, that He should lie, nor a son of man, that He should repent*" (Num 23:19, NKJV), or "*I will not execute the fierceness of My anger; I will not again destroy Ephraim. For I am God, and not man, the Holy One in your midst*" (Hos 11:9, NKJV). Their words were a bulwark against the pagan folly of gods fashioned in man's image—capricious, fickle, and earthbound. Yet now, in the luminous second volume of sacred Scripture—the New Testament's updated edition where prophecy finds its telos in fulfillment—we bear them staggering witness to a '*present truth*' that both honors and transcends their oracles: Behold, God is also now a Man—the God of heaven is also now a Man of earth—the God who formed Adam out of the dust of earth has Himself donned the dust's humble garb, the eternal Word tabernacling in temporal weakness.

What was once an emphatic 'not' erupts into an astonished 'also'—God is not merely transcendent; he is immanent, not aloof but alongside, the High and Lofty One who humbles Himself to behold the things in heaven and earth (Ps 113:5–6). In His Son, this God has savored the bitter cup of humanity to its dregs—every pang of rejection, every thorn of temptation, every shadow of sorrow—walking miles in sandals worn thin by Judean roads, his divine feet blistered by the same sun that scorches ours. No longer can he thunder from Sinai's heights, "For I am God, and not man" (Hos 11:9 NKJV)—without the echo of Bethlehem's cries and Gethsemane's sweat qualifying the claim. He knows our frame; he remembers that we are dust (Ps 103:14), because he has been dust—tasted its grit, felt its weight, borne its curse. And herein lies a solemn, eternal scar upon the divine narrative: the Incarnation brooks no reversal, no 'excarnation' to slough off the human husk like a shed skin. The God-Man remains the God-Man ad infinitum, his glorified form forever etched with the insignia of mortality's ransom. Those nail prints in his hands and feet? Not fading tattoos of a bygone ordeal, but indelible emblems of covenant love, badges of solidarity that time's river cannot erode. The spear-thrust gash in his side? An everlasting portal where mercy's fountain once gushed blood and water (John 19:34) now sealed in resurrection's victory, a testament to the atonement's finality. One day, as promised, we shall behold Him face-to-face (1 Cor 13:12), no longer through the dim mirror of faith's anticipations but in the unfiltered blaze of his presence. Like doubting Thomas, summoned from the shadows of skepticism, we too shall receive the invitation: "*Reach your finger here, and look at My hands; and reach your hand here, and put it into My side. Do not be unbelieving, but believing*" (John 20:27 NKJV). Yet ours will be the rarer grace—not groping for proof after the fact, but feasting on the banquet of belief forged in the furnace of unseen evidence, hearts ablaze long before eyes are dazzled (Rom 10:10; 2 Corinthians 5:7). And mark this: his risen frame, that flesh-and-bone temple ascended to the right hand of Majesty (Luke 24:39; Acts 1:9–11), pulses now with a life unbound by veins or ventricles. No more the crimson tide to spill, for his post-resurrection body is without blood and without water no more, because he has done all the bleeding he is ever going to do for us—emptying his blood tank, atoning for the sins of all—once and for all, the Lamb slain from the foundation of the world (1 John 2:2; Revelation 13:8). The cross's ledger is balanced; the grave's debt is discharged. What remains is an endless river of life, flowing from the throne where the Immortal Mortal reigns, beckoning us home to the scarred embrace of the One who became us that we might become like him.

THE GOSPEL: SOTERIOLOGICALLY CENTERED ON THE SINNER—THAN IT IS CHRISTOLOGICALLY CENTERED ON THE SAVIOR

Whether the Bible's primary focus on Christ excludes significant emphasis on humanity. It would seem so, for there are some who pull up short in their exegesis, asserting that since the Bible functions as a fundamentally Christocentric volume, it therefore must be all about Christ, all to the exclusion of man almost—virtually sidelining any substantial consideration of humanity's role in the grand narrative of redemption.

Objection 1: They reason that Scripture's purpose is to reveal Christ alone.

Objection 2: They repeat the religious mantra, "It's not about me, it's all about Jesus," suggesting humanity's irrelevance.

Objection 3: They proceed with parallel logic, contending that all stories are mere illuminations of Christ's role.

My educated rebuttal: While Scripture is Christ-centered, this arises because humanity's redemption centers on Christ. The Gospel of Christ is ultimately about man's salvation, making it anthropocentric in focus.

My response to Objection 1: The revelation of Christ serves man's redemption, not an end apart from it.

My response to Objection 2: This mantra overlooks that man prompts the God-Man's incarnation.

My response to Objection 3: Christ's prominence in the Scriptures enables men to see him as Savior. The Scripture's unified message is humanity's redemption via Christ.

Think of the Gospel as a bridge—Christ as the structure, but built for humanity's crossing from sin to salvation. It is also important to establish that man is the reason for the God-Man—inasmuch as the sinner is the reason for the Savior. For if there were no law, there would be no transgression; if there were no transgression, then there would be no need for atonement; if there were no need for atonement, then equally there would have been no need for the Paschal Lamb. This is not the same as suggesting that man would not need God if he were not a sinner; I am speaking strictly in the context of redemption in relation to the essence of the Christ-centeredness of the Scriptures. To make this even clearer, consider that theology, like science, builds on faith and reason: humanity's fall necessitates Christ's role, not vice versa. For not until the Fall ensued in Eden God saw no need to roll out His preconceived plan for humanity's eternal redemption—nor proclaim His promise of the Messianic Seed. Objection 4: Gospel's barely about Christ? My response to Objection 4: Yes, as the focus is man's benefit. So yes, Jesus made it all about mankind. He made His life and redemptive mission all about you and me each time he made statements like, " . . . *I have come that they may have life and have it in all its fullness*" (John 10:10 BSB). The fact that man is the sole and sovereign beneficiary of the sum totality of the redemptive work of Christ tells us it is all about him and not about Christ Himself. Think of this as a cosmic drama where the divine spotlight, though fixed on Christ as the protagonist, yet illuminates the shadowed audience of humanity. The Savior's mission is soteriologically man-centered. Like the Bible already made clear, the reason God sacrificially gave His only begotten Son is ultimately because *'God so loved the world'* (see John 3:16)—not the world of apes or monkeys but the world of human beings, indicating humanity as the reason.

While this theological school of thought clearly proposes a rather narrow lens through which to view the Scriptures altogether—*sola Christus*, one where Christ must be considered the starting point and endpoint of all biblical exploration, with all other stories and characters merely serving to illuminate His role and mission—they yet err on the side of severely underplaying the fact that the purpose and mission of the Savior, upon ultimate examination, is soteriologically centered on man—the salvation of the human soul. Quite honestly, to hear some of these voices describe it, one might think the Bible was written for Christ and solely meant for His personal reading, which is truly puzzling. Because on the contrary, like we have endeavored to demonstrate thus far, the unified message of the Scriptures is the redemption of fallen humanity, and so part of the reason the Bible is Christocentric is ultimately because the redemption of humankind is centered on Christ as the Redeemer—the ransom price for redemption. So much so that what the Bible calls *'the Gospel of Christ'* is, in its final analysis, about man, barely about Christ himself. And so, if a Christocentric portrait is being highlighted in there, it is all because God intends for Christ to essentially stand out in the entire narrative to be seen by men for whom he truly is: the Savior of the world. Which basically means that the Gospel of Christ is to a fairly large extent anthropocentric in essence, in that it makes sinful man its focus—for the salvation of man is chiefly the reason the Son of God became the Son of Man in the first place. Whereupon John, the beloved disciple, has taken it upon himself to point out that the Scriptures " . . . *are written that you may believe that Jesus is the Christ, the Son of God, and that believing you may have life in His name*" (John 20:31 NKJV). And once we grasp the revelatory truth of the Gospel about Christ ultimately being our Lord and personal Savior and come to faith in him, we join the community of the faithful who testify that " . . . *we have come to know and believe the love that God has for us. God is love; whoever abides in love abides in God, and God in him*" (I John 4:16 BSB). In essence, this highlights how the Christian story hangs together beautifully, integrating divine revelation with human experience in a way that apologetically defends the faith's internal logic, where Christ's centrality serves not as an end in itself but as the means to address humanity's deepest needs.

Indeed, the Savior is not simply emphasized in the sacred writings solely for His own glory; rather, he is spotlighted for the benefit of the sinner, the very individual to whom those texts are directed. Besides, who in sound judgment pens a passionate love letter, only to make it all about himself—entirely self-referential and self-centered, addressing it all to himself afterward, instead of the beloved object of his love? If no rational person would engage in such an act, then it is reasonable to conclude that God's love letter (the Bible) was neither written about Himself nor addressed to Himself—but to man—the object of His love. Although salvation has definitely got everything to do 'with' Christ procuring it, at the end of the day, it was nothing 'about' him needing it, thus everything about the sinner. For Christ did not come down here to die on the Cross for himself; he came all the way down because of man, and his life was clearly shown to be all about man's salvation. Come on, let us face it, he was doing pretty good in heaven, where he was before his descent into time, and did not need any saving from nothing; we needed saving from everything—even from ourselves. Therefore, the Advent of Christ was entirely focused on humanity and had no relevance to the Second Person of the Trinity, nor to the First Person, nor to the Third Person. I recognize that this truth might seem profoundly challenging for the religious mind to comprehend or embrace. One must at least inquire: if the redemptive work of the Cross of Christ is not centered on humanity, on whom then is it truly focused—God? Or on Christ Himself? Anselm was among the earliest Christian philosophers to have reflected on the question: '*cur deus homo*?' Otherwise translated: Why the God-Man? Or why did God become Man? If we are ever going to deeply understand and appreciate the overall significance of God's incarnate appearance on cosmic soil, then that question remains a valid one we cannot afford to let go unanswered today. First, it is worth considering here that even though Christ had lived 33 years of His life on earth, not a single day of those 33 years was lived for Himself—not one. But just in case you are one of those who might have been under the impression that he lived for God the Father, you will be wrong on the spot, because again, His whole life was sacrificially poured out for sinful humanity—from womb to tomb, not for God the Father and certainly not for Himself, the Eternal Son. Like Daniel's eschatological prophecy had foretold far out before His Advent, the ". . . . *Messiah shall be cut off, but not for Himself . . .* " (Dan 9:26 NKJV). In fact, the Divine love for man is the only reason why the Creator-God deigned so low as to take the form of His own creature, the most compelling reason for His incarnate appearance in man's world, such that if it were not for man's dire need of redemption and God's redemptive love for man as the only answer—both predating that very need and towering over it—He never would have been seen anywhere around here imprimis, and we never would have heard anything about the historical Jesus of Nazareth—the Most Significant Figure in Human History—even the Most Famous Man Whoever Lived. Not to even mention anything about Him being the Christ and Savior of the world.

These folks, to their credit, however, have done an exceptionally good job identifying the thematic outline of a Christocentric portrait in Scripture, but they would do even better if they went a step further to tell us exactly 'why' we have that portrait in there in the first place. We perhaps could consider such Bible exegetes to be archaeologists who often discover some rare finds in their archaeological excavations and cave explorations, one of the most historically significant being the discovery of hieroglyphs in caves—as left behind by prehistoric cave dwellers. And so, what the most distinguished fellows in the archeological field would endeavor to do is go a step further in decrypting the hidden meanings and often esoteric messages embedded in those rebuses or drawings on the cave walls or trees, as in the case of dendroglyphs drawn by native tribes. Thus and so, these Bible exegetes may have done an impressively good job at discovering the Christocentric handwriting on the wall of Biblical literature—the Rosetta Stone of Scripture, as it were—but they do much better if they venture even further to spell out the core meaning behind the handwriting on the wall, thus demystifying the ultimate significance of them being there in the first place. For there is a great gulf of difference between articulating what is observable and explaining the rationale for why what is observable takes its specific shape. So it is not enough to show us that Jesus is the Messianic figure and Savior portrayed throughout the OT Bible, you must endeavor to lay out a strong and compelling case for why God decidedly went through all that trouble to become the Jewish Messiah and the Savior of all mankind.

And as soon as you get to this juncture, the conversation shifts to a profound realization: it suddenly dawns on everyone in the room that

God-the-Son becoming a Man and the Savior of all mankind is not necessarily because man so desperately needed salvation per se—no, but because he so dearly loved man—yes. It is such that his love for man would forever stand as the most compelling Divine impetus for both His incarnate appearance and his redemptive sacrifice on Calvary's Cross. Well, did Jesus state abundantly clear that God had loved man ever before he required salvation from sin—even before he sinned—way before he was even created, like he loved him before the foundation of the world (cf. John 17:23–26). Ever before the creation of man, before the sin of man, before the Fall of man—there was love—the predestinarian love of God for man, both predating and undergirding the creation of man, and by the same token—foreseeing and guaranteeing the redemption of man. God's love, not the historical necessity of salvation, constitutes the ultimate reason for Christ's redemptive work. For the Father's storge, in its pure essence, resolves the deepest human crisis—redemption itself—wherein mere desideratum, though pressing and fundamental, fails to constitute the sufficient cause, nor could it ever adequately compel the self-emptying oblation of the Godhead. The imperative of salvation, considered ipso facto, did not dictate the origin of its bestowal upon humankind; rather, the inexhaustible love of God for man is the ultimate aetiology for its deliberate procurement, while His grace serves as the means by which this gift is universally extended, freely offered to every human person on the silver platter of sheer benevolence—without cost or condition of merit. In other words, God did not save you simply because you needed salvation; he saved you because he loves you regardless of circumstance. Besides, this love antedated the advent of transgression, arising not from any emergent compulsion. Sin did not cause God to love man, but sin and the Fall of man served to manifest the immovability and unconditionality of that love, proving it true in a way that precludes all gainsay.

This revelatory insight discloses how the necessity of our redemption is integrated into the eternal volition of God's love, avoiding simplistic interpretations of His redemptive acts as merely reparative, thereby challenging those commonplace views that reduce the Cross to a mere divine afterthought, more or less a bandage for our self-inflicted wounds—a reactive fix for our brokenness rather than as the outworking of a love that precedes and encompasses all things. When we consider this in the light of Christian tradition, this reframes the doctrine of salvation beyond the scope of human necessities, anchoring it within the eternal dynamics of divine communion, where the act of saving emerges not just as God's answer to our salvific needs alone but as a radiant outpouring of that eternal communion wherein His love, ever perfect and self-giving, spills over into the fleeting currents of time. This vision summons us to contemplate the aseity of God's love—self-existent and complete in its own triune perfection, needing nothing beyond itself, yet freely overflowing toward us in such measure that it lays bare the destitution of our own darkened human loves: those restless, grasping pursuits born of inner void, forever chasing phantoms and clutching at fleeting shadows. Envision this love as an immeasurable expanse, older than the wheeling stars, deeper than the interstellar abyss, in which God's pristine, prelapsarian affection—untouched by any stain of sin—enters into tender choreography with man's postlapsarian poverty, forming a single, harmonious *pas de deux* of grace. That primordial love, begotten before creation drew its first breath, stretches like a silken thread through the whole length of time, irrevocably binding our redemption and restored communion with God, while drawing the opening page of human history into seamless unity with the radiant consummation of God's everlasting counsel. Truly, divine love transcends any mere *coup de foudre*; it is love before sight, love beyond sight—far more ancient and profound than any love awakened at first glance. This pre-creational love of God is grounded in relational benevolence rather than mere contingency, thus revealing a teleological structure where love is not reactive but proactive, shaping creation's narrative arc from eternity.

The same divine love is what it took to bestow such eternally priceless existential value on man that only his species can boast of in all creation, and the same love is what equally considered man worthy of dying for—not slightly on the basis of merit but totally on the account of God's grace and love. For although the Jews had weighed out the sum of 30 pieces of silver to Judas as the price for which they had valued the Christ, Christ, in stark contrast, axiologically weighed out the sum of His whole life as the ransom price for which God values the life of each and every one of them. This divine valuation encompasses not only the Jewish people but every person ever born, Jew and Gentile alike. That, dear friends, is the true worth of a human life: " . . . *for one's life does not consist in the abundance of the things he possesses*" (Luke 12:15 NKJV).

And I, for one, stand in awe—utterly mind-boggled—when I contemplate this staggering reality: the redemption of mankind was purchased at the price of the life of its own Maker. At the redemption grounds of Calvary's Cross, the life of the God who became man was paid in full as the ransom for every soul. For not only did God love man so much he endowed him with the extraordinary perquisite of personhood in creation, he also went a billion steps further to crown him a person of inestimable value in redemption. The only One (the Creator-God) with the honest scale for weighing the intrinsic value of all creatures in the balance has thoughtfully weighed the value of human life against the whole universe he created and has determined that each man's life is worth more to him than the whole universe taken together—exempting nothing within and without the universe. The Creator's descent into human form ultimately affirmed the sanctity of human life and the intrinsic value of the human soul. So the next time you think about how much you are really worth—what value there is to your life—kindly think about that.

Concerning the unfathomable depths of the redemptive love and sacrifice of which we speak, William Law had made the following observations: "*View every part of our redemption, from Adam's first sin to the resurrection of the dead, and you will find nothing but successive mysteries of that first love, which created angels and men. All the mysteries of the gospel are only so many marks and proofs of God's desiring to make his love triumph in the removal of sin and disorder from all nature and creature.*" How so spot-on? Except, of course, to register my objection that the Divine love did not necessarily apply to the creation of angels and humans alike, because if it did, then the redemption of fallen angels and fallen men should have been considered equally as important to God, but that did not happen by any stretch. Because, like he touched on, the triumph of God's love was uniquely and ultimately demonstrated 'in the removal' of human sin on Calvary's Cross—barring the sin of Lucifer and all fallen angels. To this end, the Bible furnishes us with the corroborative testimony that "*For it is clear that he didn't do this for the angels, but for all the sons and daughters of Abraham. This is why he had to be a man and take hold of our humanity in every way. He made us his brothers and sisters and became our merciful and faithful King-Priest before God as the One who removed our sins to make us one with him. He suffered and endured every test and temptation so that he can help us every time we pass through the ordeals of life*" (Heb 2:16–18 TPT). Peter concurs that "*For God did not spare even the angels who sinned. He threw them into hell, in gloomy pits of darkness, where they are being held until the day of judgment*" (2 Pet 2:4 NLT). Besides, angels were not fashioned after the Divine image and likeness and are therefore intrinsically inferior creatures to God, so expecting him to love them like he loves man would be more like expecting a man to love his dog as much as he loves his dear son. Perhaps we could say rightly, in human terms, that when God fell in love with man, he was simply falling in love with His Divine image and likeness in man. Which also means that redeeming man from the Fall may also have had everything to do with restoring him to the state of glory and honor of the Divine image and likeness in which he was aboriginally created. Furthermore, it could yet be argued that Lucifer himself could do with salvation as things currently stand, owing to the fact that he had sinned in Heaven's Paradise very much like Adam later did in Eden's Paradise at the beginning, before falling face flat as a result, although, unlike Adam, he had no tempter. But then, the point is that we have never seen any sign of God rushing down to Lucifer's salvific rescue ever since he fell, like he did in the case of Adam's fall, which only came much later in cosmic time. If anything, we are told that He is impatiently waiting to have him and his hellbound emissaries punished in the infernal fires of hell for their sin of seditious conspiracy against Him. Thus, it becomes all the more remarkable that God never saw any need to become an angel to save fallen angels whom he had created up there with him in heaven, yet we could clearly see him venturing so far as to become a Man to save fallen men whom he created down here on earth. That would forever stand as an incontestable testament to the fact that man is indeed the sole creature of His Divine love. The reason for that submission is to further emphasize that, left to itself, man's need for salvation does not sufficiently account for the reasons why God would go so far as to become a Man to meet the said need—nor does it constitute sufficient grounds to compel his vicarious death on the Cross, but God's love for man does so comprehensively and most convincingly. Because after all, John 3:16 does not necessarily say or exactly suggest that God sent his Son into the world to save man because he needed salvation or a Savior; no, it rather makes abundantly clear that he did so all because of his love for man—*'For God so loved the world that He . . .* ' did something about man's dire need of salvation, not that man so desperately needed salvation that God gave His only begotten Son for salvation unto man. It explains why theist philosophers would often use such designations as the Prime Mover or Primum mobile or the Unmoved Mover to aptly describe the Creator's place in the grand scheme of things, viz., the One who alone moves all things and sets all else in motion but is Himself moved by no one and caused by nothing. And if we are to go by that philosophical proposition for God's existence, then it would also have to mean that God was not merely being 'moved' by man's need for salvation in the aftermath of the Fall, in that the need was in itself insufficient to compel His gift of His Son for a Savior, but His eternal love for man was all-sufficient in itself to compel His salvific acts—His priceless sacrifice—the gift of the Paschal Lamb. Moreover, the Scriptures also bear witness that the Lamb of God was slain before the foundation of the world, which again tells us, with some degree of certainty, that the Divine love for man predated the Fall of Man in the Garden of Eden. Thus making it even clearer that the same love is what informed His decision to save man, not man's need for salvation per se.

And as I came to discover with wonder, one of the most breathtaking revelations concerning the steadfastness and unconditionality of God's love is this: God did not wait for men to go from being sinners to becoming Saints to find them loveable, nor did he wait for the sinful man to somehow change the color of his sin-speckled skin to consider him redeemable, nor did he wait for the unchurched to finally walk through the doors of a congregational church to find him acceptable. He simply loved man with so great an everlasting love before he sinned—no less than he loved him after he sinned—no more than he loves him after he repents of his sins. Which further demonstrates beyond contradiction that divine love depends on nothing in man: it is noncontingent upon human behavior—for they are both mutable and unpredictable—independent of good deeds—for they are equally as capricious and undependable as the shifting winds. It is for the same reason also that God's love for man is said to be truly 'unconditional': unconditionally constant—timelessly unwavering—steadfastly faithful—eternally boundless. Even though men undergo chameleonic changes in their lives from time to time (whether for the better or for the worse), God's love-posture toward them never really changes with time—it has been all the same through the ages and forever will stay the same. Far from what a handful of us in Christendom might have imagined, God did not suddenly start loving you because you became a Christian or because you joined a church. No, not even the slightest. Paul, in his epistle addressed to his protégé Timothy, reminds the Church that "*For God saved us and called us to live a holy life. He did this, not because we deserved it, but because that was his plan from before the beginning of time—to show us his grace through Christ Jesus. And now he has made all of this plain to us by the appearing of Christ Jesus, our Savior . . .* " (2 Tim 1:9–10 NLT). I was going to say, like so many others have said, that God loves the good, the bad, and the ugly among the sons of men, but then it occurred to me that there was none good among the progeny of Adam—not even one. Like Jesus was quick to affirm, "*No one is good but One, that is, God*" (Mark 10:18 NKJV), for they have altogether corrupted themselves and were therefore all bad and ugly. He still loves them all anyway, and in fact, he loves them no less. And of course, that makes it all the more obvious that man was predestined according to the Divine plan to become the object of the Divine love, because the same love predated '*the beginning of time*' and definitely preexisted the creation of man.

Thus, the sin of Adam and Eve at the dawn of time did nothing to alter the unconditionality of God's love toward man, nor did it do enough to tamper with the infinitude of the same. Through the passage of time, his love for man has remained unwaveringly steadfast; present before sin, persisting through sin in Eden, and prevailing over sin through the death and anastasis of his Son. Charles Spurgeon accurately noted that "*He chose us from eternity, and He will love us throughout eternity. He loved us enough to die for us, and we may therefore be sure that His love will never die.*" This is something King Solomon already found out way back in time, which led him to conclude that " . . . *love is as strong as death . . . Many waters cannot quench love, Nor can the floods drown it* . . . " (Song of Solomon 8:6–7 NKJV). So the maxim that death is the end does not necessarily hold true for love, because love (as embodied by the Son of God) has proven to be truly indestructible—for it transcends death—having no end in sight—having historically outperformed sin by the redemptive work of the Cross and overcome death by gainrising to eternal life. Indeed, if there is anything we can all be most certain about in this life, it is that God's love for us 'will never die.' So even if you happen to be a nonbeliever reading this right this moment, I can tell you for a fact, without batting an eyelid, that he already loved you ever before you dreamt of taking your first breath and still loves you no less until now and will forever do so. But of course, what you do with his love for you is totally up to you—how you respond to the evidence of its demonstration toward you will always be your choice to make, so the ball is very much in your court and will remain so until you take your last breath. God's love for you is, in this sense of the word, your cup of tea—having been served to you hot on the platter of the cross of his Son Jesus Christ. The only fundamental difference between the Christian and the non-Christian in this regard is that the former, having heard preached the Gospel of God's love—especially as demonstrated toward him on the Cross of his Son—has given the due response of faith—as though saying to God, *'I love You too, Heavenly Daddy,'* while the latter is yet to do no more than just that. And until he does so, the divine love for him will continue to go unrequited.

And there you have it. I may have just succeeded in painting you a prosaic picture of God's only heartbreak—watching his love for the sinner go unrequited for the whole duration of his lifetime on earth, or as they say, watching a sinful man die roaring for a priest. Especially not after all he has done to prove his love beyond all reasonable doubt, in the cruciform death of his Son, whom he sent down here on earth for that specific purpose. Sadly, this is by far the greatest human tragedy under heaven—the most heartbreaking existential catastrophe on the face of the earth! So again, if truth be told, the most popular verse of the Bible—John 3:16—was actually not addressed to Christendom but to the sinful world; besides, the first audience to whom Jesus said those astonishing words were themselves not Christians. The text does not necessarily say that God gave his only begotten Son because he so loved the Church world—full of saints—but because he so dearly loved the unchurched world—full of sinners. That might be hard for the religious mind to accept, but it is the truth of the Gospel nonetheless. With that taken into account, it suddenly becomes much clearer to us that Jesus died not for the churchful but for the churchless—not for the Saint but for the sinner—not for the godly but for the godless—not for the righteous but for the unrighteous. There was not one righteous person in the world anyway, so how could he have been laying down his life for nonexistent people? Like Himself made clear, "*It is not the healthy who need a doctor, but the sick. I have not come to call the righteous, but sinners*" (Mark 2:17 BSB). Bravo! For we all were morally and spiritually plagued by sin-sickness and were equally in desperate need of the healing touch of the Divine Physician, who alone has all that it takes to heal not only our fallen humanity but our fallen land as well. And in the same way and manner in which none among the Jewish mob who had taken up stones to bethwack to death that adulterous lady who had been caught in the very act were able to look at the Son of God in the eye and stake the claim that they had no sin, likewise shall no man, whether Jew or Gentile, be able to look at God the Father in the eye on the Day of Judgement and say, *'I had no sin and therefore, I needed no salvation nor Savior'* (cf. John 8:1–11).

But then again, the same folks who are often caught up in the habit of shifting the focus of the Gospel away from the sinner to the Savior merely for religious reasons or for whatever else their motivations might be would have no difficulty, one may imagine, acknowledging the fact that the whole world is itself prima facie man-centered—'man's world,' as it is often so-called. Further prompting the question: since the world is so self-admittedly man-centered, and clearly, God decidedly became a Man in order that he might legally step into a man-centered world to save all mankind, how then can a book written about man and man's place in the universe—as inspired by God himself and addressed to man—be said to be any more centered on the Divine Guest—the God-Man—than it is centered on the cosmic landlord—man (cf. Ps 115:16)? That syllogism does not quite seem to add up, does it? Because if we say that the Bible is about the Savior, and it turns out that the Savior himself has proven beyond all reasonable doubt to be all about the sinful man for whom it is written and the salvation of his soul, then of course, it must follow that the Book is soteriologically centered on man—no less than the Savior himself had proven to be in his redemptive mission. Now we can better understand why Spurgeon unabashedly ventured so far as to make the bold submission that "*The sinner is the gospel's reason for existence.*" And who would want to argue with that, with the fact that the Gospel's primary focus is fallen and sinful humanity, given how much the life and death of the Savior has conclusively been shown to be all about the salvation of the same? So much so that what we call *'the Gospel of Christ'* today is, at the end of the day, so man-centered that it could alternatively be called the gospel of man's salvation—" . . . *the gospel of your salvation* . . . " as Paul phrased it in his Letter to the Church at Ephesus (cf. Eph 1:13 & Romans 1:16). The Gospel is so man-centered that God literally had to become a Man in order to be able to procure man the much-needed salvation. Well, if part of the reason they are shifting the message of the Cross from the sinner is to impress God, they should know that God is not the least bit impressed, given how much he already made the whole thing about man when he decidedly became a Man himself to guarantee man's salvation by dying on the Cross. So to make the Gospel any less about man than God himself already made it is to distort the truth of the Gospel.

It does not get any more anthropocentric than that. Although the content and substance of God's promise of the gospel is the God-Man—the Seed of the woman—yet the reason for the gospel is man—the one to whom the promise of the Seed was made imprimis. That is to also clarify that God did not make the promise of a Savior to the Savior himself; he made the promise of a Savior to the sinner who needed salvation. So yes, you, the sinner, are the reason for the Savior. Because that gospel that was first preached to Adam and Eve in the Garden in the aftermath of the Fall, and then to Abraham as far back as the Book of Genesis Chapter 12, and runs its course throughout the OT and right into the New, has always had the sinner at heart way more than it has had the Savior in mind. Quite obviously, the very existence of the Savior is rooted in the reality of human sin; without sinners, there would have been no need for a Savior. Thus, the message of the Cross is profoundly good news primarily for the sinner who stands in desperate need of salvation, rather than for the Savior who accomplished it. The redeemed sinner rightly exclaims, "Thank God, I am finally saved!"—a testimony of personal deliverance, not one centered on the Savior's experience. Even when Jesus declared that the Law, the Psalms, and the Prophets all pointed to him, he emphasized that their ultimate purpose revolves around the sinner: "*Thus it is written, that the Christ should suffer and rise from the dead the third day, and that repentance and remission of sins should be preached in His name to all nations, beginning at Jerusalem*" (Luke 24:46–47 NKJV). In essence, his brief summation of the Pentateuch and the numerous Messianic prophecies contained in the entire OT centers on the Savior's ultimate purpose in delivering sinful humanity, all rooted in God's love. This reinforces my argument that the gospel is more soteriologically centered on man—the sinner—than it is Christologically centered on the God-Man—the Savior. In sum, Scripture's Christocentrism serves anthropocentric ends, where God's love manifests in human rescue. As demonstrated, the writings' unity lies in humanity's redemption, hence Christ-centered because restoration is Christ-exclusive. Thus, the "*Gospel of Christ*" addresses humanity chiefly. Thus, the narrow lens errs by underplaying this. Besides, Jesus did not come down here to show us how much God really loved him, because if that were to be his mission objective, then it is safe to say that he failed miserably in that effort, given that God ended up abandoning him on the Cross at the time when he desperately needed him the most. He rather came to show us how much God really loves each and every one of us, enough to heartwrenchingly abandon his own Son on the stake for our sake—loving us to the point of turning his back on his Beloved to procure us eternal redemption. Just let that sink in for a second. Because that is the central focus of the gospel: sinful humanity occupying the center stage of the heart of God's love. And not only does man occupy a special place in God's heart, he also stands as the cynosure of his creation. Further substantiating my point that man equally finds himself occupying the center stage of attention throughout the book of the Bible—no less than he occupies the center stage of the heart of the Grand Author himself. In other words, the Grand Artificer of creation, who had made man the centerpiece of his works of creation, is no different from the Grand Author of the Bible, who equally made man the center of attention in his work of literature. For the depth of the love of Creator-God for mankind remains unfathomable to the human mind as of yet; you just cannot wrap your mind around it. Even when Satan essentially offered to make Christ the cosmic superstar in the whole human story, so to speak, by enticing him with the glory of man's world and the Adamic authority to rule over it, he declined the offer and took no glory unto himself as a Man, chiefly because he was all about God's redemptive business—the business of procuring the cosmic landlord the much-needed salvation (cf. Luke 4:5–8).

MAN'S SPECIAL PLACE IN THE HEART OF CREATION—MIRRORS HIS SPECIAL PLACE IN THE HEART OF THE CREATOR

And when we speak of man as the cosmic landlord, does it not fill your soul with overwhelming wonder that, though our own Solar System boasts eight major planets, though the observable universe enfolds an estimated two trillion galaxies, though the Milky Way alone harbors between one hundred and four hundred billion stars—yet scientific and cosmological evidence converges to reveal that Earth's ecosystem alone has been exquisitely fashioned to sustain life? Consider the precision of the Goldilocks Zone, the habitable sweet spot; the razor-thin atmospheric equilibrium; the astonishing richness of biodiversity; the finely tuned physical constants that permit the existence of liquid water—the sine qua non of biological life. All harmoniously conspiring to produce the rare "just right" conditions. Nevertheless, the gaze of the Almighty has never, in any age, been fixed upon any of those innumerable stars or myriad planetary orbs; his undivided attention has rested solely upon this tiny, seemingly insignificant speck called Earth. What does this astonishing reality declare to us? Beyond furnishing powerful philosophical and theological testimony to a deliberate, man-centered design—lending fresh vigor to the teleological argument for Earth's singular place amid cosmic immensity—it proclaims with unmistakable clarity the supreme truth: the Creator-God pours out his unreserved focus upon this one small world for one reason alone—because his heart belongs wholly and exclusively to man, devoted in boundless, particular love to mankind and to no other part of creation. If you want to uncover where someone's treasure is buried, simply find the place where their heart calls home—mankind is God's most valued treasure, and earth is the sacred ground where it is 'buried,' so we can understand the divine fixation. Even the Son of God Himself agreed in principle that "*For where your treasure is, there your heart will be also*" (Matt 6:21 NKJV).

God's heart is overly fixated here because planet Earth is home to the single most valuable treasure of his heart—housing the unimpeachable occupant of the heart of his love—man. So the only reason in the world that planet Earth alone boasts of having what I would prefer to call the Badge of Special Planetary Status, so to speak, in the midst of all other planetary bodies in the sidereal universe, to the point of being treated like a divine treasure chest or Godzone almost, is because it houses the Creator's most treasured possession in both the seen and unseen universe—the crown jewel of his entire work of creation. Actually, if the Creator's image bearer deserved a special place in his heart, we can understand why he deserves no less a special place in his creation. You might also find it interesting to know that the Creator-God also answers to divine titles such as *'the God of heaven and earth'—'Lord of heaven and earth,'* and *'the God of heaven and the God of the earth.'* He is barely ever called the God of Mars or the God of Jupiter or the God of the numberless planetary bodies or stars out there in the vast universe, even though he equally created them all. And that, in itself, is enough to suggest that he has some special interest in planet earth particularly, and that special interest has everything to do with the one for whom he created the earth—again, man (see Ezra 5:11; Acts 17:24; Genesis 24:3; Psalms 115:16). It does not end there; it also explains why he eventually ventured down here on earth to die an atoning death for the sins of mankind, yet another timeless testament to the fact that his heart ultimately lies with the man of earth—the cosmic landlord.

Further coupled with the fact that God has hardly ever been seen or heard visiting any other planet in the universe, much less making anywhere else in the vast universe His point of focus, which again, goes to show that his universe revolves around man—his unbridled attention is centered on the human species. Simply put, man's special place in the heart of creation mirrors his special place in the heart of the Creator.

For these are some of the contemplations that, I believe, soon led King David the Psalmist to start asking such pointed and thought-provoking questions as, "*When I consider Your heavens, the work of Your fingers, The moon and the stars, which You have ordained, What is man that You are mindful of him, And the son of man that You visit him?*" (Ps 8:4 NKJV). It turns out the Psalmist was not by himself in that; the Fatiloquist, Job, is yet another individual who also found his wandering mind wondering wide afield, contemplating the very same question: "*What is man, that You should exalt him, That You should set Your heart on him, That You should visit him every morning, And test him every moment?*" (Job 7:17–18 NKJV). The timeless validity of such insightful existential questions makes it not only relevant to bygone generations but even more so for us today. This is especially striking when we recall that both Job and David lived before the incarnation of Christ and thus never witnessed the ultimate revelation of God's love displayed on the Cross—yet they grasped, by divine illumination, the astonishing depth of God's affection for humanity.

All the more awe-inspiring when we reflect that God, having made the unprecedented and unparalleled investment of his divine image in the human species in creation, doubles down on that effort with priceless investment of his life in the redemption of their souls—thereby establishing human beings as the singular object of his highest affection, the pinnacle and treasure of all his works from creation through redemption. The greatest investment that there is, ever was—and ever will be—is the investment of the Trinity in humanity: the creative investment of God's image, the redemptive investment of his Son, and the Pentecostal investment of his Spirit. While his redemptive investment came to redeem and restore the initial investment of his image in mankind, his Pentecostal investment came to secure and seal it forever. Evidently, God stands as the greatest investor in human capital. This also confirms that when Scripture declares man was created in God's image and likeness in the beginning, it meant every single word of it. No one has greater faith in God's image-bearer than God himself. You would never invest so deeply in something you had no faith in—neither does God. He has never at any point in time regarded man to be anything less than his image-bearer—his *imago Dei* incarnate.

CUPIDITY VERSUS CHARITY: THE DEGREES OF LOVE FROM SELF-INTEREST TO SELF-DIFFUSIVE DILECTION

Fundamentally, love expresses itself in two distinct forms: the superior one is termed the love of benevolence (or goodwill), while the inferior is called cupidity. The love of cupidity refers to that self-centered affection in which we value something solely for the temporary benefits or worldly advantages we expect to gain from it—a pursuit rooted in personal gain and fleeting gratification. In sharp contrast, the love of benevolence stands as that virtuous and selfless affection whereby we earnestly seek the authentic good of the beloved solely for its own inherent value, free from any ulterior motive or hope of return. For what, indeed, is the love of benevolence if not the profound, heartfelt yearning for another's true flourishing and welfare, an echo resonant with the eternal, self-diffusing love of the Creator-God himself? When this love of benevolence is proffered without demand for requital from the beloved—extended in selfless profusion—it merits the designation of the love of simple benevolence; conversely, when it encounters a reciprocal effusion of affection, it ascends to the dignity of the love of friendship, a harmonious bond forged in mutual regard. This reciprocal interplay, however, rests upon three indispensable pillars: friends must harbor a profound love for one another, mutually discern and acknowledge this love within each other's hearts, and cultivate open communication, deepening familiarity, and intimate communion. Should we cherish a friend without according him precedence over others in our affections, the friendship abides in its elemental form as simple; yet, when we deliberately prefer him—elevating him in deliberate choice above the multitude of cherished entities—this friendship attains the elevated stature of dilection, emblematic of a chosen love, wherein we select this singular one amid the panoply of valued things and hold it in singular esteem.

Further, when this dilection does not greatly prefer one friend over others, it is called simple dilection. Yet, when we elevate and venerate one friend to a degree far surpassing and transcending the esteem accorded to others of his ilk, this exalted friendship ascends to the nomenclature of dilection by excellence or singular predilection, a deliberate and discerning elevation amid the chorus of cherished relations. If the esteem and preference for our friend, though great and unmatched, still allows comparison with others, the friendship is called eminent dilection. Yet, if this eminence transcends all comparison and proportion, surpassing every rival in the incandescent intensity and consummate perfection of its devotion, it is adorned with the august title of incomparable, sovereign, and supereminent dilection, which we call charity, the pinnacle of self-diffusing benevolence. Such, in its transcendent archetype, is the unparalleled manner of the love that the Creator has lavishly, exclusively conferred upon humanity, meticulously singling out the human species from the teeming manifold of creatures birthed from his creative fiat. This sublime act of divine election, eternally rooted in the inscrutable yet unerring counsel of God's sovereign will, unveils and exemplifies his omnibenevolent nature—an inexhaustible fount of universal goodness—which irrevocably ordains humanity for the paramount telos of eternal communion with the Triune Godhead, the perichoretic fellowship of Father, Son, and Holy Spirit. This love, cascading in effulgent profusion from the uncreated source of all subsistent being, catapults man above the myriad hierarchies and forms of creation, not through any antecedent merit or desert but through the sheer gratuity of grace, as the luminous reflection of God's free and sovereign volition to disseminate his ineffable beatitude—the consummate felicity of divine life—across the chasm of contingency. This love bursts forth with vivacious splendor in the sacred verses of the Song of Songs, wherein the bride, interrogated by her companions—"*What is your beloved more than another beloved, O fairest among women? What is your beloved more than another beloved, that you thus adjure us?*"—responds with fervent eloquence: "*My beloved is all radiant and ruddy, distinguished among ten thousand*" (Song of Solomon 5:9–10 RSV). His luminous distinction elevates him as the singular elect amid the throng of suitors, a beacon of unparalleled allure.

In analogous majesty, humanity—imprinted with the divine image as a rational creature endowed with the sublime capacity to know and love its Creator—stands sovereignly chosen by the Creator's boundless love, meticulously singled out from the intricate, vast spectrum of creation, a privileged election echoed in Christ's own proclamation: "*I chose you out of the world, therefore the world hates you*" (John 15:19). Thus, when John 3:16 resounds its clarion trumpet that *'God so loved the world,'* it proclaims with unerring specificity not the realm of apes or monkeys, but the world of humans in particular—the human cosmos, fraught with frailty and promise. This divine choice, eternally anchored in the inexhaustible reservoir of God's love, unveils humanity as the paramount object of a supereminent affection, inexorably ordered toward the eschatological consummation of intimate union with God, wherein the soul's ardent longing finds its rapturous fulfillment in the beatific vision of his transcendent glory. Soothfastly, all divine acts—from the primordial symphony of creation to the crimson crescendo of redemption—resound as harmonious testimonies to this supereminent love of God for man, an eternal refrain weaving through the cosmos. Eke, the fact that the creation of man on the sixth day is what officially marked the end of the Creator's emprise or adventurism with His work of creation, is, in itself, evidence enough to suggest that man is the crowning glory of all of his works. And I say that for several reasons.

First, it is quite significant that the works of creation from Day 1 through Day 5 were generally considered good by the Creator-God, until, of course, man came along on Day 6, and then all of a sudden, the Divine appraisal shifted exponentially—upgraded from 'good' to 'very good' (cf. Gen 1:31). In English grammar, the adjective 'very' is referred to as the superlative of superiority, primarily used to highlight the degree of surpassing quality of one entity in comparison to numerous others. In this particular context, it highlights the intrinsic quality of the human person, amplified to the nth degree over the rest of God's creation. Man, in this sense, came along as the perfection of the works of God's hands, because up until his species was introduced in the Hexameron, the phrase 'and God saw that it was good' had only been employed 6x in describing the state and quality of his works, but when man was eventually fashioned in his Divine image and likeness, then the word 'good' appeared for the seventh and final time, but with the adjective 'very' prefixing it this time around (cf. Gen 1:4, 10, 12, 18, 21, 25 with 1:31). As many students of Scripture recognize, the number seven carries profound symbolic weight throughout the Bible, representing divine perfection, wholeness, and completion. This theme originates in the creation account itself, where God brings the universe into existence over six days and then rests on the seventh, signifying that his work has reached its flawless fulfillment (Gen 2:1–3). In this sacred narrative, the seventh day stands as a divine seal of approval—a declaration that creation, in its entirety, is not merely good, but perfectly complete and harmonious under God's sovereign design. This climax of divine perfection finds its pinnacle expression in the events of the sixth and seventh days. On the sixth day, God creates humanity (Gen 1:26–27)—forming Adam's body from the dust of the earth and breathing into him the breath of life on the seventh day of rest (Gen 2:7). This act elevates humankind above all prior works: the light and firmament, the seas and land, the plants and celestial bodies, the creatures of sea and sky, and even the land animals. Man emerges as the undisputed crowning glory of God's creative labors—the exquisite masterpiece, the centerpiece of the cosmos, endowed with dominion over creation and reflecting the very likeness of the Creator Himself (Ps 8:3–8). Yet the narrative does not end with the sixth day. On the seventh, God ceases from his labor, blessing and sanctifying the day as holy (Gen 2:3). This rest is not born of weariness—God is omnipotent and never tires (Isa 40:28)—but of absolute satisfaction in a creation now perfected through the inclusion of humanity. The seventh day thus encapsulates the divine perfection that humanity's creation brings to completion: God's works, culminating in his image-bearer, are declared very good (Gen 1:31), forming a symphony of order, beauty, and purpose that reflects the eternal excellence of the Divine Artist. In this light, the creation week reveals not just the origins of the world, but a profound theological truth: humanity, as God's final and finest act before and into his Sabbath rest, occupies the central place in his redemptive plan—a plan that points forward to ultimate rest and perfection in him (Heb 4:1–11).

Creation on Day 6 is now considered doubly good, or better still, perfectly good in comparison to the state in which it was the 5 days before the creation of man. Let us say God created all things good from Day 1 to Day 5, but on Day 6 he created someone very special—viz., man. So not only did the creation of man on the 6th and final day of creation mark the completion of the work of creation, it also marked the perfection of God's creation. Such that creation, even though it was altogether good from Day 1–5, yet could not be considered good in and of itself without man or good enough as a standalone without man, just the same way man could barely ever be considered good enough to be by himself alone without God (cf. Gen 2:18). Put more forcefully, creation could neither be perfected without man nor considered complete without him. The whole thing was all about humanity after all—the whole process was initiated because of him from the get-go. Calling God's creation complete or perfect without man on the scene is akin to calling a wedding feast a total and complete success even without the bride and the groom being present. The wedding is all about them—centered about them and nobody else for that matter, so even with all the guests and special guests being present and all the merrymaking going on, the wedding will still not be considered complete without the bride and groom being present and will definitely remain inconclusive until they show up. In the heart and mind of the Creator-God, no way in the world was the work of creation ever going to be considered complete or perfect without man being on the cosmic scene.

Perfection-in-completion was ultimately going to be achieved in creation as soon as God's image-bearer was created. Hence the reason I often refer to man as the crowning achievement of God's creation—most befittingly wearing the crown of Divine perfection amidst all of his works. And part of what that also means is that the work of creation cannot possibly be improved upon once the Creator was done creating man in his image and likeness. This is all the more true when we bethink that God cannot possibly create an entity any better than the analogical reflection of himself. Because, as the Hebrew words tselem (image) and demut (likeness) altogether imply, man was uniquely created to reflect Divine resemblance—mirroring Divine nature. In consequence, the creation of man in his image and likeness became the zenith of his work of creation—the best he could ever come up with. Man was simply God's finest and no less. It will be no exaggeration to refer to man as *'the perfection of beauty'* in creation—the reflector of the Creator's glory and beauty in creation. Yet another reason the work of creation was said to be very good on the 6th day, after the creation of man, is because all creation being good in the first place was all for man's very good, or shall we say, for man's sake. Especially given that every piece of work God had undertaken from Day 1 to Day 5 in the creation narrative was all centered about this entity whom he was going to be creating on the sixth day. The multifarious works of God's creation recorded from Genesis Chapter 1 and verse 1 all the way down to verse 25 had been all about man all the time—all made good for his sake. And suddenly we can tell, just by reading further down the chapter from verses 26–31, that God's signature creation has got man's name on it and man's name alone—custom-made to fit man—tailored to meet all of his needs. That is to say, even though creation has God's signature on it, it nevertheless has man's name on it, because he created them all for man in the first place. Creation was essentially signed, sealed, and delivered to man by the Creator himself when he said, "*Then God said, "I give you every seed-bearing plant on the face of the whole earth and every tree that has fruit with seed in it. They will be yours for food*" (Gen 1:29 NIV). It therefore is no coincidence at all that man ended up at the top of the food chain. And here is a prose poem I recently wrote to help convey the imagery of this Biblical idea, which perfectly captures the teleological order in creation:

> *'Let the plants exploit and draw sustenance from the inanimate elements all they can, and let the animals take turns in feeding on the plants without care or limit, and let the flesh-eating predators in the wild feast on the flesh of the prey to the limits of their appetite, but at the end of the day, all roads lead to man's communal table—where flora and fauna are destined to end up in his stomach for a meal—there he consumes without fear or worry of ever being consumed. All the while, the abiotic forces preoccupy themselves with balancing out the ecosystem to make life ultimately conducive for him still—crafting a universe that bows to humanity's sacred dominion. In this Divine order, man is destined to be food for no other—for all are in one way or the other subservient to him who remains unchallenged as the pinnacle of God's handiwork—the supreme masterpiece of the Creator's craftsmanship.'* (by Israel E. Nwachukwu)

That dovetails with Thomas Aquinas's observation that "*But plants exist for the sake of animals, some animals for the sake of others, and all for the sake of man.*" Precisely the sense in which I have identified man to be the sovereign beneficiary of all God's goodness in creation. Not to even begin to mention the work of redemption, which equally has man's name on it, because everything the Son of God accomplished through the work of his cross was all for man and for man alone—all that God accomplished in his Son when he raised him from the dead and made him sit at the right hand of his throne was all for man. Think about that! So by simply leaving the creation of man for last in the hexameral narrative, God was essentially letting us know he was reserving his best work for last. Now we can understand why God would consider man worth the redemptive exchange: sacrificially giving up his best—his Son—in order to save his best—his image bearer. Essentially what the Bible means when it tells us in the hexameral narrative of creation that God only saw the need to conclude his works of creation just as soon as he was done with creating man on the sixth and final day—thus entering into his Sabbath Rest on the seventh. The exact words are: "*And on the seventh day God ended his work which he had made; and he rested on the seventh day from all his work which he had made*" (Gen 2:2 KJV). In essence, man is the only creature who had all that it took to stop the Omnificent Creator from experimenting any further with his work of creation, because it was only as soon as he had him fashioned in his image and likeness that all Divine experiments ceased. This would also have to mean that God cannot possibly create any creature better than man (the bearer of His image and likeness). Because in principle, he cannot possibly create any being greater or more sublime than himself; hence, the best he could come up with is a creature who would mirror his image—reflect his likeness—embody his Divine nature and personhood. Thus are we told that "*So God made man like his Maker. Like God, did God make man; Man and maid did he make them*" (Gen 1:27 TLB). As far as the nature of 'beings' goes, it does not get any better or greater than being fashioned in the image and likeness of the Creator-God, whose personhood is Sublime—being the Most Perfect Being forever. To really understand the depth of God's love for man, it is first important we understand how much value God places on him and why.

Secondly, quander also that there would have been absolutely no need for the Creator-God to undertake or initiate the very first course of action we see him embark on in Genesis Chapter 1 and verse 1 if it had not been for his preconceived idea to create man—his image bearer. That is to say, man had been at the front and center of God's thoughts and plans ever before the cosmos made any appearance on the canvas of divine imagination. For not only is man the reason for the creation of the earth, he is the reason for the creation of the heavens also—the reason God ever saw the need to create the heavens and the earth in the beginning. Because it was not until he thought of creating man '*in the beginning*' that the need arose to create the heavens. In fact, man is the reason there was ever a beginning in the first place; the preconceived plan to create an image bearer is what necessitated the beginning. All the more true when you consider that the Creator is eternal and inhabits eternity (Isa 57:15)—having no beginning and no end—no beginning of life nor the end of days. For the One who is in and of Himself '. . . *the Beginning and the End, the First and the Last*'—the same who brought about the beginning and would be there to see it through to the end—needs, himself, to have no beginning nor an end (Rev 22:13 NKJV). So man is the only reason God seemingly stepped out of eternity—breaching timelessness—initiating the beginning of time—stepping into time, and functioning within the dimensions of spatiotemporal reality. To this end, God created nothing within the dimension of time for himself. Heaven itself was created in time, that is—in the beginning. So God could not have created heaven for himself but for man. Hence the reason he brought heaven down here on earth for man in the Garden of Eden—Paradise on earth. The Garden of Eden represented a cosmic alliance between heaven and earth. It was meant for man, because God actually wanted the heaven-on-earth experience for man and never wanted man to live outside the four walls of Eden's garden. So again, yes, the ultimate reason God initiated the "*beginning*"—bringing forth a space-time dimension—was entirely because of man. This foundational act was not simply the birth of the cosmos; it was the commencement of the great human story—the very inception of a creation purposefully centered upon humankind, the true incunabulum of a man-centered universe. Far from concealing this profound orientation, the Creator-God boldly proclaims it without the slightest insecurity or hesitation, openly declaring humanity's privileged and central place within the vast tapestry of creation. This unapologetic disclosure flows from divine confidence and generosity: God has no reluctance in affirming man's special status. It is precisely for this reason that he has graciously bestowed his written Word upon us—an enduring testimony that persists through the ages, continually illuminating the grand design of creation and our exalted yet responsible role within it. Through Scripture, we are constantly reminded of the big picture: a cosmos fashioned with humanity in view, called to reflect God's glory and steward his handiwork in grateful communion with him.

It is as though God is speaking directly to every single person, saying: "You—yes, you—you are the very reason the entire material universe exists; everything in creation was made for your sake." I would take it even a step further: without humanity, there would have been no real point in having this Bible we hold today. No rational being would have existed to record or inspire its writing in the first place—and even if God had directly inscribed it (as he did with the Ten Commandments using his own finger), there still would not have been any intelligent person capable of reading, understanding, or receiving it. Yet in case anyone overlooked or failed to grasp this profound truth revealed through God's act of creation, he drives the message home even more unmistakably through his work of redemption, making it crystal clear. We essentially see the same dynamics at play again in Christ's redemptive work, in that God could not possibly have given any sacrificial gift greater than himself, so he gave himself as a ransom for man's redemption—in a rare and unparalleled expression of his love for man. And by the same redemptive sacrifice, confirming the human species to be indeed the best he ever made—essentially crowning man the best he ever had in creation. But should you ever bump into anything else or anyone else in the universe that you think is more valued or treasured by the Creator-God above and besides man, kindly let me know; that would make for the greatest discovery in all of history. But as far as we can tell, there is no other creature besides man—none nearly as intrinsically valued as the human species—none in heaven and none under heaven. We all can agree on the fact that the value of a commodity is the actual price you pay in exchange rate for it. In the words of one of the world's most renowned investment bankers, Warren Buffett: "*Price is what you pay; value is what you get.*" In consequence, the ransom price that the Creator-God was willing to pay and did pay for the redemption of the human soul is what ultimately determined and forever established the intrinsic worth of each human person. Let us not even begin to get into the value of the investment of his Holy Spirit in man at Pentecost—the third Person of the Trinity as a denizen of the human heart—the hearts of the faithful. The human soul is unarguably the most precious thing there is in the universe. It will, therefore, make for no less than the greatest miscalculation under heaven to think that the value of our human lives could merely be determined by the amount of money we have in our bank accounts or the monetary value of the estate or assets we own. Therefore, the only reason in the world God would value man as much as he does is if he genuinely loves him. As the value and dignity he bestows on the human person can only be a reflection of his love for the same. Even we humans tend to value those we love and care deeply about. Thus, the intrinsic value and esteem for human life can only be a function or an outgrowth of the Creator's love. What this piece of agglomerative evidence ultimately does is come together nicely in testifying forcefully that man's special place and status in creation mirror his special place and status in the heart and mind of the Creator-God.

The first sip of God's love that humanity was ever privileged to have was the savory taste of the sweet wine of his creative love, a primal potion so graciously poured into molding us to mirror his majestic image at the dawn of time, long before the privilege was granted us to drink from the New Testament cup of his bittersweet redemptive love, that costly vintage poured out in the fullness of time from the pierced veins of Immanuel Himself. Even before love would reach its climactic crescendo in the work of redemption, its gentle traces were already discernible in the act of creation. Thus the earliest scriptural witness to God's loving deed is found not in the drama of atonement but in the narrative of origins—his creative love—because long before redemption answered the cry of humanity's fall, the very constitution of our being already bore the intricate embroidery of divine affection woven into the fabric of human existence.

Though present then only in faint yet unmistakable outline within the mystery of the imago Dei, this love—by which humanity was begotten in God's likeness—stood as the eternal pledge and sure foundation guaranteeing the promise of redemption should mankind ever wander astray. In this divine economy, God indeed saved the best wine of his love for last—reserved and poured forth in full measure into the chalice of the New Covenant at the appointed hour of consummation. God's creative love, rooted in divine wisdom, prepared us to further receive the gift of redemptive love, which perfects our nature toward its ultimate end—the *summum bonum*—the theopoesis of person between the Creator and the creatures of his love. Having humanity fashioned in his own image and likeness stands as an eternal testimony of God's love, an act of divine intentionality that exclusively positioned us as the recipients of his redeeming grace. The *imago Dei,* a radiant reflection reflecting the Triune love, necessitates that the love proper to the members of the Triune Community be communicated to us, beckoning us into communion. If we were not wondrously wrought in God's likeness, the outpouring of his love would be totally foreign to us, for only a creature bearing the Divine likeness can participate in the eternal fellowship of divine love. In the absence of God's likeness, the bestowal of his love on mankind would be philosophically incoherent, if not ontologically impossible. Thus, the *imago Dei* stands as an everlasting signature, testifying of God's unchanging love from creation's Genesis to redemption's Revelation—ensuring that humanity, created and redeemed, is eventually drawn into the eternal fellowship of the Godhead's boundless love.

The immensity of divine love and affection and even providential care we see bestowed on the human species is unlike anything ever witnessed with any of God's other creatures besides. And that, also, would seem to explain why God would go so far as to assign each human person a guardian angel at birth to attend to them throughout the course of their cosmic journey through life (see Matthew 18:10; Acts 12:15; Hebrews 1:14). In Psalms 91:11, for example, it states unambiguously that "*For He shall give His angels charge over you, To keep you in all your ways. In their hands they shall bear you up, Lest you dash your foot against a stone*" (NKJV). I am pretty sure none of us would be hiring the high-end services of a bodyguard to protect our cats or keep watch over our dogs twenty-four seven. Which promptly leads me to this next question: what really do you think God's guardian angels are constantly mounting guard over—some worthless garbage bin, some empty treasure chest, or some subspecies the Creator-God does not really care much about? Definitely not! If we humans would not so much as pay for the services of some trained security personnel to mount guard over our empty safe deposit box or anything else we do not actually care much about, neither would the only wise God. So the fact that we have guardian angels watching over humans further makes my case that each human person is indeed of some immense value—if not totally of immensurable value to the Creator-God—and is hence considered to be worth the level of providential care and divine protection so assigned to them from cradle to grave. At the very least, this scrupulous level of care and unbridled attention tells us one thing: that God's vested interest in humanity is uniquely unparalleled. Perhaps because they are distinctively the bearers of his *imago Dei*—the Grand Poobah among all his created species, or just maybe, who knows, for some other reasons far much deeper than we may have realized. For not only is it significant that man was created a 'person,' but even more than that, it must also be that he is an essential person of special interest to the Creator-God.

And the reason I say that is because no other species that we know of in the universe enjoys anything resembling the kind of privileged treatment and divine attention that humans receive from God exclusively; none comes even close. Think of it this way: if the angels are apotropaically watching over humans like those bodyguards with whom we are familiar down here, in contrast, who then is bodyguarding the guardian angels, do you think? Well, from what we already know by the Scriptures, they too, like all other impersonal creatures, enjoy no such privilege, for that is uniquely reserved for humans. Judging with the benefit of hindsight today, we can now understand even better that part of the reason the Scriptures say concerning the Israelites that "*Indeed, he who watches over Israel never slumbers or sleeps*"—is simply because—" . . . *the Lord your God has chosen you [Israel] to be his own special treasure*" (Ps 121:4; Deuteronomy 7:6 NLT). In other words, God is essentially keeping a watchful eye over a distinct people he holds very dear to his heart and considers a divine treasure. And when we apply that as a rule universally to all humanity, we could perhaps say that the Creator-God is basically being a Guardian-God—one who is constantly mounting guard over a distinct species he considers deeply special and treasures the most and holds so dear to heart—like ." . .*a hen protects her chicks beneath her wings . . .* " (Matt 23:37 NLT). Our governments, for example, go to great lengths, both making it a point of duty and as a critical aspect of national security, to ensure we maintain some of the highest levels of security protocols around the premises of our financial institutions and Federal Reserve buildings, clearly reflecting the immense worth we place on the valuables and cash reserves that are being housed within those vaults. None of which they would be doing if it were not considered significantly valuable enough, as the same robust safeguards are noticeably absent from places like national parks, for example.

By the same analogy, therefore, no one goes to great lengths to safeguard anything they really do not cherish or consider to be of some value. Hence, if man were a noman, God would not be having his guardian angels watching over him 24/7/365. But given how much the human species is considered his most valuable treasure in the universe, we can understand why he constantly has them under the Divine radar and tutelage of his watchful eyes. The fact that we have the eyes of God's divine attention and the heart of his sacred affection both centered on nothing else in the universe but man remains a testament to how much each man uniquely means to him. Even in the aftermath of the Fall into sin and rebellion in the Garden, which resulted in God losing that human soul he considers so precious and even priceless, his guardian angels never left still—they were never recalled back to heaven but were left here to further help each human person navigate through the maze fields of life until they eventually find the redemptive pathway back to their Maker. And as far as the redemptive transaction at Calvary's Cross goes, God went on to spend his life buying back the human soul because of how much it deeply meant to him—everything. Yes, you heard that right; man means everything to God, else he would not have gone to the length he did or paid the hefty price he paid redeeming their human souls from eternal ruination. Just the same way we ourselves would not be spending our hard-earned currency on buying back anything that is of little or no value to us, we will only consider buying back things that are of great value or some pecuniary significance to us. Likewise, God, whose Son would not have ventured so far as sacrificially laying down his life as a ransom price for the redemption of the human soul, except, of course, to demonstrate that it is truly considered to be of inestimable value to the Creator-God.

THE ALL-EMBRACING ARMS OF GOD'S LOVE: JEWS AND GENTILES UNITED IN WELCOME

It is a matter of no small theological consequence to revisit the precise terms in which the Lord addressed the sage-king Solomon on the occasion of the First Temple's inaugural consecration: "*I have chosen and consecrated this temple so that my Name may be there forever. My eyes and my heart will always be there*" (2 Chr 7:16 NIV). Of course, from our vantage in the unfolding drama of salvation history, informed by the prophetic intimations of the OT and the fuller Christological disclosures of the NT epistles, it is clear that this divine commitment was never confined to the physical contours of Solomon's architectural masterpiece—or indeed any other edifice erected by human hands—made of quarried stone and crafted mortar and whatnot—but extended, in typological anticipation, to the profound mystery of the human person as the true dwelling-place of God. In consequence, every believer today, responding in faith to the gospel of God's self-giving love, embodies this antitypical reality—thus the treasure of his heart and the apple of his eyes. To be 'the treasure' of God's heart denotes an unparalleled intimacy and valuation—where he holds you so dear to heart; to serve as the apple of his eye signifies perception unmediated by anything other than benevolent love—for God only sees man through the eyes of his love. This motif harks back to the promise He made to the OT covenant community (the Israelites), one that has since gone on to find fulfillment in the NT ecclesia of Christ: " . . . *you shall be a special treasure to Me above all people; for all the earth is Mine*" (Exod 19:5 NKJV). A disciplined reading of Scripture, attuned to the revelations of the Spirit, beyond the literality of the letters, yields the insight that God's entire engagement with the Jewish minority in the OT—whether in favor of or against—from his acts of deliverance, guidance, and even judgment upon them, was providentially oriented toward the salvation of the majority in the NT dispensation of grace—encompassing both Jewish and Gentile constituencies in equal measure. For the only possible means by which to procure such universal salvation for the majority of the sinful human population could only have been through the gift of a Savior, but then, the Savior had to have been born a man, and that man had to have come from some lineage somewhere, given the fact that it was actually a man (Adam) who originally caused all of humanity's woes from the incunabulum of the human story. It is this salvific genealogy that lies behind Jesus' candid acknowledgment: "

. . . salvation is from the Jews" (John 4:22, NIV)—in that the birth of the incarnate Word was genealogically channeled through the Jewish race—through the matrix of Israel's calling—God's distinct people, as it were: "*. . . from whom, according to the flesh, Christ came, who is over all, the eternally blessed God. Amen*" (Rom 9:5, NKJV). In further highlighting the uniqueness of the role played by the nation of Israel in God's salvation plan for all nations, the Psalmist makes the following submission: "*He has revealed his word to Jacob, his laws and decrees to Israel. "He has done this for no other nation; they do not know his laws. Praise the Lord*" (Ps 147:19–20 NIV). Here, we encounter not an arbitrary favoritism, but a strategic election: the particular serving the universal, the historical prefiguring the eschatological—the covenantal few midwife the salvific many, in a divine economy where God's faithfulness to one people becomes the ground of hope for all. It becomes clear that the election of the minority (Jews) signifies not exclusion of the majority (Gentiles) but a universal embrace of all, and herein, the whims of history bow to the unyielding call of redemption.

In the light of this essential revelation, we come to appreciate more fully the divine intent underlying the Lord's command to Moses, directing him to announce these words to the Jewish congregation at the wake of their Hegira from Egypt: "*God wasn't attracted to you and didn't choose you because you were big and important—the fact is, there was almost nothing to you. He did it out of sheer love, keeping the promise he made to your ancestors. God stepped in and mightily bought you back out of that world of slavery, freed you from the iron grip of Pharaoh, king of Egypt*" (Deut 7:7–8 MSG). The specific '*promise he made to your ancestors*' mentioned here ultimately centers on God's commitment to extend the grace of salvation to every nation and people on earth through the Seed of the Semitic forefather—Abraham—who is also the founder of the Jewish nation and the head of their covenant. It is especially telling that the promise of salvation for the entire human race predated the birth of the nation—Israel—itself, as well as the giving of the Law and the covenants via Moses, which only came much later. Apparently, God's unilateral covenant with Abraham had always had an eye looking out for the entire human race. Hence the reason we have such recurrent emphasis included in the articles of God's covenant promises to the patriarch: "*And in you all the families of the earth shall be blessed*"—"*In your seed all the nations of the earth shall be blessed, because you have obeyed My voice*"—"*since Abraham shall surely become a great and mighty nation, and all the nations of the earth shall be blessed in him*" (Gen 12:3b; 22:11–18; 18:18 NKJV). This was obviously beyond Abraham and his biological descendants; it highlights the universalist scope of God's covenant relationship and partnership with Abraham. And also, the Abrahamic 'Seed' in question is no different from the Adamic Seed whom God had promised all humanity in the Protevangelium, who later became the Davidic Seed—the Greater Son of David and the Messianic King who embodied the Jewish Expectation—revealed as *Yeshua ha-Mashiach*, or Jesus the Messiah. We hence can understand why the Evangelist, Matthew, would commence his Gospel with the following genealogical introduction: "*The book of the genealogy of Jesus Christ, the Son of David, the Son of Abraham*" (Matt 1:1 NKJV). By spotlighting David and Abraham, he presents Jesus as the long-awaited fulfillment of God's covenant promises to Israel—the royal heir and the seed through whom all nations would be blessed. In striking contrast, Luke's Gospel uniquely traces the Messiah's lineage all the way back to Adam, "the son of God" (Luke 3:38), thereby linking the Second Adam to the first. This deliberate extension of the genealogy beyond Israel's patriarchs affirms that Jesus, the Second Adam, identifies fully with the entire human race. In this careful detail, we glimpse the beauty of God's meticulous design—one might say, with a smile, that the Lord truly is "in the details," weaving purposeful threads even through what might seem the fine print of Scripture.

None of this is a coincidence at all, because, as it turns out, the Bible is a book substantively bookended by the progressive revelations of God's redeeming love for mankind—prefiguratively going from the exclusive redemption of the Jewish race under the mediatorial headship of Moses—antitypically arriving at the all-inclusive redemption of the entire human race under the mediatorial headship of Christ, the Redeemer of both the Jewish and Gentile races. The doctrine of God's love serves as the essential hermeneutical lens for picturing every facet of Scripture—the indispensable prism through which everything else must be discerned and depicted. Consequently, viewing and comprehending each biblical teaching in the light of God's love allows us to behold all realities in their authentic form, significantly leaving very little or no room for hermeneutical margin of error, doctrinal distortion, misinterpretation, or misguided conclusions. Since God Himself is love, every dimension of his divine character—his justice, his power, his patience—demands ultimate interpretation from the vantage of that boundless love, and every tenet of faith must yield to its unerring adjudication. Matter-of-factly, every divine intervention encountered in the Biblical corpus is grounded in God's love for humanity; every profound scriptural verity emanates from this same source; and the entirety of the divine economy pivots upon a substantive comprehension of his inexpressible love for humankind. Thus, whether individuals succumb to perdition or ascend to glorification, the outcome hinges upon their personal responses to God's perennial love—the love extended to our singular, cherished species: the human race. This narrative bears no relation to assertions of racial superiority, the exaltation of one ethnicity over another, or pitting one religion against another, as some who happen to have read their eisegesis into the Scriptures have suggested; rather, it pertains unequivocally to God's salvific love for the whole human family, transcending distinctions of ethnicity, creed, tribe, or language. In this regard, divine love is impartial—blind—race-blind—color-blind—religion-blind; it is no respecter of persons and it knows no racial favorites; it is all-accommodating to any human person (created in God's image and likeness) who would receive it with the open-hearted embrace of childlike faith. This divine impartiality is corroborated by the scriptural affirmation: "*From one human being he created all races of people and made them live throughout the whole earth. He himself fixed beforehand the exact times and the limits of the places where they would live*" (Acts 17:26 GNT). I, for one, formerly held the misconception that God's love for humanity commenced only in the New Testament with the advent of Jesus Christ; however, I now acknowledge this view as erroneous.

Though the cross represents the supreme and clearest display of God's love toward all nations, tribe and tongue, we must not overlook a vital truth: the Lord would never have righteously commanded Israel, "*You shall love the LORD your God with all your heart, with all your soul, and with all your strength*" (Deut 6:5 NKJV), had he not already loved them with incomparable depth and priority. It would, in fact, be morally incoherent for a holy God to demand total devotion from his people without having first set his heart upon them in covenant grace. Thus, the command to love God wholly rests on the prior, gracious reality that he has first loved his chosen people—a love that both enables and obligates their heartfelt response. Indeed, this paramount injunction—the Shema—presupposes the antecedent divine love toward the Jewish people in the OT era. Only on this basis could God evade the moral indictment of exacting an undue reciprocity or requiring of them what he had not first bestowed upon them. The God of Scripture stands unrivaled as the greatest, most transformative Leader conceivable in any era—past, present, or future. In his flawless example, he never requires of humanity to walk a path he has not pioneered or make a sacrifice he has not made. Unlike the hypocritical Pharisees, who imposed crushing obligations while refusing to lift a finger to help—they essentially "*bind heavy burdens, hard to bear, and lay them on men's shoulders; but they themselves will not move them with one of their fingers*" (Matt 23:4 NKJV)—Christ leads by perfect participation, having gone ahead and carried the fullest burden on our behalf, he empowers us to walk behind him in obedience through his own completed work. He calls us to holiness because He has embodied it, to sacrifice because he has offered it, and to love because he has loved us to the uttermost. Of course, it would be absurd to require heartfelt devotion from someone we ourselves treat with indifference or barely care about—just as insisting on loyalty while withholding our own would fracture any relationship from the start, for no such imbalance could sustain any meaningful relationship. Yet herein lies the breathtaking wonder of the Gospel: before the foundation of the world, God eternally purposed to give his only Son, the Lamb slain from the foundation of the world (Rev 13:8), as the atoning sacrifice for the sins of all humanity—Jew and Gentile alike. This predestined act reveals a boundless, initiating love that needs no prior merit from us. Although God's covenant relationship with Israel was contractual in nature, often outlining stringent conditions such as—" . . . *keeping his covenant of love to a thousand generations of those who love him and keep his commandments*"—"*If you listen to these regulations and faithfully obey them, the LORD your God will keep his covenant of unfailing love with you, as he promised with an oath to your ancestors*" (Deut 7:9 & 12 NLT)—the new covenant in Christ flows from God's unconditional determination to love and rescue the undeserving, securing forever those who trust in him.

From Genesis onward, God's redemptive story has been moving decisively—slowly but surely toward one glorious destination: the cross, where his immeasurable love for all humanity is forever displayed in the atoning death of his Son—the turning point of all history. The covenants established with Israel served as prophetic foreshadows, graciously pointing forward to the far greater reality accomplished in his Son: a complete and universal redemption, secured through the atoning power of Calvary to forgive sins and reconcile sinners to God. Thus, the Abrahamic covenant existed for the sake of the Abrahamic Seed—Christ Himself—the same who grew into the fruit-bearing tree of eternal salvation for the world, the living fulfillment of John 3:16. The major takeaway in all of this is that God loved the Jewish minority no more and no less than he loved the majority of the human population; rather, he sovereignly chose them as the instrument through whom the Messiah would come, demonstrating at the cross his equal, infinite love for every nation. The God of Israel, we could rightly infer, was essentially going somewhere with his love to happen; he was headed to Calvary's Cross to demonstrate his eternal love for the entire human race. However, should we fail to acknowledge Israel's irreplaceable yet temporary role as the divinely appointed instrument through whom salvation would reach all mankind, we risk misunderstanding their unique, servant-like calling as the conduit for the world's Savior. This can render the Old Testament deeply confusing, seemingly contradictory, or even disturbing. A preoccupation with surface-level historical analysis, without discerning the Spirit's unifying message, risks losing sight of the forest for the trees. In the absence of this historical clarity, it becomes all too easy to accuse God of capriciousness, moral inconsistencies or legalistic severity—a grave error that tragically obscures the radiant thread of his steadfast, sacrificial love woven throughout Scripture for the entire human race—a love that gave everything for everyone.

Once again, the penetrating words of the Apostle Paul come vividly to mind, reminding us that true understanding of Scripture does not reside merely in the external text but in the illuminating work of the Holy Spirit. As he declares, " . . . *the letter kills, but the Spirit gives life*" (2 Cor 3:6 NKJV). This timeless principle guards us against a cold, legalistic reading that brings only condemnation, while inviting us to receive the life-giving revelation that the Spirit alone imparts—transforming hearts and unveiling the glory of Christ in the Gospel. Essentially re-echoing the words of the Master: "*It is the Spirit who gives life; the flesh profits nothing. The words that I speak to you are spirit, and they are life*" (John 6:63 NKJV). Never a word spoken so true. Yet, even today, some persist in pinning the blame for Jesus' death exclusively on the Jewish people, overshadowing the Gospel's core proclamation of God's boundless love for every ethnicity. The Synoptic Gospels, however, leave no room for such racial stereotypes—they portray both Jewish and Gentile actors as equally culpable in this tragedy. In Luke's Gospel, for example, we are told that "*Then He took the twelve aside and said to them, "Behold, we are going up to Jerusalem, and all things that are written by the prophets concerning the Son of Man will be accomplished. For He will be delivered to the Gentiles and will be mocked and insulted and spit upon. They will scourge Him and kill Him. And the third day He will rise again*" (Luke 18:31–33 NKJV). This passage delineates a collaborative culpability: for both the Jews who led the Lamb of God to the place of slaughter—to 'be delivered to the Gentiles' for slaughter—and the Gentiles who ended up slaughtering the Lamb stand equally as complicit in His death. The same fact is repeated in Mark's Gospel: "*Behold, we are going up to Jerusalem, and the Son of Man will be betrayed to the chief priests and to the scribes; and they will condemn Him to death and deliver Him to the Gentiles*" (Mark 10:33 NKJV). The Bible unequivocally affirms that both Jewish and Gentile hands bore responsibility for Jesus' crucifixion—a profound symbol of humanity's collective complicity, encompassing even you and me, though we stood absent from Calvary.

This truth underscores our shared culpability, mirroring the universal stain of sin upon every soul. None of us emerges as untainted or exemplary in righteousness; none acted in love. Both Jews and Gentiles perpetrated the greatest act of injustice against an innocent Man in malice. The whole point of God going on the record to emphasise the parity of Jewish and Gentile guilt in the crucifixion of his Son, given their unholy alliance in the conspiracy to make it all happen—epitomised by the eleventh hour friendship between King Herod and Pontius Pilate—as well as the strategic collusion forged between the Jewish Religious establishment and the Secular Roman empire working in cahoots; is to let us know that all humanity—including all who are alive today, irrespective of temporal absence from the scenes of the Cross, yet cannot exonerate ourselves from the guilt of His bloodshed. This theological motif receives explicit corroboration in the apostolic prayer recorded in Acts 4:27–28 (NKJV), uttered amid threats from the same Jewish authorities prohibiting proclamation in Jesus' name: "*For truly against Your holy Servant Jesus, whom You anointed, both Herod and Pontius Pilate, with the Gentiles and the people of Israel, were gathered together to do whatever Your hand and Your purpose determined before to be done*" (Acts 4:27–28 NKJV). The same Jewish leaders, in a futile bid to deflect culpability, later remonstrated with the Apostles of Jesus: "*We gave you strict orders not to continue teaching in this name, and yet you have filled Jerusalem with your teaching and you intend to bring this Man's blood on us [by accusing us as His murderers]*" (Acts 5:28 AMP). Yet their efforts proved unavailing; the act was irrevocable—the damage irreversible, and no subsequent disavowal could cleanse the stain of innocent blood.

Indeed, the Jewish populace, alongside their leaders, had invoked precisely this consequence during Pilate's interrogation of Jesus, declaring, "*His blood be on us and on our children*" (Matt 27:25 NKJV). And as they had said with their mouths, so was it done unto them—their words became their curse—standing up in judgment against them in the universal court of justice, indelibly binding them to that innocent blood. As it turns out, Jewish elites are not alone in that, for not even Pontius Pilate, who supposedly washed his hands off the prosecution case in a performative gesture of absolution, managed to exonerate himself from the moral accountability of bloodshed before the Sovereign Judge. Despite going so far as to declare explicitly, "*I am innocent of the blood of this just Person. You see to it*" (Matt 27:24 NKJV), he nonetheless remained ensnared, no less culpable than absent contemporaries or posterity. Moreover, his self-exculpation rings hollow, as his earlier assertion remains all that is needed as evidence to pin him down. If you remember correctly, during that brief interrogation he had levied on Jesus in the inner chambers of his cavaedium, he went so far as to braggadociously admit *sub rosa*: " . . . *Do You not know that I have power to crucify You, and power to release you?*" (John 19:10 NKJV)—a statement that, in strict legal terms, was accurate. For he was indeed correct in recognizing his sole authority under Roman law—specifically the *jus gladii* (the right of the sword) vested in him as Prefect of Judea during Passover, A.D. 33—to pronounce final judgment. This power granted him full discretion to evaluate the evidence, recognize Christ's manifest innocence on both legal and moral grounds, and order His immediate release. The charges leveled against Jesus, far from amounting to the capital crime of *maiestas* (treason against the Empire), were entirely unsubstantiated. Pilate was thus well within his lawful jurisdiction (*intra vires*) to adjudicate the case on evidentiary merits and secure Jesus' acquittal. Yet, confronted with mounting political and socio-religious pressures orchestrated largely by the Sanhedrin and amplified by the incited crowd, he capitulated, surrendering principle on the altar of pragmatism, thereby prioritizing political expediency over equity—self-preservation over the weightier matters of justice.

At the end of the day, after all is said and done, history attests that " . . . *Pilate, wanting to gratify the crowd, released Barabbas to them; and he delivered Jesus, after he had scourged Him, to be crucified*" (Mark 15:15 NKJV). Clearly, his actions ended up betraying his own words; gratifying the Jewish masses and their leaders is precisely what he did. In essence, this passage powerfully underscores the inescapable solidarity of human frailty that binds Jews and non-Jews together, making any claims to personal innocence as pointless as those made by witnesses then—or by us now, or anyone throughout history—in the grand ledger of collective wrongdoing. There is just no way of getting off the hook for any of us, for in the crucible of that fateful hour, each of us would have mirrored the deeds of those present, ensnared by the same shadows of the heart. Hence, like Judas, the betrayer, we are all better off coming clean, unvarnishedly admitting our guilt of bloodshed before the divine tribunal: "*I have sinned by betraying innocent blood*" (Matt 27:4). Yet, in stark contrast to his despairing end, we are beckoned to emulate the Psalmist's liturgy of contrition—a fervent supplication for divine clemency: "*Deliver me from the guilt of bloodshed, O God, The God of my salvation, And my tongue shall sing aloud of Your righteousness*" (Ps 51:14 NKJV). Consider, then, the oracle of Zechariah, which might at first glance appear confined to the covenant people: "*And I will pour on the house of David and on the inhabitants of Jerusalem the Spirit of grace and supplication; then they will look on Me whom they pierced. Yes, they will mourn for Him as one mourns for his only son and grieve for Him as one grieves for a firstborn*" (Zechariah 12:10 NKJV). Such a narrow reading, however, conceals the prophecy's far-reaching end-times significance. Observe its parallel in the apocalyptic imagery from the island of Patmos, addressed to both Jews and Gentiles alike: "*Behold, He is coming with clouds, and every eye will see Him, even they who pierced Him. And all the tribes of the earth will mourn because of Him. Even so, Amen*" (Rev 1:7 NKJV). The blanket phrases 'every eye' and 'all the tribes of the earth' encompass all humankind, regardless of heritage. In other words, every person will grieve over the horrors inflicted on that spotless Lamb of God—a sweeping indictment against the entire human family for our shared responsibility and universal culpability of bloodshed.

Very much like those of the past, we too would have known no better at the time, for ignorance of the truth plagued all humanity in equal measure. That is precisely why the Son of God, in His agony, urgently interceded: "*Father, forgive them, for they do not know what they do*" (Luke 23:34 NKJV). This sweeping charge of guilt ties directly to the fall of humanity in Eden, affecting us all—from the humblest to the mightiest, from the tiniest newborn to the eldest soul. We nailed our Creator and Redeemer to the cross for our own failings—pause and let that sink in. If that is not the ultimate embodiment of love, the unparalleled outpouring of grace, it is difficult to imagine what could be. The reality that Jesus was executed by Roman authorities under Pontius Pilate's governorship is an undisputed cornerstone of history, supported by early church fathers and ancient historical analysis, and affirmed by a broad array of scholars even today. Consequently, this makes you just as guilty a Jew as I am a Gentile; we thus stand equally deserving of God's mercy, grace, and pardon. It also represents the unalterable principle of the Christian message, resistant to superficial interpretations. The letters of Paul articulate this clearly: "*What then? Are we better than they? Not at all. For we have previously charged both Jews and Greeks that they are all under sin*" (Rom 3:9 NKJV), a lament over comprehensive human fallenness that creates an even ground for redemption (see Romans 3:10–18). Embracing this core truth of the Gospel would protect the modern-day Church from the poison of cultural prejudice and spare many in our time from straying into error on this delicate topic—specifically, from wrongly pinning the blame for Christ's crucifixion and death solely on the Jewish people. The same centuries' old, poisonous antisemitic canard—one that, unfortunately, has historically never failed to morph into supersessionism (the misguided notion of Replacement Theology) or, worse still, outright accusations of blood libel.

Given how much Paul knew how racially charged and religiously sensitive this issue tends to be, he felt compelled to address it head-on by posing the following question to those of his generation: "*Or is He the God of the Jews only? Is He not also the God of the Gentiles?*"*—to which he firmly answers, "Yes, of the Gentiles also*" (Rom 3:29 NKJV). Because, again, like he elaborated elsewhere on a similar note, expanding on this theme of inclusive relationship: "*For there is no difference between Jew and Gentile—the same Lord is Lord of all and richly blesses all who call on him, for, 'Everyone who calls on the name of the Lord will be saved'*" (Rom 10:12–13). Well and truly, the ecumenical tent of God's love is big enough to accommodate each one of us, regardless of what tribe or tongue—race or ethnicity. God is no respecter of the persons of men, but he certainly is a respecter of his covenants with men, and as per his covenant with the ancestors of the Jewish people, he will not break his word of promise to the patriarch Abraham; he will not alter it. For this reason, we have no difficulty agreeing with Paul's conclusion: "*For I do not desire, brethren, that you should be ignorant of this mystery, lest you should be wise in your own opinion, that blindness in part has happened to Israel until the fullness of the Gentiles has come in. And so all Israel will be saved, as it is written: "The Deliverer will come out of Zion, And He* *will turn away ungodliness from Jacob; For this is My covenant with them, When I take away their sins*" (Rom 11:25–27 NKJV). At its deepest core, the gospel radically reverses every human expectation of divine invitation. No longer is the call reserved for the righteous or the devout—"*O come, all ye faithful*"—but rather it resounds to the broken and undeserving: "*O come, all ye unfaithful.*" For Scripture solemnly declares that there is none righteous, no, not one—neither Jew nor Gentile possesses any inherent faithfulness (Rom 3:10–12). This sweeping indictment levels every distinction of birth, culture, or tongue, clearing the ground for grace alone. The Savior's beckoning love extends without precondition to every sinner, inviting all—exactly as they are—to receive forgiveness and new life in him.

To strip the Cross of Christ of its central message—God's boundless love for all mankind and not some select few—is to strip it bare of whatever significance it has, reducing it to a lifeless stake—a hollow relic devoid of salvific efficacy and power. Love is the pulsating heart of the Cross's redemptive work—the quickening spirit that stirs every deed of the Messiah—the very cause that moved God to take upon himself the form of man and to walk among us as one despised and unknown. To sever the Cross from its redemptive framework, where it ultimately heralds the evangel of God's agape love for humankind, is to risk dismantling its salvific essence and Christological significance, rendering it a silent, shadowed relic of some antiquated story in history. Behold, the Cross, where love crosses out all human sin, stands as the crux of salvation's story. To uproot it is to uproot likewise the hope of eternal reconciliation with God, to hush the hymn of salvation, leaving naught but faint whispers of everlasting truth. In effect, symbols like the crucifix—a vivid icon of Christ's cross-bearing sacrifice—and the Christogram—a solemn glyph of his divine identity—once vibrant with symbolic potency, would equally fade into historical obscurity, languishing as mere curiosities, stripped of salvific significance. Leaving their theological potency and evocative force lost to a world wandering far from faith's foundational font, bereft of the beauty that binds the human heart to heaven. Love, for the Cross, is not merely a theological proposition nor is it a religious debate to be had but the very essence of the Gospel it heralds. Love is the universal language of the Cross, deeply resonating with every human person as the most native tongue of the heart. Without God's love, the Cross could not sing, because by then it would have no voice—love gives eternal voice to the salvation song of the Cross, a melody that never fails to resonate in the deepest chambers of the human heart. Without love as the most recurrent theme in all sixty-six volumes of sacred Scripture taken together, the doctrine of salvation and everything else about the Gospel falls apart. Sithence, the proposition that *'God is love'* remains a necessary universal truth, not tied to a time or tribe—neither confined to the Old Testament's covenant with Israel nor limited to the New Testament's Church. It stands eternally immutable—unchanging and unchangeable as God himself. In no way, shape, or form could the gospel of God's love be considered anachronistic in its application, because love is ultimately who God is today—who he was yesterday—and will be forever. He is no chameleon by nature; therefore, he changes not. To miss the central message pertaining to the universality of God's love in the biblical storyline is to miss the heart of God himself, casting us adrift upon seas far from his faithful word.

This love is the only reason compelling enough to account for why the God of Israel would come down to the lost sheep of the house of Israel in the 1st century A.D., travelling across land and sea—traversing the vast expanses of mountains and valleys to reach the lost in good time for a salvific rescue. Just when the question was raised in the heavenly council of the Triune Godhead, "*Whom shall I send, And who will go for Us?,*" God's love for man stood towering tall as the only answer—the only response echoing through the corridors of eternity. For the resounding response of God the Son who embodied God the Father's love was *"Here Am I! Send Me"* (Isa 6:8 NKJV). That call of God is one that no son of man was fit to answer—a divine summons none of us had what it took heed, save the Son of God. Truly, God's love knows no distances, no barriers nor boundaries, having journeyed across distances no man would ever dare to journey—traversing vast, uncharted territories that no mortal would dare attempt, thereby bridging distances that would otherwise have remained forever apart—reconciling two fundamentally disparate worlds that would have remained eternally irreconcilable. As the songwriter Rick Founds captured so vividly in 1989:

> *"You came from Heaven to earth*
> *To show the way.*
> *From the Earth to the cross,*
> *My debt to pay.*
> *From the cross to the grave,*
> *From the grave to the sky"*

Indeed, come all the way down he did—and go all the way up on the Cross he also did—even going out his way to pay the sin debt owed by sinful humanity. The magnanimity of divine love is the only ample explanation for why the Creator-God had ventured to such unfathomable depths to be identified with these puny little creatures of his—seemingly insignificant specks of dust dotted all across the earth's surface. In all honesty, we could hardly make any concrete sense of the Cross of Christ besides the redemptive love of God for man. Because again, absent that love, the Cross would essentially be no more than an empty, meaningless piece of lumber—a crude instrument of death, once reserved for the execution of common criminals and rabble-rousers. In fact, it was not until Christ was crucified on it that it suddenly began to be ascribed any significance whatsoever, at which point it transformed entirely, acquiring profound new meaning ever since. For the love of God for man is what gave the Cross its true meaning and whatever soteriological significance and historical relevance it ended up having today. The Cross only made history when Love finally made His way up the Cross—it etched itself into the annals of eternity that pivotal moment when the body of the God incarnate hung on it for all humanity.

Someone like Paul would even dare to argue that altruism without love is essentially empty and therefore, profitable for nothing—availing naught to giver or receiver. In his words: "*And though I bestow all my goods to feed the poor, and though I give my body to be burned, but have not love, it profits me nothing*" (I Corinthians 13:3 NKJV). An engaging modern take from The Message version echoes this: "*If I give everything I own to the poor and even go to the stake to be burned as a martyr, but I don't love, I've gotten nowhere. So, no matter what I say, what I believe, and what I do, I'm bankrupt without love*" (I Corinthians 13:3 MSG). Quite literally, the very same critique could apply to Christ's self-sacrifice at Calvary, had it not been for the fact that it was all centred about the demonstration of God's redemptive love for the human race—aimed squarely as a means towards the achievement of salvific ends. Were it not for the cross of Christ, I—and countless others—would remain in profound ignorance of what true love actually is and how immeasurably far it is willing to go. The cross alone unveils love in its purest, most self-sacrificial form: a love that traverses infinite distances—from the throne of heaven to a Roman execution stake, descends to unimaginable depths—from eternal glory to shameful death, and endures the utmost cost to redeem the utterly undeserving—the Passion of the Cross. Apart from Calvary, love would remain an abstract ideal; but there, in the suffering of the Sinless One, we behold its breathtaking reality and boundless reach.

THE CONQUEST OF ALMIGHTY LOVE ON CALVARY'S CROSS

The unparalleled display of love and self-sacrifice on the Cross of Christ transcends all human acts of altruism or humanitarianism ever recorded in the history books. For although Jesus was historically not the first to have been crucified on a stake, nor was he the last, yet his crucifixion is on par with that of no one else in history. And why? All because of divine love! God's redemptive love for the human race is what essentially made all the difference in the crucifixion and death of his Son. This self-giving love is what it took to divest the Cross of that stigma of shame and contempt that once defined it, purging it of its anathemic curse and transforming that antiquated symbol of ignominy into an eternal symbol of love's lasting legacy—love's lofty landmark. For the conquest of divine love on Calvary's Cross is what turned the story of this crucifixion in favor of the Crucified—crowning the victim, the victor; the humiliated, the glorified; the Suffering Servant, the Supreme Sovereign. By the same token, rendering the crucifixion of Christ the most iconic death the world has ever witnessed—the most heroic act ever known to man—the supreme emblem of self-sacrifice—the soul-stirring symbol of eternal salvation. The Cross, crowned by love's eternal triumph, forever stands as history's greatest triumph. For love, indeed, is the only force in the universe strong and powerful enough to have had the God incarnate impaled crosswise to the patibulum, hoisted lengthwise to the staticula, thrusted through with the pilum on the side of his torso, and left hanging cruciform on the Crux immissa, just as he waited upon his own death in excruciating pain and intense physical exhaustion, not the Roman soldiers—certainly not the Jewish civilians. Like he personally affirmed, "*Therefore My Father loves Me, because I lay down My life that I may take it again. No one takes it from Me, but I lay down it of Myself. I have power to lay it down, and I have power to take it again. This command I have received from My Father*" (John 10:17–18 NKJV). For man could not have succeeded in crucifying his own God and Maker had he not already been crucified by the resignations of his own love for man, nor could impotent creatures manage to overpower the Omnipotent Creator had he not already been disempowered by the constraining force of his own love for them, nor could the weak and frail somehow conquer the Strong and Almighty had he not already been conquered by his all-conquering love. And yes, God is love, and indeed he conquers all, but he could himself be conquered by no one; hence, only his consummate love for mankind had all that it took to have him conquered into surrendering his own life in abject abandonment into the hands of sinful men—all for sin, sin—none of his own—but all of their own. Only Love (God), the all-conquering One, had all that it took to have himself conquered, and so he decidedly allowed himself to be conquered by the ones whom he loves—all for the sake of the same ones whom he loves. God, the All-consuming Fire, whose infinite essence none can consume, willingly surrendered himself to be consumed on the altar of Calvary's cruel crucible, in the consummate demonstration of his love. Consumed, as it were, not by anyone else or by anything else beyond him but by the fervent flame and fervor of his own love for a fallen race—the passion and compassion of his own grace. This divine drama, where grace's passion dances with compassion, reveals a paradox: by single-handedly allowing himself to be conquered by his own love for man on Golgotha's Gibbet, Christ decisively conquered the whole world, i.e., the triumph of divine love over the rebellion and sins of men. This self-consuming act of Christ, where love's luminous light vanquished vile venom, reveals redemption's radiant reality: that divine devotion, deeply rooted in eternal essence, forever foils fallen fury, forging a path where grace's gentle grandeur guides the soul to salvation's sweet summit.

Forsooth, the Omnipotent God is the Greatest Conceivable Being whose love has indeed conquered all—not so much on the bloodied battlefields of military warfare but at the blessed battlefield of Calvary's Cross; for even the most rebellious of men have indeed been conquered hands down into submission at the foot of his Cross—not by the greatness of his Divine armipotence, which could rend the heavens, but by the greatness of his Divine love; and yea, even the most obstinate of sinners have equally been conquered hands up in surrender at the foot of his altar—not by the Omnipotence of his might, which could shatter the fabric of creation, but by the Omnibenevolence of his love—even the extravagance of his grace. For what no army general in the world could ever aspire to accomplish with the combined military might of thousands upon thousands and tens of thousands of heavily armed soldiers and squadrons of galloping horsemen at his command, Jesus accomplished without ever commanding an army—without ever wielding a weapon—without ever swinging a sword.

What the greatest of swordsmen, warlords, and fabled war heroes, the likes of Alexander the Great and even Napoleon Bonaparte, could never have dreamt of accomplishing with their master swordsmanship and knightly chivalry, Christ accomplished with just an innocuous stake—the cruciform weapon of his love and grace. At the foot of the Cross of God's love is right where the thrones of all powers that be and the altars of all religions that exist have historically come bowing down on their knees in heart-surrender—without any shots fired, without any coercion applied, and without any violence employed. Here, mighty monarchs and most zealous devotees bow in reverence, transformed by the eternal depth of his mercy, which conquers without combat and reconciles without restraint. Through the profound mystery of his divine mission, Christ prevailed where earthly power falters, conquering the human heart not by brutal battle but by the boundless beauty of his blessed love. This triumph, wrought without violence—unmarred by bloodshed—vanquishes vice, converting wayward wills to worship. Unveiling the profound mystery of God's radiant love—brighter than battalions, more lustrous than legions—drawing souls from defiance to devotion through the transformative radiance of his grace, which surpasses all human strength and establishes eternal reconciliation. At the sacred altar of that blood-stained tree, God's love, a power more potent than power, woos the wildest wills to wondrous worship, transforming turbulent trespassers into trembling devotees, who, kneeling at the soles of his feet, find their defiance dissolved by the unfathomable depth of divine devotion. There, this divine affection, a radiant force for good—a force more forceful than force itself—subjugates the recalcitrant spirit, with hands raised in righteous retreat, leaving the wayward heart, once hardened in defiance, bowing in reverent acquiescence and silent awe, enraptured by the poetic grandeur of the love that transforms rebellion into reverence.

For the power of Love is the greatest, and the dominion of Love is indeed matchless, for Love is the Conqueror of the unconquerable, the Savior of the unsavable—the Redeemer of the irredeemable—the Conciliator of the irreconcilable—the Governor of the ungovernable. So "*Do not doubt the power of Almighty love,*" said Spurgeon! And yes, do not underestimate the matchless might of All-conquering love, seconds Israel (pg. 59). Verily, love governs all other human passions with a gentleness most sublime—a sweetness unsurpassed, for love's lovely lure lacks the locks of enslavement and the lashes of servitude, yet lures all living under its lordship with a power so pure and sublime, so potently pleasing, that as nothing matches its mighty measure, so too no strength rivals its tender dominion. This love—luminous and limitless, this love—leading all lesser longings, this love—lordly and lasting, governs the heart's harmony, drawing every desire to its dainty dominion, not by bitter bonds nor with harsh hegemony but by the blissful beauty of its boundless being, heralding the height of holy might. It is the eternal archetype of caritas, the divine self-donation incarnate in Christ's sacrifice, uniting humanity to God in perfect relational harmony. It is easy to see how Paul would have quickly arrived at the conclusion that "*Three things will last forever—faith, hope, and love—and the greatest of these is love*" (1 Cor 13:13 NLT). For lo and behold, Love is the greatest—the conquest of Love the ultimate—the triumph of Love indisputable. On Calvary's holy cross, not only do we witness Love stooping so humble and lowly in order to conquer the so high and mighty sinner, we also see him suffering all—for the sake of all sinners—in order to conquer all sins. Yet, to achieve the ultimate conquest over every dominion and foe, Love himself was compelled to pioneer the path by first suffering all things with unflinching resolve, bearing all things in steadfast solidarity, believing all things with unshakeable fidelity, hoping all things amid unrelenting shadows, and enduring all things through the crucible of unyielding trial (cf. 1 Cor 13:7).

And through his resolute endurance of the searing pain and excruciating agony inflicted by the Cross, through his audacious conquest of the searing shame and profound humiliation woven into the fabric of his own crucifixion—even the abject ignominy of his death upon that cursed timber—followed by his resplendent triumph over the adamantine grip of death and the yawning maw of the grave across the momentous three days that ensued, Christ has, in solitary magnificence, irrefutably demonstrated to the solitary seeker as much as to the vast throng of humanity, that in truth, precisely as the sacred Scriptures have proclaimed with timeless authority: "*Love never fails . . .*" (1 Cor 13:8). Yes, Love never fails to conquer all because Love knows to overcome all evil with good—all wickedness with kindness—all ill will with goodwill—and above all, all hatred with the boundless expression of himself—agape (cf. Rom 12:21). Although humanity, in its corrupted essence, had mustered every last strand of rancorous hatred, venomous spite, and unbridled malice from the depths of its fallen nature against the Son of God upon the Cross of his boundless love—unleashing an unrelenting deluge of its profoundest enmity straight upon his person—yet, in the climactic finale, his love surged forth to conquer every adversary, his grace cascading in unassailable triumph. Hallelujah, love always wins! Wherefore, to wage war against Love is a contest no mortal can ever expect to win, rendering it utterly impolitic, or at the very least disastrously ill-advised, for any man to dare pick a fight with him. To fight against Love is to fight against oneself—to bet against one's own interest, because at the end of the day, Love will always be found looking out for every man's interest way better than any man could ever look out for his own. This truth resonates all the more profoundly when you consider that Love " . . . *is not self-seeking* . . . " (I Corinthians 13:5 NIVUK). Precisely as he himself attested with unwavering clarity: "*For I have come down from heaven, not to do My own will, but the will of Him who sent Me*" (John 6:38 NKJV). This has got to be love at its finest, and yes, it is—love at its most exquisite and enchanting loveliness—love exalted to the sovereign summit of its consummate expression—agape love unveiled in its transcendent essence.

Perhaps, the triumphant conquest of Almighty Love upon Calvary's Cross in the First Century A.D. finds its most vivid and resonant encapsulation in that legendary proclamation from Julius Caesar's triumphant dispatch to the Roman Senate, penned in the immediate aftermath of his decisive victory in the Battle of Zela against King Pharnaces II in 47 B.C.: '*veni, vidi, vici*'—that is, I came, I saw, I conquered. For truly, Christus Victor came into the shadowed realm of man's fallen world; he saw its every anguish and aberration in unflinching clarity; he endured its every torment and trial with unwavering fortitude; he accomplished its every redemptive demand with sovereign fidelity—all orchestrated impeccably according to God's unerring will—and ultimately, he conquered its every foe and fetter in resounding finality, all secured indelibly for the sake of mankind's eternal liberation. Hence, from that victorious hour, his blessed assurance to every weary human heart has since been and forever will be, " . . . *be of good cheer, I have overcome the world*" (John 16:33 NKJV). For unlike Caesar, whose conquests were forged in the crucible of imperial ambition, the descent of Love incarnate into this fractured realm was singularly purposed to vanquish the pervasive sinfulness ensnaring the sinful world—all executed unswervingly on behalf of sinful humanity, scarcely for his own sake, nor for the hollow pursuit of self-glorification, nor for the fleeting laurels of vainglory alone. Should we adopt John Maxwell's incisive paradigm of success—"*Success in life has nothing to do with what you gain or accomplish for yourself. It's what you do for others*"—then Jesus, beyond any shadow of dispute, must don the laurel of the supremely successful Man who ever graced the annals of existence, not least owing to the unrelenting altruism that defined his every stride, for in all he undertook, he labored ceaselessly for others, with precious little regard for his own personal stake or self-serving agenda. And therein lies one awe-inspiring reality concerning the Man of Galilee—a prodigious truth that has unfailingly stirred multitudes of men to stand transfixed in reverent wonder, each soul inwardly wrestling with the same profound, inescapable query—whilst murmuring in hushed astonishment: "*What manner of man is this . . . ?*" (Matt 8:27 KJV). Verily, a manner of Man unparalleled, utterly singular, like no other who ever trod the dust of earth or graced the annals of eternity. History further attests to this timeless intrigue, revealing that Napoleon Bonaparte stands among those eminent figures who have paused in awe-struck contemplation, wrestling with the fathomless profundity of that epoch-shattering accomplishment—the singular, historically unprecedented feat—that Jesus achieved through naught but that innocuous cruciform stake of his boundless love and atoning sacrifice, together with the matchless, enduring sway he continues to exert, even in the wake of his earthly sojourn, upon the souls of humanity across every stripe of disposition, every race and ethnicity, every dialect and dominion, as the radiant outgrowth of that transcendent act.

In juxtaposing the parabola of the revolutionary, world-altering force of Jesus's earthly life and the age-enduring legacy of love and sacrifice he bequeathed to generations against the martial and imperial imprints left by other luminaries of history's pantheon, he found himself inescapably drawn to this stark conclusion: "*Alexander, Caesar, Charlemagne, and I have founded empires. But on what did we rest the creations of our genius? Upon force. Jesus Christ founded his empire upon love, and at this hour millions of men would die for him.*" In truth, the indomitable militancy of divine love has undeniably proven itself to be vastly superior in efficacy to any arsenal of conventional military stratagems devised by human ingenuity, precisely because its mission objective has always been one of conquering hearts and not conquering territories—its goal to win countless souls and not wage endless wars—its strategy to triumph through softhearted compassion rather than stonehearted conquest. Hence, its resounding battle cry will always be one of "*. . . take up the cross, and follow Me*"—even as it resounds in stark juxtaposition with the clarion call: "*Put your sword back in its place because all who take up a sword will perish by a sword. Or do you think that I cannot call on My Father, and He will provide Me at once with more than 12 legions of angels?*" (Mark 10:21b NKJV;

Matthew 26:52–53 HCSB). And the rationale for steadfastly embracing this resolute posture of nonviolence is neither obscure nor contrived, for it rests squarely upon the pivotal reality that " . . . *the Son of Man did not come to destroy men's lives but to save them*" (Luke 9:56 NKJV). Indeed, notwithstanding that God's unchanging, eternal plan remains for all men to be saved and come to the profound knowledge of the truth enshrined in his Son, he nevertheless " . . . *will not save them by bow, nor by sword, nor by battle, by horses, nor by horsemen*"—but rather by the triumphant arsenal of love, by the boundless torrent of grace, by the fathomless well-spring of mercy, and by the liberating pardon of sins (Hos 1:7 KJV). As if that was not clear enough, though, Simon Peter, a devoted disciple of the Christ who happened to be one of those hanging out with him in the shadowed garden of Gethsemane's ancient olives on the night of his betrayal and arrest, impulsively drew his sword and struck one of the palace guards attempting to enforce his Master's arrest, severing his ear on the spot, in his bid to make an a baculo case against his apprehension. Some might cheer and commend Peter's fervor, perceiving it as a gallant gesture, arguing that it was a befitting zealous defense of justice against the encroachment of worldly power.

Yet, such commendation falters when weighed against the eternal truth pertaining to Christ's kingdom, where righteousness is not wrought by the sword's fleeting might but by the meekness of divine love. To his fault, however, Peter should have at least realized that might never makes right with Jesus—the resort to violence is barely ever considered a viable option in his pacific kingdom. For not only does this Divine Peacenik go by the title *'the King of Righteousness,'* he is also called 'the Prince of Peace'—and of the increase of his " . . . government and peace . . . ," we have been told that " . . . *there shall be no end*" (See. Hebrews 7:2; Isaiah 9:6). Moreover, the fact that he would rather speak the language of peace and not war is all part of the reason he has always had his sword in his mouth and never in his hands (see Revelation 19:15, 21). Unlike those bloodthirsty men of war, savage swordsmen who are predisposed to violence, whose blood-drenched swords revel in slaughter and find no rest nor quiet in their scabbard from being made drunk with the blood of their enemies—satiated with devouring the flesh of their foes in the field of battle. The sacred sword of God's Christ is a sword of peace and justice, not a sword of violence or villainy. And for the interest of peace, he makes it his aim and mission objective to keep his sword back from bloodshed—denying it any opportunity of ever having to relish the taste of blood—keeping it sheathed and unsoiled by bloodshed for good—idle and unemployed in his scabbard for the greater good. Thus, giving peace all the chance it deserves to reign in men's hearts and in man's world. By withholding his blade, Christ cultivates peace in hearts and the world, weaving a divine narrative where justice silences violence, allowing peace to reign supreme, thus uniting humanity in God's redemptive harmony—forever crowned by the triumph of divine love. This peace is part of the parting legacy he left behind. Addressing the fears of his disciples in a world of Roman oppression and Jewish unrest, on the eve of his crucifixion, grants them his divine, enduring peace. Saying: "*Peace I leave with you, My peace I give to you; not as the world gives do I give to you. Let not your heart be troubled, neither let it be afraid*" (John 14:27 NKJV). This promise, rooted in his cosmic mission, assured them of God's unshakable presence beyond the Cross, preparing them for the challenges of proclaiming the Gospel in a hostile world.

That said, far from the reaction you would often expect to get from most people in such a situation, the Master did not particularly seem thrilled nor impressed about this incident at all, as his unrehearsed response instead was, "*Permit even this." And He touched his ear and healed him*" (Luke 22:49–51 NKJV). Imagine restoring the ear of a man who came for your arrest and obviously meant you no goodwill. As it turns out, experiencing such undeserved kindness from Jesus is not something that is common to Malchus alone, as Saul of Tarsus (who later became Paul the Apostle) is someone else who can also relate to that on a much deeper level, for it took the same Jesus whose radiant appearance had left him blind during his now famous Damascus Road encounter to also go on to lovingly restore his sight. He, like so many others, had just enjoyed the privilege of witnessing firsthand how easily divine love could convert a foe into a friend—a persecutor into a preacher—an adversary into an ally. In reflecting on this life-changing encounter he had with Jesus, he would later go on to pen down the following thoughts, almost as though expressing his gratitude *in memoriam*: "*For you have heard of my former conduct in Judaism, how I persecuted the church of God beyond measure and tried to destroy it . . . But when it pleased God, who separated me from my mother's womb and called me through His grace*" (Gal 1:13, 15 NKJV). And that, in itself, proves yet again that, truly, love " . . . *does not hold grudges and will hardly even notice when others do it wrong*" (1 Cor 13:5 TLB). It even goes a step further to explain why it just so happens that despite all that, Jesus ended up suffering at the hands of men—all the barbaric torture he was put through at the hands of the Romans—he was yet never once seen or heard threatening payback but would rather go on to commit his righteous cause into the hands of the righteous Sovereign Judge—even God (see 1 Peter 2:23). A testament to the fact that he came in peace and was all for peace, never for war. One can certainly almost picture him being in prayer before God during those final moments leading up to his Passion and having to recite word-for-word this particular Psalm, which said, "*Too long have I lived among those who hate peace. I am for peace; but when I speak, they are for war*" (Ps 120:6–7 NIV). Indeed, Love is for peace and not for war and would pursue peace at all costs, no matter where it leads. And for the same reason also, David the Psalmist had no qualms vouching that "*He makes wars cease to the end of the earth; He breaks the bow and cuts the spear in two; He burns the chariot in the fire*" (Ps 46:9 NKJV). For the pacific militancy of God's love is the only force for good in the universe that is guaranteed to usher in the reign of peace in man's world—establishing *modus vivendi* as the New World Order—whilst having the hearts and minds of all men garrisoned with such levels of Divine peace that surpass all human understanding. In fact, if love were to be assigned an inseparable working companion, that would be none other than peace: the Divine love fosters a peaceful coexistence among men—between friends and foes alike.

Now we can better understand why the unassailable moral examples of Christ, among others, forever stand as the *beau idéal* for the Christian life and virtue. For the uncompromising posture of God's love toward mankind will always be anchored on the creedal text: " . . . *on earth peace, goodwill toward men!*" (Luke 2:14 NKJV). Reasons also for which Paul, in a number of his epistles, would interchangeably refer to the gospel of Christ as '*the gospel of peace*.' In one such instance, you could almost literally feel his heartfelt commitment to the cause of peace as he writes to fellow Christians by way of commendation, expressing so much joy and delight about "How beautiful are the feet of those who preach the gospel of peace, Who bring glad tidings of good things!" (Rom 10:15 NKJV). Of little surprise is it then to also discover that the divine title "*the God is peace*' is ascribed to the Christian God more times in the NT than any other title we could think of. On the grounds of the above agglomerative evidence, we can sufficiently make the case that the Christian God is demonstrably not the God of war that many have imagined Him to be, but the God of peace—as seen in all his churches. And like they say, the proof of the pudding is in the eating. In contrasting between the hawkish kingship of David and the irenic kingship of his son who was to succeed his throne, not Solomon per se but his Greater Son who is Jesus the Messiah, the Scriptures essentially witnessed that he shall be a man of peace (having rest from wars during the day of his reign)—unlike David, who was euonymously considered a man of war, with far too much bloodshed on his hands. Hence the reason he was considered unworthy of building God a temple, even though he had it in his heart to do so at the time (cf. 1 Chronicles 22:9–10). Consequently, by simply highlighting the ephemeral nature and the transient legacy of those empires that were historically built on the backs of military conquest, in contrast to the Pacific Kingdom that Christ came down here to establish on the conquest of the Divine love, Napoleon reinforces the idea that agape is indeed the ultimate—the Ultimate Conqueror—even the King of hearts—the master key to every human heart. Throughout the history of the Church, love has clearly been shown to be that one master key that unlocks the hearts of men great and small to the acceptance of Christ as Savior—to the eternal embrace of his salvation. For the triumph of the Christian faith through the ages has neither been by the greatness of the Church's military might nor by the strength of her power, but by the fervent labor of her love and her love alone.

That is all the more true when you consider that Love has never really waged war with any man yet in the effort to win their heart, nor has Christ ever forced himself upon anybody yet in order to convert them over to his kingdom, nor has God trampled down the free will of any man by brute force in order to compel submission to do his Divine will, despite the fact his moral will and eternal purposes are altogether righteous. Which further demonstrates that divine love is firmly entrenched on the foundations of freedom—dutifully upholding the fundamental principles of free choice. What am I, a creature endowed with reason, to make of the fact that there is an omnipotent Big Guy up there somewhere who could effortlessly bend my will to his own, causing me to do or say anything he wishes—yet chooses not to? He has every resource necessary to override my freedom, but he deliberately restrains his power. Once again, the big four-letter word (written in all caps) is all that comes to mind: LOVE. For God, in his infinite understanding, recognizes a fundamental truth: genuine love is impossible in the absence of freedom. Forced devotion is no devotion at all; therefore, his love honors my freedom, inviting rather than imposing, so that any response of love from me might be real and heartfelt. By the very same token also, the Son of God was himself not forced to the Cross against his own will—love led him there—love compelled him to journey there by the shadowed valley of the *Via Dolorosa*—his love, fervent and free, kept him hanging in there and then up there until his salvific mission was accomplished. Unlike Samson, who was hoodwinked into his own death by a strange woman, that femme fatale by the name of Delilah, with whom he was blindly besotted, Christ it was who willfully and knowingly surrendered himself into the hands of the son of perdition, that greedy man by the name of Judas Iscariot, along with his co-conspirators, who were hell-bent on doing him harm and wanted him dead. Far from being constrained by any necessity outside the divine will, he did it all for love, flowing graciously from the unity of Father and Son—all for the love of God's one and only beloved creature—mankind. Far from what Judas might have imagined at the time, it was Love who, for no price, had his Son delivered into the hands of those who had him crucified, not himself who had done so for the meager price of 30 pieces of silver.

And like Paul was quick to affirm, it was God " . . . *who did not spare His own Son, but delivered Him up for us all* . . . " (Rom 8:32 NKJV). Simon Peter, seconding that motion, sets the records straight before his Jewish countrymen, by stating emphatically clear that: "*Men of Israel, listen to these words: Jesus the Nazarene, a Man attested to you by God with miracles and wonders and signs which God performed through Him in your midst, just as you yourselves know—this Man, delivered over by the predetermined plan and foreknowledge of God, you nailed to a cross by the hands of godless men and put Him to death*" (Acts 2:22–23 NASB2020). Yes indeed, God, out of his own benevolent volition and goodwill toward mankind, had his Son delivered over to slaughter as the sacrificial lamb for the sins of men. But then again, unlike Samson, whose love for Delilah was to a fairly large extent 'blind'—no less blind than blind Bartimaeus, one might say. God's love for humanity was all clear-eyed, for Christ knew exactly what he was getting himself into before venturing down here—way before venturing up there on Calvary's rugged Cross. Quite similarly, in sharp contrast to Isaac, who had to be first blindfolded before being led unawares up Mount Moriah's sacrificial altar, where he was supposedly going to be sacrificed by his father, Abraham, Christ was by no means blindfolded when he journeyed up Golgotha's sacrificial altar to be sacrificed by his Heavenly Father for the sins of all mankind. He was fully aware of the high stakes and was yet in total submission to the Father's will, even unto death, for the salvation of all. Without mincing words, he said to the few epigones whose listening ears he had at the time, "*Behold, we are going up to Jerusalem, and all things that are written by the prophets concerning the Son of Man will be accomplished. For He will be delivered to the Gentiles and will be mocked and insulted and spit upon. They will scourge Him and kill Him. And the third day He will rise again*" (Luke 18:31–33 NKJV). Clearly, he was by no means blindsided about what awaited him at Jerusalem; he yet remained resolute all the way there. Moreover, very unlike the retributive measures Samson felt compelled to take whilst hanging on his own version of the Cross during the final moments leading up to his death, shackled between the twin-pillars of an indoor coliseum as it were, he made a revanchist last-wish, in his Hail Mary prayer to God, that he might at least be able to summon every last ounce of strength he had left within him, in receiving a pound of flesh from all his foes who had relished the pleasure of watching his woes, as they cheered on in glee—rejoicing in schadenfreude; their eye for his eye—their tooth for his tooth—their death for his death, he vengefully demanded.

Christ saw absolutely no need to take out revenge against his enemies whilst hanging on his cross in insufferable pain. He, rather, would most graciously and lovingly go on to make the most benevolent prayer you would ever hear proceed from the lips of any man for his fellow men, shortly before laying down his life for them all: "*Father, forgive them, for they do not know what they do*" (Luke 23:34 NKJV). As though dramatizing his most famous Sermon on the Mount, in which he majored on the Beatitudes, saying, " . . . *love your enemies, bless those who curse you, do good to those who hate you, and pray for those who spitefully use you and persecute you*"—or simply just living by what He preached (Matt 5:44 NKJV). Symbolically, we see displayed on the Cross of Christ two opposing extremities—extreme vice alongside extreme virtue, and by that I am simply referring to the greatest display of man's hatred and rebellion toward God on the one hand, alongside the greatest display of God's love and humility toward man on the other. Because just when men were at their worst in sin, pride, and rebellion against God, God was at his finest in love, grace, and forgiveness toward them all. Very well do the Scriptures maintain that where the sins of men abound, the grace of God abounds even much more (cf. Rom 5:20 NKJV). What is more, out of the seeming foolishness and shamefulness of the crucifixion and death of God's Divine Son came forth the most impressive display of the unfathomable depths and brilliance of God's wisdom: for the same God who had caused light to be made manifest in the midst of darkness in the beginning has in these last days caused life to spring forth from the midst of death—the death of his Son. But up until the Savior came down to our rescue, we were more or less living in sin like an endangered species, almost at the verge of pushing ourselves off the cliff of existential damnation—about plunging ourselves into the death of extinction. Well and truly, God is all about love, and his Son, in demonstrating his Father's love for mankind, conquered this sinful, hateful, and wicked world with love. Doubtless, the Divine love forever stands as the only thing in the universe that had all that it took to have man's sin of rebellion against God conquered on the Cross of Jesus Christ—with Divine judgment averted—and Divine wrath assuaged. The conquest of the Son of God on Calvary's Cross essentially represents the conquest of God's love over human sin and all manifestations of hate. And with Christ forever seated at the right hand of the throne of God, God's love, we could also say, has eternally been enthroned over all the mortal and spiritual forces of vice and would forever reign in triumph over them.

CHRISTUS VICTOR: THE ONE-MAN ARMY – THE SOLO SAVIOR'S UNACCOMPANIED TRIUMPH

Behold the audacious and all-sufficient design of divine redemption: nothing but Jesus and his Cross—nothing added, nothing subtracted—the breathtaking theater of God's saving work unveiled in full! See him, the invincible One-Man Army, raising high the tree of tears, that rough-hewn emblem soaked in the scarlet grief of ages; behold the steadfast Lone Soldier, armed with nothing save the stake of sorrows, that twisted wood tempered in the crucible of utter abandonment, where the unrelenting blaze of love's holy fury disarmed the hosts of darkness and flung wide the gates of glory. In this titanic contest of cosmic consequence, where the eternal destiny of souls hung trembling in the balance of divine justice, God did not summon vast legions of angelic might nor unleash the thunderous host of heaven's warriors; instead, he accomplished the salvation of the whole world through a solitary, unconquerable force—one Man alone, an impregnable army distilled into the person of his only begotten Son. This Lone Strategist pressed forward in a righteous campaign, charging single-handed into the fury of spiritual warfare to secure humanity's final deliverance. Truly he stood in solitary grandeur as the One-Man Army, displaying matchless courage and unbreakable determination; he fought the decisive battle entirely unaided as the Lone Soldier, confronting the powers of darkness in magnificent isolation; and he secured the resounding victory in peerless solitude, sustained only by the invincible might of his cross and the boundless, life-transforming power of his sacrificial love— which shattered every fetter of captivity and ratified forever the decree of grace. Holy Scripture thunders this enduring truth: "*Nothing can hinder the Lord from saving, whether by many or by few*" (1 Sam 14:6 NIV).

Picture it this way: just Jesus and his Cross of suffering, with no armies marching in behind him in thundering ranks—no legions of light bolstering his flank—for he stands as the quintessential One-Man Army from Heaven's unassailable ramparts, who puts everything on the line in reckless, redemptive abandon to redeem earth from its chains of darkness. He embodies the Lone Soldier who went to battle for humanity at his own expense with his stake of sorrows, bearing the full weight of redemption's Holy War and the cost of crimson sacrifice alone in solitary majesty. Consider the faithful scribe, that tireless teacher of Tarsus, who asked a heart-piercing and thorn-sharp question that resounds through the corridors of military archives and spiritual warfare: who, pray tell, goes to battle at his own expense in a campaign not fueled by gain or glory—plunder or prestige—but by pure devotion? (1 Cor 9:7). Well, the answer to that question has historically been updated, polished to perfection, and eternally etched upon the sacred tablets of redemptive history; we eventually found one in the fullness of time—the world's only Lone Soldier—the peerless unaccompanied Crusader who went to war at His own expense without a whisper of recompense or reward from the fray—one from which he stood to gain nothing in personal aggrandizement or selfish triumph but gave all in unparalleled generosity.

He engaged the enemy and emerged victorious in a conquest that shakes the earth and shatters the foundations of sheol—he won a victory not his own in isolated vindication, but for a world who did not so much believe in him with fervent conviction—a people who had no faith in his righteous cause that championed the least and the lost—for brother-in-arms who would not get behind him in unwavering phalanx to march to Calvary's sacred battleground to clinch redemption's conquest over the principalities of perdition in a clash that echoes eternally. The *Christus Victor* is the epitome of solo military might who persisted in solitary determination, apart from all allies—he stood all by himself and waged this Holy War in unyielding isolation, yet not for himself in narcissistic pursuit of personal praise or isolated glory—but for those who would not rally behind him in solidarity in redemption's fierce battle against the gates of hell, to deliver the Fallen Creation from its fetters of gloom. It was just him against the world in cosmic confrontation—*Christ Solus*, Christ the Solo Savior, versus a world full of sin that saturates every crevice like a venomous flood, dominated by Satan's despotic sway that enslaves the masses, and plagued by death's insidious grip that casts a pall of despair over every dawn.

Within the grand amphitheater of God's unfolding plan of redemption—as chronicled from Genesis to Revelation, where the dire consequences of the age to come—judgment's unyielding verdict—dangle like an ever-looming peril akin to the fabled sword of Damocles over the entire human narrative, the Savior's complete arsenal for this redemptive warfare crystallizes into a single defining artifact: the Cross, that cruciform armamentarium that transmutes suffering's scourge into sovereignty's scepter. This singular armament emerges as the cruciform icon of his agapeic passion that penetrates and tears apart the thick curtain of enveloping gloom and spiritual blindness, allowing light to flood in where shadows once reigned supreme—his arsenal distilled to the singular cartridge, the prophetic utterance of truth that booms as the shofar's ancient summons, rallying the covenant people from bondage. Outfitted completely, from head to toe, armed to the teeth with scriptural verity, a force so potent it crumbles the mightiest fortresses of deception and falsehood, brick by brick, as foretold in the Psalms of deliverance—unleashing these salvific shafts steeped in the steadfast love, truth-laden projectiles discharged with a love that heals the wounded rather than harm the innocent—swinging the two-edged sword of the Spirit, that instrument of justice, with redemptive grace that cuts asunder the heavy chains of sin's tyranny and resurrect the dry bones of the valley, fulfilling Ezekiel's vision—securing redemption's victory in resplendent triumph—not for vainglory in solitary enthronement, but for the ingathering of nations in the renewed Eden of Revelation's promise. The redemptive weapon of the God's love, in its transcendent and all-conquering potency, strikingly evokes the memory of the five smooth stones that David chose from the brook—five chosen stones forged into one devastating, unerring shot upon his shepherd's sling—that selfsame David's slingshot, which, by heaven's hidden hand, brought low the towering Goliath in catastrophic and total defeat—hurling the Philistine giant down into the dust of irrecoverable ruin. So too, the love of God, stretched to its utmost tension across the wooden crossbeam of Calvary, unleashes its flawless and invincible arrow, completely shattering the dominion of sin and destroying Satan the adversary's kingdom through the perfectly aimed, never-failing missile of redeeming love and saving grace.

Observe closely: Christ, the Greater David, never once raised arms against any man in carnal enmity or personal vendetta—he rather fought against the malevolent forces of darkness who fought against every man in unseen, relentless warfare—against every man's eternal destiny that teeters on the precipice of perdition or promise. Echoing Ephesians' battle cry with granite-hewn resolve as hard as forged steel and a clarity of vision that shines like a lighthouse through the fog of war, he affirmed in the strongest possible terms that his battle was never against *'flesh and blood'* in ephemeral strife but against the hierarchical principalities that govern evil, against the ruling powers of darkness that enforce its dominion, and against the spiritual forces of wickedness that lurk in the heavenlies and ensnare the earthly. And in the climactic resolution, he conquered them utterly in a cataclysm of divine overturning—not by flexing the muscles of his unlimited power in brute, overwhelming force that crushes without mercy, nor by parading his might in flashy, attention-grabbing spectacles meant to awe and intimidate—but by the voluntary outpouring of his own pure, sinless blood, shed as the perfect, unspotted Lamb in an act of complete propitiation that satisfies divine justice forever, and by the unwavering word of his testimony, that bold declaration of truth which stands as an eternal, unbreakable stronghold against all assault.

Across the grand sweep of redemptive history capturing this age-long conflict—this undiminished duel between deities and dust that relentlessly unfurls from the curse pronounced in Eden's fallen garden to the triumphant revelation of the new heavens and new earth—no human blood has ever truly atoned for human sin. Not one drop shed in the endless cycle of violence and enmity that has pitted brother against brother, not even righteous Abel's blood crying out from the blood-soaked earth of fratricide's primal outrage, has possessed the power to reconcile sinners to God. Abel's innocent blood cried from the earth not for pardon but for judgment; only the spotless blood of Christ, shed willingly on the cross, speaks a better word—pleading remission instead of retribution—and atoning the sin that shattered fellowship with the Creator-God. Likewise, no human life has ever been offered as a sufficient sacrifice amid the relentless turmoil of mortal strife; not even Isaac upon the altar served as a vicarious ransom for humanity. Only his life—freely and sovereignly laid down—became the perfect, once-for-all payment that liberates us forever from sin's bondage and ushers us into the glorious freedom of the children of God. Behold the wondrous mystery: the One who formed an army of one—needed no ally, no battalion, no companion in arms—the Divine Lone Warrior who waged the fight entirely by his own sovereign self. By his sovereign power, the Victorious Messiah fought and won the battle for redemption single-handedly, not to hoard glory for himself in selfish ambition, but to bestow it lavishly upon the company of unworthy sinners. In grace beyond measure, he draws us—once estranged and helpless—into the radiant fellowship of his eternal triumph. Lo and behold, just this Jesus is all it took to win us the victory! Hallelujah!

THE LION WHO WAS TAMED INTO A LAMB BY HIS LOVE

Something else this gripping narrative of the Cross does so impressively well is unveil the profound paradox of Christ as a King—the Lion King, none other than *'the Lion of the tribe of Judah'* as Holy Scripture enshrines him (Rev 5:5)—who, in the throes of mortality's anguish—for the vicarious suffering of death—was veiled as a Suffering Servant, nay, even the Silent Lamb. For the exigencies of his redemptive mission demanded that he incarnate this Silent Lamb and Suffering Servant through a designated time—for an appointed season. Divine love is what tamed this Sovereign Lion, transforming him into a Sacrificial Lamb for the sins of men—the Paschal Lamb—and by the same token, rendering his sovereign might restrained through the reins of that very love—his sovereign will submit to God's redemption plan. Whereas "*all kinds of animals, birds, reptiles, and creatures of the sea are being tamed and have been tamed by man*" (Jas 3:7 BSB), solely the Almighty's love for humanity possessed the efficacy to tame this lion—the Lion King. His kenotic love molded him into the Lamb of God, ordained to bear away the sins of the whole world. The silence of the Lamb is never to be mistaken for a sign of weakness but must be seen for what it really and truly is: the quintessence of his love's dominion—his intentional vulnerability—his redemptive kryptonite. This theological mystery, where omnipotence bows to love's humility, probes the philosophical depths of a God whose strength embraces weakness for salvation. We stand awed by this love, the unparalleled agency capable of subjugating the Sovereign, forging him anew as the Paschal Lamb whose silence conceals inexhaustible might. No human hand could ever domesticate this Lion; it was exclusively his illimitable love for the wayward that orchestrated the victory of the Cross, weaving humanity into the sublime tapestry of grace, where love's surrender conquers sin and death in an everlasting gesture of redemption. Weakness—or more precisely, love, only insofar as it pertains to his unparalleled relationship with humans—although the selfless surrender of Christ may have been portrayed as his only weakness on the Cross, it nevertheless proved to be his greatest strength—the greatest demonstration of God's Omnipotence—displayed alongside his Omnibenevolence in redemptive harmony. This ostensible weakness and vulnerability in his love—or, to refine it, his love-weakness—has irrefutably been shown to be far much stronger than the strongest of men, constituting the apotheosis of divine authority that eclipses every vestige of earthly prowess. For God's love, not his might, is what it took and still takes to conquer the most hardhearted of men into making a heart-surrender to Christ as their Lord and personal Savior. Paul did not fail to pick up on the fact that " . . . *God's weakness is stronger than the greatest of human strength*" (1 Cor 1:25 NLT). You bet! It turns out, the Lamb of God is also a King—the true Lion King—the one who, even though had laid down his life without a fight, was yet not going to go down without a shout. Thus he died with a shout—the shout of a King. This seemingly trivial but profoundly significant detail about his final moments on the Cross was perfectly captured in Mark's Gospel, for he has it that "*And Jesus cried out with a loud voice, and breathed His last*" (Mark 15:37 NKJV). What I find particularly interesting and at the same time inspiring here is that a crucified Man who was hanging on the cross in excruciating pain, in a state of physical exhaustion, and at the point of his death was somehow able to summon the mental strength and physical energy to let out a bellowing sound—a shout signalling the parting of his ghost. Which tells me this was no ordinary shout at all.

This Man obviously did not give up his ghost in a wimp or whimper of defeat like most men are wont; he did so with an accompanying shout—a shout signalling the triumph of eternal accomplishment—signalling salvation's splendid success—his redemptive mission accomplished! And boy, was that one helluva shout, a shout that did not go unnoticed, especially not to the centurion who, given the circumstantial evidence he had been stitching together since he assumed the role of overseeing the execution of Jesus, was now being forced to admit that this was truly the

Son of God. And part of the reason he quickly arrived at this stupendous conclusion was, as Mark noted, precisely because " . . . *when the centurion, who stood opposite Him, saw that He cried out like this and breathed His last, he said, "Truly this Man was the Son of God!"* (Mark 15:39 NKJV). I particularly like that Mark did not gloss over the fact that the centurion's conviction only came full circle right after he *'saw that He cried out like this,'* which obviously left him perplexed and shaken. As it turns out, that is one transdimensional shout that was heard reverberating through all four corners of the universe—through all dimensions of reality and across all planes of existence. So significant was it that it was even heard echoing through the roofs of the third heaven. And the fact that it was significant enough to have triggered such a cosmic response from heaven: "*And Jesus cried out again with a loud voice, and yielded up His spirit. Then, behold, the veil of the temple was torn in two from top to bottom; and the earth quaked, and the rocks were split*" (Matt 27:50–51 NKJV)—is evidence enough to suggest that this was no mere human utterance by any metric but a celestial herald of love's conquest for God's beloved creation—shaking creation and shattering the sacred veil, proclaiming the love that conquered sin and death and opened the gates of heaven to men. Just like he foretold before his crucifixion: "*Do not marvel at this; for the hour is coming in which all who are in the graves will hear His voice and come forth—those who have done good, to the resurrection of life, and those who have done evil, to the resurrection of condemnation*" (John 5:28–29 NKJV). And true to His words, " . . . *the graves were opened; and many bodies of the saints who had fallen asleep were raised; and coming out of the graves after His resurrection, they went into the holy city and appeared to many*" (Matt 27:52–53 NKJV). We all know lambs do not roar, but this, more or less, was the Lamb of God roaring in the voice of a lion, just as he laid down his life in honor of doing the Father's will for humanity.

This was thus a shout like no other. And that, on the spot, puts him on record for being the first and the only Lamb who ever roared in the voice of a Lion. For the sovereign Lion King had, for the most part, been quiet all along—silent as 'the Suffering Servant' until now—even as silent as a lamb as he was being led to his own slaughter. But now that the deed had been done, for man had done the worst he could ever do—kill his body but not his soul, and his salvific mission had clearly been accomplished—there was no point in keeping silent anymore. He was now not only going to speak out; he was going to shout out loud. For even the heavens to hear him say with the full blast of a trumpet's sound, It is finished! And no doubt, it was indeed finished. Even David himself appears to have caught a glimpse of this glorious moment when he wrote, "*God has gone up with a shout, The LORD with the sound of a trumpet*" (Ps 47:5 NKJV). How you can tell he is not necessarily referring to God the Father but the Son is that the Father has never really stepped down from his throne in heaven, much less having to go back up with a shout; only God the Son did all that. So this is Jesus King David was prophesying about. Apparently, the shout of his departure only has for a parallel the shout of his re-entrance into man's world—at his resurrection when he appeared to Mary Magdalene with a shout of '*Rejoice!*' (See Matthew 28:9). You can say that again, perhaps doubling down in that effort after Paul: "*Rejoice in the Lord alway: and again I say, Rejoice*" (Phil 4:4 KJV). Rejoice because this innocent Man has just had his day in the Supreme Court of Heaven with his accusers, who had all conspired to have him killed, launching a successful appeal to heaven, as they say, and has been vindicated—totally discharged and declared guiltless from all the charges leveled against him. And guess what? Where the human verdict reached unanimously by the Sanhedrin was that "*He is deserving of death,*" his resurrection essentially came as the Divine verdict—the Sovereign verdict—a total reversal of that wicked and unjust human verdict (Matt 26:66 NKJV). So you can imagine why he would be so happy to share that joy and excitement with Mary, the first human witness of his resurrection, and with whoever else would come to believe in his redemptive accomplishments. So again rejoice, one has to say, because subject to the righteous verdict of the Sovereign Judge, death could no longer exercise any power or dominion over the precious life of this innocent Man, and hell could as such have no credible case against his sinless soul, and the grave could therefore stake no valid claims over his unblemished body: his resurrection was consequently inevitable. He has been vindicated; the Son of God has just been vindicated by God Himself. Because even though the Jews had thought, "*We have a law, and according to our law He ought to die, because He made Himself the Son of God,*" yet the resurrection verdict forever stands as His vindication, attesting with a note of finality that "*This is My beloved Son, in whom I am well pleased*" (John 19:7; Matthew 3:17 NKJV). Further allowing for Paul and others to arrive at the conclusion that Jesus was ultimately " . . . *shown to be the Son of God when he was raised from the dead by the power of the Holy Spirit. He is Jesus Christ our Lord*" (Rom 1:4 NLT). Everyone knows that death, as humanity has always experienced it, is irreversible—an inescapable end from which no one returns. History records no authentic comeback from the grave; the grave has always claimed final victory over every son and daughter of Adam. Yet astonishingly, this was not true of Jesus. The Scriptures boldly proclaim him the "*Firstborn from the dead*" (Col 1:18; Revelation 1:5), the Pioneer who shattered death's dominion and rose triumphant. Far from being the common criminal or blasphemous law-breaker his accusers falsely portrayed, he proved by His resurrection to be exactly who he claimed: the holy Son of God, victorious over sin and the grave.

In all honesty, if anyone truly deserves to be remembered and celebrated as a hero to humanity today, it is he—the unsung Hero who never received earthly acclaim for the immeasurable accomplishments he achieved on behalf of the entire human race. This brings to mind the title of James D. G. Dunn's work, *Jesus Remembered*—a title that, even judged by its cover, speaks volumes. It is worth emphasizing that the fact Jesus is still being remembered some two thousand years after his death, resurrection, and ascension is not due to any military victories or battlefield heroism recorded in history books—for he had none to boast of—nor is it merely for religious reasons. We do not remember the God Incarnate for his displays of power, though he is all-powerful; we do not recall him as a Cosmic Emperor (the sort the Caesars once aspired to become), though he created the cosmos. Rather, we remember him for his love and his sacrifice—given freely and personally for each one of us. For although God is all-powerful, he is yet not one and the same with his power; though Almighty, his personhood is distinct from his might. Though all-knowing, he is not to be equated with his knowledge; though all-present, he does not personify his own omnipresence. Yet when we declare that God is all-loving, we mean precisely this: he is one and the same with his love—his essence and his love are one and indivisible. In simplest terms, God is the living personification of his omnibenevolence, and his Son is the incarnate revelation of that very love. It is the undeniable and unforgettable impact of this love upon our lives and upon the world that explains why Christ continues to be venerated and celebrated in the hearts and minds of countless people across the globe today. A wise man once said—and the sentiment bears repeating—that it is far better to have one's name indelibly etched in the hearts of others and cherished long after departure than to have it infamously engraved on a million-dollar gravestone, only to be soon forgotten along with the memory of the self-conceited and unimpactful life you may have lived. Those whose lives have touched ours in profoundly significant ways will, without question, continue to be remembered and posthumously honored in our hearts long after they are gone. Although no tombstone or ossuary has ever been indisputably identified as belonging to Jesus of Nazareth, and no relic directly tied to him has received universal scholarly authentication—despite ongoing debate surrounding artifacts such as the James ossuary—recent archaeological discoveries beneath the Church of the Holy Sepulchre have uncovered traces of an ancient garden strikingly consistent with the Gospel accounts of his burial.

Yet in a far greater wonder, the name of this crucified Carpenter remains vibrantly alive today, spoken with reverence and treasured in the hearts of billions across the globe today—a living testimony far more enduring and powerful than any material artifact could ever be.

For he is most famously remembered and celebrated, not merely for religious reasons, but for the eternal significance of the salvific work of his Cross—his vicarious death for the sins of all mankind. Despite all of their concerted efforts by the Jewish Religious Establishment to stifle the testimony of the Apostles concerning Jesus, even going as far as imprisoning them, Luke yet records them saying, "*Did we not strictly command you not to teach in this name? And look, you have filled Jerusalem with your doctrine, and intend to bring this Man's blood on us!*" (Acts 5:28 NKJV). Again, he writes that:

> "Now when they saw the boldness of Peter and John, and perceived that they were uneducated and untrained men, they marveled. And they realized that they had been with Jesus. And seeing the man who had been healed standing with them, they could say nothing against it. But when they had commanded them to go aside out of the council, they conferred among themselves, saying, "What shall we do to these men? For, indeed, that a notable miracle has been done through them is evident to all who dwell in Jerusalem, and we cannot deny it. But so that it spreads no further among the people, let us severely threaten them that from now on they speak to no man in this name." So they called them and commanded them not to speak at all nor teach in the name of Jesus" (Acts 4:13–18 NKJV).

That is quite reminiscent of the ancient Roman punishment termed *damnatio memoriae*, which often involved using state powers for the debarment from all public life, the mention of the names and the works of those individuals who were considered traitors. Although the Jewish leaders are seen here doing everything within their powers and even going ultra vires (beyond their powers) in their attempt to forbid the Apostles of Jesus from ever preaching the Gospel in His Name post-resurrection, they failed woefully in that effort, evinced by the fact he is still being remembered today and his Name is arguably more famous today than ever before. And not only were the Apostles derring-doery about testifying of the risen Jesus, they were willing to do so at any and all cost, even when it meant laying down their lives. The only reason in the world that they were willing to venture this far is because his love and sacrifice have had a tremendous impact on their immediate lives, as well as their eternal destinies. The same is the salvation testimony of billions of Christians all around the world today concerning Christ the Savior, ultimately because they have all come to the realization and belief that everything he ever did was for them—all he accomplished in life from womb to tomb—from the Cross to the grave—and from the grave to the skies of heaven was for their sakes.

CONCLUSION

As we trace God's heart across the ages, it becomes gloriously evident that from eternity past, the Creator has desired only the highest good for mankind—his perfect best, lavished without reservation, even at the staggering cost of his own life. To him, that price was no obstacle but a willing offering of love. Thus, we can wholeheartedly affirm his solemn declaration: "*I lavish unfailing love to a thousand generations, forgiving iniquity, rebellion, and sin. But I do not leave the guilty unpunished . . .* " (Exod 34:7 NLT). The cross of Jesus Christ stands as the breathtaking fulfillment of both truths: divine justice satisfied and divine mercy unleashed, as the Father pours out the penalty for sin upon his innocent Son in the place of guilty, death-deserving sinners. The sinless Man of Sorrows was wounded and crushed not for any wrongdoing of his own, but solely for ours—pure love absorbing the wrath we deserved. Doubtless, love and self-sacrifice are one unmistakable legacy that the God-Man left behind when he walked the face of the earth. Love is what brought him down here in the first place—love is what kept him around here the whole time, only for as long as was necessary for him to turn our mission impossible into a mission accomplished. For so impossible a mission it was to find among the sons and daughters of men a sinless and morally perfect individual who would take a redemptive stand in the place of all sinful humanity—a perfect and spotless Paschal Lamb who would die a vicarious death for all sinners—until the Jesus of history stepped into time and changed all history forever. Where Adam's selfish, sinful act single-handedly made the rest of us sinners—equally as guilty—Jesus' selfless, righteous act single-handedly made all of us righteous—equally as justified and acquitted guiltless.

With this, the words of Scripture are in agreement that: "*Therefore, as through one man's offense judgment came to all men, resulting in condemnation, even so through one Man's righteous act the free gift came to all men, resulting in justification of life. For as by one man's disobedience many were made sinners, so also by one Man's obedience many will be made righteous*" (Rom 5:18–19 NKJV). So believe me when I say, without God's redemptive love for humanity, there literally would be no story to tell about the Cross at all—none worth telling here, none worth retelling elsewhere, none worth telling from the Genesis to Revelation of Scripture. The Gospel, in its final analysis, is ultimately about God's love for man, as his love is what wrought salvation for mankind. God is the personification of love, and his Son became the pleromatic embodiment of the same love on cosmic soil—the walking, talking expression of God's love for man. Almost as though God previously had all divine mysteries pertaining to his love hidden and locked away, only to have them unveiled in Christ for the world to see for the first time since the world began. Such that all Divine mysteries only finally became an 'open secret' in Christ, which now means that the Divine personhood of God can at this moment be known for the first time since time began. And so, if any man is ever going to understand whatever depths there are to the mysteries of God, he must first have to understand the depths that there are to the mysteries of his Divine love for man. But if you cannot understand the cruciform demonstration of God's love for man, then the chances are that you are never ever going to understand God—you are hardly ever going to see any rationale behind his redemptive acts. Well, if someone were to ask me, "*What is it you think God loves to do best and enjoys doing the most?*" I would simply say 'love.' God is simply at his best when he loves, and loving the object, man in particular, is what he enjoys doing the most. He derives no greater pleasure than in having the Divine love lavishly channeled toward people. Love is who God is, remember?

So he is basically being himself when he loves. So without a doubt, love is the greatest expression there is in God. After all, the greatest

Divine act on record yet hinges upon God loving man enough to become a Man first, and then every other act he may have performed in his incarnate humanity must have had to flow freely from the first historical act of Divine love: the Incarnation. God loving man enough to become a Man Himself is quite a big deal; in fact, the biggest deal in the Bible. Everything else would have to be considered secondary. That already makes for quite a landing page for our redemptive love story, quite a mouthful already, or at least so it seems, but if you would believe it, we have only succeeded in breaking the ice; we have yet to scratch the surface of the profound depths of the Divine love for man. That is to say that all we have looked at so far happens to be just one angle from which to view God's love for man altogether, but there are other angles, and very much like this one, they too are definitely worth exploring. But the truth is and remains that the depth, the height, the width, and the length of the Divine love are far too deep for utterance—a subject about which we have so much to say but so few words to express them, whereupon the gross limitations of our human vocabulary are suddenly laid bare as soon as we attempt to discuss these things adeptly and in-depth. Anyhow, that should not stop us from trying nor disbar us from making the honest effort to both contemplate and articulate the Divine love as much as we are enabled.

3

That Man Was Foreknown, Foreordained, and Foreloved by God

Divine love for man at first sight, nay, at first thought . . .

In the spirit of reverent theological inquiry, we find ourselves irresistibly drawn to ponder—within the safe bounds of orthodoxy—the eternal counsels of the Triune God before creation itself. There, right behind the pre-Adamic scenes, in the perfect perichoretic communion of Father (unbegotten), Son (eternally begotten), and Holy Spirit (eternally proceeding), a unified divine will hashed out not only the blueprint for the creation of the cosmos but also the gracious provision for the redemption of mankind. Long before the first word of Genesis sounded, the Godhead sovereignly decreed a plan whereby one of the Three would venture into time and adorn flesh to accomplish the saving work foreseen from eternity. Scripture itself encourages such careful reflection, granting us glimpses of this precosmic resolve where love, wisdom, and purpose converged to secure our salvation even before we existed.

PRECOSMIC DELIBERATIONS: THE TRIUNE GOD'S ETERNAL PLAN FOR MAN'S REDEMPTION

In the eternal deliberations of the Godhead—long before the creation of Adam and the foreseen catastrophe of his fall—the Father, Son, and Holy Spirit, in perfect unity of will and love, considered every possible path for humanity's salvation. With sovereign foresight, they discerned and unanimously affirmed that no other way would suffice: redemption required nothing less than God himself becoming man. One of the divine Persons must enter human history, take upon himself our nature, and personally bear the cost of the ransom needed to deliver Adam's fallen race. Since every descendant of Adam bears the stain of hereditary sin, no one could ever attain the sinless perfection that divine justice requires—a spotless, unblemished sacrifice. The ransom needed to redeem us was therefore utterly beyond our means: we could neither pay it ourselves nor find within our race anyone qualified to stand in our place. Humanity, in its depravity, stood bankrupt before a holy God, incapable of financing or furnishing the perfect Holocaust that justice demanded. As the Scripture testifies in the Psalms of David: "*No one can redeem the life of another or give to God a ransom for them—the ransom for a life is costly, no payment is ever enough—so that they should live on forever and not see decay. For all can see that the wise die, that the foolish and the senseless also perish, leaving their wealth to others*" (Ps 49:7–10 NIV). Seeing that no commensurate ransom would ever emerge from Adam's sin-stained descendants, the momentous conclusion inevitably followed that a Person of the Godhead must himself descend into the very essence of creaturehood, taking upon himself the very human nature destined for destruction, thereby furnishing from within the Godhead the oblation adequate to reconcile all things. This was the indispensable path if God was ever going to save the image-bearing race he had purposed and envisioned to create from dateless eternity—a people already held dear in the eternal affections of his love, preconceived and treasured before ever the worlds were framed. Thereupon, the Psalmist, moved by divine inspiration, further proclaims a sobering yet hopeful contrast: those who trust in their own strength and wealth, along with those who admire and follow them, are like sheep appointed to death—death itself will shepherd them to the grave, where their bodies decay far from earthly splendor. Yet for the upright who trust in the Lord, a glorious reversal awaits. With confident assurance he declares on behalf of all God's redeemed, "*But God will redeem my soul from the power of the grave, for He shall receive me*" (Ps 49:15 NKJV). Here shines the gospel hope foreshadowed—death's dominion broken, the righteous taken safely into the everlasting presence of God himself.

Thus, from eternity, the incarnation and atonement were settled as the only adequate remedy for the sin that had not yet occurred but was already known—a resolution born not of necessity imposed from without, but of boundless love within the Godhead itself. Such were the veiled, pre-creational, backstage deliberations of the Divine Will, destined to be unveiled in the holy oracles. These proleptic counsels, antecedent to the genesis of the visible world, reveal not merely the pre-existence of the Creator before his works, but likewise the anteriority of his love toward mankind, which antedated the molding of the first clay. Necessarily so, for the Genesis hexaemeron narrative itself assures us that humanity's origination was in no manner an improvisation or secondary notion; indeed, the human race was eternally conceived within the loving purposes of God prior to the inception of creation's labors. This implies, moreover, that God, from the exalted perch of his foreknowledge, was fully apprised in advance that the only path to fulfill this Herculean labor was through his 'Incarnation'—a descent wherein he would literally assume manhood and appear in the theater of redemptive history, humbling himself to become the very *Agnus Dei* essential for the atoning mission to secure for all humanity the remission of sins—past, present, and future—through the outpouring of his own blood. This precosmic roundtable—predating Creation, the Fall, and Redemption—is what eventually led up to the greatest divine decisions ever made, and I mean the most consequentially unprecedented decisions there ever would be in the heavens or on earth—God creating man in his image and likeness and then becoming a man to redeem the same divine image in man.

And how amazing it is to realize that the supreme act of the Divine Will has everything to do with meeting man's greatest needs: the redemption of the soul, the securing of eternal existence, and the glorious resurrection (anastasis) of the human spirit. Far from being an afterthought, the eternal counsels of the Trinity—encompassing both creation and its foreseen redemption—were profoundly centered upon man. In boundless love, the Triune God ordained all things with humanity's ultimate good in view, making the rescue and exaltation of image-bearers the very heartbeat of his sovereign purpose. Yet this was no light decision; it required the Creator to surrender everything—even his own life—because he had sovereignly judged his image-bearers worthy of such total devotion. As Jesus himself wisely taught, no prudent builder begins a tower without first counting the cost. His exact words: "*For which of you, intending to build a tower, does not sit down first and count the cost, whether he has enough to finish it—lest, after he has laid the foundation, and is not able to finish, all who see it begin to mock him, saying, 'This man began to build and was not able to finish'?*" (Luke 14:28–30 NKJV). How much more, then, did the Son—who gave this admonition—carefully reckon the staggering price of redemption long before the foundation of the world, fully aware that the toll of his forthcoming redemptive sojourn on earth, the price of securing everlasting salvation for humanity would ultimately cost him everything he held most dear—exacting the fullest measure of divine self-giving. Apurpose, it was only after pondering with utmost deliberation every avenue of grace and arriving at the staggering conviction that humanity, fashioned in God's image and likeness, was worth his priceless sacrificial oblation, that he proceeded undeterred. More confounding yet, the whisper of divine foreknowledge—that man's birth would be chased by his downfall—neither swayed the hand of the Father, nor dissuaded the zeal of the Son, nor dimmed the fervor of the Spirit from enacting the vast theodrama ordained for the yet-unformed race; nay, the Three in One surged ahead with the soteriological enterprise—undaunted by the exorbitant expenditure—the Eternal Word's descent into time, veiling his majesty in mortal flesh to effect the liberation of the captive race. This altruistic venture promptly witnessed him undertaking the most adventurous odyssey of transspatial migration—from the celestial heights of hyperborean spire to the terrestrial depths of telluric mire, on a mission of utter self-oblation, which had him irrevocably intermarry his Divinity with man's humanity.

MAN: PRECONCEIVED IN THE HEART OF GOD'S LOVE

It is worth reemphasizing that, prior to the creative acts recounted in Genesis, man was uniquely and exclusively predestined to become the object of God's love—preconceived in the heart of his eternal affection. The doctrine of predestination blooms as love's tender first whisper to the frail sons of dust—foreseeing the shadowed fall from Eden's grace, yet weaving threads of chosen redemption's embrace with fingers of sovereign grace. Despite God's prescient awareness of mankind's forthcoming lapse into transgression following the act of creation, he yet decided to foreordain us from ages unbegun that we should become recipients of eternal grace in time, marking one of his earliest, most poignant bestowals of love upon our yet-unbreathed forms. Looking at the whole roadmap of how God saves people (within the framework of the ordo salutis)—from his foreknowledge to his forelove and foreordination—we could see that his foreknowledge regarding humanity's status as bearers of the imago Dei kindled within the bottomless abyss of his heart a love primordial and profound—that forelove, wherein this forelove decisively shaped his choice to foreordain or predestine us from the get-go. Put simply, predestination is basically God's poetic way of saying "*I love you*" to us humans before we even existed. In essence, humanity's profound significance to God is evident, for their worth was matched by the love poured out upon them. Should humanity have held lesser significance in the divine estimation, one would struggle to discern the rationale behind the extraordinary commitment expended in the undertaking of redemption. Such a perspective finds robust confirmation in the biblical testimony that God already had the names of every human person ever born "*. . . written in the Book of Life from the foundation of the world . . .*" (Rev 17:8 NKJV—cf. Revelation 3:5). The phrase 'from the foundation of the world' is not necessarily referring to a literal moment when God laid a physical foundation for the earth, as if building a structure like ours, nor does it refer to any point within the six days of creation. The term "foundation," derived from the Greek *katabolē*, refers to the moment of inception or the initial conception of an idea, distinct from themelios, which pertains to a literal structural foundation (cf. Rev 21:19; Acts 16:26). Thus, *'katabolē'* signifies the first instance when an idea occurred or was first conceived in the mind of a creator or an inventor—what someone might want to call the light-bulb moment. In effect, it captures God's initial spark of thought, the moment when the idea of creation was first envisioned.

Consequently, the incunabulum of the created order, God's "light-bulb moment," for project creation precedes the six days of creative activity recorded in the hexaemeron. The pretemporal inscription of every person's name in the pages of the Lamb's Book of Life, etched before the dawn of eternity, before the world's formation and any act of genesis, bears witness that each individual was as a cherished preconception in the mind and affections of the Book's Sovereign Composer. Evidently, the Almighty's antemundane meditations on humanity were wholly grounded in his redemptive agape, with the entire architecture of existence arising from those same love-infused thoughts and antecedent inspirations tailored to humanity's redemption. This love, extended to mankind post-creation, perfectly mirrors the same love that was mutually shared among all three Persons in the Community of the Godhead before creation. Creating man to reflect the imago Dei also meant showering him with the very same love that existed in the Godhead, flourishing greatly in that community ever before the thought of embarking on Project Creation was conceived. Jesus affirmed for a fact that " . . . *You loved Me before the foundation of the world*" (John 17:24 NKJV). Divine love is the bond of perfection that unites all three distinct personalities of the Trinity together in a single, eternal, and indivisible existence. Thus, by imparting the divine similitude and form upon humanity at the point of creation, the divine will perforce extended that same divine love to humankind at the same instant. Beyond the confines of the Divine fellowship of the Father, the Son, and the Holy Spirit, this love had never ever been shared with any other entity; humanity alone claims the unparalleled sacred privilege of savoring the exquisite draught of the Creator's love—both as inaugurator and as ultimate beneficiary. Love, as certain thoughtful observers have articulated, is fundamentally a deliberate choice or willful decision, not merely an emotional impulse or fleeting affection—a series of decisions God made before the world's inception, not only to have man created after his image and likeness, but also to venture a thousand steps further in guaranteeing his redemption at the event of the Fall.

Since humanity was truly fashioned as the bearer of God's own image, divine love for man is, in a profound sense, an extension of God's love for himself. No external persuasion was ever needed for God to cherish mankind; loving the sons of men with the same intensity as he loves his own essence flows naturally and necessarily from his being—more spontaneously than any other act directed toward creation. Just as he required no counsel or anyone outside the Trinity to convince him to create us in his image and likeness, so he needs no urging to love us as he loves himself. If earthly mothers and fathers, imperfect as they are, instinctively need no convincing to love their own flesh and blood—children who merely bear their connatural likeness—how infinitely greater would God's love be for all those who are bearers of his Divine image and likeness? Ultimately, the unique reason humanity stands alone as the primary recipient of God's love arises directly from our creation in his likeness—the eternal Trinitarian resolve to form a creature that would reflect and resemble the Divine glory, thereby evoking from God a love as natural as his own self-existence. Far surpassing the fleeting spark of *coup de foudre—"love at first sight"*—that sudden infatuation born of visual meeting—God's love for humanity is better understood as "*love at first thought.*" It was kindled in the eternal counsels of predestination, long before any creature existed to be seen—a love ignited in the smithy of timeless predestination, woven into the very fabric of preexistent afflatus. The mere thought of creating image-bearers in his likeness was, in and of itself, enough to set ablaze the unquenchable fire of God's affection for mankind. Thus, humanity was cherished with infinite passion long before we were formed, loved from the very moment we were first conceived in the eternal mind of the Creator-God.

THE *IMAGO DEI:* HUMANITY AS GOD'S LIVING REFLECTION

From the get-go, God's original idea and foundational purpose was to create a unique entity other than himself—yet very much like himself—a consummate representation of his Divine Personhood, embodied in a created form—distinct from the Holy Trinity, yet bearing the indelible seal of the *imago Dei.* This rational image-bearer he called 'man.' That effectively answers David the Psalmist's question: what is man? For man is no less than a living portrait of the Creator-God, embodied in the fragile beauty of dust and breath. Now, it is easy to see why God's natural disposition toward man would be one of fervent love, unbridled devotion, and providential care, as it all boils down to the fact that he beholds no less than a reflection of himself in man and not merely a product of creation—he beholds the sole bearer of his communicable attributes among the created order—the only creature crafted from the wellspring of his divine affection. In reality, to hate or despise one's own reflection will be tantamount to self-loathing—an impossible contradiction for the God whose essence is love. Comfortingly, as any storyteller knows, no character in the tale of existence truly abhors their own reflection—not even the unchanging God who pens the plot. Thus, it stands to reason that God cannot really hate man, because hating man would essentially mean hating his own reflection and, by extension, himself. Therefore, his love for man is inevitable, rooted in the very act of creating a mirror of himself. Yet, there exists a caveat: in the case of genetic apostasy from the archetypal form—a deviation from that primal divine blueprint and resemblance in which humanity was originally fashioned—toward such, God is naturally inclined to despise, with his divine holiness recoiling in righteous abhorrence, and even worse—grief-stricken rejection. Sin constitutes a tragic apostasy from our archetypal form, provoking divine wrath against the distortion while never negating his foundational love for the image itself. A striking historical illustration of this genetic apostasy from God's image is the antediluvian perversion that triggered the hydro-cataclysm of Noah's day—a widespread contamination that corrupted the genetic fabric of the entire human population on earth except Noah and his kin, making the great flood a necessary act of retributive justice—an unavoidable prophylactic cleansing. Thereby preserving the lineage through which the uncorrupted Image would one day perfectly appear in Christ.

But so long as it bears the name 'man'—remains recognizably human—retains the indelible vestige of humanity—echoing God's faithful replica, the eternal principle holds firm: God, in his aseity and absolute simplicity, cannot but love and value the human form he first imaged forth as his undying reflection—he simply cannot withhold his love from that primal essence. In the light of this theological truth, we rightly affirm that even though God is no respecter of persons, yet, he is a respecter of his image and likeness in the persons of men. Let me explain: in his infinite justice, God exhibits no partiality in his dealings with mankind or preference for any individual predicated on worldly distinctions, superficial qualities, or personal virtues alone; instead, he holds in highest regard the manifestation of his eternal image and likeness as it resides in the hearts and forms of mortal men and women. This venerable principle of the imago Dei, representing the indelible stamp of his character upon the soul, transcends all other attributes and emerges unequivocally as the preeminent and most defining feature of mankind. Looking back, we gain clearer insight into God's profound exasperation with the unchecked teratologic degradation plaguing the Noahic generation, culminating in the expression of deep sorrow and regrets over the creation of mankind, consequently leaving him no choice but to enact severe restorative judgments to ultimately realign mankind with his redemptive plans. This is captured in the words: "*And the LORD was sorry that He had made man on the earth, and He was grieved in His heart. So the LORD said, "I will destroy man whom I have created from the face of the earth, both man and beast, creeping thing and birds of the air, for I am sorry that I have made them*" (Gen 6:6–7 NKJV). However, one should not confuse this divine regret with mere transactional dissatisfaction, as we might term 'buyer's remorse' in contemporary lingo, as this lament reflects the profound anguish of a Creator whose heart is broken: "*This is not the destiny I envisioned for you—you bear no resemblance to the man I formed you to be at the dawn of creation. Crafted to manifest the glory of my essence, you have mutated into an unrecognizable, grotesque inversion.*" Far from suggesting that God was ready to wash his hands of humanity altogether, because we need only recall His immediate promise of redemption in Genesis 3:15—the Protoevangelium spoken in the very shadow of the Fall, assuring that the seed of the woman would crush the serpent and secure ultimate victory for the fallen race. Therefore, the ominous decree in Genesis 6 cannot be interpreted as forsaking or threatening the destruction of the very race he had sworn to save. Having planted the seed of redemption—a promise of rescue that echoes through the ages—God irrevocably binds himself to our human story.

THE FLOOD'S PURPOSE: PRESERVING THE REDEEMABLE LINEAGE

But why the Diluvian destruction then? Someone may yet be prompted to ask. First, you have to understand that what unfolded pre-Flood was far much darker than mere procreation after the fallen Adamic race—this was a case of the procreation of hybrid humans—the so-called fallen "*sons of God*"—those enigmatic giants born of forbidden unions between fallen angels and the daughters of men (Gen. 6:1–4). Entities alien to the redeemable thread of God's covenant people, whose hybrid essence ultimately threatened the genealogical integrity essential for the Savior's parthenogenic conception—God's incarnation among men. By no stretch are we dealing with the same humans God was looking to redeem at some distant point in redemptive history or the fullness of time, as put in Scripture, for the genes of these monsters, by their very definition, are irredeemably corrupt—leaving them neither men nor angels in both spiritual state and bodily estate. Perforce, the Flood served as a targeted eradication to halt these hybrids from overtaking and supplanting pure humanity on the planet, particularly before the promised Savior could enter the world. Without such a purge, total corruption would have foreclosed any possibility of redemption. In essence, God was pruning the human story's wild overgrowth—those irreparably altered chimeric beings, their essence twisted beyond mending by celestial rebellion—while preserving the one uncorrupted Noachian branch: Noah and his family, the quiet carriers of the Adamic image—drifting as seeds of salvation—afloat on a wooden promise toward a renewed world, where the echoes of Eden might yet resound in the light of Christ's dawn. The deluge, accordingly, reveals itself not as blind fury but as a deliberate cleansing: eradicating the hopeless corruptions stemming from angelic defiance that nearly overwhelmed the chosen heritage, thus preserving the arrival of the God-incarnate, the ultimate aim of creation's sabbath fulfillment. In the ark of Noah, preserved as the nascent godly enclave, shines the paradigm of baptismal foreshadowing—judgmental torrents giving way to the covenantal rainbow, underscoring that God's devotion to his reflected image abides, elevated via the cross to ultimate glory.

But so long as man stays man—clinging to his essential humanity—God's own image stamped on his soul, God finds himself irresistibly compelled by the very nature of his being to mutually bestow his familial love and solicitude upon him, as though he were an intimate member of the Blessed Trinity, pulling that soul right into a communion that echoes the eternal circumincession of Father, Logos, and Pneuma. Conversely, just as soon as it defects from being a man—straying from that divine essence through apostasy from authentic human nature—he is unable to extend the same love and providential care, leaving divine intimacy withdrawn in commensurate horror—a visceral aversion mirroring the prior ardor of embrace. It is for this reason that God does not and cannot bestow his philostorgy on his angels—for the archangelic orders, notwithstanding their unfallen perfection, transcendent glory, and ethical immaculacy, remain extrinsic to the soteriological agape that pulses within the perichoretic reciprocity of the Holy Triad. Thus, establishing for a fact that God harbors no less than love in his heart for man. And part of the reason he commands each man to love his fellow man like he loves himself is because all men were created in his image and likeness. In a similar vein, he too cannot but love man like he loves himself. By parallel reasoning also, he too is bound to love and treasure mankind in the manner he loves and treasures himself. Because, God, more than everybody else, recognizes the intrinsic value of each human person, and that value stems directly from the investiture of his image and likeness in the creation of man at the beginning. Hence, this Creator, whose essence is love, channels the countless streams of his love exclusively toward humanity, underscoring the doctrine of '*imago Dei*'—humans alone bear God's image (Gen 1:26–27). This singular focus affirms humanity's unique role in his vast work of creation, re-echoing our respective call to love God and neighbor—theophilanthropism (Matt 22:37–39). If there was no value to the human person before the eyes of God, and if the investiture of the divine image and likeness in mankind meant nothing to him, then it would be difficult to see why he would go on lavishing such boundless love on the same. As is consistent with his Divine Nature, at no point did God suddenly stop seeing man as the reflection of his image and likeness, the only exception being the *Naphil* or Nephilim—neither man nor angel.

This truth also accounts for why God never abandoned the human race even after their sin and fall in Eden. Far from turning away in despair, he immediately pledged their redemption—or, more accurately, unveiled the redemptive plan he had sovereignly prepared from all eternity—because his divine foresight and foreknowledge had already anticipated every detail of what would unfold in the garden. Nothing escaped his perfect forevision—none took him by surprise; every contingency was foreseen and encompassed within his sovereign purpose. It further reveals why, even now, he remains tirelessly committed to the pursuit of the lost: he is ever the Good Shepherd who leaves the ninety-nine redeemed in the safely of the fold to go seeking the one still unredeemed, journeying to the farthest ends of the earth until that one is found and restored to the glory of his perfect image in Christ. God will never reach a point of giving up on his image-bearers, for in his eyes they remain infinitely worth dying for—precious enough that he would lay down his own life to redeem and reclaim them.

Consequently, in this gripping flood narrative of Genesis, we gaze upon this scene with a sense of holy wonder and deep respect, recognizing a form of justice that unfolds—Divine judgment dispensed not in arbitrary rage or blind destruction but in tender, purposeful love, a sovereign decree that irrevocably testifies to the unshakable commitment of God's profound love to secure humanity's ultimate wellbeing and preservation amid the deluge of depravity that threatened to engulf all. Ultimately proving that, yes, there is love even in judgment—an indissoluble union of justice and mercy where the thunder of correction resounds with the gentle cadence of affection that seeks restoration over ruin. Here, woven seamlessly into the fabric of discipline, we find threads of unbreakable bond between perfect righteousness and boundless pity, where the crashing waves of corrective thunder merge with the soft, melodic whispers of heartfelt devotion, always aiming not for mere annihilation but for the careful mending and uplifting of what was broken. In a parallel vein, the judgment of sin upon the cross of God's beloved Son Jesus Christ equally turned out to be the greatest, most transcendent expression of God's unfathomable love toward man in all its cosmic breadth and intimate depth, where the weight of divine wrath against iniquity became the crucible for eternal reconciliation and unbounded grace poured forth. Forsooth, God's judgment is always a testament to his love—for every act of divine judgment in Scripture stands as a living monument to his core essence of love—a recurring, healing melody that pulses through the corridors of time, serving as irrefutable proof of his gentle, relentless chase after the lost, not a torrent of uncontrolled vengeance but a light bent through the crystal of love itself, designed to bind up wounds, buy back the fallen, and elevate the cherished work of his hands back to the radiant glory it was always meant to reflect. In truth, nothing external compelled God to bring mankind into existence, let alone to fashion us in his own image and likeness—there was no cosmic necessity, no "or else" hanging over his decision. The creation of image-bearers was a wholly voluntary act of divine freedom, entered into with perfect foreknowledge of the overarching ramifications that would follow from granting free moral agency to creatures stamped with his imprint. He sovereignly chose to extend to this unique work of artistry the same sacred, self-giving affection that has eternally existed within the Trinity, thereby making humanity the privileged recipient of a love once shared only among Father, Son, and Holy Spirit. From these profound truths, we may justly conclude that God, being morally perfect, bears an intrinsic responsibility to love the mortal reflection of himself embodied in man—a love equal in depth to the affection he bears toward his own essence, toward his eternal Son, and toward his Holy Spirit. This love is no acquired duty but flows as naturally from his perfect nature as breath from a living soul. Indeed, in loving humanity God grants no mere favor or indulgence, any more than the Father bestows special privilege upon the Son by delighting in him from eternity. Rather, it is the inevitable overflow of divine goodness toward the unique creature fashioned to mirror his own glorious Personhood.

THE OBLIGATORY VERSUS SUPEREROGATORY ACTS OF GOD'S LOVE

From a theophilosophical perspective, virtuous deeds fall into two distinct categories: those that are obligatory, rooted in the binding claims of duty and moral imperative, and those that are supererogatory—acts of extraordinary goodness that go far beyond what is required, manifesting heroic virtue. Obligatory goodness is owed to those who, by ties of kinship or profound relational entitlement, rightfully claim our care as a matter of justice. A clear example is the nurturing love and familial care that parents owe their own children—not merely a cultural convention, but a deep moral expectation inscribed in nature itself. Supererogatory acts, by contrast, arise in the boundless realm of grace, where kindness flows freely without compulsion, extending mercy and benevolence to those who hold no inherent claim upon us. Across many cultures, especially in the structured societies of the West, the neglect of parental duty is deemed so grave that authorities may intervene, removing children from harmful environments and placing them under state guardianship, wherein custodial authority is assumed to safeguard the child's welfare. This underscores that parental care is not optional heroism but a fundamental moral obligation owed to one's offspring, so no special accolades or recognition are bestowed for fulfilling it; for parents are merely discharging the sacred stewardship inherently entrusted to them by the act of bringing children into the world. This is precisely what Jesus was alluding to when he taught parabolically, saying:

> "*And which of you, having a servant plowing or tending sheep, will say to him when he has come in from the field, 'Come at once and sit down to eat'? But will he not rather say to him, 'Prepare something for my supper, and gird yourself and serve me till I have eaten and drunk, and afterward you will eat and drink'? Does he thank that servant because he did the things that were commanded him? I think not. So likewise you, when you have done all those things which you are commanded, say, 'We are unprofitable servants. We have done what was our duty to do*" (Luke 17:7–10 NKJV).

Here, he highlights that the master of the house does not so much as 'thank that servant because he did the things that were commanded of him.' Part of the reason he would not so much express gratitude is because he owes the servant none for the performance of the duties for which he was hired. And also, the servant, in turn, having received no gratitude, nor praise for the performance of obligatory tasks, cannot then say of himself, "*I am an 'unprofitable' servant*"; he totally refrains from self-reproach in the absence of recompense. Similarly, we do not hail parents as heroes for basic child-rearing or affection—it is their baseline responsibility. Given that childbearing, perforce, begets the responsibility of childcaring. The true outlier, therefore, is the abject neglect of this parental responsibility.

By the same principle, God's love for many, before the Fall, was chiefly an obligatory virtue—an inevitable imperative flowing from the very essence (ousia) of his being, rather than a supererogatory act of extraordinary generosity. Since love constitutes the core of his nature, it necessarily pours forth toward the creature made in his image with the same intensity that characterizes the perichoretic communion of Father, Son, and Holy Spirit. To love man less would fracture the undivided simplicity of God, where nature and will are perfectly one. Human experience echoes this across cultures: a mother's instinctive bond to her child is not necessarily driven by altruism, nor does it arise from selfless generosity, but from the profound mind-body compulsion of procreation, which in turn mirrors how God's love for humanity is less a merciful act of humility and more a jubilant outpouring of infinite loving-kindness. That is to say, this love transcends voluntary charity, it is no elective benevolence but the philosophical necessity arising from God's boundless, overflowing abundance: just as Plotinus's transcendent 'One'—the ultimate, ineffable source of all reality—effortlessly emanates into the diverse multiplicity of existence without ever diminishing itself, so too does the Father's eternal love for the Son and the Spirit naturally extend and illuminate the human soul, which bears the imprint of that same divine pattern of relational unity. his love effortlessly overflows or emanates downward upon humanity in a natural, inevitable cascade of goodness and plenitude, much like light radiating from the sun or water spilling from a full vessel. Evidently, God sought to manifest the infinite expanse of his sacred affection (omnibenevolence) far beyond the intimate fellowship of the Trinity by creating a reflection of himself in some other self, deliberately fashioned as the ideal vessel for receiving the outpouring of his boundless love. Now imagine, by contrast, parents extending the same level of care and affection to a neighbor's child or an orphan bereft of kin, despite having no such obligation—this surpasses their core duties and qualifies as a supererogatory act of goodness. Caring for one's own offspring is standard; embracing another's is exceptional—a sublime altruism worthy of praise. Consequently, let us extend this framework to the dynamic between God and humanity. Initially, God's love and provision for humankind—fashioned in his image and likeness, akin to divine family—align with obligatory goodness. As bearers of his essence, humans are essentially his progeny, so his affection toward them in their original state is wholly anticipated, nothing more.

Christ himself corroborates this filial reciprocity, noting that the Father extends the same love to humanity as he does to the Son, since they belong to him by creation. His exact words: "*I in them, and You in Me; that they may be made perfect in one, and that the world may know that You have sent Me, and have loved them as You have loved Me*" (John 17:23 NKJV). Thus, God's default posture of benevolence toward unfallen humanity constitutes his obligatory good act, the baseline of his moral character. But the wonder deepens as the story unfolds to its saving end, for God did not halt his love there. Even after humanity's rebellion and fall, when they aligned with another spiritual lineage—essentially becoming offspring of Satan the devil—his commitment persisted. As Jesus declared to those under such influence, "*You belong to your father, the devil, and you want to carry out your father's desires. He was a murderer from the beginning, not holding to the truth, for there is no truth in him. When he lies, he speaks his native language, for he is a liar and the father of lies*" (John 8:44, NKJV). And again, we are told, "*He who sins is of the devil [not of God], for the devil has sinned from the beginning . . .* " (I John 3:8 NKJV—the words in parentheses are added). This indictment, though contextually aimed at a crowd in time, applies broadly to all of Adam's descendants, who, through primordial sin, cut ties with God's paternity and fell under satanic sway, much like the prodigal son who severed ties in defiance—storming off in anger. God's choice to sustain his love amid this estrangement—toward sinners no longer his own—marks a profound supererogatory gesture. The just and holy Creator withheld no affection, even as we rejected our heritage. Throughout the journey, from creation's first breath to redemption's consummate sigh, God's love for mankind has endured unchanging and utterly unwavering: he cherished us at creation—when we first belonged to him; he persisted in that love, pursuing us through the Fall, despite our adversarial adoption; and he expressed it perfectly in redemption—reclaiming us back into his filial and familial embrace. This continuity reveals a love unaltered by our waywardness, as such unchanging love defies the storms of change. Wherefore do we have the Scripture testifying to that effect: "*But God showed his great love for us by sending Christ to die for us while we were still sinners*" (Rom 5:8 NLT). Great love it is indeed—beyond the obligatory act of natural affection. The Everlasting Father, beyond all need, reached out with forgiveness unasked to those locked in rebellion's grip. On the grounds of which I further submit to you that the redemptive acts of God's love channeled toward humanity transcend obligatory virtue, embodying the pinnacle of supererogatory grace, thus, the most praiseworthy act of benevolence there is, there ever was, and there ever could be.

Consequently, God's redemptive love, far from being a debt owed to humanity or a transactional obligation binding upon him, remains a gracious bestowal flowing freely from the fountainhead of his omnibenevolent nature. Yet, it goes without saying that by making the calm and calculated decision to have humanity created in his own image, God wholeheartedly embraced the eternal commitment to love man with the selfsame intensity with which he loves himself and no less. This commitment, again, hinges upon them staying true to that divine image in which they were created. Now, it is worth remembering the words of Jesus: " . . . *You have sent Me, and have loved them as You have loved Me . . . You loved Me before the foundation of the world . . . And I have declared to them Your name, and will declare it, that the love with which You loved Me may be in them, and I in them*" (John 17:23–24, 26 NKJV), thus unveiling the mystery that God's love for mankind mirrors the eternal love of God the Father for God the Son, a love rooted in the essence of the Triune Godhead. And if that is remotely the case, then it must also mean that just as much as God's love for Jesus is eternal and immutable, his love for mankind must be equally as constant and unconditional, unshaken by any wind of opposition or storms of adversity. That aligns with some theophilosophical reflections of Thomas Aquinas, in which he demonstrated convincingly that the withdrawal of God's love from man would imply change—contradicting his nature as actus purus—viz., the ultimate being who exists entirely in actuality, possessing all perfections without any limitations or potential for change—as change implies a change from potentiality to actuality. God changes not! his divine affection for man is by no means affectatious; it is neither an act of virtue signaling nor showmanship intended to impress any man; it is just as pure as the seraphic flames encircling his sovereign throne, as genuine as his Word become flesh.

Despite the seismic rupture wrought by the Fall, however, he never once stopped seeing the enduring reflection of himself enshrined within the man he had so masterfully crafted in his own image, which tells us that he cannot but persist in lavishing his affections upon that cherished reflection of his Divine similitude, undeterred and unwavering all the same. This verity attains even greater luminosity when we contemplate that God, in his omniscient prescience, had foreknown every event, every nuance, that was destined to unfold within the verdant precincts of the Garden of Eden long prior to the dawn of creation itself, and thus he incorporated the totality of human sin—its shadows and ramifications—into the intricate blueprint of his creative design, a grand architecture that perforce demanded undergirding by the overarching, master plan for redemption, the eternal antidote woven from the very fabric of divine intent. Little wonder, then, that he traversed such extraordinary lengths in his relentless redemptive crusade—rending the heavens asunder and mobilizing the very cosmos, if need be, to secure the redemption of mankind with unassailable certainty. All of this elaborate exposition goes to show that God did not abruptly metamorphose into a loving God at the pivotal juncture of mankind's creation; he existed eternally as a loving God—immutably so—long before the inaugural contemplation of forging humanity ever graced the boundless horizons of his divine mind, and in the ceaseless torrent of ages since that decree, he has remained utterly unaltered, the same yesterday, today, and forever. From the uncharted abysses antedating the primordial stirrings of creation itself, there eternally abided God in self-sufficient splendor; God was love in the unplumbed epochs of eternity's past; God is love in the pulsating immediacy of today's present; and God shall forever remain love—unfading, invincible—in the unending expanses of all eternity's future, where his love endures as the alpha and omega of cosmic harmony.

It also follows that the thought of creating man both preceded and superseded the thought of creating man's world—an inhabitable planet he would later call home. Undoubtedly, man is primarily the reason for earth's creation, and the fact that the world was created good and very good was ultimately for his very good, his boon, and his enjoyment in God. Even our research efforts and studies in astronomy and all other related Earth scientific fields of study come together nicely in making a strong case for man's special place in the universe. One of the psalmists also appeared to have had a moment's glimpse of insight into this prehistoric divine mystery and secret about man's special place in God's heart before creation, enough to tell us that God's antecedent thoughts about mankind were altogether good and lovely. His words are: "*You made all the delicate, inner parts of my body and knit me together in my mother's womb. Thank you for making me so wonderfully complex! Your workmanship is marvelous—how well I know it. You watched me as I was being formed in utter seclusion, as I was woven together in the dark of the womb. You saw me before I was born. Every day of my life was recorded in your book. Every moment was laid out before a single day had passed. How precious are your thoughts about me, O God. They cannot be numbered! I can't even count them; they outnumber the grains of sand! And when I wake up, you are still with me!*" (Ps 139:13–18 NLT). Before any man ever got the chance to inhale the inaugural breath of earthly existence, God had already foreknown them all with unerring prescience; before any woman ever ventured to traverse even a single day within the temporal fabric of life on this terrestrial sphere, he had sovereignly foreseen the entirety of their days—each fleeting hour and epochal season—in comprehensive summation, all beheld from the eternal vantage antedating the very inception of time itself. This reality guides us to the resounding conclusion that human life constitutes no chance-accident of cosmic caprice whatsoever, nor should it be navigated or squandered through the whims of chance and contingency.

For God, in his boundless benevolence, harbored a radiant dream for your life's unfolding narrative and a crystalline vision for your unfolding future—a prophetic blueprint etched in the firmament of eternity—and he extrospectively imagined, with fervent, unquenchable passion, the resplendent future he ardently desired for you to inherit and savor in the embrace of Christ, orchestrating every intricate detail with meticulous, omniscient precision—pouring forth innumerable, inexhaustible thoughts into the sublime architecture of his Divine plan and purpose tailored uniquely for you, an eternal itinerary that arcs majestically from the primordial origins of your being to the consummate pinnacle of your destined glory. Hence, the Scriptures are having to bear witness to the fact that "*For he knew all about us before we were born and he destined us from the beginning to share the likeness of his Son. This means the Son is the oldest among a vast family of brothers and sisters who will become just like him. Having determined our destiny ahead of time, he called us to himself and transferred his perfect righteousness to everyone he called. And those who possess his perfect righteousness he co-glorified with his Son!*" (Rom 8:29–30 TPT). It is precisely for this selfsame reason that God, within the sacred annals of the OT, found no necessity to undertake a formal census in order to ascertain the precise populace inhabiting Nineveh at the juncture when he dispatched Jonah the Prophet to herald his urgent summons to repentance and deliverance unto them, for he held at the very tips of his omnipotent fingers an unerring, exacting headcount of her teeming citizenry, down to the last soul (cf. Jonah 4:11). In analogous fashion, this divine prescience is how he, from eternity's unyielding vantage, foreknew with infallible exactitude the definitive number—the veritable census headcount—of the souls destined for ultimate salvation, drawn forth from amidst all the Gentile nations scattered across the globe's vast expanse (cf. Rom 11:25). Such meticulous, pedantic precision exemplifies the boundless care with which he attends to every intricate detail pertaining to mankind, leaving no facet unattended in the tapestry of his redemptive design.

FOREKNOWN AND FORELOVED: GOD'S SACRIFICIAL LAMB SLAIN FOR FOREKNOWN SOULS

With this profound truth deeply received and contemplated, it becomes strikingly clear that the names of all those inscribed in "*the Book of Life of the Lamb slain from the foundation of the world*" (Rev 13:8 KJV) were perfectly known to God's omniscient gaze long before creation itself began. Precisely for this reason, the Psalmist articulated his conviction with unshakeable confidence that every detail of his life had been lovingly planned and meticulously prewritten and etched in the eternal ledgers well before the moment of his very conception in the womb. Yet this privilege belongs not to him alone; it extends impartially to every human soul who has ever lived, from the first breath of Adam to the final consummation. Humanity was never an afterthought in the divine design—far from it. From the very outset, God's primordial thoughts centered upon the Adamic race; mankind was the foundational purpose, the unshakable cornerstone upon which the entire cosmos was erected, the bedrock reason for which the whole majestic structure of creation was sovereignly raised in splendor and glory. By the very same token, the monumental work of creation itself was inextricably predicated upon the antecedent work of redemption, notwithstanding that creation chronologically preceded it in temporal sequence, erupting forth in pristine glory at the fiat of divine utterance, while redemption's crimson climax unfurled some four millennia hence upon the timbers of Calvary's hill. But absent the redemptive work firmly in view—and thus prehistorically assured and immutably decreed within the sacred deliberations of the Community of the Godhead—the monumental undertaking of creation itself would have been deemed utterly unworthy of initiation, at the very least when measured against the unerring counsel of God's foreknowledge and the profound reservoirs of his Divine wisdom.

Once more, this irrefutable reality overwhelmingly substantiates that humanity stands as the paramount, sovereign beneficiary of God's goodness woven throughout the fabric of creation, for every ancillary measure of goodness that other creatures might ostensibly partake in ultimately converges, in its teleological essence, toward mankind's welfare and overarching benefit. In the unadorned core of it all, nothing was organically fashioned or summoned into being to militate against man's good and boon; contrariwise, all elements of the cosmos were meticulously crafted as benign and profoundly beneficial instruments for his thriving existence—that harmonious equilibrium constituted the inviolable norm and natural order pulsating within the grand framework of creation before the cataclysmic intrusion of the Fall, with anything deviating from this pristine paradigm rightly discerned as a grotesque aberration—a grievous derailment from God's primordial intent and sovereign purpose. For, as I have already made clear, mankind—who culminated the creative symphony on the sixth day of creation—was actually the raison d'être animating every laborious act performed across the preceding five days of divine fiat; the entirety of that cosmic orchestration revolved around his race, the pulsating epicenter of it all, and should his downfall have been remotely foreknown as imminent (which, lamentably, it was) while his redemption somehow eluded guarantee within the eternal councils of the Community of the Godhead, then it would have been totally unconscionable—nay, an affront to divine rectitude—to propel forward with the comprehensive blueprint for creation, merely to witness the preeminent beneficiary of it all hurled forthwith into an abyss of untold suffering and unmitigated hurt, without any possibility for redemption and no promise of a Savior poised for triumphant rescue.

But, inasmuch as the incalculable price exacted for mankind's redemption had been thoughtfully weighed within the eternal councils—deliberated with infinite wisdom and unyielding resolve—and the sovereign decision to advance forthwith with the procurement of that transcendent redemption was thereafter irrevocably ratified, Christ himself—who stood ordained as the quintessential ransom price, the peerless oblation of divine propitiation—was, in that pivotal, timeless instant, esteemed and accounted as sacrificially slain on behalf of humanity within the profoundest recesses of the heart and mind of all three coeternal Members of the Trinity. This sublime mystery is precisely what the sacred Scriptures evoke with luminous profundity when they herald Christ as "*. . . the Lamb who was slaughtered before the world was made*" (Rev 13:8 NLT), a precreative decree where the crimson tide of Calvary's atonement cascaded eternally backward, sealing redemption's covenant before the foundations of the cosmos were ever laid in primordial splendor. That is to say, the eternal Son had solemnly pledged—crossing his heart in divine resolve—to lay down his life in humanity's place long before he ever stepped into the created cosmos. Thus, when Scripture declares the Lamb slain from before the world's foundation (Rev 13:8), it invites a bold question: for whom was this immolation eternally decreed? For mere abstractions or nameless shadows? For faceless and unknown souls veiled from the all-knowing God and the Lamb himself? Such an idea collapses into absurdity; to vow a vicarious death for the utterly anonymous and profoundly unfamiliar strains the limits of reason to the breaking point—an irreconcilable paradox that defies the very nature of sacrificial love.

Therefore, I tell you the truth: every soul whose name is written in the Lamb's Book of Life was not only foreknown but foreloved by God long before the genesis of creation. This is precisely why we may boldly affirm that humanity—specifically the redeemed—was preconceived in the eternal depths of divine love. Our Lord Jesus himself confirms this glorious truth when he prays, "*I in them, and You in Me . . . that the world may know that You have sent Me, and have loved them as You have loved Me . . . for You loved Me before the foundation of the world*" (John 17:23–24 NKJV). In these words, Christ unveils the staggering reality that the Father's love for his people is measured by the same infinite affection he bears toward the eternal Son—a love timeless and undated, predating the creation of man and rooted in the everlasting communion of the Godhead. Because it is the selfsame everlasting love that was shared among all 3 members of the Sacred Trinity *'before the foundation of the world'* that God has bestowed upon all mankind. Put differently, 'for You loved Me [Jesus] before the foundation of the world' and have equally *'loved them [mankind] as You have loved Me.'* This truth strikes the heart with special force when we consider the inherent impossibility of genuinely loving someone completely unknown to us—a mystery as baffling as falling deeply in love with a faceless stranger lost in obscurity.

For Scripture to declare that God loved humanity from eternity past, before creation's first light, necessarily means he intimately knew each soul in that timeless expanse, every individual already vividly present to his omniscience long before time began. This eternal principle is beautifully foreshadowed in God's covenant with Abraham, as particularly illustrated in the divine tutorial the LORD imparted to the patriarch when he compelled him to enact a prophetic anticipation of the fulfillment of the promise of Isaac, wherein he was urged to lift his gaze to the twinkling, star-studded nighttime skies arching over the Eastern Mediterranean's ancient horizons, with each star standing as a bespoke facial representation of future descendants yet unborn, a multitude as innumerable as the heavens themselves. Genesis 15:5 duly records, "*Then He brought him outside and said, "Look now toward heaven, and count the stars if you are able to number them.*" And He said to him, "*So shall your descendants be.*" In precisely the same way, before ever humanity was formed in Genesis, God sovereignly beheld the face of every individual—from the least to the greatest—with perfect foreknowledge and unchanging forelove. All were held in the tender, predestining affection of his eternal heart, known and cherished in exquisite detail long before the first breath of creation.

In truth, the Lamb was figuratively "*slain*" the moment the eternal counsel of the Trinity reached its irrevocable decision—solemnly recorded in the sacred Volume of the Book—declaring that the Son would one day enter human history to become the ransom for fallen mankind, paying that price through a vicarious death. Long before he ever touched the soil of creation, Christ had, in the depths of eternity, crossed his heart and pledged himself to die in our stead. This is the profound reality Scripture conveys when it speaks of the Lamb slain before the foundation of the world: not a literal crucifixion in eternity past, but the binding, foreordained commitment of divine love to accomplish redemption through the cross at the appointed time. Especially so when we recognize the absolute immutability of God's counsel—including his foreknowledge and foreordination of humanity's redemption—which stands eternally steadfast and binding upon all three Persons of the Trinity. God is not like man, who might lie or repent of a promise (cf. Num 23:19); his word is unbreakable. As Hebrews so beautifully assures us, human oaths invoke a greater authority to enforce compliance, but God, desiring to show the unchangeable character of his purpose, confirmed it with an oath—two unalterable things: his promise and his oath, in which it is impossible for him to lie (cf. Heb 6:16–18). Thus, those who take refuge in him may have strong encouragement, utterly certain that he will fulfill the salvation he has pledged. In this light, the precreative commitment to provide a ransom through the Lamb was irrevocably sealed; Christ himself would never waver or retract—come hell or high water, he was steadfastly bound for the cross from eternity to Calvary. It is precisely upon the unchangeable redemptive counsels and eternal conclusions of the Godhead that the Lord later gave Abraham the solemn assurance, "*The LORD will provide*" (Gen 22:14)—Jehovah Jireh. And what would he provide? Nothing less than the perfect ransom for humanity's redemption. This was no provisional promise but a divine guarantee, irrevocably signed, sealed, and delivered in the heart and mind of the God who cannot lie. Long before the ram appeared on Mount Moriah, the true Lamb had already been appointed in eternity, ensuring that the provision Abraham glimpsed in shadow would be gloriously fulfilled in the substance of Christ's once-for-all sacrifice.

This is precisely what the following Messianic Psalm is alluding to: "*Many, O LORD my God, are Your wonderful works Which You have done; And Your thoughts toward us Cannot be recounted to You in order; If I would declare and speak of them, they are more than can be numbered. Sacrifice and offering You did not desire; My ears You have opened. Burnt offering and sin offering You did not require. Then I said, "Behold, I come; In the scroll of the book it is written of me. I delight to do Your will, O my God, And Your law is within my heart*" (Ps 40:5–8 NKJV). The first thing to point out here is that by the phrase '*Your thoughts toward us,*' the Psalmist is not merely referring to the spontaneous thoughts of God; no, he is rather referring to precreative thoughts of God that were all grounded in his Divine foreknowledge of every human person ever born. Second, the Psalmist speaks in the voice of the coming Messiah—Christ himself—who declares that the Father never ultimately desired the animal sacrifices of the Mosaic Law, for they could never truly atone or redeem. In glad submission, the Son responds, "*Behold, I come*" into man's world to '*do*' or implement the Father's will. Joyfully embracing the role already inscribed for him in the eternal "*scroll of the book*"—the divine decree settled before creation—to enter the world and accomplish the Father's will through his own obedient life and atoning death. At its core, the Father's eternal will centers upon the Son's entrance into human history—redemptive history itself—and the voluntary laying down of his life as the once-for-all ransom for mankind's sin. The author of Hebrews, writing with the clarity of hindsight, quotes this same Messianic Psalm with heightened emphasis:

"*Therefore, when He came into the world, He said, 'Sacrifice and offering You did not desire, but a body You have prepared for Me . . . Then I said, "Behold, I have come—in the volume of the book it is written of Me—to do Your will, O God*" (Heb 10:5–7 NKJV). The added phrase "*a body You have prepared for Me*" points directly to the incarnation—the Son taking on human flesh, that very body historically battered, crucified, and offered as the perfect sacrifice whose blood alone secures the forgiveness of sins and the eternal redemption of the human soul.

REDEEMING THE INITIAL INVESTMENT OF THE *IMAGO DEI*: MANKIND'S INTRINSIC WORTH IN CHRIST

A vital question arises naturally here: was God acting as a poor investor when he lavished the priceless treasure of his own image and likeness upon mankind at creation—fully aware that Adam and Eve would soon fall, defacing that glorious imprint through pride, disobedience, and rebellion, apparently squandering the divine investment almost immediately? The answer is an emphatic no. Far from a miscalculation, the bestowal of the *imago Dei* was never regarded in the eternal counsel as a risky or regrettable venture. Though God sovereignly foreknew the Fall and its devastating consequences, he deemed the creation of image-bearers infinitely worthwhile—precisely because the greater glory of redemption through the incarnate Son had already been planned, ensuring that the temporary marring of the image would give way to an even more radiant restoration. And according to the eternal counsel of God's foreknowledge, the creation of humanity in Adam was never intended to be an end in itself but a gracious means toward the greater end: the procreation, through redemption, of a new humanity in Christ—conformed to the perfect image and likeness of the Son of God. Thus, God's original investment of his likeness in mankind was always destined to prove infinitely worthwhile, even though the redemptive cost—the sacrifice of his beloved Son—would demand everything from him. In this light, the salvation of fallen humanity can be seen as the glorious recovery and enhancement of that initial deposit of the *imago Dei*, fully vindicated through the cross. At the end of the divine accounting, every infinite "*dime*" was worth it to God—abundantly so. Clearly, then, the Creator proved no unwise investor in forming man; rather, his sovereign wisdom shines undimmed. These profound mysteries—the eternal secrets of God's foreknowing love for humanity, hidden since the foundation of the world (Matt 13:35)—were never concealed from him, but are now being progressively unveiled to us across time as we inquire and the Spirit illuminates.

Believe it or not, you were eternally cherished—preconceived in the boundless depths of God's love—long before your conception or birth. This profound reality illuminates why the Creator, guided by the counsel of his own will, chose to orient the vast panorama of creation around this one creature: enthroning humanity above all else, placing our species at the pinnacle of dominion and care. David himself stood in awe of this singular affection, compelled to ask: "*What is man that You are mindful of him, and the son of man that You visit him?*" (Ps 8:4). Yet the wonder deepens, for God not only appointed man as the cosmic Vicegerent or Suzerain Deputy over the works of his hands but crowned him with glory and majesty, a little lower than the heavenly beings, granting rule over sheep and oxen, beasts of the field, birds of the air, fish of the sea, and all that traverses the oceans (Ps 8:5–8). Here we glimpse the crowning glory of creation: mankind, uniquely exalted as the centerpiece of God's cosmic design, reflecting his image and receiving his sovereign delight. The fact that God sovereignly fashioned mankind as both the crowning masterpiece and cosmic centerpiece of all his creative works reveals why even Adam's catastrophic sin—marked by disobedience, pride, and rebellion in Eden—could not extinguish the ardent flames of divine love for humanity. The Fall, for all its devastation, lacked the power to derail or diminish God's redemptive affection. Time and again, Scripture bears witness that humanity occupies the very heart of God's cosmic design precisely because the spotlight of his unchanging love and sovereign interest shines with undimmed brilliance upon our race, drawing all creation toward the glory of redeeming and exalting his image-bearers.

For this very reason, the entire created order revolves around humanity much as the planets orbit the sun—a cosmic design reflecting man's exalted primacy. Thomas Aquinas, echoing David's wonder, aptly observed that "*But plants exist for the sake of animals, some animals for the sake of others, and all for the sake of man.*" Humanity stands not only at the apex of the food chain but also as sovereign steward over the world, exercising dominion as God's appointed vicegerent, with every creature and realm placed in loving subservience. This enthronement over creation flows naturally from a deeper reality: man was already enthroned in the eternal heart of God's love before the worlds were framed. Even more astonishing, Scripture records only two direct works of God performed solely by his own hand—creation and redemption—both centered upon man: fashioning him and his world, then redeeming both through the cross. These sacred labors God reserved exclusively for himself, never delegating them to angels, who otherwise carry out all his eternal purposes in his name. In the same way, God entrusted no part of the creation of man and his world to the angels—he neither delegated nor permitted them the slightest assistance. From the forming of the cosmos to the inbreathing of human life, he alone oversaw, executed, and completed every detail, then rested in the perfection of his finished work. This intimate, personal labor finds a poignant echo in the Psalmist's awe: "*For You formed my inward parts; You covered me in my mother's womb . . . Marvelous are Your works . . . Your eyes saw my substance, being yet unformed. And in Your book they all were written, the days fashioned for me . . .* " (Ps 139:13–17 NKJV). The preciousness of God's thoughts toward us reflects his direct, loving craftsmanship. Likewise in redemption: no angel was commissioned to save fallen humanity or restore the broken world—the Triune God accomplished it entirely himself, Father, Son, and Holy Spirit working in perfect, undivided harmony.

UNCAUSED YET PURPOSEFUL: THE RATIONAL ROOT OF DIVINE AFFECTION

Even in the shadowed light of Old Testament revelation, David perceived with remarkable clarity that God had crowned mankind as the pinnacle of his magnificent creation—adorning him with a royal diadem of glory and honor in a breathtaking act of investiture. Yet what lay beyond his full comprehension was the profound reason for such extraordinary elevation. One cannot help but imagine the depths of awe that would have overwhelmed him had he beheld the ultimate display of divine love in the redemptive sacrifice of Christ—the triumph of grace over the grave. Nonetheless, we must acknowledge that David touched upon something eternally momentous in Psalm 8, posing questions of piercing insight that continue to echo with undimmed power across the centuries, inviting every generation to marvel at the mystery of God's heart for man. Certain questions retain their urgency across the ages, inviting us afresh to inquire along the same reverent path: why did God choose humanity as the crowning object of his love? Why not the majestic companies of angels, or the apes that mirror us in form, or any of the diverse creatures populating earth's fullness or the boundless sidereal heavens? Nothing inherent in the created order demanded that man alone should be singled out—nothing in the intricate fabric of the universe constrained the Almighty to lavish his singular, paramount love upon us rather than upon any other being. There was no cosmic necessity, no external compulsion, dictating that humanity must become the supreme object of divine affection—absolutely none. This sovereign freedom shines with particular brilliance when we consider that within the eternal Godhead there has never existed the slightest trace of limerence—no romantic longing, no infatuation—either before humanity's creation or at any moment since. The perfect communion of Father, Son, and Holy Spirit has always been complete in itself—needing nothing beyond itself, utterly fulfilled in boundless love. It is therefore impossible to portray God as lovesick or compelled by loneliness or driven by emotional lack; humanity was not created out of divine necessity, was never fashioned to fill some aching divine emptiness or meet some existential need within the Godhead community. God is no lovesick suitor seeking completion; our creation sprang solely from the gracious liberty of a God whose love is complete, choosing to share his fullness out of pure sovereign generosity.

The Bible only goes so far as telling us clearly that the reason we love God is because *'He first loved us'* (see 1 John 4:19); but when it comes to answering the million-dollar question—why, pray tell, did He first love us with such prodigal intensity, even from the unformed epochs before the foundation of the world?—it is there that the veil thickens, and the mystery deepens into realms both tantalizing and elusive. On that contemplative note, permit me to venture this clarification: initially, I had envisaged God's love for humanity as utterly without a cause—devoid of any discernible motive, a Divine mystery bereft of apparent rationale; he simply adores man in a random, capricious flourish, merely for existing as one among his manifold creatures, and no deeper significance thereto. But as revelation unfolded in fuller measure, I soon discerned that this was not precisely the case; rather, God's love for mankind emerges neither as uncaused nor misplaced, but as profoundly anchored in a rational and coherent purpose, attuned with exquisite precision to man's unparalleled station within the grand hierarchy of creation. Far from the caprice of whimsy or the flutter of fleeting fancy, God's love for us reflects the purposeful intentionality of his sovereign design and the inexpressible dignity he has exclusively bestowed upon us as the sole creatures bearing his divine image and likeness. This profound, sacred bond—both resonant and revelatory—escaped my full grasp for far too long, yet now it shines with transformative light, anchoring divine affection in the eternal wisdom of the Creator rather than in arbitrary preference.

Though no shadow of doubt remains that God's love for humanity is utterly unmerited—flowing with the same sovereign freedom as his grace, which by definition is bestowed without regard to human worthiness—this does not mean it is altogether uncaused or, in any sense, misdirected. To call it unmerited highlights one glorious facet of the mystery: it springs lavishly apart from any human effort or deserving act. But to term it uncaused would plunge us into a different abyss, suggesting it lacks all rationale, purpose, or intentional direction. Were we to ask the Almighty, "*Why do You love mankind exclusively?*" he would not stand speechless, unable to offer coherent reasons for singling out the human race amid the vast creation for such preferential affection and care. Thankfully, that is not our reality—his love is both gratuitous and profoundly purposeful. If God's love for mankind were truly uncaused or irrational—a mere capricious whim detached from divine wisdom—then it could just as easily shift its focus to any other creature at eternity's fancy, perhaps redirecting its intensity toward the beasts of the field or the angelic hosts above. Yet history bears no witness to such fickleness, nor will eternity ever display it. God's immutable character ensures that the unparalleled depth and intimacy of his love remain steadfastly reserved for humanity alone. In this exclusive, unchanging devotion we discern a profound and compelling rationale—his love is neither arbitrary nor transferable but purposefully anchored in the unique dignity he has sovereignly bestowed upon man. The singular and exclusive outpouring of God's love upon humanity springs inexorably from the foundational truth that we were originally created in his image and likeness. This carries profound, far-reaching weight: whenever God looks upon us, he sees a luminous mirror of himself dwelling within this distinctive creature, drawing forth from him the same fervent affection he bears toward his own infinite essence. Consequently, he cannot but cherish us with the same intensity and delight with which he eternally loves his own uncreated being. Herein lies the deepest purpose for crafting a divine image-bearer: a creature uniquely suited—and sovereignly appointed—to receive the very love that has forever flowed in perichoretic bliss among the three coeternal Persons of the Trinity.

If there resides any spark of glory within the human frame, it emanates unequivocally from the radiant glory of God's own image indelibly imprinted upon him; if there lingers any beauty worthy of rapt contemplation in his being, it derives from the exquisite beauty of being meticulously fashioned after the transcendent likeness of his eternal Maker. The old saying "*love is blind*" finds no application here—God's love for humanity is anything but sightless. He gazes with unflinching, sovereign clarity upon the brilliant reflection of his own divine nature embodied in man, cherishing with deliberate joy the majesty and splendor of his likeness uniquely vested in this singular species. Here beats the very heart, the living essence, of God's infinite love for humankind. This truth supplies the unshakeable reason why his sovereign, lavish affection—directed with such deliberate prodigality toward man as its primary and primordial object—cannot be redirected or transferred to any other creature or order of being. This insight carries immense weight: if nothing else, it shields us from the subtle danger of reducing divine love to fleeting whim or caprice, while steadfastly guarding its unmerited, gratuitous splendor. At the same time, it reveals the majestic depth of God's love as profoundly purposeful and teleologically grounded—never descending into the cold exchange of transactional bargaining or *quid pro quo*. Throughout this discourse, I have steadfastly maintained that God's descent into humanity—his becoming man—stands as an event of incomparable magnitude—a moment of unparalleled wonder in redemptive history. To this I add with equal conviction: the original creation of humanity in God's image and likeness is no less monumental—a groundbreaking miracle of foundational, cosmic significance. This truth casts brilliant light on why the Almighty would embrace without reservation the form of this unique creature—incarnating as man Himself. The profound mystery finds its roots in the eternal reality that humans were fashioned as bearers of the divine image, exalted to a kinship with God's own essence, members of the "*Godkind*" in reflection and destiny.

By an incalculable measure, God's becoming man stands as one of the most eloquent witnesses to the foundational truth that humanity was originally forged in his divine image and likeness at creation's dawn. This alone provides the transcendent reason why mankind was deemed worthy of such costly redemption—worthy that the infinite price of the cross should be paid on our behalf. Even after the catastrophic Fall grievously marred and tarnished that sacred imprint, God never ceased to regard us as his cherished image-bearers; he never stopped beholding the enduring reflection of himself within the human soul, nor did he ever diminish his estimation of our intrinsic worth from the glorious valuation he held before sin entered the world. Thus, God never for a moment ceased loving humanity, nor did he ever abandon hope of restoring us to the pristine glory and status in which we were first created. His love has remained steadfast across the ages, enduring every trial and tribulation. Consider it this way: at creation, God made an initial divine investment by imparting his own image and likeness to mankind—a profound theomorphism that marked us as reflections of his essence. Undeterred by the Fall, he doubled down with the ultimate redemptive investment: the offering of his Son's life to reclaim and renew that original imprint. Finally, in the climactic Pentecostal outpouring, he sealed his purpose with the indwelling Holy Spirit—a transformative investment that effects true theopoesis, drawing redeemed humanity into living union with the divine nature. The resounding fact remains: God felt no compulsion to abandon or forsake mankind in the wake of the Fall; instead, he immediately covenanted to redeem us. This resolute tenacity stands as one of the most sublime and irrefutable witnesses to the immense significance the Creator attached to fashioning humanity in his own image and likeness—an eternal investment of such profound weight that humanity itself could scarcely comprehend its magnitude. It reveals how highly God valued that original endowment, deeming it entirely worthy of the infinite price he later paid in the sacrifice of his Son upon Calvary. Would any of us risk our lives to redeem a pet cat or dog? Hardly—and neither would God expend such disproportionate devotion. The unassailable reality endures: he loves mankind with unparalleled intensity precisely because we were sculpted in his image and likeness from the beginning, and he cannot but love us with the same depth and fervor with which he eternally loves his own uncreated essence—no less, but in boundless, inexhaustible measure.

It is precisely because of this same boundless love that the supreme, self-sufficient God would lay down his life as a ransom for creatures seemingly insignificant—beings he had no inherent need of—yet cherishing them as though they were the very center of all reality and beyond. To affirm, with Christ, that God loved you before the foundation of the world is to declare that his love preceded any right or wrong you could ever do. If your actions—good or evil—held no sway over his affection when you were yet unaware of it, why should they now obstruct it when you have joyfully entered his embrace? Christianity, at its heart, is never about our merits or failures; if our sins truly barred his love, God would have exacted punishment upon us, not upon his innocent Son in our place. Instead, he poured out wrath upon Christ so that sin might never again hinder his love, and now he assures us with divine certainty that nothing—"*tribulation, or distress, or persecution, or famine, or nakedness, or peril, or sword*"—can ever separate us from the everlasting arms of his love (Rom 8:35 NKJV). And as if that were not sufficient, Paul presses further: " . . . *neither death nor life, nor angels nor principalities nor powers, nor things present nor things to come, nor height nor depth, nor any other created thing, shall be able to separate us from the love of God which is in Christ Jesus our Lord*" (Rom 8:38–39 NKJV). This is grace in its most breathtaking form—love in its most unconditional splendor. Not only did God love humanity so profoundly that he made us the sole bearers of his divine image, but he went even further, graciously allowing us to bear his divine Name—calling us by his own sacred Name. Through faith, every believer becomes part of the people identified with him, named after Christ himself, privileged to invoke his Name in prayer and spiritual warfare as though it were our birthright—a wondrous inheritance secured through union with the Son.

In the OT, God's explicit command to the Aaronic priesthood was profound: "*So they shall put My name upon the children of Israel, and I will bless them*" *(Num 6:27 NKJV). Centuries later, this divine* naming finds echo in the promise: "*If My people who are called by My name will humble themselves, and pray and seek My face, and turn from their wicked ways, then I will hear from heaven, and will forgive their sin and heal their land*" (2 Chr 7:14 NKJV). Notice the intimate correlation: the priestly act of placing God's name upon Israel transitions seamlessly into the people being identified as those "*called by My name*." The Israelites were, in essence, named after their God—bearing His sacred identity. Yet marvelously, the Almighty is "*not ashamed to be called their God*" (Heb 11:16 NKJV), embracing with unreserved delight the very people who carry his name, a foreshadowing of the greater privilege granted to all who are named after Christ. One might understandably wonder: does God not fear that sinful humanity, by bearing his sacred name, could tarnish his flawless reputation? Is he unconcerned that unrighteous lives might cast shame upon his holy Name, or that calling imperfect believers his sons and daughters could drag his glory into disrepute? He is fully aware of every such possibility—yet his sovereign response silences all concern: "*Love covers all sins*" (Prov 10:12 NKJV). His love for mankind "*bears all things, believes all things, hopes all things, endures all things . . . [and] never fails"* (1 Cor 13:7–8 NKJV). This enduring, covering love is pure and unconditional, free from hidden motive or reservation—a sacred testament to the boundless, self-giving heart of God.

Though Scripture nowhere hints that God is jealous over any other creature, it repeatedly affirms a holy jealousy reserved solely for the unique object of his affection—humanity. In his own words: "*You shall worship no other gods, for the LORD, whose name is Jealous, is a jealous God*" (Exod 34:14 NLT), guarding with passionate fidelity the intimacy of his covenant relationship with us. This revelation is profoundly illuminating: God has wholly committed himself to mankind in love, burning every bridge of retreat. He will never revoke his decision, never alter his stance toward us—for any reason in heaven or on earth, neither now nor through all eternity. This sacred agape bond—this divine romance between God and mankind—lies at the very heart of what enrages Satan, driving him to the brink of frenzied madness. Excluded entirely from this intimate love shared between the Divine Lover and his beloved image-bearers, he is left seething on the outside, unable to partake in even the smallest portion of that exclusive affection. In his fury, he conveniently forgets his own created station: a glorious angel, yet never fashioned in the divine image and likeness reserved uniquely for humanity. But dare not remind him of this painful truth—it cuts like a blade to the core, a wound he refuses to acknowledge. This truth—that humanity alone bears God's image and receives the singular focus of his love—sounds stranger than fiction to the devil, and he will have none of it. In prideful defiance, he persists in claiming a special status never granted him, revealing the depths of his arrogant and rebellious heart. Had he but heeded the divine principle—"*Whoever exalts himself will be humbled, and he who humbles himself will be exalted*" (Luke 14:11 NKJV)—he might have spared himself eternal ruin. Even now, as we ponder these mysteries, we can be certain that David's awe-struck question—"*What is man that You are mindful of him?*"—has tormented Satan across the ages, a piercing reminder of his own humbled station that robs him of rest and deepens his anguish whenever it crosses his mind.

Nothing bewilders and enrages Satan more than the impenetrable mystery of God's choice: "Why mankind and not me? Why has God lavished such singular love upon man, making him alone the bearer of the divine image and the exclusive object of his eternal affection?" Unable to get himself to reconcile with the divine rationale or the heart behind this preference, Satan finds the matter an utterly closed book—his mind forever barred from understanding God's sovereign purpose. We can only imagine the depths of his bitter, cantankerous frustration, for no answer has ever sufficed to calm his malicious outbursts or temper his seething hatred toward humanity. Were it not for his adversarial presence, human history would unfold precisely according to God's gracious predestination; all things equal, without the devil's orchestration of evil and adversity, God's good plan would proceed unhindered—but tragically, the adversary exists, and mankind must contend with his relentless opposition. Is it not strikingly ironic that the very architect of evil and orchestrator of adversity in human lives is euonymously named "*your adversary the devil*" (1 Pet 5:8)? His title alone betrays his notorious character and contemptible reputation. Yet, amid all his malicious intent, there remains an unshakable saving grace for every soul: none other than the Savior Himself, Christ Jesus. When these truths dawned upon me personally, I resolved within my heart that no temptation—no cunning serpent—could ever bribe or persuade me to trade away my God-ordained purpose and destiny for fleeting gain, as Esau tragically bartered his birthright for a mere bowl of stew. Mark Twain's famous words—"*The two most important days in your life are the day you are born and the day you find out why*"—ring profoundly true when understood as the moment we discover God's eternal plan and call for us in His Son, Christ Jesus. As Pascal so wisely declared at the outset, it is only through Jesus Christ that we truly know God, ourselves, life, and death; apart from Him, all remains veiled and unknown.

LUCIFER'S SCORN: JEALOUSY OVER MAN'S PRIVILEGED PLACE IN GOD'S HEART

Building upon these prior meditations, we can scarcely imagine the storm of turmoil that must have raged within Lucifer's mind as the Godhead's august counsel unfolded its anthropocentric design for creation. Can we, even for a moment, suppose that he felt the slightest thrill at the prospect of Adam's formation, or that he offered the remotest welcome to God's gracious plan for this new creature called "man"—a being destined to receive the priceless gift of true moral freedom, that heavenly prerogative God sovereignly reserved for humanity alone? This was the very liberty Lucifer coveted with desperate intensity, the one treasure he would have traded everything to possess for himself rather than see bestowed upon this nascent race emerging onto the cosmic stage. To deepen the sting, the newly formed Adamic race was destined to surpass the angelic orders in ultimate glory—eclipsing even Lucifer himself in his lofty archangelic splendor. It was likely at this very moment in eternity's timeless counsels that the poisonous seed of jealousy and root of bitterness first took hold in Lucifer's heart, sprouting into the rebellion that would forever mar his once-exalted station. One can almost envision Lucifer seething inwardly: "*How dare this creature—man—be fashioned to eclipse me in glory, after I have long submitted to the yoke of divine authority since my own creation? Why must I now suffer the added indignity of inferiority to this newborn race, whose nature I can scarcely comprehend?*" I propose this reconstruction because the multifaceted truth of God's love for humanity illuminates so much; it casts crystalline light upon the hidden motive driving Satan's ceaseless contempt for mankind—his ferocious pursuit of Adam's sons resembling the bitter malice of a jilted lover. For when his implicit bid to become the exclusive object of God's affection—in place of man—was summarily rejected without hesitation, dead on arrival and devoid of any consideration, it ignited an unquenchable rage born of wounded pride.

Yet Satan embodies no true lover in the proper sense, for angelic beings were never created in the divine image and likeness from the beginning. By their very constitution, they are intrinsically unsuited for the profound relational intimacy that God extends to mankind—the sacred communion rooted in shared similitude. This fundamental difference renders angels incapable of receiving or reciprocating the covenantal depth of love reserved exclusively for image-bearers, highlighting the unique privilege humanity alone possesses in the heart of the Divine Lover. Yet, inasmuch as the archangel Lucifer refused to relinquish his grievance or reconcile himself to the inexorable reality that the divine love for man stands both irrevocable and unyielding in its fidelity, he succumbed to an all-consuming covetousness; thereafter, filled with toxic rage and acrid bile, thereby allowing darkness and hatred to creep into his soul, irredeemably corrupting his default programming altogether. This innate corruption of the soul also serves to explain how it came to be that, he, even though was created an angelic being of light, *hêylêl* in the Hebrew tongue—literally the 'morning star', from whence English derivations like luciferase and luciferous trace their etymology—he devolved inexorably into a lucifugous abomination: a creature of darkness who harbors an intrinsic revulsion toward the light and cannot stand the light of God's truth. Precisely as Jesus incisively diagnosed, he "*. . . does not stand in the truth, because there is no truth in him. When he speaks a lie, he speaks from his own resources, for he is a liar and the father of it*" (John 8:44 NKJV). And therein resides incontrovertible evidence that Satan, indeed, loves darkness rather than light, ultimately because his deeds are evil—perpetually and unrepentantly so (cf. John 3:19).

This stands as an unassailable foundational truth: "*Everyone who does evil hates the light and will not come into the light for fear that their deeds will be exposed. But those who practice the truth come into the light, so that it may be clearly seen that what they have done has been wrought in God*" (John 3:20–21 BSB). At its core, Satan the adversary perpetually relies upon the shroud of darkness—whether the veil of ignorance or the mantle of deception—to conceal his destructive schemes and wicked intentions, lest the piercing light of discernment should reveal their true, repulsive nature and lay them bare before the gaze of truth. Scripture is thus fully vindicated in condemning every scheme of the adversary—and all those craftily executed through agents under his sway—as nothing less than "*works of darkness*" (Eph 5:11). These are invariably conceived and carried out in secrecy and shadow, in stark opposition to the good works of God, which always unfold in the open light of day—most perfectly in the radiant light of truth itself. It is therefore no surprise that Jesus charged His disciples: "*What I tell you in the dark, speak in the light; and what you hear whispered in your ear, proclaim from the housetops*" (Matt 10:27 NKJV). In these words shines His complete transparency and utter freedom from any need for concealment—a defining mark of the One who is Himself the Light of the world. At His core, the Lord has nothing to hide and no requirement for the cover of darkness to act. It is those harboring hidden motives, usually inclined toward mischief, who depend on secrecy and shadows to succeed. This profound insight undergirds Jesus' open command to His followers: "*Let your light so shine before men, that they may see your good works and glorify your Father in heaven*" (Matt 5:16 NKJV). Yet if the devil were permitted to advance his schemes without restraint, the radiant gospel truth of God's fervent love for humanity would remain perpetually hidden, prevented from penetrating the human heart. We wrestle against an adversary who takes pleasure in raising towering edifices on the unstable sands of falsehood and establishing vast kingdoms on the foundation of deceit. In the Tower of Babel and the expansive empire of Babylon, we see archetypal emblems of human pride—grand constructions and sprawling cities erected on the false notion that mankind could fashion an earthly paradise apart from the sovereign Lord of heaven and earth. What interpretation, then, shall we assign to the emerging vision of "15-Minute Cities" in our contemporary age, if not as the twenty-first-century manifestations of that ancient Babylonian delusion: a quest for human dominion and supremacy, aspiring to a theocracy stripped of the Divine, where the Father of Lies assumes the throne as unchallenged God-Emperor, lording over souls ensnared in self-deifying rebellion.

EMPTYING THE ALABASTER BOTTLE OF GOD'S LOVE ON MAN: ENRAGING SATAN THE DEVIL AS JUDAS ISCARIOT

To grasp the depth of the antagonistic hatred Satan harbors against frail humanity, we must consider this central truth: God loved us with such extravagant, unconditional passion that he made his love for us the non-negotiable cause worth dying for. In the cosmic drama of redemption, he literally gave his life on the cross—the ultimate symbol of self-emptying love—sparing no expense in lavish generosity, pouring out every drop of divine love from the fountainhead of his veins until nothing remained in reservation—no remnant spared for any lesser creature of his own creation. Again, this perfectly illustrates what it truly means to call humanity the sole object of God's love—heaven's hallowed heartthrob: Christ, in supreme devotion, poured out his precious blood upon the cruel crest of Calvary, the hillock literally called "*the hill of the skull*," in a cosmic demonstration of God's love for you and me. Nailed in naked agony on that notorious hill, he fell head over heels in utter devotion for the only creature that uniquely captures God's heart and delight in all the universe. There, atop that fateful hill, Christ deliberately broke to pieces the alabaster bottle of divine love like a precious vessel shattered in extravagant generosity, graciously emptying upon us every ounce of the priceless fragrant ointment of God's love contained therein—down to the very last droplet that lingers in sacrificial completeness—down to the deepest dregs drained in devoted depletion. For God spared no expense, holding nothing back, hoarding no drop of heaven's heartfelt hemorrhage, he poured out every pulse of his liquid love through the shed blood of his Son—the perfect atonement for our sins. And in that infinite outpouring,

Lucifer lies lacerated, lashed by the luminous love he yearns for yet can never lay hold of. This truth finds beautiful harmony in the inspired words of that great man of God, Pastor Dr. Chris Oyakhilome, DSc. DD., who so poetically described divine love as "*liquid love*"—a living river flowing from the throne of God, yes, from Emmanuel's very veins. To sharpen this vivid picture, the alabaster flask represents nothing less than Christ's own body, broken, battered, and marred beyond recognition for our sake upon the cross in perfect prophetic fulfillment; the precious, fragrant ointment within symbolizes His priceless blood, poured out in extravagant love for the forgiveness and remission of our sins. Thus, at the inaugural Eucharist, Jesus spoke with tender finality: "*Take, eat; this is My body which is broken for you; do this in remembrance of Me*" (1 Cor 11:24 NKJV), and "*This cup is the new covenant in My blood, which is shed for you*" (Luke 22:20 NKJV)—words that resound through the centuries as a sacramental invitation to partake of the love that redeems and restores. In that sacred moment, he symbolically and prophetically instituted what would later become the antitypical, fulfilling Pesach or Passover in its eschatological glory, essentially a Dominical redefinition of the whole redemptive framework—now commonly known and cherished as the Eucharist or the Holy Communion in Christianity, a feast that transcends time in tasting eternity.

Amid these profound revelations, one truth stands out with unmistakable clarity: the extravagant outpouring of God's liquid love upon humanity at Calvary casts brilliant light upon the abysmal depth of Lucifer's grudge and burning hatred toward mankind—a festering wound upon creation's canvas. In covetous fury, he had yearned for that divine affection to be lavished solely upon himself in selfish isolation. In bitter anger, he finds himself excluded, denied even the smallest taste of the cake representing the divine romance between God and man. His reaction mirrors Judas Iscariot's hypocritical indignation over Mary's costly alabaster ointment poured in lavish worship upon the Beloved Son at Betsaida's banquet—feigning concern while seething at love freely given to another. Lucifer's indignant revolt arose from raw, unchecked jealousy—a serpent-like, gnawing envy—coupled with a venomous hatred for humanity and a pride that swelled like a malignant growth. He could not rest content in the exalted angelic station God had graciously appointed him within the heavenly harmony; instead, he coveted ascension beyond his ordained place in rebellious ambition. By contrast, Judas's complaint sprang from shortsighted human greed—a grasping after sordid gain that cloaked itself in betrayal's shadow, betraying the Master for fleeting silver rather than aspiring to divine heights. This same insidious dynamic sheds profound light on Lucifer's tragic descent into the malevolent misanthrope he became—plummeting from his exalted station as one of heaven's highest archangels, radiant in celestial splendor, to the archdevil enthroned in the abyss of eternal damnation. In this fall, he fittingly assumed the name "*Satan the devil*," a title that reveals his character as the direct opposite of the Divine Philanthrope—God himself, the true Lover of mankind. From this sacred origin springs the modern term "*philanthropist*," now often diluted yet still echoing, however faintly, the boundless, self-giving love of the Creator for His image-bearers. God's divine philanthropy reveals His omnibenevolent heart toward humanity—an infinite, all-embracing goodness and unfailing love that pursues the wandering prodigal to the uttermost ends of the earth. In stark contrast, Satan's deep-seated misanthropy manifests as omnimalevolence: a boundless expanse of evil, irredeemably wicked at its core, intent only on devouring and destroying. Thus, the Latin phrase *odium generis humani*—hatred of mankind—most characteristically captures the devil's true character: the most resolute and unrelenting enemy of mankind. If God is the perfect embodiment of love in its most unalloyed and holy form, then Satan stands as the chilling personification of hatred in its vilest guise and most depraved expression. The contrast is stark and uncomplicated—unvarnished truth, sharp and unrelenting as a hidden blade in the night, revealing the eternal opposition between light and shadow, grace and malice.

Pay particular attention to a subtle yet profound detail in Scripture: the Bible never refers to Satan merely as *"a devil"* in generic terms but consistently employs the definite article—"*the devil*"—with deliberate precision. This grammatical choice carries deep theological weight: any other creature of God that will end up becoming a devil—descending into mephistophelean depravity—will invariably be taking cues, guidance, and inspiration from Satan the devil himself, imitating his malice as the archetypal source and exemplar of evil. In essence, Satan holds an absolute monopoly over the realm of wickedness and hatred—no other malevolent entity could ever function independently, detached from his Svengali-like sway, that insidious puppetry that pulls strings from the abyss. Is it any wonder, then, that Jesus portrayed him with such piercing clarity: "*He was a murderer from the beginning, and does not stand in the truth, because there is no truth in him. When he speaks a lie, he speaks from his own resources, for he is a liar and the father of it*" (John 8:44 NKJV)—a vivid exposure of the original deceiver, the fountainhead from whom all falsehood and destruction flow. Far from simply stating that Satan "is" a murderer in the present, Jesus reaches back into primordial history to reveal that he "*was a murderer from the beginning*"—from the very moment of his fall—and has remained implacably committed to that path ever since. With relentless, unyielding malice, he pursues the destruction of human lives, finding a perverse sport and twisted satisfaction in his ceaseless assault upon the objects of God's love. Satan's culpability runs so deep that his fingerprints are unmistakably upon the inaugural murder in human history, and he has never ceased from that path. Ever since, he has roamed the earth as the marauder-in-chief—the father-of-mischief—the murderer-in-chief, restlessly seeking his next victim, ensnaring through cunning lies, and then destroying without remorse (cf. 1 Pet 5:8). This relentless prowling reveals the depth of his fallen nature, forever opposed to the Author of life and intent on undoing the works of God's love. John the Evangelist echoes this solemn verdict in perfect harmony, urging believers: "*For this is the message you have heard from the beginning, that we should love one another—not as Cain, who was of the wicked one and murdered his brother. And why did he murder him? Because his own works were evil and his brother's righteous. Do not marvel, my brothers and sisters, if the world hates you*" (1 John 3:11–13 NKJV). With unflinching clarity, John declares that Cain "*was of the wicked one,*" revealing that the first recorded fratricide in human history was carried out under the dark dominion and malignant influence of Satan himself—the spirit of hatred that opposes the light of righteous love. Thus, Satan transcends mere wickedness; he is, in his very essence, '*the wicked one*'—the Voldemort and grand puppeteer behind every act of wickedness, to such an extent that no perpetrator of wickedness could ever really be considered free from his iron-fisted control and Svengali influence.

This sobering reality undergirds the apostolic declaration: "*He who sins is of the devil, for the devil has sinned from the beginning. For this purpose the Son of God was manifested, that He might destroy the works of the devil*" (I John 3:8 NKJV). Such insight, in turn, clarifies why Jesus evinced no flicker of sentiment in branding one of His innermost companions as '*a devil.*' As John's Gospel recounts: "*Jesus answered them, "Did I not choose you, the twelve, and one of you is a devil?" He spoke of Judas Iscariot, the son of Simon, for it was he who would betray Him, being one of the twelve*" (John 6:70–71 NKJV). Judas Iscariot devolved into a devil (viz., an underdevil) precisely when he began imbibing directives straight from Satan *'the devil'* (viz., the archdevil), who loomed as the shadowy *éminence grise* or ventriloquist dictating his every move. This hierarchical distinction is precisely what the Pharisees invoked when they slanderously accused Jesus of colluding with Beelzebub—the ruler of the demons (Greek: *archōn daimonion*)—the very entity he was exorcising from those ensnared by demonic possession. In their accusation: "*This fellow does not cast out demons except by Beelzebub, the ruler of the demons*" (Matt 12:24 NKJV). Bear in mind, these were the equivalents of modern-day Bible scholars, steeped in scriptural acumen regarding spiritual authority and celestial hierarchy; thus, they grasped full well that every devil operates beneath the overarching authority and insidious influence of Satan the devil himself—the same architect who orchestrated the audacious coup of seducing a third of God's angels into his celestial rebellion against the Almighty, only to be ejected from the heavens. Consequently, what Judas embodied was nothing less than the Devil's marionette or shall we say—the Devil's underdevil. And this inexorably draws us to the sobering inference that the ancient narrative of Cain and Abel in Genesis 4 was, at its core, Satan outsourcing his dirty job to Cain—betrayal and murder—mirroring the scheme he later replicated with Judas in the Gospels. His perennial *modus operandi* entailed infiltrating the innermost sanctum of Cain's heart, then diabolically manipulating the levers that propelled him to slaughter his own flesh-and-blood brother in cold blood—a fiendish parallel to how he infiltrated Judas' psyche, compelling him to betray his own Lord with ruthless cupidity. All of this dovetails seamlessly with John's vivid depiction of the climactic tableau at the Last Supper, mere hours before the betrayal and apprehension of Jesus, wherein he discloses, "*Jesus responded, 'It is the one to whom I give the bread I dip in the bowl.'*" And when he had dipped it, he gave it to Judas, son of Simon Iscariot. When Judas had eaten the bread, Satan entered into him. Then Jesus told him, "*Hurry and do what you're going to do*" (John 13:26–27 NLT). In truth, every deed Judas enacted on that fateful, doom-laden night transpired not from his autonomous volition but under the oppressive, heavy-handed influence of the Devil—with the dark shadow of satanic manipulation enshrouding his every step—beclouding his every judgment.

Yet far more grievous than Judas' outright betrayal was the infamous "*Judas kiss*"—that insidious and deceptive means by which the whole perfidy was executed in chilling proximity, masked under the guise of a kiss of friendship or the traditional religious kiss of peace. In the end, it revealed itself as nothing less than a kiss of death—a Stoic, phlegmatic sign language that silently delivered his Master to mortal doom, while betraying not a single trace of emotion, not even a fleeting flicker of remorse or inner conflict. Paradoxically, this act known as the "*kiss of Judas*" has lived on through history's corridors as the classic, eponymous symbol of the supreme betrayal—of friendship, comradeship, and even mishpocha itself, that most intimate and covenantal expression of brotherhood (cf. Matt 26:47–48). And oh, what a duplicitous frenemy that ultimately rendered Judas in the stark light of truth—covetously ensnared in the clutches of Jesus' archenemy (Satan the devil), bartering his soul for profane profit. As chronicled in Matthew's vivid recounting of the harrowing events that unfolded on that fateful Maundy Thursday night, Jesus, undeterred by the treachery, would nonetheless address this duplicitous betrayer with piercing candor: "*Friend, why have you come?*" (Matt 26:50 NKJV)—a question that may have carried a faint undercurrent of sarcasm on this occasion. Across all the earlier seasons of ministry, even into the fateful final week—the now-notorious week of His Passion and trial—this apparently devoted companion had followed Him with relentless closeness, trailing Him as an inseparable confidant, resembling that rare friend Scripture calls closer than a brother in the intimate bonds of true affinity (cf. Prov 18:24). With timeless wisdom, King Solomon captured this peril: "*Faithful are the wounds of a friend [who corrects out of love and concern], But the kisses of an enemy are deceitful [because they serve his hidden agenda]*" (Proverbs 27:6 AMP). Though Judas, in his final act of pretended devotion, greeted Jesus as "*Master*"*—as the Gospel solemnly records: "And forthwith he came to Jesus, and said, Hail, master; and kissed him*" (Matthew 26:49 KJV)—in the unmasked reality of his divided heart, he had already pledged allegiance to a rival master, the one to whom his true love and loyalty belonged. And that treacherous overlord was none other than money—the glittering lure of those thirty pieces of silver to which he bowed in abject servitude, trading the Pearl of Great Price for fleeting, tarnished gain. His tragic mistake lay in the grand illusion that he could serve two masters—the Christ and the coin—completely disregarding the solemn warning Jesus had declared with piercing clarity: "*No one can serve two masters; for either he will hate the one and love the other, or else he will be loyal to the one and despise the other. You cannot serve God and mammon*" (Matthew 6:24 NKJV).

Beneath Judas's honeyed words lurked a profounder devotion to the unrighteous mammon—the idolatrous deity of avarice—that inexorably commandeered his loyalties, ensnaring his heart in its icy vise and compelling him to abandon the authentic Master for the hollow mirage of ephemeral riches. And herein resides a faintly dramatized evocation of how the Messianic Figure (Jesus) is limned in the Psalms, voicing a poignant lament over Judas' perfidy: "*It wasn't an enemy who taunted me. If it was my enemy, filled with pride and hatred, then I could have endured it. I would have just run away. But it was you, my intimate friend—one like a brother to me. It was you, my advisor, the companion I walked with and worked with! We once had sweet fellowship with each other. We worshiped in unity as one, celebrating together with God's people. Now desolation and darkness have come upon you. May you and all those like you descend into the pit of destruction! Since evil has been your home, may evil now bury you alive!*" (Ps 55:12–15 TPT). Echoed with resonant sorrow in Psalms 41:9 (TPT): "*Even my ally, my friend, has turned against me. He was one I totally trusted with my life, sharing supper with him, and now he shows me nothing but betrayal and treachery. He has sold me as an enemy.*" In the vernacular of contemporary mediaspeak, we might aptly dub Judas a frenemy of Jesus who masqueraded as fren with an unwavering facade for a time and a season, only to be eventually unmasked as a nonfren through and through. Yet, amid the frostbitten tableau of that harrowing night, by no conceivable measure could Jesus be deemed caught off guard or blindsided, for as he had foretold with unflinching prescience over the solemn precincts of the Last Supper, "*Assuredly, I say to you, one of you will betray Me*" (Matt 26:21 NKJV). He required no special revelation or tutelage to foresee and identify in advance the one ordained to betray Him—the so-called son of perdition—who would arise from within the intimate circle of the Twelve. This is evident in His high-priestly prayer during that Passion Week: "*While I was with them in the world, I kept them in Your name. Those whom You gave Me I have kept; and none of them is lost except the son of perdition, that the Scripture might be fulfilled*" (John 17:12 NKJV). Scripture issues no fixed, irrevocable decree predestining any particular individual to become the son of perdition in all his tragic infamy. The prophetic role remained open until Judas, driven by his own rapacious greed, tragically stepped into its contours—his insatiable covetousness molding him with sorrowful precision to fulfill the foretold betrayal. One might observe, with a touch of wry reflection, that his avarice fitted the prophetic pattern with an almost providential exactness, sealing his destiny in the very furnace of his chosen desires.

Only a heart utterly devoid of love could commit the horror of murder, and with Satan established as the original father and inexhaustible wellspring of all hatred, this venomous enmity inevitably flows forth as the outward expression of his dark, twisted nature. He channels it insidiously through men and women who are hoodwinked into becoming willing instruments and complicit partners in his relentless campaigns against the beleaguered human race. With this sobering insight, the Psalmist could hardly contain his grief-stricken cry over such irrational, cruel, and wholly undeserved hatred: "*Those who hate me without a cause are more than the hairs of my head; those who would destroy me, being wrongfully my enemies . . .* " (Ps 69:4 KJV). The poignant phrase '*without a cause*' derives from the original Hebrew *chinnâm*, which evokes the idea of laboring for naught, or in vain, or to no avail. Completely lacking any substantive motive or justifying grounds, much less a fruitful outcome. The Lord provides a second, striking confirmation of this truth in His second dialogue with Satan over the righteous Job: "*Have you considered My servant Job, that there is none like him on the earth, a blameless and upright man, one who fears God and shuns evil? And still he holds fast to his integrity, although you incited Me against him to destroy him without cause*" (Job 2:3 NKJV). In the resounding final clause of that verse, one discerns how the LORD unreservedly discloses that Satan harbored a singular, pernicious intent '*to destroy him [Job] without cause*'—in other words, without any legitimate cause or justifiable reason, but purely for spite and for sport, an exercise in gratuitous malice. Even though no trophies awaited his grasp—no laurels or rewards dangled as enticement—he remained hell-bent on annihilating the blameless man for absolutely nothing, deriving a perverse, intoxicating pleasure from the exquisite pain inflicted upon others and a macabre happiness from the raw hurt he orchestrated, not because such depravity augmented his own essence in any measurable way, but solely because it afforded him a fleeting, warped solace that no sane soul could ever hope to comprehend or reconcile within the confines of rational thought. This grim tableau figuratively embodies the futile folly of inheriting the wind—the whirlwind of utter nothingness—by doggedly pursuing a trajectory of action from which one inevitably reaps absolutely nothing in the end, a barren harvest sown in the tempests of vanity. Thus, it compellingly warrants the Wise Preacher to interpose this piercing rhetorical question amid his meditations on life's enigmas: " . . . *And what profit has he who has labored for the wind?*" (Ecclesiastes 5:16 NKJV). The answer, crystalline and incontrovertible even to the blind, rings forth with inexorable finality: it is none—no profit whatsoever, only the echo of squandered toil reverberating into oblivion. In the same vein, this unyielding truth aligns seamlessly with what the Apostle Paul evoked when he decried Satan's machinations as " . . . *the unfruitful works of darkness* . . . " (Eph 5:11 NKJV). The evocative term "*unfruitful*," rendered from the Greek akarpos, literally signifies "barren" or "fruitless"—a sterile void yielding no harvest, no proliferation of life, but only desolation's sterile hush.

This harrowing account of Job's trials further lays bare, with chilling clarity, the abysmal depths to which Satan is willing and eager to descend in his unquenchable hatred for mankind, given even the slightest unchecked opportunity. In a single, devastating day, he orchestrated catastrophic ruin upon that righteous servant's life—stripping away family, wealth, and health in one merciless onslaught—all without gaining anything, all devoid of reward or purpose, driven solely by the venomous malice that consumes him. With timeless sagacity, the Scriptures steadfastly affirm, "*For there shall be no reward to the evil man; The candle of the wicked shall be put out*" (Prov 24:20 KJV). The Good News Translation renders this same verse with stirring contemporaneity: "*A wicked person has no future—nothing to look forward to*"—a verdict with which I could not concur more emphatically, its resonance echoing through the soul like a divine echo. We must reaffirm this solemn truth: that Satan stands irredeemably lost—utterly beyond the pale of repentance—irrevocably beyond the reach of salvation. He knows full well that his case has long been judged and consigned to the annals of a hopelessly lost cause, and he also recognizes that his relentless atrocities against humanity yield him no profit, only deeper entanglement in ruin. Having thus resigned himself to the inexorable, grim kismet that the everlasting infernal fires of hell await him and his demonic minions with unrelenting, scorching fury for the most inglorious and utterly unglamorous reception imaginable. No Grammys or red carpet welcome parties await the damned in hell—only the desolate silence of irreversible loss and unending sorrow. Meseems we stand at a crossroads where someone must plainly declare to the devil that evil offers no true payoff; wickedness leads only to a hollow, self-inflicted abyss. His enmity toward humanity is both causeless and disturbingly obsessive—a hellish preoccupation with extinguishing lives for twisted pleasure alone, rendering it all the more profoundly sinister and inexcusable. And herein, for me, resides incontrovertible evidence to posit that the eugenicists of this modern-day era are merely imbibing insidious cues from their spiritual progenitor, the devil—" . . . *the spirit who now works in the sons of disobedience*" (Eph 2:2 NKJV). In our troubled age, we cannot fail to notice those individuals—men and women alike—who display a fervent, almost feverish zeal in advancing the cause of death, tirelessly spreading a culture that celebrates destruction across the globe. Their life's chief mission seems to be the large-scale extinguishing of human lives, the orchestration of widespread loss of soul and breath. To my deep sorrow, I have encountered such figures, and what heightens the dismay is their prominent presence on our screens in these turbulent times. I would wish the very best of fortune to anyone daring to probe the abysmal depths or scale the vertiginous heights of Satan's malevolent hatred toward humanity—for just as our finite minds can never fully comprehend or contain the infinite expanse of God's boundless love for us, so too the adversary's enmity remains an impenetrable mystery, a dark enigma forever beyond the reach of human understanding.

If we can confidently affirm with Scripture that "*God is light and in Him is no darkness at all*" (1 John 1:5), then by the same measure we may rightly conclude that since "*God is love*" (1 John 4:8), there can be no hate in Him whatsoever. The parallelism is profound: just as the perfect purity of light admits no compromise with even the faintest trace of darkness—neither tolerating its presence nor permitting it any foothold—so the flawless integrity of divine love excludes every possibility of hatred, allowing it neither entry, expression, nor influence within the flawless harmony of his eternal relational being. Here, God stands revealed not merely as a source but as the living embodiment, the radiant archetype of light itself, intertwined inseparably with the personal, pulsating vitality of love that defines existence at its core. It is this very identity—God as love—that seals the verdict: no hate dwells within, no antipathy lurks in the recesses, for such would fracture the very foundation of that nature. Hatred or enmity, after all, wears the unmistakable garb of love's direct inversion, its polar negation, rendering any imagined coexistence not just improbable but metaphysically impossible within the seamless unity of the Divine character. And when we elevate this to the doctrinal pinnacle of Divine omnibenevolence—that majestic affirmation of a God whose lovingkindness permeates every facet of his being, not as an occasional attribute but as the throbbing pulse of his eternal essence—we find ourselves inescapably drawn to the conclusion that hate clashes irreconcilably with every outflow, every expression, every act proceeding from that essence, branding it as an alien intruder, a conceptual impossibility for God to embody or enact in the manner we mortals grasp through our shadowed lenses.

It follows as surely as night follows day that every occurrence of "hate" or its cognates when applied to God across the full sweep of inspired Scripture calls for our most careful, prayer-drenched exegetical labor—unpacking its layers, situating it within its immediate narrative and broader theological context, lest we misinterpret the Divine heart through the fog of our limited human language. Take, for example, the striking phrase "*the foolishness of God*" (1 Cor 1:25): at first glance it shocks the intellect, for foolishness in its ordinary sense—irrational absurdity—seems irreconcilable with the limitless wisdom that governs creation—how then could such a word be applied to the All-Wise without contradiction or degradation? Yet when we look more deeply into Paul's apostolic intent, we discover not a literal attribution but a brilliant rhetorical device, intended to highlight the vast chasm between heavenly wisdom and earthly folly, just as "*the weakness of God*" serves to underscore the infinite distance between divine omnipotence and human frailty. Paul, in these daring expressions, walks the tightrope of language's limitations, using paradox to exalt rather than undermine the divine perfections. It is precisely this kind of hermeneutical care that has fueled the passionate conviction of many theological voices across the centuries: they insist, with strong reasoning, that what superficial readers or skeptics may quickly label as "malice" or the fierce blaze of divine displeasure or wrath in Scripture is, in reality, nothing other than the measured, righteous unfolding of heavenly equity—God's justice wielding its gavel in holy response to the devastation wrought by human rebellion and sin, a justice that flows from the very same wellspring of love that seeks restoration amid the wreckage of sin.

Something else profoundly worth remembering here is that the Bible unequivocally teaches that hatred is manifestly a sinful work of the fallen human nature, standing in diametric opposition to the righteous work of the Spirit of God—or, as the Apostle Paul electively designates it, '*the fruit of the Spirit*' (Gal 5:22)—as against 'works of the flesh' (Gal 5:19). This stark juxtaposition inescapably implies that for God to grant hatred even the slightest foothold or expression within his immutable nature, he would perforce be indulging in the very works of the flesh that he expressly proscribes and condemns in his infallible Word—a prospect that borders on the inconceivable, utterly at odds with the impeccable moral character we have come to revere and affirm in him. For Paul's missive to the Galatian Church articulates this truth with razor shape precision: "*Now the works of the flesh are evident, which are: adultery, fornication, uncleanness, lewdness, idolatry, sorcery, hatred, contentions, jealousies, outbursts of wrath, selfish ambitions, dissensions, heresies, envy, murders, drunkenness, revelries, and the like; of which I tell you beforehand, just as I also told you in time past, that those who practice such things will not inherit the kingdom of God*" (Gal 5:19–21 NKJV). Without pause, he transitions in the very next verse to delineate love as the foremost attribute among the Spirit's verdant fruits, a living testimony to the transformative power at work within the redeemed. Thus, through this luminous contrasting of hate as the pernicious work of the human flesh against love as the sublime work of the Spirit of God, Paul lays bare the profound incompatibility at the heart of the matter: hate, rooted in the soil of human fallenness, is fundamentally at odds with God's transcendent nature and, as a matter of eternal principle, could harbor no scintilla of expression within his being—can claim no territory, no sliver of legitimacy, within the untainted precincts of his divine nature. This truth gains even greater weight when we contemplate the profound relational harmony subsisting among the Father, the Son, and the Holy Spirit—a triune fellowship of absolute accord, where divergence in purpose or inclination is utterly inconceivable.

Paul's Epistle to the Galatians dovetails seamlessly with the solemn admonition issued by John in Chapter 2 of his First Epistle: "*He who says he is in the light, and hates his brother, is in darkness until now. He who loves his brother abides in the light, and there is no cause for stumbling in him. But he who hates his brother is in darkness and walks in darkness and does not know where he is going, because the darkness has blinded his eyes*" (I John 2:9–11 NKJV). Observe keenly how he inextricably associates hate with the enveloping shroud of darkness and love with the illuminating blaze of light. And this luminous dichotomy, in turn, fortifies our conviction beyond cavil that hate is fundamentally incompatible with God's nature, for he is light incarnate, and in him there resides no darkness at all—not the faintest shadow or whisper thereof. Hence, love, beyond any shadow of doubt, emerges as the paramount, unrivaled expression there is—and ever could be—within the boundless expanse of God. Every expression emanating from God draws its vital inspiration from love—every divine act surges forth from a heart overflowing with love, unadulterated and inexhaustible. This inexorable truth extends even to acts of divine judgment, for even the most cataclysmic divine judgment unveiled across all Scripture—the unsparing judgement of sin upon the cross of Jesus Christ—unfolds, upon closer inspection, as the supreme, unparalleled demonstration of God's love toward mankind. Apropos to this profound paradox, the Scriptures proclaim with resounding clarity: " . . . *God demonstrates His own love toward us, in that while we were still sinners, Christ died for us*"—and this redemptive act he sovereignly undertook—"*to demonstrate at the present time His righteousness, that He might be just and the justifier of the one who has faith in Jesus*" (Rom 5:8; Romans 3:26 NKJV). This dual revelation further illuminates with great lucidity that both the greatest act of Divine judgment and the greatest act of Divine love that we witness in all Scripture were inexorably intertwined and simultaneously unveiled, side-by-side, upon the sacred scaffold of the Cross of Jesus Christ. And that speaks directly to the unassailable righteousness of God's judgments, proving irrefutably that divine judgments are never dispensed in the venom of hate or the sting of malice, never doled out in the shadow of ill will or solely for the crude mechanics of retribution, but invariably executed in the tender embrace of love and apportioned with scrupulous equity on the unyielding basis of merit.

With a touch of irony, we might wish the best of fortune to anyone bold enough to believe they could alter God's steadfast commitment to love humanity; not even the beguiling serpent, despite his Herculean efforts, could accomplish such an impossible feat; his efforts vanished into complete futility and vanity. Though God created Lucifer as an impersonal creature, just like every other heavenly messenger in his celestial host, Lucifer dared to take offense at the intimate, overflowing manner God lavished his love upon mankind. He took the matter far too personally, plunging into an extravagant overreaction wholly unbecoming and grotesque for an angelic creature of his exalted origin. Not only could Satan not tolerate the sight of divine love poured out so exclusively upon mankind, but he himself is fundamentally incapable of expressing or embodying genuine love in any true sense—leaving him a lovelorn wretch, utterly loveless by essence and intrinsically unlovable by indelible nature. Far from the romanticized notion some have embraced, the fallen angels did not descend in Genesis 6 to interbreed with human women simply because they were captivated by their beauty or overcome with romantic affection. Far from it—their actions stemmed from something far darker and more sinister than any spark of awe-struck love. In utter contrast, the opposite reality prevailed: the fallen angels pursued these abominations not from any spark of affection or admiration, but from pure, unfiltered spite and malice. Their corrupted hearts seethed with all-encompassing hatred toward the entire human race, driving them to sabotage our genetic integrity through envious corruption. Perhaps they also yearned for some vicarious participation in the human experience—the embodied, somatic privilege eternally withheld from their purely spiritual existence—thus seeking to defile what they could never possess.

Thus, those fallen beings accomplished their dark purpose with devastating success, plunging the earth into such profound corruption that it compelled God to reach a sorrowful yet unavoidable conclusion: "*I will destroy man whom I have created from the face of the earth, both man and beast, creeping thing and birds of the air, for I am sorry that I have made them*" (Gen 6:7 NKJV). The earth had become utterly corrupt before God, filled to overflowing with violence. When the Lord looked upon it, he saw that every inclination of the flesh had become corrupted, and so he declared to Noah, "*The end of all flesh has come before Me, for the earth is filled with violence through them; behold, I will destroy them with the earth. Make yourself an ark of gopherwood; make rooms in the ark, and cover it inside and outside with pitch*" (Gen 6:11–14 NKJV). In this solemn decree, divine grief and righteous judgment intertwined, paving the way for both destruction and the preservation of a righteous remnant. As we trace the sacred narrative to its luminous horizon within these pages, a sobering truth emerges unadorned: nowhere in the whole of Scripture—neither in direct statement nor in the faintest implication—does God ever express love, not even the smallest measure, toward any of his angels—from the most exalted archangel to the humblest among the rank and file—nor toward any other creature in the vast tapestry of his creation. It is thus incumbent upon us to underscore this foundational principle: the Creator-God is under no obligation whatsoever to extend love to any of his impersonal creatures—neither can he be compelled, persuaded, or constrained into such grace by any power or plea. The sovereign right to designate the exclusive recipient of his divine love rests entirely and irrevocably with him alone, a prerogative that belongs to his unchanging will and no other.

CONCLUSION

To wisse, we arrive at the sobering and enlightening conclusion: for untold ages Satan has dwelt in unquenchable inner torment, utterly beside himself, consumed by a fury he cannot extinguish—the deepest root of his anguish being his utter refusal to accept the unassailable reality that God's heart belongs wholly and supremely to mankind. This irreconcilable truth constitutes a vital strand in the tapestry of his ruin: it was precisely this scandal—that the Creator's supreme delight rests upon those fashioned in his image—that precipitated his catastrophic fall from the pristine heights of celestial splendor. As the Lord Jesus himself testified with sovereign authority, *"I saw Satan fall like lightning from heaven"* (Luke 10:18 NKJV). Such is the tragic consequence of arrogant disdain toward the one whom God cherishes with infinite tenderness: the Almighty will suffer no insolent hatred to be directed against his beloved image-bearer. Therefore, following Satan's brazen insurrection against his Maker, he was cast down from the heavenly realms with swift and irrevocable judgment. This also reveals a crucial timeline: Lucifer's descent—from the radiant angel of light to Satan, the angel of darkness—commenced only after the creation of man in Genesis. It was precisely at that moment, when humanity was formed in God's image, that the seed of jealousy first took root in his heart, growing swiftly into the towering tree of bitterness and hatred that would define his eternal rebellion. As Martin Luther King Jr. so beautifully observed, love begets love—yet in a profound and tragic irony, it was precisely God's boundless love for man that begot deep-seated hatred within Lucifer's heart toward the human race. The very affection that the Creator lavished upon his image-bearers became the spark that ignited the adversary's unrelenting enmity, transforming divine benevolence into the root of cosmic rebellion and malice. As though God lacks the rightful authority to bestow his love as he pleases, as if he requires counsel or permission to choose its object! One can almost hear the echo of Jesus' words to the disgruntled worker in the parable of the vineyard: "*Is it not lawful for me to do what I wish with my own things* [love]? *Or is your eye evil because I am good?' So the last will be first, and the first last. For many are called, but few chosen*" (Matt 20:15–16 NKJV—the word in parenthesis is added).

Satan's eye, like that of Judas, became evil precisely because God lavished the costly fragrance of his alabaster love upon mankind alone.

For although Lucifer was fashioned 'first' in the order of creation, he consequently became 'last' in the order of divine favor; though God 'called' forth many creatures into existence, his heart sovereignly set its affection upon the chosen one—man. In this divine reversal, the exalted archangel found himself surpassed by the humble image-bearer, a testament to the Creator's free and purposeful choice to lavish his love upon humanity alone or whomever he elects. Apparently, he had remained in his exalted angelic station until the birth of God's image-bearer—mankind. This abrupt and catastrophic fall essentially transformed him into an exponentially more dangerous and depraved being—not merely a ruin to his own fractured essence, but a relentless, pervasive threat to every creature under the divine canopy. His corruption grew so grievous that he drew a third of the angelic host into his rebellion, dragging them down with him into the abyss of insurrection (cf. Rev 12:4, 9; Matthew 25:41). Once more, we are irresistibly drawn to compare Satan's unrelenting malice toward mankind to the fierce wrath of a jilted lover. Because the deeper you comprehend the measureless depths of God's love for you, the more evident it coincidentally becomes why Satan harbors such fierce hatred toward you. For were it not for God's extraordinary affection, there would be no such enmity. Otherwise, we would witness the adversary pouring all his malicious energy into tormenting other creatures—perhaps the wild beasts of the field—rather than reserving his unrelenting malice exclusively for God's image-bearers. His hatred is not random; it is precisely targeted at those whom God has uniquely loved and marked with his own likeness.

One might hope he could restrain himself, but he cannot—his enmity flows as naturally and irrepressibly as jealousy itself, often awakened by the presence of a perceived rival. Precisely as Solomon captured in his proverb: "*For jealousy arouses a husband's fury, and he will show no mercy when he takes revenge*" (Prov 6:34). This striking parallel reveals the depth of the adversary's envy—not born of any prior love betrayed, but ignited by the exclusive divine affection poured out upon mankind alone—driving him to a vengeful fury, one that admits neither compassion nor restraint. So great is this jealousy that God, in his wisdom, explicitly warned the people of Israel against provoking such wrath in human relationships, incorporating safeguards within the Mosaic law to guard against the destructive force of a jilted lover's rage. In this denouement, the serpent's shadow lengthens across the garden's threshold, revealing the Adversary's true peril: in truth, he metastasized into a peril far too acute even for his own beleaguered survival, forfeiting every vestige of meaning and benignity intrinsic to his primordial existence, emerging forthwith as an existential cataclysm to both his own shadowed self and, preeminently, to mankind—having abjectly floundered in his desperate attempt to supplant humanity's exalted station within the heart and mind of the Almighty. Yet, tragically, Adam and Eve, ensnared in utter obliviousness to Satan's true, malevolent colors—his serpentine duplicity veiled in cunning allure—proffered him the unguarded right hand of fellowship within the verdant sanctum of the Garden, a grievous misstep they ought never to have committed, one that the Adversary seized upon with predatory alacrity, cunningly leveraging that ill-fated opening to usurp mankind from their privileged perch as the centerpiece in the heart of God's resplendent creation—having ignominiously faltered in his prior, vainglorious bid to dislodge them from their singular, cherished abode within the heart of the Creator-God himself.

From the silent dawn of creation's genesis, across the upheavals of angelic revolt and the brokenness of humankind, this chapter has led us inexorably to witness the unconquerable triumph of a love that prevails above every shadow cast by cosmic strife. Now, in the radiant unveiling of divine revelation, the veils of antiquity are drawn back to reveal a love eternally purposed—a love that, before time began, appointed us to be the chief treasure of God's affection in Christ, our redemption foreordained and inscribed as an essential, unalterable provision within creation's original design from the first instant of the eternal counsel. In this glorious arrangement, the dark reality of sin is inseparably joined to a foundation resting wholly on God's self-diffusing, outgoing love—an exuberant benevolence that constitutes the living pulse of the created order. This exalted vantage point floods our theological vision with rich philosophical depth, enthroning the love of God as the sovereign reality and ultimate substance of all that is. In this light, divine love stands revealed as the paradigmatic principle that transcends and fulfills every causal framework—eclipsing Aristotle's efficient cause (the originating power) and final cause (the directed end)—and thereby redirects the entire course of human history toward the intentional, comprehensive embrace that the Father has eternally intended for us in Jesus Christ his Son. As the chapter closes, let us abide in wondering adoration at the edge of this mystery: in the intertwined threads of election and exile, our summons into the heart of the Creator stands as both sheer, unmerited gift and irrevocable vocation—where the storms of defiance melt into the quiet melody of grace, and the unchanging, resolute gaze of God beckons us homeward through the pierced side of the Lamb.

Soli Deo Gloria!

4

That God Became a Man to Meet Man's Greatest Needs

Meeting the most essential human needs ever to have arisen in the history of the human experiment

To properly place the discussions that follow within their broader context and offer a bird's-eye perspective, it is essential to briefly underscore the prevailing theme that threads its way like a golden cord through every page and chapter of this work. At its heart lies what the author identifies as some of the most foundational existential needs ever to emerge in the human experiment since the Fall. These needs were so profound that they drew forth God's own incarnation from heaven to earth, providing eternal answers: the existential need for the redemption of the human soul, the existential need for the rebirth of the human spirit, the existential need for the perpetuity of human existence, and the delicate pre-Fall need for God's Paraclete—the Holy Spirit Himself. Together, these form the bedrock of '*The Doctrine of Man,*' underscoring revealing mankind's desperate and unparalleled need for salvation in Christ Jesus. So vast and central are these needs that nothing else rivals them in magnitude; no other human longing approaches their gravity. Universal in scope, these soteriological necessities bind every person across time and space—regardless of race, ethnicity, social standing, or creed—defining the deepest shared realities of human existence, both temporal and eternal. They are so vital to man's earthly life and ultimate destiny that their absence represents the greatest existential peril to every soul, past, present, and future. Grounded in God's act of becoming human, this teaching reveals our dependence on his love to find meaning, showing our reliance on the Savior's redemptive sacrifice. No human ambition, worldly pursuit, or temporal gain can rival these needs, which stand as the foundation of human purpose, guiding us through our earthly journey and toward our eternal home, uniting us from the dawn of creation to the horizon of eternity.

SALVATION: THE MOST FUNDAMENTAL HUMAN NEED

Given their nonelective nature and supreme importance, these redemptive needs surpass all others in rank and paramountcy. Without their fulfillment, human life on earth would lack any telos and existential substance. All other needs that arise in a man's life are largely secondary—fleshly and material, concerned with mundane questions such as "*What shall we eat?*" or "*What shall we drink?*" or "*What shall we wear?*" (Matt 6:31 NKJV). These questions captured principal concerns for many in Jesus' day, but how much more do they dominate in modern times? Today, such subjacent needs often take pride of first place in countless lives, while the fundamental needs that should concern us most are neglected and relegated to the back benches of life. Modern culture has enculturated many to adopt an intellectual posture of indifference or nescience toward the existential questions of life, sidelining eternal truths that define our purpose and destiny. This leaves humanity adrift in a sea of fleeting, material pursuits devoid of ultimate meaning. People simply just care more about bread-and-butter issues, and the rest can wait or be forever damned in the silos of irrelevance. Yet, a fundamental existential need like the salvation of the human soul transcends this world and man's spatiotemporal subsistence. It is an aeviternal need, cutting across the borderlines between man's earthbound and eternal existence. For the human soul occupies the borderline between two natures—spiritual and physical—with one foot in eternity and the other in time, one foot in the ethereal regions and the other in the corporeal world. As an interminably ageless and ceaseless spiritual entity, the soul's eternal salvation ought to be of utmost importance, essential to both man's interminable spiritual existence in the hereafter and his transmigratory corporeal existence in the here-and-now.

This truth sheds light on why Jesus could stare right into the eyes of full-blown adult men and women encumbered by responsibilities—families to cater for—with urgent and relatively pressing needs often requiring great care and attention, and yet have the chutzpah to say to each one of them, "*Take no thought for your life, what ye shall eat, or what ye shall drink; nor yet for your body, what ye shall put on. Is not the life more than meat, and the body than raiment?*" (Matt 6:25 KJV). First, it is worth pointing out here that he is not to be considered censuring the whole industry of thinking, given how much he knew that God endowed humanity with the faculties of noesis to apprehend divine verities. He is rather reorienting every man and woman's concern and life's priorities away from those parochial needs that so easily beset us to the far more fundamental human needs that he, for one, considers supremely essential to man's cosmic existence, such as eternal life, spanning the here-and-now to the eschatological kingdom age and beyond. This divine summons to seek first the eternal reveals the very heart of God's redemptive plan: the salvation of the soul surpasses every earthly consideration in value. Consider the poignant encounter between Jesus and the rich young ruler, who ultimately rejected the priceless gift of eternal life—the only assurance of perpetual existence—because he deemed something else far more precious in the hic et nunc. The Gospel records his sorrowful departure: "*Completely shocked by Jesus' answer, he turned and walked away very sad, for he was extremely rich*" (Mark 10:22 TPT). In the final balance of his heart, he weighed his affluence ad valorem to be worth more than eternal life, choosing the temporal over the everlasting. Speak of being penny-wise, yet pound-foolish; this he exemplified to the nth degree, being totally incognizant of the fact that not a single penny—not a single cent—nor even a single kobo of his moolah would be accompanying him through death's exit door, whenever he finally gets to take a bow out of this cosmic scene. It all would eventually mean absolutely nothing to himself or anyone else in the afterlife, but God's gift of eternal life in His Son is all that there is to essentially guarantee him the perpetuity of existence beyond this life. This choice underscores humanity's need for divine grace to recognize the eternal over the temporal, for only through Christ's sacrifice can we attain the life that endures beyond the grave, securing our place in God's eternal kingdom where his love reigns supreme.

Like myriad souls adrift in today's tempests, this young man's heart was overcharged with the cares of this life and the deceitfulness of riches, which binds his soul, making it nearly impossible to embrace the Gospel's truth. So bleak was his case that Jesus had to say to His disciples, "*Assuredly, I say to you that it is hard for a rich man to enter the kingdom of heaven. And again I say to you, it is easier for a camel to go through the eye of a needle than for a rich man to enter the kingdom of God*" (Matt 19:23–24 NKJV). It should, however, be noted that the problem with this rich dude is not so much his riches as it is his 'trust' in his riches and the illusion of perennial security that it offered him. In other words, even though the Jews were self-assured monotheists by religion, yet unbeknownst to him, he had made for himself another 'god'—the false god that Jesus specifically referred to in another place as the '*unrighteous mammon*'—the god of avarice. Utterly neglecting the fact that "*No one can serve two masters. For you will hate one and love the other; you will be devoted to one and despise the other. You cannot serve God and be enslaved to money*" (Matt 6:24 NLT). Sadly, countless individuals have been beaten down in life to the point that they have internalized the prevailing cultural lie that "*money rules the world*"—or, more personally, that money rules their world. For them, every decision, every pursuit, and every step is dictated solely by what money demands and where money directs. Money has become the absolute master, reducing them to willing servants in its kingdom. In their relationship with wealth, money reigns supreme, issuing commands to go here or there, to steal, or even to kill—as Judas ultimately did. Their entire existence orbits around money, leaving no room in their hearts for God's righteous laws; money alone calls the shots (cf. Psalm 10:4). God, the divine Architect, fashioned man, and man in turn created money as a practical instrument for earthly exchange. In the intended order, money should serve man, while man renders worship to God as the supreme Sovereign.

Yet tragically, many live in a reversed reality—a topsy-turvy world where wealth usurps God's place—money is exalted as master, and God is reduced to a mere tool for transactional convenience. Unwittingly, they have enthroned money as lord, only to discover it becomes a ruthless tyrant, poised to destroy the very soul that serves it. This inversion lies at the heart of Jesus' solemn warning. While recognizing the legitimate role of temporal authority in human affairs—Caesar's domain in the earthly realm—Jesus firmly declares that no such authority may ever be placed above God's sovereignty. We are to render to Caesar what belongs to Caesar, but to God what belongs to God (cf. Matt 22:21)—giving earthly rulers their due while reserving ultimate worship for the Creator alone. Thus, in enthroning wealth above God, the rich young ruler transgressed the supreme and foundational commandment of Scripture: "*Hear, O Israel: The LORD our God, the LORD is one! You shall love the LORD your God with all your heart, with all your soul, and with all your strength*" (Deut 6:4–5 NKJV). By choosing earthly riches over the LORD Himself, he failed to render the wholehearted, exclusive devotion that God alone deserves, demonstrating how the lure of temporal gain can tragically displace the eternal priority of loving the one true God with every fiber of one's being. Perhaps he needed a gentle nudge on his right shoulder for just a friendly reminder that, hey, " . . . *Life is not measured by how much you own*" (Luke 12:15 NLT). Were he to accuse us of wielding Scripture too zealously or of being the often so-called '*Bible basher*,' as some might in the bustling streets of Swansea or the busy thoroughfares of London, we could summon a voice from Chicago or San Francisco to reframe the truth in urban lingua franca: Life isn't all about the Benjamins, buddy! Capisce? You may have to pardon my French there, but this is the unvarnished truth.

THE ULTIMATE VALUE: NOTHING IN CREATION MERITS THE SACRIFICE OF THE CREATOR-GOD EXCEPT THE HUMAN SOUL

I have said that in order to also say this, in the entire universe of creation, only the soul of humanity justifies the death of God the Creator. Christ's crucifixion on the cross at Calvary was not aimed at redeeming or founding any religion—though countless religions have since arisen. Nowhere in the four Gospels does Jesus ever state or imply such a purpose; his sacrifice was for something far more profound—the eternal redemption of the human soul, the one created thing whose value demanded nothing less than the very life of God. On the contrary, Jesus stood in resolute opposition to religion itself, repeatedly confronting the religious authorities of his time who placed rigid customs above living truth and elevated ceremonial ritual over authentic spiritual reality. His life and ministry were marked by a radical insistence on the heart of God's kingdom rather than the outward forms of human tradition, exposing the emptiness of piety that lacks genuine devotion. His mission, oft-repeated in words that echo through eternity, was to offer himself as the sacrificial Lamb, not for the privileged few but for the salvation of all humanity—irrespective of their religious persuasion, political affiliation, socio-economic status, academic qualification, racial background or ethnicity, tribe, or tongue. In his very own words: "*Thus it is written, and thus it was necessary for the Christ to suffer and to rise from the dead the third day, and that repentance and remission of sins should be preached in His name to all nations, beginning at Jerusalem*" (Luke 24:46–47 NKJV). In other words, his Passion, death, and resurrection were to suffice as the necessary and sufficient condition for the remission of the sins and the redemption of the souls of all mankind. He likewise affirmed, "*for the Son of Man has come to seek and to save that which was lost*" (Luke 19:10 NKJV). The phrase 'that which was lost' in the above verse refers to the lost souls of all mankind—lost in the life of sinfulness and lost in the most distant separation from God. So whether one identifies as a religionist or an irreligionist, atheist or agnostic, Judaist or Buddhist, Mahometan or Zoroastrian, Shintoist or Shaman, secular humanist or existential nihilist, or just whatever the case may be, it does not matter; we all need the redemption of our human soul, the eternality of our human existence, the rebirth of our human spirit, and the help of God's Paraclete alike. Without these, our relatively short earthly existence, however industrious or illustrious, amounts to a fleeting shadow, a vain pursuit that crumbles into nothingness.

Even our very lives and transient existence will be uberly devoid of any ultimate significance whatsoever, and as perfectly captured in one of the most famous quotes by the Wise Preacher, King Solomon, it will all just be "*Vanity of vanities, all is vanity*" (Ecclesiastes 1:2 NKJV). The proper rendering for that should be: Vanity upon vanities, all is vanity. And what that simply means is that filling emptiness (vanity) with more emptiness will only end up leaving whoever does so with emptiness and even more emptiness. Man's existential emptiness must therefore be filled with substance: Christ is needed here! And yes indeed, without the redemption of our human souls and without any divine guarantees as to the perpetuity of our human existence, our relatively short-lived existence here on earth will mean no more than that—vanity—existential emptiness, and all the numerous activities that may have taken over our lives will eventually account for nothing more than the so-called '*Vanity Fair*.' So, for a fact, without the salvation of the human soul that God alone guarantees in Christ, the whole enterprise of the human experiment will eventually account for no more than wasted lives expended in wasted times, all amounting to nothing but extraneous exercises in futility, ultimately signifying pointlessness, emptiness, worthlessness, shallowness, and even meaninglessness. Because without having the aforementioned fundamental human needs met, man's journey of life on earth could most characteristically be summarised into some aimless circuitous wandering about the proverbial La-La Land, somewhat similar to that generation of the Israelites who had needlessly spent or perhaps wasted 40 years of their lives traipsing and circumambulating the mountains of the Sinaitic Peninsula, very much like Cain before them, who for example, had this to say about himself, after God was done describing for him what life was going to reduced to, living outside His Divine plan and purpose: "*Today you are driving me from the land, and I will be hidden from your presence; I will be a restless wanderer on the earth . . .* " (Gen 4:14 NIV). That certainly does not sound like anything he was cheering about; it is an informed lamentation rather. But oh, that this generation will come to realize how much of an existential restlessness and taedium vitae plagues that man or woman who has yet to find his or her rest in God through his Son!

All the more so, without some raison d'être to our lives or what the Japanese term ikigai, we would be no more than aimless and noctivagant vagabonds in the earth—having no sense of origin or destination in our perilous odyssey through life—no eternal plan or purpose to all of our cosmic peregrination whatsoever—essentially coming from nowhere and heading nowhere. On that account, it is God alone who confers on human existence its true and perduring meaning, even the objectivity of meaning. And only 'in' him do our collective expressions of dasein as creatures (especially as personal creatures) find their true meaning—never outside him and certainly not besides him. Very well do the Scriptures testify to the effect that " . . . *in him we live and move and exist. As some of your own poets have said, 'We are his offspring*" (Acts of the Apostles 17:28 NLT). In other words, both the origin and destiny of each man's existence are unilaterally hedged within parameters of God's divine ubiquity. Also, his omnifarious attribute comfortably places him and himself alone above and beyond the multifarious expressions of existence that are extant within the whole created order, such that every genus of his creatures can only coherently find their ideal expression of life's reality within him. Inferably, it would take no less than the One Who single-handedly grants men existence to equally grant them both meaning and purpose to their existence. Considered in that light, it must have to be that the Preexistent God is solely in the place and position to predeterminately confer on the existence of his creatures whatever meaning and cosmic coherence they are to experientially have in reality, and were predetermined to have by intelligent design and purposeful intent, all on the basis of his Divine goodness (cf. Col 1:17). But good luck accounting for the provenance of your transient existence outside the Preexistent God—much less making head or tail of your life without him. Moreover, it behooves us to remind ourselves at this point that nothing suddenly pops into existence from out of nowhere and without any explanations whatsoever, even our observable human experiences, as well as our scientific research efforts, all come together nicely in historically confirming *ex nihilo nihil* to be the case. Further corroborated by the overwhelming evidence of 'intelligent design' in the natural order of things in the world around us. Hence, the Creator is most beseemingly referred to in Scripture as the "*. . . God who gives life to the nonliving and calls into existence the nonexistent*" (Rom 4:17b, My Translation), and, like he further confirms in the first person, "*I have made the earth, And created man on it. I—My hands—stretched out the heavens, And all their host I have commanded*" (Isa 45:12 NKJV). Beyond controversy, everything we as a species have historically come to know and scientifically understand about our own existence and that of the created world around us was altogether authored by God himself as the Divine Auteur—handcrafted by him alone as the Divine Artificer. This I say to one and to all alike: may you find success in the impossible task of intellectually defining your own existence without God, or in philosophically discovering any lasting meaning for your life apart from him.

Even theistic philosophers, through their sustained and profound intellectual labors, have consistently succeeded in proving by reasoned argument that God is the ens entium—the Being of beings, the Person of persons, the Spirit of spirits, the God of gods, the King of kings, and Lord of lords—although the central reality stands out with unmistakable force regardless of which of these titles is employed. And that he is, in fact, the Greatest Conceivable Being. The First Cause (the Self-Caused who causes everything), the Uncaused (who is caused by nothing)—causa sui—for nothing is ever caused to come into being except by him. Also, he is the Prime Mover who sets all beings and things in motion, but he himself is moved by no one. For the same reason also, the ancient Greek term "theogony" is almost immediately rendered fundamentally inapplicable to the context of all considerations appurtenant to God's existence; for the preexistent and eternal deity cannot be confined or boxed up within the existential boundaries of origin and destiny to begin with, not especially given the fact that he is literally "*without father, without mother, without genealogy, having neither beginning of days nor end of life . . .* " (Heb 7:3 NKJV). Thereupon, the theological term 'emanation' is most characteristically employed in distinguishing between the incarnate generation of the Son (filiation) and the Pentecostal procession of the Holy Spirit (spiration) from God on the one hand, totally differing from the natural origination (procreation) of the sons and daughters of men on the other hand. It is simply futile trying to have our finite minds wrapped around God's Omnitude—his Divine allness. So again, he is ultimately the reason for being, the reason for everything, such that all creatures simply exist for his good pleasure—all under the aegis of his goodness. And that perfectly corresponds with the testimony of Scripture that "*You are worthy, our Lord and God, to receive glory, honor, and power, for you created all things, and for your pleasure they were created and exist*" (Rev 4:11 TPT). Not only were all creatures in heaven and on earth brought into being by the creative acts of the Creator-God, but their continuum existence is also altogether preserved by his sustaining act—all by the instrumentality of his Divine fiat, exactly what Peter was alluding to when he said in passing that: "*But the heavens and the earth which are now preserved by the same word . . .* " (II Peter 3:7 NKJV)—the same word of God that engendered creation at the beginning of time also preserves it in time—even until the end of time. As you can readily see, the Creator-God is to all his creatures over and above anything a potter could ever be to the pots or vessels of his own craftsmanship—above and beyond anything any workman could ever aspire to be to the work of his own workmanship (cf. Isa 29:16; 45:9; 64:8; Jeremiah 18:1–10).

THE VANITY OF HUMAN STRUGGLES SANS THE SAVIOR'S SALVATION

All our striving, all our accomplishments, fade into vanity without the redemption Christ offers. His death and resurrection stand as the sole pathway to true meaning, giving every person a chance to escape a wasted life and embrace an eternal purpose firmly rooted in God's boundless love and abounding grace. Only by recognizing this transformative truth can humanity break free from the illusion of a purposeless life and embrace the fullness of its intended destiny, a glorious life that transcends temporal constraints and ascends toward eternal significance and purpose. At any rate, we might as well just own up to the fact that without God and without his redemptive programme for humanity, nothing we do down here on earth will end up being of any significance whatsoever, it will all just be inconceivably vacuous; for though we supposedly find ourselves mindlessly thrust into the arms of cosmic existence by the so-called 'Mother Nature' through birth or evolution (as the Secular Humanists and Evolutionists would have us believe), it is only so that we may just live and simply die—live for a relatively short lifespan and eventually die off and forever evanesce into the oblivion of nonexistence or nothingness like the fleeting puffs of cigarette fumes and then irretrievably lost in the silos of the past like yesteryears—lost in the black hole of auld lang syne, the Scottish man may want to say in agreement. For though our kingdoms come, it is only so that they may come and go—forever gone as soon as they came, as though they had never really come; for though our empires rise, it is only so that they may rise and fall—ephemerally rising so high like the Tower of Babel, only to be eventually razed to ash heaps like the cities of Sodom and Gomorrah, the sooner they rose. And have you ever pondered over such questions as, where are the once great and renowned Babylonian, Assyrian, and even Grecian kingdoms of yesterday? Whatever happened to the preeminent Caesarean dynasties of the past? What is left to show for the hegemonic powers and expansionary ambitions in which the Roman Empire once boasted herself? And what else is there to remember the Pharaohs of Egypt for but the relics of their past glories—perhaps the Pyramids of Giza or the Pharos of Alexandria they most famously built and faddishly left behind? Although we keep on building civilization after civilization, it is only so that we may watch them eventually come down to ruinous ends and then get buried and forgotten under the refuse heap of history, and that particularly resonates with the principle underpinning the idiomatic expression: What goes up must come down. But one has to at least ask, how high can we really go without the Most High, and does it really matter how high we get on our own without him? Because at the end of the day, without him in our ascent, though it be towering as high as the Tower of Babel, it will only end up being short-lived, and by then our descent will be all the more guaranteed.

King Solomon was quick to both insightfully and fatidically point out that "History merely repeats itself. It has all been done before. Nothing under the sun is truly new. Sometimes people say, "*Here is something new!*" *But actually it is old; nothing is ever truly new. We don't remember what happened in the past, and in future generations, no one will remember what we are doing now*" (Ecclesiastes 1:9-11 NLT). If history is any reliable guide at all, we may safely foretell that this present generation, like so many that have preceded it, will prove to be more like those little kids who went down to play at the beachside—devoting long hours to the patient construction of elaborate sandcastles with beach-sand, only to watch the rising tide at eventide sweep in relentlessly, wave upon crashing wave, dissolving every turret and rampart they had so carefully shaped until nothing remains but smooth, unmarked sand. In the same manner, the inexorable tides of time and changing seasons have historically surged against the proud works of successive generations, burying their labors beneath the accumulating rubble of forgotten ages, eroding every trace of their strenuous exertions, and leaving behind no lasting fruit from their toil. Surely there must be something more substantial to this earthly existence—something solid, something truly tangible upon which the soul may securely rest—lest we continue merely planning and building, sowing and reaping, feasting and celebrating, marrying and giving in marriage, only to meet the same desolate end that overtook the generation of Noah: a people who beheld with their own eyes the Diluvian floodwaters rising at the very thresholds of their ancient civilization, sweeping away every monument of their ingenuity and enterprise, sparing neither their toilsome labour borne under the scorching summer-heat nor their backbreaking toil braved through the biting winter-cold. Quite sobering to realize that they ended up inheriting nothing but the wind of nothingness—reaping no more than the fruit of futility, having ignored Noah's prophetic warnings for no other reason than their Cassandra complex. Solomon was also quick to have clairvoyantly picked up on this, for he had this to say in congruence, but first, I must admit that I am particularly hard-pressed to quote him ad verbum here and could hardly resist the need to do so at considerable length, given the pertinence of the text to the point at issue, so kindly bear with me:

> *"I, the Preacher, have been king over Israel in Jerusalem. And I set my mind to seek and explore by [man's] wisdom all [human activity] that has been done under heaven. It is a miserable business and a burdensome task which God has given the sons of men with*

> *which to be busy and distressed. I have seen all the works which have been done under the sun, and behold, all is vanity, a futile grasping and chasing after the wind. I said to myself, "Come now, I will test you with pleasure and gratification; so enjoy yourself and have a good time." But behold, this too was vanity (futility, meaninglessness). I said of laughter, "It is madness," and of pleasure, "What does it accomplish?" I explored with my mind how to gratify myself with wine while [at the same time] having my mind remain steady and guide me wisely; and how to take control of foolishness, until I could see what was good for the sons of men to do under heaven all the days of their lives. I made great works: I built houses for myself; I planted vineyards for myself; I made gardens and orchards for myself and I planted in them all kinds of fruit trees; I made pools of water for myself from which to water the forest and make the trees bud. I bought male and female slaves and had slaves born in my house. I also possessed herds and flocks larger than any who preceded me in Jerusalem. Also, I collected for myself silver and gold and the treasure of kings and provinces. I provided for myself male singers and female singers, and the delights and pleasures of men—many concubines. So I became great and excelled more than all who preceded me in Jerusalem. My wisdom also remained with me. Whatever my eyes looked at with desire I did not refuse them. I did not withhold from my heart any pleasure, for my heart was pleased because of all my labor; and this was my reward for all my labor. Then I considered all which my hands had done and labored to do, and behold, all was vanity and chasing after the wind and there was no profit (nothing of lasting value) under the sun"* (Ecclesiastes 1:12-14—2:1-11 AMP).

What a Stygian indictment of the generality of human activities under the sun, a floccinaucinihilipilification of man's cosmic experience in the sheer absence of some ultimate significance. And what that also helps establish is the fact that there could be no happy ending to the human story without the eternal redemption of the human soul. As the entirety of man's fleeting cosmic existence would have been devoid of any ultimate significance had redemption not become part and parcel of the human story at some point. Without the promise of eternal life or some life hereafter, man's journey through life would essentially amount to some pointless and hopeless waste of time and effort. Besides the advent of the God-incarnate in the 1st century A.D., the 4000 years B.C. history of man's existence on planet earth would doubtless have amounted to nothing but a sheer exercise in futility—all 'vanity' according to the Wise Preacher. Thus highlighting the tragedy of the human story without Christ the Savior. Without Christ, the story would just be the same for all of us, as our lives would most characteristically boil down to making money and paying bills, but at the end of the day, the story tragically ends in "*Naked I came from my mother's womb, And naked shall I return there*" (Job 1:21 NKJV). In other words, man basically has no profit from all of his labor and arduous toil from sunrise until sundown—he stands to gain nothing for all of his life's activities from cradle to the grave—nothing of substance to take away with him in all of his journey from womb to tomb. Naked and empty-handed he was born, and naked and empty-handed he is guaranteed to leave the cosmic scene. Not even the richest billionaires in the world will be taking a dime with them out of this place. So without Christ, life is essentially empty—it all comes down to heaping up vanity upon vanity, all amounting to vanity. Only Christ makes it full and meaningful; only he makes man's cosmic existence worthwhile—only he makes man's cosmic experience make any sense at all. The sense in which I refer to him as the substance of man's existence—the only substance with which every man can fill out his empty and otherwise miserable life—the substance with which to fill that gaping existential void of meaninglessness and worthlessness. Like he said, "*I have come that they may have life, and have it to the full*" (John 10:10 NIV). Without him, our lives are essentially empty and devoid of any meaning and purpose whatsoever. Christ is the only thing of substance every man can take with him whenever he journeys out of this place and into the nether regions. he is all God gave us—he is all we needed all along—he has been the missing link in our humanity all along—one without whom our cosmic human story would be hopelessly incomplete. So not only did Christ save our souls from eternal damnation, he also saved us the trouble of having a pointless and hopeless cosmic human experience—he saved us the everlasting contempt of living meaningless and empty lives. Because at the end of the day, all the activities of a man's life would only have been in vain without him—utterly meaningless, hopeless, and devoid of any substance whatsoever. But just in case any one of us might be jetting off thinking that these existential challenges only plague those belonging to the lower rung of society, who are overly preoccupied with 9-to-5 working shifts, well, not according to what the wealthiest man in history is saying here; so whether blue-collar or blue-blooded—baseborn or wellborn—patrician or plebeian, all are equally as affected.

CONCLUSION

I should also point out, in a note of finality, that identifying these barefaced realities bothering around human existence and sounding off an alarm about them does not necessarily make Solomon, myself, or anyone else who so does an alarmist, a Capehanger, or the often so-charged prophet of doom, because, as the saying goes, the messenger is not to blame for merely delivering the message, no matter how much it turns out to be a bitter pill to swallow down. Besides, his ratiocination about the fact that the entirety of man's cosmic affairs will essentially amount to no more than 'futile grasping and chasing after the wind' or what I preferably would term existential sciamachy is no longshot away from the warning tintinnabulum Jesus had repeatedly sounded off in the ears of His own generation, saying: "*And as it was in the days of Noah, so it will be also in the days of the Son of Man: They ate, they drank, they married wives, they were given in marriage, until the day that Noah entered the ark, and the flood came and destroyed them all. Likewise as it was also in the days of Lot: They ate, they drank, they bought, they sold, they planted, they built; but on the day that Lot went out of Sodom it rained fire and brimstone from heaven and destroyed them all. Even so will it be in the day when the Son of Man is revealed*" (Luke 17:26-30 NKJV). This is especially the case in the sheer absence of some ultimate significance or objective meaning to life, and it is why God knew so well that he had to price the redemption of the human soul far over and above the whole universe of things he created. So profoundly significant is that truth that his Son had to pose what I believe to be one of the greatest existential questions ever asked in the history of the world: "*And what do you benefit if you gain the whole world but lose your own soul? Is anything worth more than your soul?*" (Matt 16:26 NLT), good question! He was not merely comparing apples to oranges by placing in apposition the whole world taken together on the one hand and the soul of just a single individual on the other hand.

Quite obviously, the human soul is worth more than anything else in the world—way more valuable than the entire universe of things taken together, at least in the very eyes of the One who made them all, to wit, when weighed in his sovereign scales of existential value. Well, for all that this truth is worth, the One who once said, *'Follow Me and I will make you,'* is still very much in the business of making something of eternal substance out of the transient nothingness of man's cosmic existence—something of great worth and meaning out of the worthlessness and meaninglessness of the life of every human person ever born. Proud to say that His Name is Jesus. For in Christ and Christ alone are all men to potentially discover their intrinsic value and existential worth, including the divine purpose and objective meaning of their lives, because only then shall all existential crises of man's soul be brought to a standstill—even to the grinding halt of eternal stillness—with all existential threats to man's eternal destiny bidden the hush of everlasting silence. As if to say to the troubled waters of man's weary soul and to the boisterous winds of adversity billowing against the straight course of man's sail to eternal destiny: 'Peace, be thou still!'

5

That Christ is God's Final Answer to Man's Greatest Needs

Jesus Christ is the answer: in Him alone, God has accomplished everything necessary and sufficient to fully satisfy every existential human need

PERHAPS YOU HAVE NOTICED that I intentionally refrained from including Christians among the various stereotypical groups and made no mention of Christianity within the array of religious persuasions and philosophical worldviews surveyed in the preceding chapter. This omission arises not from any bias—though I openly and unapologetically confess my allegiance to the truth they proclaim—but from a careful recognition of Christianity's singular and unique manner of addressing humanity's deepest existential needs. The Christian faith and worldview stand apart in that they present Christ alone as the universal and all-sufficient answer to these longings—the one true and complete remedy for the soul's profoundest yearnings. Truth be told, no other religion or creed feigns any pretense about meeting any of the profound spiritual human needs so far identified. Through the annals of time, none has ventured the audacity to lay a finger of care on any one of them, as fundamentally important as they are to our collective human experience. Solely within Christianity's purview do they receive explicit attention and are addressed with unflinching resolve—exclusively via Christ Jesus, the Redeemer, do they attain consummate fulfillment, as our colloquy and forthcoming expositions shall further attest. Eternal salvation, the emancipation of the human spirit, constitutes no ancillary proposition to be tabled or trivialized; it reigns supreme as the apex exigency of corporeal tenure, its attainment beyond the machinations of mortal agency or barter. Of such bedrock importance is this demand that it necessitated a transcendent scheme exempt from the limits of time and space. More precisely, these exigencies were so primordial in essence that they compelled a protohistoric divine blueprint transcending the spacetime framework altogether. To expound: the Creator, in his aeonian omniscience, foresaw that Adam was going to end up plunging both kin and kind alike into the wreckage of sin and death, discerning the imperative for redemption. Accordingly, the full blueprint for redemption was strictly prehistorically predicated on the love of God for mankind; out of that limitless benevolence, he conceived a reparative mission before the universe's inception, a design rooted in his unwavering commitment to humanity's thriving. This pretemporal act of divine grace addresses the fracture of human existence with a solution as profound as the need itself, offering hope to all who embrace it. As our inquiry progresses, the unique power of this redemptive vision will unfold, revealing a pathway to wholeness that resonates with the deepest aspirations of the human soul, anchored in the eternal God's indescribable love.

THE PROTOEVANGELIUM: GOD'S SOVEREIGN PROMISE OF REDEMPTION IN THE SHADOW OF THE FALL

It becomes immediately and unmistakably evident that when Adam and Eve committed sin and experienced their tragic downfall in the lush Garden of Eden, God was far from being merely reactive or improvising in response to what had unexpectedly unfolded, as if he had been totally caught off guard or unprepared by the sudden crisis. No, he was deliberately proactive and strategically sovereign, operating light-years ahead of the unfolding situation in his divine foreknowledge and wisdom, since he had long before established and set in motion a comprehensive, eternal plan of redemption and restoration for humanity. As a direct consequence of this divine foresight, everything we witness him methodically orchestrating and progressively revealing in the post-fall (postlapsarian) sections of Genesis was nothing less than the step-by-step rollout or dramatic unveiling of that redemption plan he had already meticulously prepared and held in readiness from eternity past. And at the very heart and climax of the entire plan's immense weight and sacrificial cost, it was destined to be carried entirely on the willing shoulders of his only begotten Son, Jesus Christ—who is prophetically identified right there as the promised *'Seed of the woman'* in the pivotal curse-turned-promise of Genesis 3:16: "*And I will put enmity between you and the woman, And between your seed and her Seed; He shall bruise your head, And you shall bruise His heel*" (Gen 3:15 NKJV). That is God essentially making the commitment on behalf of humanity to establish an ongoing hostility and irreconcilable conflict between the serpent (symbolizing Satan) and the Messianic Seed in a transgenerational clash that would eventually have him fatally and decisively bruise and crush the serpent's head, destroying his power and authority forever. Therefore, this verse fundamentally establishes the promise of Christ the Savior as the very first and singular piece of fantastic news that the almighty Creator-God extended to a now-fallen and hopeless humanity in the immediate aftermath of their rebellion, which is precisely why esteemed theologians and Bible scholars have fittingly labeled this Scripture passage the *Protevangelium*—literally meaning 'the first gospel' or 'proto-gospel,' God's inaugural proclamation of salvation through the coming Redeemer.

That original, foundational (protological) gospel message, which received its maiden divine announcement within the foundational books of the Pentateuch (the first five books of Moses), would subsequently progress to its climactic, end-times (eschatological) fulfillment in the incarnate life, atoning death, victorious resurrection, and redemptive ministry of Jesus of Nazareth—all faithfully chronicled and preserved for our instruction in the Tetrevangelium (the Fourfold Gospel accounts of Matthew, Mark, Luke, and John), narrated as if inscribed in the vivid *'red ink'* of the precious blood that graciously poured forth from the sacrificial fountain of Immanuel's (God-with-us) pierced veins on the Cross. The Apostle Paul would later go on to echo this truth in a poignant reminder, affirming that the gospel of God—which he sovereignly promised beforehand through His faithful prophets across the expanse of the Holy Scriptures—centered chiefly on "*His Son Jesus Christ our Lord, who was born of the seed of David according to the flesh*" (Rom 1:1–3 NKJV, emphasizing the human lineage fulfilling divine prophecy). Given this unbroken thread of revelation, it comes as absolutely no surprise whatsoever that both the Tetrevangelium and the subsequent NT Epistles collectively embody and expound what is aptly designated *'the Gospel of Jesus Christ'*—a phrase the Apostle Paul repeatedly and affectionately employs throughout his inspired letters to the early churches. Yet, as I have just highlighted, even the majority of the OT Scriptures themselves constitute an essential, interwoven component of the Gospel of Jesus Christ, wholly depending on the interpretive lenses or Christ-centered perspective through which one reads and understands them. And Jesus Himself explicitly validated this reality in the Gospel of Luke, as well as in various other Gospel passages, declaring with authoritative finality, "*These are the words which I spoke to you while I was still with you, that all things must be fulfilled which were written in the Law of Moses and the Prophets and the Psalms concerning Me*" (Luke 24:44 NKJV). It is extraordinary to realize that, while every passage of these Scriptures was ultimately authored and composed with Him—the Messiah—at their very center, in their full essence and overarching substance, they were never written apart from you—the reader and beneficiary. They were never detached from your personal life story in view, nor oblivious to your God-ordained destiny and eternal hope held in focus.

At the very heart of his divine mission and incarnate purpose, Christ was unquestionably and profoundly all about you—the individual soul he came to redeem. It is you, in your fallen condition and desperate need, who ultimately and eternally became the paramount reason he sovereignly chose to step down from the unapproachable light of heavenly glory into the dust and darkness of this sin-cursed earth—lowering his throne to taste death and the tomb for trembling, broken humanity. And if ever there was a living fulfillment of the ancient idiom "*carrying the weight of the world on one's shoulders,*" look no further than Christ himself. Throughout his entire earthly life and ministry, he bore the crushing, indescribable burden of all sin, all sorrow, and all human lostness upon his shoulders—for the sake of every single soul he came to save. As the Savior of the entire world, the eternal destiny of the human race rested heavily upon his 33-year-old shoulders; he single-handedly shouldered the monumental weight of mankind's salvation, performing the impossible, redemptive labor we could never accomplish ourselves. This is the heart of what theologians have so fittingly called the substitutionary work of the Cross—the divine act where the innocent One took upon himself the full weight of the world's guilt and grief. Whenever we casually or figuratively speak of "having a heavy cross to bear" in everyday conversation, we must pause in solemn reverence and remember that no burden—however great—can ever compare in depth, agony, or redemptive significance to the singular, matchless cross that Christ alone bore upon his sinless shoulders. It comes as no surprise, then, to the heart that knows him, that the eternal, omnipotent Father experienced no hesitation or reluctance whatsoever in prophetically entrusting the full weight of his sovereign universal government—his righteous and just kingdom without end—to rest squarely and securely upon those very shoulders of his beloved Son (cf. Isa 9:6: "*The government will be upon His shoulder*").

Indeed, the entire work of the Cross was fundamentally a do-or-die affair of cosmic proportions—not so much for Christ in terms of his immutable divine nature or eternal security, but irrevocably and desperately for every one of us as fallen, dying sinners. We all—without exception—found ourselves confronted with a stark, binary choice: life or death, a fate-sealing moral dilemma and inescapable crisis that none of us possessed the power, righteousness, or capacity to resolve or fulfill in our own strength. Thus, Christ was either going to graciously, voluntarily, and self-sacrificially undertake and perfectly accomplish the full work of the Cross on our behalf—to secure our eternal salvation once and for all—or else we were tragically and irrevocably left with no alternative but to perish forever in the unquenchable flames of damnation. For as Scripture solemnly declares, "*the wages of sin is death*" (Rom 6:23)—that inevitable, spiritual, and eternal payment required by divine justice—so it was either Christ sovereignly chose to bear upon himself the full, imputed penalty of our sins and died our death in our place, or we each had no other path but to personally pay the infinite penalty with our own hell-bound lives in unending torment. And there was just no conceivable way of getting around it—no loophole, no evasion tactic, no merciful sidestep to circumvent or elude the long, inexorable arms of the Universal Law—that immutable, divine statute pertaining to human sin and the penal consequences it inevitably called for under the righteous decree of Heaven. For we all were equally and universally found as guilty beyond reasonable doubt and damnworthy as divinely charged—to wit, the indictment of original sin (inherited from Adam's federal headship) and our accumulated personal sins was all irrefutably fair, squarely just, and morally unassailable in the court of divine equity. And just as the state government exercises its inherent legal prerogative to apprehend, try, and justly punish the criminal for his heinous crimes against society, so too the sovereign God of the universe held the unassailable moral and judicial prerogative to condemn and punish the sinner for his grievous offenses against the holiness of Heaven. But strictly on the unshakable grounds of his infinite Divine love, boundless mercy, and compassionate lenity, he opted for and orchestrated the redemptive legal route that culminated in Substitutionary Justice—which consequently afforded him the judicial wiggle room and righteous basis to pour out his full, unrelenting wrath and penal substitution upon his own beloved Son instead of the utterly helpless, hell-deserving sinner. That, in its raw, transformative essence, is precisely what the Cross of Jesus Christ was unapologetically and redemptively all about—the spotless, innocent Son of God willingly stepping into and taking the exact place of the guilty, hell-bound, and spiritually bankrupt sinner—vicariously receiving and enduring the full, imputed wages for the sins he personally did not commit—and ultimately dying the multiplied, substitutionary deaths that the sinner alone deserved under divine justice. Condemned to a shameful, unjust death sentence by the corrupt human authorities at Gabbatha's merciless courthouse (Pilate's judgment hall)—and utterly damned and forsaken in divine wrath by God himself at Golgotha's blood-soaked slaughterhouse, where the Lamb of God was sacrificed for the sins of the world.

CHRIST: THE LIVING EMBODIMENT OF HUMANITY'S SALVATION

What is notable in the narrative of redemption is that it took this humble Man from Galilee—the incarnate Word made flesh—to self-sacrificially assume the driver's seat at the helm of man's fallen humanity. As he manned the wrecked vehicle of the human soul, destined for eternal damnation, he steered and redirected it—not just averting disaster, but guiding its course to eternal salvation—as the Champion and Savior of the world. To this purpose he is called "*the Captain of our salvation*" (cf. Heb 2:10), the archetype of leadership and deliverance. Upon this Captain—Jesus—the Pilot and Commander of redemption—faith for salvation is anchored like an anchor in the storm. Under his guidance, the lost ship of the human soul, which had strayed into the waters of God's wrath en route to eternal damnation, has now been guided to a course correction, sailing homeward to the haven of eternal salvation upon the waters of God's grace, arriving at God's destination, all secured and centered in Christ alone. The Scriptures hold to this testimony: "*You were wandering like sheep without a shepherd, but now you have returned to the Shepherd and Guardian of your souls*" (1 Pet 2:25). In recognition of his protection and intervention, he earned the title: "*the Guardian of the Human Soul*"—the champion of its eternal salvation. The redemption of the human soul was man's greatest priority, given the threat of eternal damnation over every person born under Adam's curse. Christ faced a battle of cosmic magnitude—a war for the redemption of souls across generations. He knew the stakes from the beginning. Whether the human soul would be redeemed depended on this one man—the God-Man Jesus Christ—and on every step he took, from his virgin birth in Bethlehem to his death on the cross at Calvary. He was willing and committed to the work required, in the name of God's love for fallen man—even when it meant confronting death to secure the salvation of mankind from eternal damnation. The rider on the white horse in Revelation 19:11—called Faithful and True—is the one who executed God's cause for man's salvation on the cross. He remained faithful and true to the cause until the end. He not only achieved salvation through his atoning work but also embodied it in his person. His name, Yeshua, means "the LORD saves," a testament to who he is as Savior. The patriarch Jacob was the first to invoke this name prophetically, declaring in his blessing, "*I wait for your salvation, O LORD*" (Gen 49:18)—where "salvation" translates the Hebrew word for Yeshua, the first mention of the term in Scripture.

The sacred Scriptures—spanning the profound depths of both the venerable Old Testament and the revelatory New Testament—come together in perfect, harmonious symphony and unbreakable unity, irrevocably giving us the unwavering, Divine guarantee and eternal assurance that: "*whoever calls on the name of the LORD shall be saved*" (Rom 10:13 NKJV)—and, amplifying this gospel truth even further—"*If you declare with your mouth, "Jesus is Lord," and believe in your heart that God raised him from the dead, you will be saved*" (Rom 10:9 NIV). In foundational principle and doctrinal essence, all of this redemptive promise and salvific pathway is strictly based upon the rock-solid, exclusive reality that "*Salvation is found in no one else, for there is no other name under heaven given to mankind by which we must be saved*" (Acts 4:12 NIV)—a declaration that shuts the door on every false hope and alternative savior. Interestingly—and profoundly so—in the narrative richness of Luke's Gospel, we intimately learn of a certain devout, righteous Jew by the revered name of Simeon, who had been faithfully, longingly waiting and watching for the glorious arrival of the promised Messiah on the cosmic, redemptive scene of human history. And he had this much—this Spirit-breathed, prophetic utterance—to say the very moment that the Holy Spirit divinely assisted and illuminated him in unerringly identifying the particular Jewish newborn infant who had only been ceremonially christened according to the ancient Mosaic Law and officially named *'Yeshua'*—some precisely 33 days earlier on the eighth day of his sacred birth, as commanded in Leviticus: "*Sovereign LORD, as You have promised, You now dismiss Your servant in peace. For my eyes have seen Your salvation, which You have prepared in the sight of all people, a light for revelation to the Gentiles, and for glory to Your people Israel*" (Luke 2:29-32 BSB)—a *Nunc Dimittis* (Latin for 'Now dismiss') that echoes through eternity as the old man's triumphant farewell upon beholding the Light of the world. This prophetic encounter would also irrefutably have to mean that ever before the fiery prophet John the Baptizer had even had the divine opportunity of fulfilling his pivotal ministry as the heraldic Forerunner and bold Revealer of the Messiah to all of expectant Israel—proclaiming in the wilderness, *'Behold the Lamb of God'*—Simeon had literally enjoyed the exalted, once-in-history privilege of beholding Him in the flesh—the living personification of the salvation of all mankind, miraculously encased in a fragile, innocent flesh-and-blood infant's body, cradled in Mary's arms at the Temple.

It therefore should come as no surprise whatsoever to any discerning reader of the sacred text to learn that the very day and precise moment in redemptive history that the fully grown, mission-accomplishing Man—Jesus the eternal Messiah—boldly walked right into the humble, tax-collector's home of Zacchaeus the chief publican, he was unhesitatingly bold and authoritatively confident enough to declare to him and every single member of his extended household by way of intimate, self-referential proclamation that: "*Today salvation has come to this house . . . for the Son of Man has come to seek and to save that which was lost*" (Luke 19:9-10 NKJV)—a divine visitation that transformed a traitor's heart instantly. Whoever ever spoke with such unmatched, divine authority and compassionate certainty as Jesus! And guess what—in the face of skeptical doubt—he was deucedly right and was by no means blustering, boasting, or speaking empty words, obviously because man's universal, eternal salvation was literally and inseparably embodied by the Savior himself—the relentless, seeking, and saving Shepherd who descended from glory on a daring, divine rescue mission and irrevocably became the very source and substance of salvation to all nations, peoples, tribes, and tongues of the earth. Moreover, everything he just declared to them in that pivotal moment is theologically equivalent and prophetically resonant to the eternal God of Israel himself thundering from the throne: "*. . . I AM your salvation*" (Ps 35:3b)—or, better still and more precisely in its covenantal depth, "I AM" is your salvation—the self-existent One becoming the personal deliverer. And that declaration is quite profoundly significant and laden with redemptive weight, because the sacred deonym (divine name-title) 'I AM'—*Yahweh*, the covenant name—was eponymously—as a namesake of deliverance—linked inextricably to the miraculous salvation and exodus of the Jews from their oppressive Egyptian slavemasters (cf. Exod 3:13–15, where God reveals, "*I AM WHO I AM . . .* "). Such that what we reverently call the Exodus today—that archetypal liberation from Pharaoh's chains—irrevocably foretypified and prophetically prefigured the universal, eschatological salvation of all mankind that was destined to be wrought, achieved, and consummated in the singular Person of Christ—the archetypical, Greater Moses of the New Covenant (see Deuteronomy 18:15–18; 1 Corinthians 10:1–11, where Paul explains the Exodus as a typological shadow). For both the Savior himself and the salvation he graciously offers and imparts are essentially one and the indivisible same eternal reality, such that you cannot possibly receive or lay hold of salvation in any authentic sense without the full, personal acceptance and embrace of the Savior. The heart-deep, volitional acceptance of the Savior—trusting in his person, work, and Sovereign Lordship—is precisely and comprehensively what it biblically means to be saved—rescued, redeemed, and restored to eternal life in fellowship with God.

Not only did the living Embodiment of Salvation himself arrive at Zacchaeus's home that pivotal day in person—bringing immediate redemption to the tax collector and his household—but on a universal scale, he arrived at the doorsteps of all fallen humanity the moment the Savior was born into this sin-shadowed world. Salvation walked through the metaphorical and literal doors of man's cosmic home on the day the uncreated God passed through the womb of the Virgin Mary, entering a fallen and morally bankrupt world undeterred by its sin, darkness, and depravity. The Apostle Peter, reflecting with post-resurrection clarity and Spirit-illumination, realized the immense privilege he and countless others—from the Twelve to the multitudes—had enjoyed in having Salvation present with them in living person: walking dusty roads, sharing meals, and teaching truths. With a note of holy regret, he lamented the missed opportunity to address and attend to him as befitting his divine personhood as God-with-us. Unlike the patriarchs, prophets, and saints of old, who only prophesied his First Coming from afar—never witnessing or meeting Him face-to-face—Peter articulates their longing: "*This salvation was something even the prophets wanted to know more about when they prophesied about this gracious salvation prepared for you. They wondered what time or situation the Spirit of Christ within them was talking about when he told them in advance about Christ's suffering and his great glory afterward. They were told that their messages were not for themselves, but for you. And now this good news has been announced to you by those who preached in the power of the Holy Spirit sent from heaven. It is all so wonderful that even the angels are eagerly watching these things happen*" (1 Pet 1:10–12 NLT). This testimony elevates New Covenant believers above the old as recipients of fulfillment rather than mere custodians of promise. It confirms that Christ, the prophesied Seed of the woman who crushes the serpent's head, is in his very person the living Evangel—the good news bearer—at the heart of God's Gospel to humanity.

He is the eternal Savior, the exclusive gospel of salvation, and the only hope for every fallen soul. It becomes even more glorious when we realize that the entirety of his earthly life, ministry, suffering, and triumph was expended to meet humanity's deepest salvific needs. In this sense, he was all about man's salvation: all about humanity, all about you the individual, all about our personal, communal, and universal salvation. This truth lies at the core of soteriology, embracing election, atonement, faith, and glorification for all who believe. With pastoral care, and without intending to offend any religious sentiments or traditions, it must be said that the common claim "*Christmas is all about Christ*" is not biblically accurate in its absolute form, even though it sounds comforting. Christmas is inextricably tied to Christ as the demonstration of God's covenant love, shown in the gift of his only Son—the supreme expression of divine generosity and redemption. Yet Scripture does not present Christmas as solely or ultimately about Christ in a self-referential way, as if the narrative centers only on his personal glory apart from purpose. Christ himself—the humble Servant-King—never made his birth, mission, or death about himself in isolation. He intentionally made it all about fallen humanity in its need. This may be a paradigm shift, but it is the liberating truth of the Gospel. Christmas celebrates the birth of a Savior whose entire incarnate life was purposefully spent securing man's salvation and soul redemption. Therefore, both Christ and the Christmas season are essentially about humanity—about its desperate plight—and the glorious salvation of every human soul.

Man—every single person, every successive generation—is unmistakably the intended recipient and beneficiary of the full redemptive drama enacted in Christ's birth and vicarious death. All that he did—from his lowly birth in the stable, through his atoning death on the cross, to his victorious resurrection—was accomplished for man, in the name and outpouring of God's unrelenting, unconditional love. Theological precision demands the question: What was the ultimate purpose behind this Gift? Why did God give his only begotten Son to a race enslaved by sin? First, the newborn Jesus—God with us—was sent forth from the Father's initiating love for man; hence the Scripture names him "*the Son of His love" (Col 1:13 NKJV). Second, if Christmas commemorates* the virgin birth of Christ, and Christ is the greatest personal Gift ever given by God to man, then Christmas is logically and theologically centered upon man—the cherished recipient, the prodigal race for whom the Child was prophesied and born, to whom the Son was given in covenant promise. We often quote Isaiah's magnificent words: "*For unto us a Child is born, Unto us a Son is given . . .* " (Isa 9:6 NKJV), yet we can easily miss their deeply anthropocentric thrust: the entire event is "unto us," viz., for us and all about us—the beloved objects of divine love. The prophet was simply declaring that the birth of the promised Child, who would go on to become Jesus Christ, was wholly for mankind. If Christ is the reason for the season of Christmas, and God's love for man is the reason he gave Christ as a redemptive gift for salvation, then it is biblically imperative to say that Christmas is essentially centered around man—around humanity's story—and the historical demonstration of God's love toward the sinner. The eternal Logos became the Lamb of God's love because he was born out of God's infinite love for man—a love that preceded the foundation of the world. To insist that Christmas is exclusively about Christ, excluding the recipient, adopts a posture of false humility and repeats unexamined religious platitudes that miss the relational heart of the gospel. But to claim that Christmas is exclusively about Christ—while excluding the recipient of the Gift of Christmas—adopts a posture of false humility and perpetuates unexamined religious clichés that overlook the deeply relational heart of the gospel. The birth of Christ is not a self-contained divine act; it is God's deliberate act of love directed toward humanity. To remove man from the narrative is to strip Christmas of its true meaning: God sending his Son to us, for us, in pursuit of us—the wayward recipients whose need and value moved the heart of God to act.

Beyond all the storytelling, however beautiful, stands this weighty and inescapable truth—one that weighs heavily upon every human heart and calls for an answer: Christ is the beloved Son whom God has given personally to you—so receive him. Open your heart wide and welcome the fullness of God's transforming love. You may feel unworthy of him or of the redemption he won for you on the Cross, yet the one true response is to believe it, embrace it, and receive it with thankful surrender. At that exact moment in history, God gave his only begotten Son because he loves you—has chosen you—with a love that beats all imagination. Christmas is redemptively about you—about God's extravagant love-gift of Christ the Savior to die vicariously for you on Calvary, sealing your eternal redemption. It is ironic that during the festive Christmas season of gift-giving and holiday cheer, we receive and express gratitude for every other gift—from toys under the tree to presents from loved ones—except the supreme divine Gift that matters most eternally: the beloved Son of God's love, Christ our eternal Savior and Redeemer of lost souls. Even the angels, who do not celebrate Christmas in the earthly sense, showed a more in-depth understanding of its true meaning than many Christians. On the first Christmas night in Bethlehem, they announced to shepherds and sinners alike, "*Do not be afraid, for behold, I bring you good tidings of great joy, which will be to all people. For there is born to you this day in the city of David a Savior, who is Christ the Lord. And this will be the sign to you: You will find a Babe wrapped in swaddling cloths, lying in a manger*" (Luke 2:10–12 NKJV). Notice the emphasis: "I bring you"—personal delivery; "to all people"—global scope; "born to you this day"—covenantal gift; "the sign to you"—tailored confirmation. The birth of the Savior, Christ the Lord, is in its final analysis—wholly for you—all about God's particular love for you, the cherished object of his redemptive pursuit.

And there you have it—in plain gospel simplicity—that is what Christmas is fundamentally about: the prophesied birth of the Messianic Savior who procures and secures your personal salvation, all accomplished in the name and expression of God's unfathomable love. With that timeless truth firmly grasped, Christmas and the extended Christmastide season would be stripped of superficial trappings—from the myth of Santa Claus, frenzied shopping, ornamented trees, and casual pleasantries—and restored to its biblical purpose: a sacred, reflective time of thanksgiving to God for the priceless gift of his only begotten Son, and to the obedient Son for faithfully fulfilling the Father's eternal redemptive plan for your soul's salvation from sin's dominion. In truth, the day we begin to see Christmas from God's sovereign, redemptive perspective—through the lens of divine economy rather than cultural consumerism—we would celebrate the Eucharistic Meal, the sacramental feast of remembrance, on December 25th with far greater fervor and Spirit-led passion than our traditional Christmas dinners, which pale in eternal significance. It seems, with sorrow, that the universal Church's understanding of Christmas has long been distorted and sidetracked from the pure purpose intended by the early Church Fathers through centuries of cultural drift. Even Christ himself would likely grieve to see Christmas celebrated as most do today—lost in secular pageantry rather than sacred proclamation. I say this with sober conviction: the only divinely ordained sacrament he personally instituted and entrusted to the Apostles and the Church for the perpetual remembrance of his sacrifice is the Eucharist, the Holy Communion—the memorial feast of grace—not a seasonal Christmas dinner. Bread and wine at the Lord's Table, symbols of his broken body and poured-out blood, were specifically instituted to commemorate his vicarious death for the remission and forgiveness of our sins, binding us to his cross in perpetual covenant.

In contemporary Christendom, professing Christians load their Christmas Day menus with every imaginable meal and dessert—from gourmet roasts to exotic sweets—yet omit the one sacred meal Christ himself instituted and commanded for his perpetual remembrance: the hallowed bread and wine, symbolizing his broken body and poured-out blood in vicarious atonement. Jesus Christ, in his essence and redemptive mission, is all about God's boundless love for man—especially for the lost sinner, for all have sinned and fallen short of God's glory. Christmas, the incarnational pinnacle of divine grace, should reflect this same gospel-centered focus. The unfathomable love of God for man is the foundational reason for creation—from galaxies to DNA—and remains the paramount reason for the entire drama of redemption, from Eden's promise to Calvary's triumph. Read the Scriptures for yourself and see if you reach any different conclusion. Even the Eucharist, the ordinance meant for solemn remembrance of himself, Christ made about you—the recipient of grace—saying, "*Take, eat; this is My body which is broken for you; do this in remembrance of Me*" (1 Cor 11:24 NKJV). In plain terms, the breaking of his body and the shedding of his blood were wholly for you—for your eternal salvation—not for himself. As often as you partake in this memorial feast, your thanksgiving, and praise will abound toward God for all his Son accomplished for you in the name of God's unconditional love. The purpose of this exposition is not to make Christmas artificially about yourself—God already did that in the person and work of his incarnate Son, and cultural tradition typically does so unconsciously—but to urge you to make it less about temporal pursuits and self-indulgence and more about the Father's eternal business: his compassionate love for the broken sinner and the salvation of his soul.

That is precisely what God's Christmas Gift is ultimately about—the personal salvation of humanity from sin's tyranny. Have you ever, in a moment of gospel courage, told a stranger on the street during Christmastide, "Sir/Madam, do you know Christmas is really about you—because God's boundless love for you is why Christ was born in a stable"? Observe the reaction: shock, wonder, a stirring of the soul—and the lasting impression that truth may leave, perhaps kindling faith. If the universal Church would humbly abandon self-righteous postures and proclaim to the desperate world that Christmas has always been about them—that the reason for God's gift of Christ was their personal salvation and liberation from death—hearts would open more readily to embrace the Gospel of God's love, the Gospel of their own salvation, prepared from eternity. Without agape love at its core, Christmas becomes an empty shell of festivity. Without God's redemptive love for the sinful world shining through us as living epistles, most Christmas celebrations remain hollow and devoid of eternal weight. God's pursuing, transformative love for the repentant sinner is the reason for Christ's birth and sacrificial death—the alpha and omega of the Advent story.

THE KING OF KINGS WHO STOOPED TO CONQUER BY BECOMING THE SERVANT OF SERVANTS—THE SERVANT OF MEN

I share the deep affection that spans generations of believers for Christmas hymns—those lyrical masterpieces that proclaim Christ's centrality in the Nativity. They are enduring anthems that conjure peace amid earthly toil, and I hold them dear, with no dissent against their declarations of devotion. This fondness grows when we reflect that the Eternal Son descended not to exalt himself or claim acclaim as a mortal, but to magnify his Father through obedience to the Father's redemptive decree of mercy for humankind. As he himself illuminated for his loyal followers in the dawn of resurrection victory, "*These are the words which I spoke to you while I was still with you, that all things must be fulfilled which were written in the Law of Moses and the Prophets and the Psalms concerning Me . . . Thus it is written, and thus it was necessary for the Christ to suffer and to rise from the dead the third day, and that repentance and remission of sins should be preached in His name to all nations, beginning at Jerusalem*" (Luke 24:44–47, NKJV). An Eastertide exposition that lays bare the Scriptures' Christocentric thread. His agony culminating in execution, his conquest over the sepulcher, and the summons to contrition yielding pardon form his own précis of what his incarnate life was about, in agreement with what the Old Testament writings prophesied across centuries of anticipation. Coming from the resurrected Lord himself, such affirmation carries gravity. By this progression, we arrive at this verdict: fallen yet cherished humanity stands as the impetus for the Deity's entry into time as Jesus the Christ, the incarnate Divine-Human. Since the Savior is depicted as devoted to humanity's deliverance, it follows that we—lost souls—are the core purpose of his advent. For Christ did not come down from heaven's throne to save himself, but to save you and me—the objects of grace—and so we are the reason he endured suffering, poured out his blood in agony, died a criminal's death, was buried in a borrowed tomb, and rose from the dead on the third day as foretold. Yet, as previously observed, this truth does not require us to transform the Yuletide into a self-indulgent spectacle—far from it—because although both the Redeemer and his commemoration are centered on us—on our deliverance—we purposefully redirect the celebration toward him in homage to him and in gratitude to the Father for every victory won on our behalf through the labor of his Crucifixion. When we delve deeply into Scripture, we discover that the prophetic writings about the Anointed One describe what he would accomplish in time—not for the enhancement of his divine fullness, but for the salvation and eternal well-being of all mankind. This is the evangelical truth the angel declared to Joseph when revealing Mary's conception of the Deliverer, to be named Jesus the Messiah: "*She will bear a Son, and you shall call His name JESUS, for He will save His people from their sins*" (Matt 1:21 NKJV). To redeem mortals from the penalty of sin would require the sacrifice of his own life, as he himself declared: " . . . *the Son of Man did not come to be served, but to serve, and to give His life a ransom for many*" (Matt 20:28 NKJV). That statement expresses the very creed of the Servant-King.

Behold with awe-struck reverence the King who, in supreme condescension, came not to be served but to serve his undeserving servants—the Creator-God who cared not for his own salvation but the salvation of his sinful creatures—mankind! For he did not deviate one iota but came precisely as was prophesied long ago—ever before he came; for he only came walking those humble, dust-trodden steps of sacrificial humility in unwavering service to broken humanity. And just about every single step he took throughout his thirty-three-year incarnate lifetime were all love-propelled steps headed in the singular direction of the demonstration of God's love lavished upon all mankind—narrow steps of agape love strictly taken in lockstep with the prophetic blueprint meticulously tailored to fit the fulfillment of God's redemptive plans; giant steps of amazing grace unwaveringly journeying toward the shadowed gates of death's domain. Going from being the Most High God to becoming the most lowly Galilean—that Man of Galilee who went from the serene shores of Galilee to the tormented garden of Gethsemane—from Gethsemane's sweat-drops-of-blood agony to Gabbatha's unjust Roman judgment hall—from Gabbatha's unjust courthouse to Golgotha's cruel slaughterhouse by the heart-wrenching *Via Dolorosa*, the sorrowful path of suffering lined with mocking crowds and heavy timbers. All the while destined for no fate shy of his horrific crucifixion—the most historically consequential, cosmic-altering crucifixion in the annals of time, which soon saw him descend from Golgotha's curse-laden stake to the cold, silent Grave wrapped in Graveclothes—further plunging from the tomb's darkness to the abyssal depths of Gehenna—the place of the damned—only to soon be found victoriously risen-alive from Gehenna's gripping chains back to his once-sealed Gravesite in a blinding blaze of resurrection glory. In what swiftly became the most gloriously iconic resurrection in human history—shattering the finality of death—the victorious Man then ascends from the ancient, weathered stones of Jerusalem's elevated ground, returning to his rightful place as God: the sovereign God he eternally was. This peerless God-Man now sits triumphantly and royally enthroned at the right hand of the majestic throne of God the Father's unfading glory, exalted far above the highest reaches of the Empyreal Heaven and transcending the unseen splendor of the third heaven.

In a fallen world ruled by arrogant men obsessed with aspiring to become like God through imitation, the humble Sovereign God, in an act of profound humility, became fully human for the sake of all mankind—to raise every person to the dignity of divine sonship, making them co-heirs with Christ in everlasting glory. Manqué deities—such as the Caesars and self-proclaimed "*God Emperors*"—were devoured by hubris, fixated on seizing crowns of self-deification and demanding divine honors from their subjects. By contrast, the true God-Man—whose life stands as a direct refutation of their pride and ambition—fulfilled the Father's redemptive will, reconciling creation to its Creator in peace and inviting all mankind to participate in divine sonship, the family of God. This evocative sequence is not a mere alliterative flourish or rhetorical device; it is historically factual and biblically accurate. I am simply drawing attention to what is already present—plainly evident in sacred Scripture, written in the words of the Word himself, calling us to deeper devotion. We must also consider deeply, that as a humble, self-emptying Servant to fallen men, he essentially had to deliberately stoop to the absolute depths of humility in order to conquer and subdue utterly; stooping as low as it possibly gets in divine condescension, so as to triumphantly conquer all sworn, implacable enemies of the vulnerable human soul—sin, death, Satan, and the grave—and thereafter—as the victorious, eternal King—ascend as high as it eternally gets, in Olympian, cosmic triumph and unrivaled exaltation over them all, securing redemption's crown for his beloved subjects. Very well, do the inspired Scriptures concur and harmoniously affirm this profound mystery of the kenosis and kyrios:

> *"He existed in the form of God, yet he gave no thought to seizing equality with God as his supreme prize. Instead he emptied himself of his outward glory by reducing himself to the form of a lowly servant. He became human! He humbled himself and became vulnerable, choosing to be revealed as a man and was obedient. He was a perfect example, even in his death—a criminal's death by crucifixion! Because of that obedience, God exalted him and multiplied his greatness! He has now been given the greatest of all names! The authority of the name of Jesus causes every knee to bow in reverence! Everything and everyone will one day submit to this name—in the heavenly realm, in the earthly realm, and in the demonic realm. And every tongue will proclaim in every language: "Jesus Christ is Lord Yahweh," bringing glory and honor to God, his Father!"* (Phil 2:6-11 TPT).

The early church's ancient hymn celebrating Christ's humiliation and exaltation, resounding through the ages. In essence, this reveals

God's triumphant elevation of his beloved Son and his joy in the victorious Son—prevailing over every archenemy, principality, and power that opposes mankind's eternal welfare. What emerges here is a classic illustration of the timeless principle: no cross—no crown. The pain, shame, and suffering of the redemptive Cross constituted the only predestined path by which the incarnate God—Emmanuel—would once again be crowned with the glory and honor he eternally held before entering the confines of time and flesh. For his Royal Majesty, the King of Glory—who sovereignly reigned over heaven's throne of unapproachable splendor—harbored no insecurities, no trace of doubt or hesitation in his divine mind. He willingly left behind his celestial kingdom, laid aside his glory, to venture into the fractured kingdom of man's fallen world in low profile, as though a nameless nobody amid the throng. Having turned his back on the streets paved with gold in the heavenly Jerusalem, only to come down here to walk the streets ridden with dust in the earthly Jerusalem—having taken off his gilded crown of glory, only to have his pate mounted with the goaded crown of thorns. As the Servant of all servants, he even stooped lower still to wash the dust-caked feet of his disciples with simple basin water, ultimately as a prophetic symbolic gesture that betokened the imminent reality that he was soon going to be washing clean all of their sins, not merely with ceremonial water this time, but with the purifying liquid of his own blood—shed on Calvary's Cross for the remission and erasure of sin. And so when impetuous Peter was suddenly, Spirit-illuminated, made to realize the salvific significance of the whole feet ablution ritual, he quickly made a run for the altar of grace—as though answering a divine altar call in revival fervor, exclaiming with surrender: "*Lord, [in that case, wash] not only my feet, but also my hands and my head!*" (John 13:9 AMP). This is actually his Lord and Master—the divine Messiah—washing his calloused feet—my God and your God stooping to wash our filthy feet, nothing short of the almighty Creator-God himself stooping as low as it gets to personally wash man's sin-fouled feet clean—the very same feet he himself had crafted and formed from the dust at the dawn of creation in Eden's garden. Wow—what grace!

But wait a minute, with theological acuity, when we say that Christ became a 'Servant of servants'—a devoted Servant to depraved men who are not even worthy to untie the dusty straps of his sandal straps—does that not sound very much like the solemn curse levied on hapless Canaan by the aged patriarch Noah, for no fault of his own but his Dad's (Ham's) act of voyeuristic exposure, in the post-flood narrative of Genesis where it unambiguously says: "*Cursed be Canaan; A servant of servants He shall be to his brethren*" (Gen 9:25 NKJV)—a patriarchal pronouncement that rippled through generations like a dark undercurrent. Oh, right—with insight! Christ must have borne on his agonizing cross that ancestral curse too. He sure did, without reservation or recrimination. As it turns out, not only did he take upon himself the curse of the Mosaic Law instead of the covenant people, the Jews, but also the array of just about every generational or transgenerational imprecation, anathema, or divine judgment ever pronounced against the entire guilty human race was imposed upon him alone on Calvary's hill. This is the radiant Son of the Blessed—and I mean, equally, the Blessed One himself—in and of himself the ultimate Blessing, the source of all benediction—who willingly became a curse for all mankind (Jews and Gentiles alike in universal scope), so that we all might become recipients of the blessings of salvation channeled through the patriarch, Abraham, and his Seed (the preeminent Christ, fulfilling Galatians 3:16). Even though he was born the only King—of unblemished Sovereign Royal Pedigree, not merely *'the King of the Jews'* as the Oriental Magi had narrowly imagined at the time of their star-guided pilgrimage (cf. Matt 2:1–2), but the King of the Whole Wide World, as Elvis Presley titled his iconic 1962 song—evoking a universal dominion that transcends ethnic bounds; he yet had no qualms, no divine reluctance whatsoever, going from being the King of all kings to becoming the ultimate Servant of all servants—the most highly esteemed, worshiped King who voluntarily became our most lowly, despised, rejected Servant, fulfilling Isaiah 53's suffering Servant motif. Now do not dare tell me that this singular Man is not *'the Most Significant Figure in Human History'*, and I do not mean nominally as a matter of bagging an honorary title, conferring accolades, or flinging laurels where none is truly deserved, but to state on the basis of fact and logic that the Man who alone was divinely able to meet, address, and satisfy the greatest existential, soul-shattering needs ever known to man—from sin's forgiveness to death's defeat—has got to be the greatest, most influential Man who ever graced this sin-cursed planet with his holy presence. And who could possibly argue with that truth? Zilch, as you and I can plainly imagine, whether in the hush of inner reckoning or beneath the torch of ages past. So, ladies and gentlemen—with gravity and proclamation—I am humbly presenting to you Jesus the Christ, the Beloved Son of the Living God—the Greatest Man Who Ever Lived—on the grounds of the significance of the redemptive work of his Cross and what it irrevocably means for every single human person ever born into this fallen world—from Adam's firstborn to the last soul before time's consummation.

For his crucifixion, vicarious death, burial, and glorious resurrection altogether account for the most unparalleled significant thing to have positively happened to the entire human race ever since the catastrophic Fall transpired in the genesis of the created world—that primal rupture in Eden's garden, shattering, reorienting, and changing the entire arc of history forevermore—from B.C. to A.D. in redemptive ripple. All the more significant when you consider that what we desperately had on our hands was that one existential problem that has historically defied every humanly devised solution known to man—from philosophic treatises to technological utopias—and so, him stepping up to the plate as the embodied, personified solution in his very self is got to be the most epoch-making, paradigm-shattering, and newsworthy event in all of cumulative history considered together—the pinnacle of divine intervention in human narrative. Because where the salvation of the human soul is man's greatest need—even the most fundamental human need amid the void of sin's dominion—prosecuting that sacred cause in order to meet that salvific need has got to be the greatest accomplishment that any human person could possibly make in the grand theater of existence. And that is exactly what Christ achieved by his substitutionary death and vindicated resurrection—the clincher of eternity's wager. Throughout the annals of history, no mortal man—no sage, conqueror, or visionary—has come anywhere close to accomplishing that salvific feat for the rest of humanity at large—save the singular Man Jesus Christ and him alone, the exclusive Architect of our souls' freedom. The God-Man was a man on a divine mission—the redemptive mission to save and restore the entire human race from perdition's brink. And so he had his eyes on the redemptive ball all the time—with his gaze transfixed on the purchase—the acquisition—of human salvation throughout his incarnate life, and not for a second did he flinch, falter, or take his eyes off the redemptive goal that loomed from Bethlehem to Golgotha. His heart of servitude in humble servantship is simply a heart of gold—incorruptible, radiant, and selfless to the core.

If that is not the quintessential definition and living embodiment of authentic greatness, then one would be left scratching their head in bewildered wonder, searching for what else could possibly bear that exalted title. For, as history irrevocably reveals, Jesus was—and eternally remains—the living embodiment of greatness itself: the Supreme Greatest who humbly walked our dusty, sin-stained streets, teaching with authority the truths of God's peaceful, shalom-filled kingdom. Yet we failed utterly to recognize or honor him for the transcendent greatness he embodied in fleshly humility, much less to give him the reverence due his Name that shakes the foundations. As he taught his disciples in a defining lesson on kingdom leadership: "*You know that those who are considered rulers over the Gentiles lord it over them, and their great ones exercise authority over them. Yet it shall not be so among you; but whoever desires to become great among you shall be your servant. And whoever of you desires to be first shall be slave of all. For even the Son of Man did not come to be served, but to serve, and to give His life a ransom for many*" (Mark 10:42–45 NKJV). This is nothing less than a blueprint for upside-down greatness that inverts the world's pyramids of power. He is right—with divine authority—especially when contrasted with historical figures like Alexander the Great, whose fleeting renown came through brutal conquest and military might, whereas Christ—the Prince of Peace (Eirenarch)—established, proclaimed, and embodied God's non-violent kingdom of shalom through love, humility, and sacrificial service to humanity's broken multitudes. This cosmic act of chivalry even drew wistful admiration from Napoleon Bonaparte in his reflective exile. His pattern of attaining sublime greatness through unparalleled servitude stands as an enduring testimony—resounding across millennia—that has baffled, stirred, and transformed countless souls. Through the greatness of his service to humanity in its lowest state, he has reclaimed—in his fully incarnate humanity—the pristine glory and radiant splendor that was eternally his by divine nature, essence, and uncreated right—the timeless splendor of the Alpha and Omega.

GOD'S UNGLAMOROUS GLORY: VEILED BENEATH THE MASQUE OF THE ORDINARY

What is more—and profoundly so—in what appears like the most self-effacing posture known to fallen man throughout the annals of human experience, the eternal God Incarnate—Emmanuel—contented himself with humbly living without a shred of earthly honor or acclaim: "*. . . in his own country, among his own relatives, and in his own house*"—dwelling unassumingly amongst us as though a nobody amid the throng of ordinary lives (Mark 6:4 NKJV). In which case—given such radical self-abasement—we humanity, in collective blindness and hard-heartedness, esteemed him not at all—rather, we contemptuously rejected him in every place and moment where he deserved our honor as the undisputed King of the universe—the cosmic Sovereign whose throne spans galaxies—despising him where he merited our acceptance as the promised Savior of the world, the Redeemer of every nation and tongue. In a foreboding portrait that bleeds with anticipated rejection, the Prophet Isaiah was spot on with prophetic precision when he remarked that the coming Messiah would be " . . . *despised and rejected by men, A Man of sorrows and acquainted with grief. And we hid, as it were, our faces from Him; He was despised, and we did not esteem Him*" (Isa 53:3 TLV). Because after having voluntarily stripped himself of his glory and majesty, he then " . . . *had no beauty or majesty [left] to attract us to him, nothing in his appearance that we should desire him*" (Isa 53:2 NIV). That truth ties in with what John alluded to with lamenting depth when he penned, "*He was in the world, and the world was made through Him, and the world did not know Him. He came to His own, and His own did not receive Him*" (John 1:10–11 NKJV). Now, consider the profound humility that stirs the depths of the soul upon encountering the paradox: that the transcendent God of all aesthetic beauty and majestic elegance desired no outward aesthetic beauty whatsoever to grace the mortal masque of his advent—the Divine Designer who designed the concept of beauty itself and fashioned the beautiful into existence did not lust after, covet, or hoard beauty's charm nor its grace and glory for his incarnate humanity, opting instead for unadorned simplicity in place of display.

Such insight further unveils that God, in his incarnate semblance, looked nothing like what many of us might have conjured in our fancies and would barely fit into our preconceived religious or sociocultural expectations of what a majestic 'God' figure should appear—in countenance, stature, or mien. For the Word made small, in the fullness of man's littleness, wore no laurels of our longings—those painted Christs we beseech in the secrecy of our pleas, nor strides the stage of synagogue or senate as our storybooks decree—his countenance unblazoned by murals of decree, his stature unhewn as giants of dominion, his gait unrobed in the glory of earthly lords—unarrayed like King Solomon in all his glory, but a quietness that quiets all, teaching this pilgrim—as well you, my fellow seeker—the lesson that God veils celestial mystery not in the veils of allure, but in the humble garb of the commonplace—conceals his essence not in the fanfare of glory, but in the quiet hearth of the unassuming—shrouds his holiness not in the ostentation of the ornate, but in the simplicity of the ordinary. In fact, the Scriptures make clear enough that He bore no resemblance to any of the modern-day *bona omi* or glamorous pin-ups that grace the front cover of lifestyle magazines—nor did he look anything like those airbrushed superstar versions of Hollywood's fictional creation we see in blockbuster movies depicting his life and ministry. He simply did not come here to show off the transcendent beauty, unveiled glory, and splendor of his eternal Divinity, else he would not have taken on himself the defaced form of man's fallen, sin-marred humanity. He came with resolve to conduct the bloody business of having his sinless body put through torture and then impaled and nailed to the Cross for the sins of all men across every generation and nation. Now we can better understand why they found him unattractive, repellent to behold, and thus failing to recognize him for who he was—despising and rejecting him in unbelief. But boy—oh, what a cosmic reversal!

Had Pontius Pilate, those Roman soldiers, and even the Jewish religious elites had any clue who that unassuming Man really was in his divine essence, they would have considered it a privilege to venture close to him, close enough to genuflect before his Presence in obeisance, casting down the crowns of their earthly power in surrender, while praising his Sovereign Lordship—with praise that shakes thrones—worshiping his Divine parsonage in solemn worship—the highest latria of adored deity. And then crowning it all off with hosanna shouts of 'All hail the King, all hail King Jesus, all hail the King of the world!' Kissing his glorious feet and having them anointed with the most extravagant fragrance oil, like that devoted Mary from Bethany had done unto him, should not be ruled out in such a scene of repentant adoration (cf. Matt 27:27–31). Only if these hardened men had caught the faintest glimpse of revelation about who he really was at the time, even as little as had those tormented demonic spirits who screamed in terror at him, saying, "*Let us alone! What have we to do with You, Jesus of Nazareth? Did You come to destroy us? I know who You are—the Holy One of God!*" (Luke 4:34b NKJV)—whenever he conducted those public exorcisms that shattered darkness. Their reactions would have been no less than what was seen with Thomas, who, after having doubted the resurrection, soon found himself on his knees before Him, confessing: "*My Lord and my God!*" (John 20:28 NKJV). But alas—even this truth about his Messianic identity and heavenly origin had to be hidden from them all, at least for the sake of protecting the sanctity and integrity of his salvific mission—the grand arc from manger to cross. And even after Peter had caught a glimpse of the revelation pertaining to his true Messianic identity and incarnate sonship, confessing: "*You are the Christ, the Son of the living God*" (Matt 16:16 NKJV)—he yet would go on to forbid him and the rest of the Twelve from divulging that information to the public, at least until his salvific mission was fully accomplished. According to Matthew's Gospel account: "*Then He commanded His disciples that they should tell no one that He was Jesus the Christ*" (Matt 16:20 NKJV).

CONCLUSION

When heaven's divine clock marked the climactic conclusion of the redemptive drama of the Cross—where the Father's Son proclaimed *"IT IS FINISHED"* from Calvary's summit—the Roman centurion pierced the veil of denial. Amid the fury surrounding the Savior's agony—the quaking earth that rent the temple curtain—these miracles shattered his resistance, compelling him to echo Peter's confession: "*Truly this was the Son of God!*" (Matt 27:54 NKJV). In that moment, a Gentile executioner turned to faith at the very heart of heaven's verdict. Actually, it does not seem like there was any other possible conclusion to draw from all the events that have just unfolded before his own eyes. Quite clearly, the incarnate posture of the Son of God was one of radical self-effacement, total self-abnegation, and ultimate self-sacrifice in humble servitude to wayward humanity, precisely as foretold in Isaiah's Four Servant Songs (cf. Isa 42:1–9; 49:1–13; 50:4–11; 52:13–53:12). This is Jesus the Christ—the divine revelation anticipated through the ages. What stands before us is a masterful portrait of the eternal Savior and King of the world, rendered in the crimson ink of his own blood—the red thread that weaves redemption through history. When the Gospels record that ordinary people flocked to him from countryside, highways, and byways, we must not credit social polish, political allure, status, or charisma; their attraction stemmed from the magnetic pull of divine grace upon his life—God was with him, baptizing him with the Spirit of grace and truth, the anointing that drew sinners like moths to a flame. At this point in our reflection on Calvary's harvest, let it be declared: God has accomplished every stroke against sin—completed all that he will ever do for humanity's redemption. He has poured out superabundant grace, an overflowing reservoir. The sacrifice of his Son is more than sufficient—Christ is the all-sufficient One. In the vast ocean of divine love resides the architect of this universal deliverance, encompassing every nation and tongue. What remains is the invitation: for every soul—man or woman, young or old—to recognize the grandeur secured in their place and to claim it through faith in the finished atonement.

6

That Christ Gulped Down the Punitive Cup of Human Sin

Down to the Very Dregs of Death

It must be stated plainly: the resolve to undertake the salvific mission—to suffer and die for humanity's redemption—was no light decision but one of immense cosmic weight, involving profound and agonizing deliberation even for the incarnate Son of God. The entire redemptive undertaking proved an arduous, uphill struggle, destined to culminate in his ascent to Golgotha. The path to redemption was indeed a steep, sorrow-laden climb toward the summit of sacrifice, bearing crushing woe yet requiring total surrender. In a moment of deep vulnerability, when the weight of this calling bore down heavily upon him, Christ naturally felt the pressure and cried out to the Father for any possible alternative to the harrowing ordeal. Yet the path remained singular—marked by the crushing burden of the crossbeam and the torturous 2.5-mile journey from Gabbatha uphill to Golgotha, where the upright stripes awaited him outside Jerusalem's walls for the most defining moment in human history. Tragically for him, yet redemptively for us—to the sorrow of his heart and the eternal benefit of humanity—no other way existed, no alternative route appeared, no escape from the crucible of suffering. This was the only passage ordained for the salvation of a fallen race. Only through this agonizing way could he become the true Path—the Mediator who alone guides every soul to reconciliation and into a filial, familial relationship with the one true God.

GETHSEMANE'S CRUCIBLE: THE INESCAPABLE CUP OF REDEMPTIVE SURRENDER

The Gospels grippingly record his anguished plea as he fell prostrate and prayed: "*O My Father, if it is possible, let this cup pass from Me; nevertheless, not as I will, but as You will*" (Matt 26:39 NKJV). To his closest disciples—Peter, James, and John—he confided that his soul was overwhelmed with sorrow, a grief so intense it approached death itself: "*My soul is exceedingly sorrowful, even to death. Stay here and watch with Me*" (Matt 26:38 NKJV). There, in that desolate hour, he sighed and bidding their watchful care in that woeful hour. In this moment, the crushing weight of human sin and divine necessity met, revealing the profound mystery of redemptive love. The sorrow described as reaching unto death exposed the deep existential tension between his divine calling and his human dread. The issue was so personally wrenching that he returned earnestly to prayer a second and then a third time, repeating the same dolorous petition—each repetition underscoring the unbearable tension of the moment: "*O My Father, if this cup cannot pass away from Me unless I drink it, Your will be done*" (Matt 26:42 NKJV). Yet, God's will offered no reprieve; the cup of suffering was inescapable. And as per the question encapsulated in his poignant entreaty—the answer would have to be a no—no because this cup will not be passing him by. This cup of his suffering, brimming with the bitter bane of human sin, was drunk to its fullness—gulping it all down to dregs for sinful and undeserving humanity. The way of wounds—the way of woe—became the way of redemptive wonder, a testament to love's triumphant travail, an act of ultimate love that would transform the sufferer into the very embodiment of salvation's only way. Yet God's will granted no relief; the cup of suffering could not be avoided. In response to the earnest question embedded in his poignant plea, the answer was a resolute no—this cup would not pass him by. This cup of his suffering, brimming with the bitter bane of human sin, was drunk to its fullness—gulping it all down to dregs for sinful and undeserving humanity. The way of wounds—the way of woe—became the way of redemptive wonder, a powerful testimony to love's victorious labor, an act of supreme love that transformed the Sufferer himself into the sole and sufficient Way of salvation.

This punitive cup—this cruel chalice—filled to the brim with galling grief and piercing pangs, laden with bitter burdens and woeful weights, Christ was destined to drink and drain down to death's dire dregs, so that humanity, dead in sins and trespasses, might be spared the sting of eternal damnation and restored to life. While it remains true that all things are possible with God—within the bounds of his will, nature, and moral character, as Jesus prayed in Gethsemane: "*Abba, Father, all things are possible for You. Take this cup away from Me . . .* " (Mark 14:36 NKJV)—yet when it came to this cup of suffering and death passing from him for the sake of sinful humanity, there was simply no possible way around it, not even within the sovereign will of Almighty God himself—no alternative path could bypass the necessity of this sacrificial act to accomplish humanity's redemption. For the sacrificial act was indispensable—an absolute, non-negotiable foundation in the architecture of redemption. Had any other path been possible, the Father, in his infinite love, would have spared his Beloved the excruciating torment, for no joy resides in the suffering of the Innocent. Yet, according to the principle of divine justice, because one man's disobedience plunged humanity into moral ruin, only another Man—sinless and perfect—could bear and pay the immense price required for redemption.

Actually, what fallen humanity needed was not a 'god' to undergo vicarious death on its behalf, but a man—simply and precisely a man. Graciously, the Son of God assumed full humanity as the representative and archetype of mankind, becoming the one Man perfectly suited to shoulder the burden of atonement—the sole individual qualified to settle redemption's immense debt. Suffering unto death for the sins of all mankind and thereby paying the costly price of redemption became for Christ the inevitable course of action—a categorical imperative, if you will. Though the prospect of death's agony tested his resolve to its limits, and I mean, tested to the hilt, he stood unyielding, refusing to falter under the crushing weight of humanity's plight. He neither buckled nor succumbed to the mounting pressures that more naturally and overwhelmingly would have dictated he gave up on sinful humanity and cry out for his own salvation from the Cross instead. In spite of being fully aware of the horrors awaiting him—even before the time—he yet chose to brace for impact, facing head-on the prophetically foretold horrors of his own crucifixion—even the imminent tragedy of his own death. In describing the unbendingness of his iron-will to have God's redemptive will for man done here on earth as it is in heaven, plus his uncompromising resolve and unwavering commitment to the cause of man's salvation, the Bible goes on to record that his face was firmly set like a flint toward Jerusalem's slaughter ground—the ground zero for the punitory work of his Cross (cf. Luke 9:51). Even when things got so tough, with the weight of scorn and derision pressing upon him, even worse, the voices of those for whom he was actually bearing this insufferable burden taunting him to his face, "*If You are the King of the Jews, save Yourself*"—"*If You are the Christ, save Yourself and us*" (Luke 23:37 & 39 NKJV). He yet did not throw in the towel in frustration, but with a composure echoing the Stoic apatheia of ancient sufferers—combined with the self-abandoned perseverance of Job, he gently reminds them: "*Daughters of Jerusalem, do not weep for Me, but weep for yourselves and for your children*" (Luke 23:28 NKJV).

In other words, his journey to Jerusalem's slaughter ground (Golgotha) was both for the salvation of Jerusalem's daughters and their children, and more broadly, for all the sons and daughters of men, but barely ever for himself in the slightest. He took our bullet—the penal bullet of our death sentence for sin—vicariously dying our due death and then proceeding even further to take our rightful place in hell. Into the jaws of justice he journeyed, descending deep to deliver divine satisfaction; thus was substitutionary justice for sin duly served and fully satisfied in Christ. Guaranteeing that every guilty sinner who would believe in what he has accomplished for them gets to walk scot-free and at the same time guiltless—omnitemporally discharged and acquitted of sins past, present, and future. For Christ is that Physician who although was severely bruised and left wounded in his Passion, yet would not as much lift a finger to administer healing to himself by his own stripes—that Savior who, amid the throes of death upon the Cross, yet chose not to exert even the slightest effort to save himself, not for the lack of power nor because he lacked the ability to save his own neck, but because of how much he understood that his stripes was meant for the healing of man's fallen humanity and his death for the salvation of man's soul from eternal damnation. The healing work of this Physician was certainly never concerned with his own needs but was completely and exclusively devoted to mankind—his fallen moral and spiritual patient. This stands as a central redemptive truth, forming the very core and essence of the Gospel of Christ for a sinful and guilt-ridden humanity. In principle, this is simply a textbook case of one person reaping the full benefits of another's labor—strikingly similar to what he was alluding to when he said, "*Thus the saying 'One sows and another reaps' is true. I sent you to reap what you have not worked for. Others have done the hard work, and you have reaped the benefits of their labor*" (John 4:37–38 NIV). The same principle applies directly to the substitutionary work of his Cross: as our perfect Substitute, he endured the intense heat of the day, painstakingly performing the punitive labor that divine justice required for the expiation of our sins and the eternal salvation of our souls.

And now we are graciously gathered, hearts thrown open wide, to feast upon the abundant harvest of a divine labor—forged in the fiery furnace of sacrifice, where no human hand has hewn—where mortal hands have sown no seed. Every soul is invited to come and partake of the fruit born from the intense toil of Christ's Passion and Cross—the saving work accomplished through his blood, sweat, and tears. Yet while the Latin principle *cui bono* typically holds that the originator of an action will also be its primary beneficiary, strangely enough, we find this axiom profoundly subverted in this redemptive narrative. Although the divine Initiator conceived and carried out this redemptive plan from the depths of eternity, humanity alone stands as the recipient of its boundless grace—the sole and sovereign beneficiary of the Redeemer's salvific work. Remarkably, the Instigator (God) in this unique case stands to gain absolutely nothing, even though he undertook every aspect of the work, bore every burden of effort, and made every sacrifice himself. This paradox reveals a divine economy grounded in self-giving love, in which the Initiator shoulders every cost yet seeks no reward beyond restored fellowship with his creatures. In this way, the act of divine selflessness stands in sharp contrast to religious systems that portray deities as the ultimate beneficiaries of human devotion and piety. This theological reality, rooted in divine love, overturns human ideas of merit and reward, revealing a love that surpasses all transactional reasoning. The divine act becomes the supreme expression of generosity, redefining justice as restorative rather than retributive, and calling us to contemplate a kingdom formed by sacrificial love, where the Creator's ultimate purpose is the eternal flourishing of the beloved. By the same juridical principle that brought humanity under death's dominion through the primal fault, so also does it rise to life through a righteous act (cf. Rom 5:17). This labor, beautiful in its extravagant generosity, unveils a divine heart that seeks not personal gain but the gentle, loving gathering of the lost.

THE FLINT-FACED RESOLVE: CHRIST'S VICARIOUS BURDEN FOR HUMANITY'S ETERNAL REST

What precisely do you suppose the Savior was occupied with during those solitary forty days of fervent fasting and passionate prayer in the barren wilderness? Or what wondrous work was being accomplished when he agonized and interceded with intense anguish in the garden's darkness for three harrowing hours before the divine tribunal? Was he, by any stretch, pleading for personal desires or reciting the self-focused gimme-gimme petitions that echo through modern halls of devotion? Far from it! In his unique role as the one Mediator between God and mankind, Christ was not praying primarily for his own sake; instead, he was actively carrying out the Father's sovereign redemptive plan for the human race. His intercessions were never self-directed but flowed from the urgent salvific needs of a lost and broken world. Through his life, death, and ongoing advocacy, he brought his mission into complete harmony with God's eternal purpose: to reconcile creation and bring fallen humanity back into covenant relationship with the Father. Even in his darkest hour, as he faced the crucible of suffering, his heart remained fixed on humanity's deliverance, not his own reprieve. So for him, it was always the case of "*I pray for them . . .* " (John 17:9 NKJV)—was hardly it ever one of 'I pray for My . . . '—a profound display of selfless advocacy that stands in vivid contrast to the self-centered prayers so common in our time. The redemptive work attributed to the cross was humanity's debt—a debt of justice owed by a guilty race. Yet, the sinless One bore this burden, assuming the penalty meant for sinners, fulfilling the demands of divine justice. With the joy of accomplishing this cosmic reconciliation before him, he embraced the cross, despising its shame (Heb 12:2)—thereby sparing humanity the everlasting consequences of its rebellion. When we speak of "*lifting the weight off one's shoulders*," no image more perfectly captures the idiom than Christ himself on the cross. Single-handedly, he removed from the shoulders of sinful humanity the crushing burden of every punitive consequence sin deserved—the insurmountable weight of moral guilt, the unbearable pressure of striving to keep God's righteous laws, the heavy yoke of laboring to please God in order to earn his acceptance, the impossible demand for flawless moral perfection, and every other burden we could name. He bore it all, leaving no obligation unmet, no righteous demand unsatisfied, and no stone unturned in the work of redemption.

And having substitutionally done all—the judicial heavyweight lifting that was required to satisfy the universal claims of justice against sinful humanity, he now turns to every weary soul—every Tom, Dick, and Harry—and says with the supreme confidence of the only Redeemer, "*Come unto me, all ye that labor and are heavy laden, and I will give you rest. Take my yoke upon you, and learn of me; for I am meek and lowly in heart: and ye shall find rest unto your souls. For my yoke is easy, and my burden is light*" (Matt 11:28-30 KJV). A more contemporary English version would make it sound like this: "*Come to me, all of you who are weary and carry heavy burdens, and I will give you rest. Take my yoke upon you. Let me teach you, because I am humble and gentle at heart, and you will find rest for your souls. For my yoke is easy to bear, and the burden I give you is light*" (Matt 11:28-30 NLT). At long last, a redemptive rest for our lost and weary souls—phew! In this invitation, the Mediator offers a share in divine rest, where the soul, freed from the overbearing weight of sin and the burden of guilt, participates in the eternal order of grace, finding peace through the merits of his redemptive act, accessible to all who approach with faith. Such insights reinforce the gratuitous nature of God's grace, philosophically distinguishing it from the human concept of meritorious justice. Salvation, sweet salvation, shatters the saying that nothing good is gained without a grueling grind. Freely given, freely received, this gift of grace flows abundantly from Christ's cross—costing creatures nothing yet costing the Creator his everything—his very life. The redemptive act of Christ stands as a miracle that transcends every earthly economy of exchange: it demands no payment from human hands, yet was purchased at the infinite, immeasurable cost of the Savior's own life—every expense fully borne at the Cross. Now it is freely served to one and to all alike upon a golden platter of divine ease—the effortless, unearned gift of grace itself.

Anyone receiving this all-expenses-paid salvation of Christ today experiences something akin to Herodias being presented with the severed head of John the Baptist on a silver platter—yet with a world of difference. In John's case, his life was taken involuntarily, snuffed out against his will; in Christ's case, it was the Creator-God himself who voluntarily and vicariously laid down his own life for the sinful creatures he so deeply loves. This supreme sacrifice is now freely served to each one of us on the silver platter of his grace and love—offered without price, without condition, as the ultimate gift of redemption. For he said plainly that "*The Father loves me because I lay down my life that I may have it back again.*

No one can kill me without my consent—I lay down my life voluntarily. For I have the right and power to lay it down when I want to and also the right and power to take it again. For the Father has given me this right" (John 10:17–18 TLB). From this we may also discern a solemn parallel: the joint demand of Jews and Gentiles to crucify Christ mirrors Herodias' wicked insistence on receiving John the Baptist's head on a platter. In both cases, the "*head on a platter*" and "*body on the cross*" serve as stark euphemisms for the giving up of life—yet where John's death was taken by force, Christ's was given in sovereign, voluntary love, the Father's beloved Son laying down his life that we might live. Of course, Christ's sacrifice far transcends the martyrdom of John the Baptist—noble and righteous though John's death was, it lacked the divine efficacy to atone. The Cross stands as the supreme locus of atonement, where human sin is met with divine justice and transformed into overflowing grace. It therefore costs us nothing but the humble profession of faith in the finished work of Christ's Cross—because he alone bore the full brunt of the punitive demands of the Cross, shedding his blood, sweat, and tears, so that salvation might be freely given to all who believe. Let us lift our voices in blazing gratitude to Jesus for the priceless gift of salvation! When believers proclaim this Gospel as free, they do not imply it is cheap—because even though we get to receive it all at zero cost to our pockets, yet it cost the Savior everything—it cost him his all—his precious life poured out unto death. Whoever willingly offers his own life on the altar of sacrifice for others has truly given everything, for at that moment he holds back nothing—nothing any more dear to him than his dear life.

Having surrendered his very life, there remained nothing left for him to withhold. There is an old adage warning that a one-eyed man dare not give up his single remaining eye in an act of charity, lest he plunge into total blindness; yet what God did in giving up his one and only Son stands in staggering parallel—he offered the irreplaceable, the singular, the beloved, as the full demonstration of his love for mankind. In perfect symmetry, the Son willingly laid down his life as the ransom for the redemption of all humanity, holding nothing back, giving everything. Therefore, the salvation secured by Christ stands as the most priceless reality in all the universe—because it cost the Creator-God nothing less than his very life. When he laid down his all in the surrender of his life, he did so to redeem and preserve the lives of every member of fallen mankind, making this gift of grace the most costly and precious treasure ever bestowed. It was love alone—love without measure—that compelled

Christ to embrace the Cross. The Scriptures abound with God's heartfelt affirmations of his love for man, and few are more intimate than Isaiah 43:4: "*. . . because you are precious to me. You are honored, and I love you*" (NLT)—a passage that feels like a personal love letter from God addressed straight to you and to me. As I noted at the outset, God has demonstrated his love for humanity not merely through words but through powerful, visible acts, proclaimed like a blazing cosmic billboard on the hill of Calvary—where he sovereignly met and satisfied all the greatest, most essential needs of human life. He got them all covered, all of our deepest needs addressed *en bloc*—our most fundamental moral and spiritual needs met ne plus ultra. This redemptive work, all-inclusive and all-conclusive, resolves our greatest dilemmas through God's masterstroke of divine genius in his Son, uniting justice and mercy in a single, eternal act of love that restores creation to its divine purpose.

Let it be clear: the Creator-God did not suffer and die on the Cross to merely address ordinary bread-and-butter matters or temporal wants. His sacrifice was for the salvation of the human soul. All secondary needs—material provision, physical well-being, earthly security—he could have supplied without ever moving a finger, without ever becoming man, and certainly without facing the horrors of the Cross. The Cross was for something far more profound: the eternal redemption of the soul from the power of sin. Of all the necessities that arise across a human lifetime, none rises higher than the soul's eternal, transcendent call for salvation—unmatched by any fleeting or illusory want. This singular, all-defining need, born of humanity's fallen condition, so stirred the divine heart with passionate love that the Creator took on mortal flesh, entering the weakness of our humanity to offer himself as the sacrificial atonement that alone could answer it. No other need—material or otherwise—could compel such an act of cosmic surrender. Case in point: God made King Solomon the richest man who ever lived—to date, without moving a single muscle, without shedding a single tear, without shedding a single drop of his blood. Likewise, God proved this to be the case in the lives of both micro-Adam (Adam in the Garden of Eden) and macro-Adam (Israel in the Promised Land). In essence, the Architect who fashioned Paradise on earth required something infinitely greater than Paradise itself to redeem the souls of men; the Creator of the land flowing with milk and honey needed something far surpassing milk and honey to ransom the souls he cherished so deeply; the Maker of all the gold and silver in creation understood from the beginning that no gold could suffice, no silver could match the price necessary to buy back the souls of those he loved with everlasting love. Redemption required a price much more costly than gold and far more precious than silver—it demanded tooth for tooth—life for life.

Graciously, Christ made the conscious decision to stake out his life on the stake of Calvary and burn at the stake for the salvation of mankind. That salvation, surpassing all else, became the supreme showcase of man's matchless merit in the Creator's sight—for the Omnificent God crushed the cruel captors of sin, death, and darkness on behalf of humanity alone. This stands as irrefutable proof: everything else the Almighty had created and fashioned held little or no weight when placed upon the scales of divine value and preference beside the one creature formed in his own image and likeness—man. In this redemptive testament of God's love, the expression 'you are worth more than a king's ransom' finds its true meaning indeed. God can very well afford to meet every other need that may arise in the life of his creatures without moving a finger, but when it came to the redemption of the human soul, he simply found no way around it. He had to get his skin in the game, because he either loved man enough to become a man to die for the redemption of man's soul, or he might as well have kissed mankind an eternal goodbye. But given the bleeding heart that God had for the human predicament, he was, of course, compelled to cast off all limits in demonstrating how much he really loved mankind, going so far as to pour out his life as a redemptive sacrifice for the sins of all. In acknowledging this to be indeed the case, Peter reminds us human redemption was purchased "*not with perishable things such as silver or gold that you were redeemed from the empty way of life handed down to you from your ancestors, but with the precious blood of Christ, a lamb without blemish or defect. He was chosen before the creation of the world but was revealed in these last times for your sake. Through him you believe in God, who raised him from the dead and glorified him, and so your faith and hope are in God*" (1 Pet 1:18-21 NIV).

SALVATION'S SOVEREIGN PARADOX: THE CREATOR'S ALL-COSTING GIFT TO THE FALLEN SOUL

Thuswise, the redemption of the human soul transcends all conceivable blessings within the finite scope of human supplication, standing as the supreme gift divine love could bestow, far exceeding any petition humanity might dare to voice. The redemptive work of Christ answers to a soul-deep longing so profound that no human heart could ever fully articulate it, a need so deep it surpasses even the most daring prayer. Imagine for a second, perhaps for arguendo: that humanity suddenly awoke to the full horror of its desperate plight and realized that only the Creator's incarnation and sacrifice could effect its rescue. Could any soul muster the audacity to beseech the Creator-God to descend, assume mortal form, and endure torment for their salvation? How does anyone even begin to get himself to voice such audacious prayer as: "O Lord God Almighty, we lie dead in trespasses and sins—would you, in your mercy, leave the heights of heaven, clothe yourself in our weak and mortal frame, and suffer us to torture and crucify you upon the cross of Calvary, that your blood might ransom our souls and secure the forgiveness of our iniquities"? No—not in a thousand lifetimes! Such a request would border perilously on sacrilege, an unthinkable blasphemy whereby fallen creatures presume to command the death of their infinite Creator-God. Such words would rightly provoke the righteous indignation of heaven: "How dare you!" Envision the outrage of a created being boldly entreating its Maker to lay down his life in its stead—an act of presumption so vast it defies all reason. It would be comparable to one of Elon Musk's most advanced creations, Optimus, turning upon its inventor and insisting that he forfeit his life to save it; or a lowly valet-de-chambre in Pharaoh's court demanding that the king's head be severed and presented on a platter, in the manner Herodias sought John the Baptist's. The very conception of such a plea is an unthinkable violation, a brazen assault upon the transcendent dignity and unchallenged sovereignty of the eternal God. Even Simon Peter—ardent disciple and loyal follower—when granted a fleeting glimpse of Christ's divine identity, recoiled in visceral horror at the prospect of his sacrificial death. With fervent dismay he rebuked the Lord, passionately forbidding any thought of humiliation and crucifixion on behalf of sinful men, unable to bear the intolerable vision of his beloved Master laid low and slain for the unworthy. His protest, though rooted in incomplete understanding, sprang from the instinctive human incapacity to grasp that the Creator might willingly suffer for the creature. In that raw surge of emotion, Peter's anguished cry found expression: *"Far be it from You, Lord; this shall not happen to You!"* (Matt. 16:22 NKJV)—spoken only after Jesus had begun to reveal to his disciples *"that He must go to Jerusalem, and suffer many things from the elders and chief priests and scribes, and be killed, and be raised the third day*" (Matt. 16:21 NKJV).

The divine disclosure of the Savior's necessary suffering, death, and resurrection unveiled a mystery so overwhelming that it stirred both profound awe and instinctive resistance in equal measure within the heart of even the most devoted disciple.

This holy, trembling awe—born of glimpsing the divine majesty of the Savior—mirrored Peter's first encounter with the Creator's power on the Sea of Galilee, when the miraculous abundance of fish in the net-breaking catch left him breathless. Overwhelmed by his own unworthiness before such holiness, he fell to his knees in worship, imploring: "*Depart from me, for I am a sinful man, O Lord!*" (Luke 5:8 NKJV)—almost echoing the humble confession of the Roman centurion: "*Lord, I am not worthy that You should come under my roof . . .* " (Matt 8:8 NKJV). The question still lingers with force: could any soul that truly comprehends the divine identity of the Messiah ever allow him to walk the road of shameful death, or summon the audacity to pray for such a fate? I find it hard to believe—reverence itself would forbid it. Such a prayer would feel profoundly wrong—almost sinful—like asking the very One who formed you to lay down his life for your sake. It strikes the soul as deeply odd, if not altogether offensive. For this same reason, Peter later resisted the foot-washing at the Last Supper, overwhelmed by his sense of unworthiness in the presence of such holiness. Yet with the light of divine revelation, we now see clearly: Christ's redemptive sacrifice stands as the supreme pinnacle of love—not summoned by any human prayer, but sovereignly initiated by God's eternal will before time began. No mortal mind could ever conceive or dare request such a thing; only divine love, transcending all human thought, could enact this redemption, restoring the soul to eternal union with its Origin. This redemptive act, arising wholly from divine initiative, forever stands as God's eternal answer to a human need too deep for utterance, a need no human mind could ever have shaped into prayer. The sheer scale of the sacrifice—offered freely, unmerited—places it beyond the reach of comprehension, a gift of grace without parallel. From this truth springs humanity's deepest gratitude: the divine deed was never owed, but poured out solely from the boundless, overflowing love of God. Especially given that no being—finding themselves in God's shoes—could ever bring themselves to do anything approaching what he has done for humanity. None would dare stoop so low as he did in the incarnation; no one could muster the munificent generosity to sacrifice even half as much as he did for the redemption of the human race. No creature—whether human, divine pretender, or angelic—could ever rival the Creator's boundless benevolence, which stooped to depths beyond imagination in the incarnation and the cross. The Creator's love, unmatched in its omnibenevolence, towers above every imaginable act of generosity; singular in its self-emptying humility, it surpasses every conceivable act of sacrifice—for no other being would so abase themselves for their own creation. This divine self-giving, rooted in infinite love, remains a mystery that forever eludes full comprehension, continually drawing the soul into the gravitational pull of unmerited, transforming grace.

Therefore, when we Christians proclaim that Jesus Christ died on the cross for the atonement of the sins of all mankind, his vicarious death must never be placed on equal footing with some random individual altruistically giving his life for his fellow men in service of a humanitarian cause. Nor should it ever be compared to the passionate, romantic self-sacrifice so common in love stories—such as the enamored lovers in countless amourettes, or the overly dramatized portrayals in Hollywood adaptations of Shakespeare's Romeo and Juliet, where the besotted pair take turns dying for one another, or even the iconic scene of Jack giving his life for Rose in the Titanic. Christ's death stands utterly apart—singular, divine, and eternally efficacious. Nor should Christ's vicarious death ever be placed on the same level as those random instances of men giving their lives in esprit de corps or brotherhood-in-arms for nationalistic or patriotic causes they deeply believed in. History is filled with such examples—Spartan warriors and Roman gladiators stoically laying down their lives in warfare and adventurism pro patria, out of love for country and unwavering loyalty to the emperor. Yet these acts, noble though they may be in human terms, pale entirely before the divine, substitutionary sacrifice of the Son of God, whose death was not for a temporal cause or earthly allegiance, but for the eternal redemption of souls. None of the examples above even remotely approaches or comes close to what we witness in Christianity: the very God who created man becoming man himself, so that he might die a substitutionary death for the sins of the very mankind he brought into being. The sovereign Lord of all creation taking the form of his own creatures in order to serve as the ransom price—the Paschal Lamb necessary for their atonement—and thereby securing the redemption of their race from eternal damnation—this stands on an entirely different plane, forever remaining an unmatched demonstration of benevolent love and self-sacrifice.

What makes the vicarious death of Christ on the Cross so staggeringly unique and infinitely weighty—second to none and seconded by none in all of human history—is the sacrificial shedding of the spotless, pure blood of the Son of God, utterly unlike the futile spilling of the tainted blood of mere mortals. Man's salvation could therefore only have been God's own sovereign idea, rooted solely in the ineffable love and boundless goodness of the Creator toward his creatures. This also illuminates how God could dare to answer prayer requests that no human would ever have had the audacity to voice: long before the need even arose in the flow of time, he had already met it. Precisely as he declared through the prophet Isaiah: "*I will answer them before they even call to me. While they are still talking about their needs, I will go ahead and answer their prayers!*" (Isa 65:24 NLT). How perfectly true—it unfolded in redemptive history exactly as foretold. Even the Son of God himself did not hesitate to most solemnly confirm for the rest of us that " . . . *your Father knows the things you have need of before you ask Him*" (Matt 6:8 NKJV). It therefore follows that long before any person ever recognized their need or formed a prayer, the Father had already foreseen it—anticipating and providing answers to the greatest necessities that would ever confront mankind, both the monumental and the seemingly small. Before any soul wandered into the shadows of transgression, the Eternal Architect, in the timeless council of divine wisdom, had already fashioned a cosmic blueprint for redemption, weaving a tapestry of grace to reclaim every heart. Way before any man ever sold off his soul to the devil for naught, God had prehistorically worked out a redemptive plan for the payment of the ransom price to buy back the souls of all mankind. Ere the dawn of human frailty, he had orchestrated a provision surpassing all need, ensuring life's restoration through an unmerited gift of divine love. And right before any man ever died the death of living a sinful life, the Redeemer equally already had the resurrection and the life waiting for them for a gift of grace. That strikes the lyrical chords of yet another classic hymn, done by Thomas O. Chisholm (1923) this time around, with the title—Great is Thy faithfulness:

Great is Thy faithfulness!
Great is Thy faithfulness!
Morning by morning new mercies I see;
all I have needed Thy hand hath provided:

great is Thy faithfulness, Lord, unto me!

The fourth line unveils a profound doctrinal reality: the sovereign hand of God, in its perfect providence, has already supplied every necessity—above all, the salvation of the soul—long before any cry of need was ever raised. Before any human heart could even conceive of praying, the God who is both the origin and final destiny of all things had foreseen humanity's greatest lack and met it with prevenient grace, securing eternal redemption. Long before the first shadow of human want ever fell, the Creator had prepared an abundant gift of life—a grace that overflows every temporal need and reaches into eternity. Before the first breath of creation was drawn, the Alpha and Omega—he who stands beyond all time—had already foreseen humanity's profoundest need and met it with the ceaseless river of his grace and love. The Beginning and the End, in his sovereign initiative, embraced the divine resolve to satisfy man's greatest longings before the dawn of time itself, ensuring that from eternity's first light to its final consummation, every soul might find its true home in his kingdom—here in the fullness of time, and ultimately at the end of time. Thus he secured an eternal path to glory, sustained by a love that precedes, enfolds, and infinitely surpasses all human understanding. We now see more clearly how the Scriptures unite in their witness: " . . . *His works were completed from the foundation of the world [waiting for all who would believe]*" (Heb 4:3 AMP). This statement reaches far beyond the works of creation alone; it embraces both creation and redemption, even though redemption unfolded much later in the timeline of history. In other words, God's masterplan for the redemption of man was eternally settled and fully accomplished in the divine counsel—every detail determined, every provision made, nothing left unfinished—long before it was ever manifested in time. It stood complete and waiting, ready to be revealed and prosecuted in redemptive history at the appointed hour.

Thus, in Jesus Christ, God has sovereignly encapsulated every solution to the countless problems that would ever confront humanity—wrapping up within the gift of his Son all the answers to the profoundest questions that would ever rise in the hearts of men and women of all stripes and calibre. This truth further confirms that the apostle Paul spoke with no exaggeration when, under the inspiration of the Holy Spirit, he declared in Ephesians that God is " . . . *able to do exceedingly abundantly above all that we ask or think, according to the power that works in us*" (Eph 3:20 NKJV). A testament that the Divine capacity far exceeds every human longing or imagination. The Amplified Translation renders it even more adapted to the point at issue: "*Now to Him who is able to [carry out His purpose and] do superabundantly more than all that we dare ask or think [infinitely beyond our greatest prayers, hopes, or dreams], according to His power that is at work within us*" (Eph 3:20 AMP). It must therefore follow that the greatest gift God could ever bestow in the redemptive sacrifice was the gift of himself—in the very Person of his Son. Wrapped within that Babe laid in swaddling clothes in the manger was nothing less than the fullness of God himself. That gift embodies the very best of God—the pinnacle of his best—his all in all—his everything encapsulated in the giving of his only begotten Son, Jesus. No wonder the Holy Spirit once spoke reassuringly to my heart: "*God has done you more good than you could ever wish yourself good.*" Oh, how blind I had been to this truth, but now I see—now the light shines clear as day! And because of this, I can look any person in the eye and say without hesitation: God does not need to do one more thing to prove his love for you—he has already done it all in Christ.

CONCLUSION

In summary, everything God accomplished for us through and in his incarnate Son is something no single one of us could ever have achieved for ourselves—far exceeding any feat the human spirit could have imagined across endless ages. This selfless act of redemption—shouldering the crushing weight of humanity's every failing—stands as an utterly unique and unmatched witness to divine love, a sacrifice no human heart would ever dare to contemplate, even on behalf of oneself, much less for a neighbor. It reaches far beyond anything any person would have had the courage to undertake, beyond what human willpower could ever have entertained, and infinitely beyond any accomplishment our ingenuity or cleverness could have devised. For no mortal will, however resolute, could muster the audacity to undertake such a redemptive mission, nor could human ingenuity devise a plan so profound. On the grounds of which I further submit to you that there is none among the sons of men who compares to the Man of Galilee. That explains why God had him anointed '*with the oil of exultation*' above everyone else, because none who could have been selflessly daring enough to do any of what he did for the rest of us—no not one (cf. Heb 1:9 Berean Literal Bible). His descent into human form, not in an era of comfort but in a time of primitive hardship, further underscores the humility of this act.

He did not step into a twenty-first-century world of technological ease and automobile convenience but into the harsh first-century Graeco-Roman reality—lacking the cooling relief of mechanical invention, swift transport, or instant communication. Picture him traversing dusty paths Nazareth, Galilee, all the way through Jerusalem under a merciless sun, bereft of mechanized relief—no engines to hasten his journey, no devices to ease his labor, no opulent vessels to offer respite on tranquil waters. This was no accident of timing but a sovereign choice: to enter a world where suffering remained raw, unsoftened, and unmitigated by modern comforts. His death was no dignified end but a grotesque, shameful spectacle—far worse than any punishment society today would deem fitting for the lowest criminal—yet perfectly suited to the divine purpose of securing redemption for all. Crucifixion would be deemed far too barbaric, cruel, and unconscionable—utterly inadmissible—under the standards of any modern criminal justice system. Such a method defies human reason, which instinctively recoils from suffering and clings to comfort and dignity. Yet Christ willingly chose this path—not for his own benefit, not to secure his own glory, but entirely for ours. He entrusted himself to the hands of conspirators and crucifiers, enduring the cross for the salvation of all, so that we might be spared the eternal consequences of sin. Throughout his journey, he spoke with unwavering resolve—to himself and to any who had ears to hear—" . . . *But for this purpose I came to this hour*" (John 12:27 NKJV). This profound act of divine condescension unveils a love so immense that it willingly forgoes every temporal comfort, choosing instead the crucible of human suffering to accomplish the cosmic plan of redemption. Philosophically, it confronts our natural instinct for self-preservation, calling us to ponder a love that places the other above self—even to the point of death. Divine foreknowledge, which could have charted a far less painful course, was willingly set aside in favor of humanity's ultimate and eternal good—making this act the supreme expression of selfless devotion. It remains a profound mystery that invites the soul to contemplate the fathomless depths of divine mercy and the striking paradox of omnipotence willingly clothed in vulnerability.

7

The Protevangelium Promise Made

The Protevangelium Promise Kept!

THE PROTEVANGELIUM, IN ITS essence, stands as God's gracious proclamation to a fallen and weary humanity: Jesus is the answer to the Fall—God's decisive, all-encompassing reply to the greatest existential longings of the human heart, his conclusive solution to the myriad crises confronting humanity, and his sovereign antidote to the pervasive sin-disease woven into fallen nature. Through this primal promise, God reveals Christ as the singular, sufficient remedy for every wound and want of the soul. And consider the timeless truth that "*a friend in need is a friend indeed*"—God has demonstrated himself to be exactly that for mankind in our hour of deepest darkness and greatest need. Through the cross, he proved himself a friend indeed. We can now more fully grasp what Jesus meant when he spoke to his disciples: "*No longer do I call you servants . . . but I have called you friends . . .* " (John 15:15 NKJV). For He immediately added the measure of such friendship: "*Greater love has no one than this, than to lay down one's life for his friends*" (John 15:13 NKJV). By giving his life, Jesus embodied the truest friendship—laying down everything so that we, his friends, might live. That is a profound truth that has encapsulated within it the reminiscent sounds and gospel-esque echoes of Joseph Medlicott Scriven's (1855) classical hymn, "*What a Friend We Have in Jesus.*"

Across the vast sweep of redemptive history, the truth shines with unmistakable clarity: Jesus has proven himself—quite literally—the truest, most faithful Friend mankind has ever known, standing with us in every hour of need, bearing our burdens, and walking beside us through every trial. In the language of today's everyday speech, he has shown himself to be man's ultimate BFF (Best Friend Forever), stepping forward precisely at the darkest moment in human history—right when our most towering salvific and existential needs arose. Towering above the entire human experiment, God rose supremely over and beyond them all, meeting every single one with perfect sufficiency, leaving no stone unturned. This profound truth found its consummate expression when Jesus Christ rose triumphantly from the grave, utterly vanquishing humanity's three archenemies: Satan, sin, and death. Drawing from the ancient Latin maxim *Amicus meus, inimicus inimici mei*—today commonly rendered "The enemy of my enemy is my friend"—Christ is unmistakably demonstrated to be man's best Friend in the truest sense, the God who brings salvation, and therefore the one true God. By rising as the conqueror of our greatest adversaries, he established himself as our faithful Defender, our Redeemer, and the sole divine Sovereign deserving of all allegiance.

CHRIST'S TRIUMPH OVER SIN: THE DEVIL'S DEFEAT AND HUMANITY'S HOPE

From the cradle of human existence—ever since the Fall of Adam, only one Man has had all that it took to stand up to the devil and emerge victorious. Christ alone was derring-do enough to go head-to-head with all three archenemies of mankind in a full-on mano-o-mano combat and lived to tell the tale afterward—the glorious tale of his triumph for mankind. For he is the first and the last Man to have mustered the moral authority to cast a stone of judgment and a sentence of condemnation on the devil, declaring, "*Concerning judgment, because the ruler of this world is judged*" (John 16:11 ESV). Further doubling down on the heels of that effort, He yet was able to stand tall to his face and assert, "*. . . for the ruler of the world (Satan) is coming. And he has no claim on Me [no power over Me nor anything that he can use against Me]*" (John 14:30 AMP). Obviously because he was morally immaculate and thus had no sin, and that meant that the devil had nothing on him and could find nothing with which to pin him down morally or spiritually. Where sin is the Tempter's greatest weapon of power and leverage over sinful men, and this particular Man had none, then, of course, he was immediately rendered powerless over him. This truth establishes Christ as mankind's only saving grace against the devil's malicious agenda for the human race. We can now more clearly see why Satan's strategic posture toward humanity had to shift almost immediately—from general anti-man hostility to a focused antichrist opposition. The one Man called Christ had iconically stood in his path, bringing a decisive end to the era of his reign of terror over the world and over human lives. All of this he accomplished for us—because the story of his triumph over the powers of darkness now spells out the gospel of hope for every person who will believe in his cruciform victory on their behoof. While the majority of the world's religions readily acknowledge that the existence of evil poses a universal and intractable problem—and many even concede the pervasive reality of sin, with some going so far as to admit that Satan the devil must play some role in it—none of them can point to any concrete, tangible action they have taken to address these core moral and spiritual crises facing humanity. Not one has offered any real remedy for the problem of sin or any decisive confrontation with the primordial mastermind and tireless architect of evil in the human world (Satan). None—absolutely none—except the Son of the Christian God.

Thankfully, according to the Christian gospel—as depicted in the story of the Good Samaritan—God literally showed up in good time for man's rescue, just at "*the fullness of time*" (Gal 4:4), in the incarnate humanity of his Son, Jesus Christ (cf. Luke 10:30–37). Being the only One in the seen and unseen universe who was compassionate enough to neither turn a blind eye nor walk past mankind in the hour of its greatest existential need, choosing rather to empty on us the bowels of his mercy and compassion in order to guarantee the eternal salvation of our race. This breathtaking act of grace resounds in the joyful refrain of Tim Godfrey's song—Goodness:

> *"I have seen the Lord's goodness*
> *His mercies and compassion*
> *I have seen the Lord's goodness*
> *Hallelujah praise the Lord"*

Oh, goodness-gracious indeed! Jesus Christ is the true Divine Good Samaritan with a heart overflowing with nothing short of mercy and compassion—love and forgiveness for us all sinners, enough to compel him to turn to us at that critical hour of dire need—picking us up from the roadsides of sinful life, where we were found wounded, bleeding, and abandoned to go on languishing away in pain and suffering, thus binding up our festering wounds of suffering and gaping bruises of pain with the healing balm of his redemptive love—administered, not as a temporary band-aid or some makeshift Aesculapian solution, but as an ever-lasting Divine panacea that guarantees us moral, spiritual, and physical healing forever—a one-stop healing meant to piece back together the broken pieces of our fallen humanity. This same overflowing heart of compassion also compelled the Great Physician to journey tirelessly across the roads and regions of Galilee, Judea, and Samaria—bringing good to the afflicted, liberating the oppressed, and restoring health to every sick and suffering soul, restoring hearing to the deaf and sight to the blind. The Synoptic Gospels repeatedly note how Jesus, when he looked upon the multitudes, was deeply " . . . *moved with compassion for them, because they were weary and scattered, like sheep having no shepherd*" (Matt 9:36 NKJV). That compassion drove Him to travel " . . . *about all the cities and villages, teaching in their synagogues, preaching the gospel of the kingdom, and healing every sickness and every disease among the people*" (Matt 9:35 NKJV). In essence, the Son of God, in profound compassion, willingly left the comfort zone of his heavenly abode to plunge into the discomfort and brokenness of our earthly time zone. He descended not to fish for the countless multitudes of creatures in the ocean world, but to seek and rescue the countless lost souls adrift in the vast ocean of humanity's fallen existence.

RELENTLESS PURSUIT: THE SHEPHERD'S HEART IN SEARCH OF THE LOST

And by the time he was done fishing himself, here is what else he promised to do and has since done to ensure that not even a single lost or straying human soul is left behind unreached and unrescued from the ocean of man's fallen world: "*Behold, I am going to send for many fishermen," declares the LORD, "and they will fish for them; and afterward I will send for many hunters, and they will hunt them from every mountain and every hill and from the clefts of the rocks*" (Jer 16:16 NASB2020). Exactly as depicted in the Parable of the Lost Sheep, he is that good Shepherd who would literally spare nothing and stop at nothing in his unrelenting effort to seek and to save that one in a hundred sheep that is yet lost and straying farther afield, including venturing as far as climbing high up the rough terrains of " . . . *the mountains to seek the one that is straying?*" (Matt 18:12 NKJV)—even after having successfully rescued and secured the salvation of the ninety-nine that were previously just as misguided. Now that is really remarkable; it makes quite an indelible impression, does it not? Because at the very least, the above salvific posture puts in perspective the relentlessness of God's love in his pursuit of the lost souls of all men world over, it further explains and substantiates the undeniable fact that he is indeed " . . . *not willing that any should perish but that all should come to repentance*" (II Peter 3:9 NKJV)—and that is ultimately so because He " . . . *desires all men to be saved and to come to the knowledge of the truth*" (I Timothy 2:4 NKJV). Thus, the oft-repeated declaration that "*God is good*" is far more than a mere religious catchphrase or shibboleth—it is a truth firmly anchored in actual history. God did not remain distant; he literally showed up in the course of human history on a deliberate search-and-rescue mission for the human soul, coming to save and redeem it from eternal peril.

When we speak of perfect timing and the flawless precision of God's appointed hour, the timing of his Good Samaritan rescue mission for wounded and dying humanity stands as the epitome of divine punctuality. It serves as the *locus classicus* of everything the parable truly signifies—because no other place or person so fully embodied its meaning as did the life and ministry of Jesus Christ. He was always precisely on divine schedule—moving in perfect alignment with God's timetable for the purpose of his life and the fulfillment of his redemptive destiny. Especially when you consider that just about all the events and circumstances that had transpired in his cosmic life were preplanned and pre-scheduled to fit perfectly into God's redemptive calendar and then ordered aright according to the perfect timings of God's Holy Spirit, who dwelt in him. A case in point would be when he said the following to his epigones as he mustered the courage to face head-on the grim cruciform fate that lay right ahead of him: "*Now My soul is troubled and deeply distressed; what shall I say? 'Father, save Me from this hour [of trial and agony]'? But it is for this [very] purpose that I have come to this hour [this time and place]. [Rather, I will say,] 'Father, glorify (honor, extol) Your name! . . .* " (John 12:27-28 AMP). He was also heard saying to those about to crucify Him, "*This is your hour, and the power of darkness*" (Luke 22:53 NKJV). In a profound irony, their hour of apparent triumph coincided precisely with his appointed hour of suffering and death—granting the forces of darkness the long-desired opportunity to unleash the full fury of hell upon the God-Man, all for the sake of humanity's salvation. This moment mirrored the darkest hour in history: the Fall in Eden, when man's greatest need for redemption was first created. The necessity of rescue began with Adam in the Garden, and now, at Calvary, the powers of darkness were permitted to rage—viz., to "*bruise His heel*" (Gen 3:15 KJV)—yet unwittingly served the eternal purpose of divine redemption.

FROM PROMISE TO PERFORMANCE: THE PROTEVANGELIUM FULFILLED IN REDEMPTIVE HISTORY

What we behold here is nothing less than the single most defining moment in the fate of the human race—the most epoch-making hour in all of human history—the decisive, pivotal moment when Christ took upon himself the full responsibility to meet humanity's most desperate needs and to resolve the deepest existential crisis confronting every person, from the greatest to the least, every Tom, Dick, and Harry. This is when God, in his incarnate humanity, had essentially shown up to do the needful and was going to be confronting all three archenemies of mankind head-on, first in his servant posture as the Paschal Lamb who gave himself up in weakness for crucifixion and finally, in his Junoesque posture as the Lion of the tribe of Judah who soon rose triumphantly and exultantly over all three archenemies of mankind—with our victory eternally secured in his coffers. We all know that the darkest part of the night comes just right before dawn; likewise, in figurative terms, the darkest hour of the life of Christ—the hour of his death and descension into the bottomless depths of hell—came right before the dawn—the new dawn of his resurrection and ascension unto the highest heights of glory. In 3 days, he transitioned from dust to glory—with his body undergoing transformation from the dust of human mortality to the glory of Divine immortality. Exactly as foreseen by the prophets and foretold in the Scriptures: this is nothing short of a textbook case of the Protevangelium promise made—the Protevangelium promise kept! Because God is here votively keeping to his promises encapsulated in the Protevangelium, one that he made to mankind at the hour of its greatest existential need and humanitarian crisis in the Garden: to crush the head of the serpent, the figurehead of all nemesis of mankind—symbolically representing the root cause of all the troubles plaguing humanity. God literally became an adversary to all of man's adversaries who had ultimately endeavored to stand in the way of his redemptive plans for man's race, an antitypical representation of what he had done for the Jews during and after their hegira from Egypt, in fulfillment of the promise, "*But if you indeed obey His voice and do all that I speak, then I will be an enemy to your enemies and an adversary to your adversaries*" (Exod 23:22 NKJV).

This also happens to be a fact congruously captured in the content and substance of Zechariah's prophecy about Immanuel's epochal visit in redemptive history, recorded in Luke 1:68-75 (NKJV): "*Blessed is the LORD God of Israel, For He has visited and redeemed His people, And has raised up a horn of salvation for us In the house of His servant David, As He spoke by the mouth of His holy prophets, Who have been since the world began, That we should be saved from our enemies And from the hand of all who hate us, To perform the mercy promised to our fathers And to remember His holy covenant, The oath which He swore to our father Abraham: To grant us that we, Being delivered from the hand of our enemies, Might serve Him without fear, In holiness and righteousness before Him all the days of our life.*" The timing for the fulfilment of his promised Divine visitation could not have been anymore perfect—even pluperfect. And he did not just show up empty—he showed up to deliver the goods—he showed up to do what is necessary—he showed up with all the redemptive answers to man's greatest existential needs—he showed up in good time to deliver on all the promised deliverances contained in the Protevangelium. We can therefore affirm with the Apostle Peter and countless believers before and after him, "*The Lord does not delay [as though He were unable to act] and is not slow about His promise . . .* " (2 Pet 3:9 AMP). Just as the prophet Ezekiel, speaking by the Holy Spirit long before Jesus' birth, proclaimed, "*Therefore say to them, Thus says the LORD God: None of my words will be delayed any longer, but the word that I speak will be performed, declares the LORD God*" (Ezek 12:28 ESV), so in Jesus, God has since gone from promise to performance—gloriously taking his prehistoric redemptive plans from prophecy to fulfillment within the timeline of redemptive history. If ever there was a moment for those in the amen-corner to raise their voices in a resounding "Amen!," this is it—Hallelujah!

KINGDOM REALIZED: CHRIST'S DEMONSTRATION OF HEAVEN'S POWER ON EARTH

Markedly, the arrival of that singular redemptive event some two thousand years ago stands utterly without parallel in all of human history;

indeed, it did not merely mark a moment but forever transformed history itself, reshaping the Greco-Roman world of that era and beyond. That transformation has continued without interruption across the centuries—right up to our present day—and all available evidence confirms that it remains vibrantly active in the world around us, depending on where one chooses to look. But go ahead—look around the whole landscape of history and see if you can identify any other religious figure or faith tradition that has exerted such a profound, sweeping influence on human dignity and the condition of the world, fundamentally elevating the human experience as Christ has done so overwhelmingly. None—not a single one. The most many of these other religionists have managed to offer is the vague promise of some distant "*nirvana*" or heavenly realm somewhere out there. Yet that promise is ultimately empty and self-defeating: *nirvana* could never have created itself, nor can it explain its own existence, much less account for ours, nor give any meaningful answer to the fundamental question of why we are here at all. Why in God's name should anyone believe or cling to the promise of some distant "*thy kingdom come*" if it offers no power to touch or transform my life right here and now, in the *hic et nunc*? As the saying goes, the proof of the pudding is in the eating—and I agree. If nirvana or any other promised realm is real, show us something concrete, something visible, just as Jesus did when he demonstrated the realities and verities of the kingdom of heaven on earth.

Before ever heading to the cross, he moved among the crowds—preaching publicly to every soul who would listen: "*Keep turning away from your sins and come back to God, for heaven's kingdom realm is now accessible*" (Matt 4:17 TPT). And, of course, he backed those words with tangible acts that changed lives, healed bodies, and restored hope in the present moment. Continuing along the same lines, Jesus further instructed his disciples that they too could pray to God, their Heavenly Father, and believe for the realities of his kingdom to become manifest in their lives on earth in the meantime. He taught them to pray in this way: "*Our Beloved Father, dwelling in the heavenly realms, may the glory of your name be the center on which our lives turn. Manifest your kingdom realm, and cause your every purpose to be fulfilled on earth, just as it is in heaven*" (Matt 6:9–10 TPT). His message of the kingdom stands utterly unique in the history of religion—one that can be genuinely experienced and lived out right here on earth. That is the kind of promise I can believe in and hope for—because talk is cheap, and anyone can make empty declarations, but Jesus offers a kingdom that is real, tangible, and presently accessible. Now I see clearly why that faithful servant of Christ, Paul, had to insist with such force: "*For the Kingdom of God is not just a lot of talk; it is living by God's power*" (1 Cor 4:20 NLT), and as the Passion Translation renders it: "*For the kingdom realm of God comes with power, not simply impressive words*" (1 Cor 4:20 TPT).

This declaration powerfully distinguishes Jesus' testimony about God and his kingdom from that of any other religious figure one might name. While others may offer eloquent teachings or moral philosophies, only in Christ does the kingdom arrive with tangible, transformative power—demonstrating that God's rule is not mere rhetoric but a living reality that changes lives. Further riding on the wings of his newly found confidence in the demonstrability of God's kingdom message, Paul goes on to say to the congregational church that he planted and pioneered in the middle of the 1st century A.D.: "*And so it was with me, brothers and sisters. When I came to you, I did not come with eloquence or human wisdom as I proclaimed to you the testimony about God. My message and my preaching were not with wise and persuasive words, but with a demonstration of the Spirit's power, so that your faith might not rest on human wisdom, but on God's power*" (I Corinthians 2:1, 4–5 NIV). His evidence for the reality of God's kingdom invading man's world lies ultimately in the demonstration of the miraculous power that was manifestly engendered by God's Spirit through him, so that the faith of his congregants should not have to rest on some eloquently delivered pie-in-the-sky speech or some empty promises of egg in the moonshine.

CONCLUSION

Not only did Jesus announce the glad tidings of God's heavenly kingdom; he himself brought heaven down to earth, rendering its reality near at hand and attainable to every soul. No longer need we lift our gaze heavenward in distant longing, awaiting "Thy kingdom come" in some far-off sweet by-and-by; the God of heaven has descended to us in the likeness of our humanity—in the very Person of His eternal Son—making the kingdom no longer a remote hope but a present, tangible, and intimately accessible gift for all who will receive it here and now. As the Church Fathers perceived—Irenaeus in the recapitulation whereby the kingdom is restored through the incarnate Word who gathers all things into Himself;

Athanasius in the divine descent that unites heaven and earth in the one Person of the Son, making the inaccessible accessible; Augustine in the kingdom as the inner reality of grace already present and operative in the regenerate soul—this incarnation stands as the decisive event that abolishes the chasm between God and man, bringing the eschatological kingdom into the midst of time as a present power and living promise.

8

God's Good Samaritan Approach

Love and Compassion for Fallen and Suffering Humanity

In order to prevent well-meaning people from mistakenly equating or conflating the living essence of Christianity with the multitude of other religions extant in the world today—or the transformative power of the redemptive Cross with the varied tenets of competing religious worldviews and philosophies—it is absolutely essential, indeed non-negotiably vital, that these foundational truths be proclaimed with the utmost clarity of expression and urgency of delivery, sweeping away any remaining confusion once and for all. Let me begin this essential discourse by declaring with unshakable conviction: the greatest revelation any man could ever receive or experience in this earthly journey is the profound revelation of God's infinite love. The most sublime divine revelation any man can aspire to receive from the Almighty, remains, by far, the earth-shattering disclosure of his only begotten Son, Jesus Christ—the Logos made flesh. The uniquely Christian confession that "*God is love*" is therefore far more than a doctrine supported solely by unassailable biblical testimony and scriptural witness; it is also—and with equal weight—a verifiable fact of history and lived reality, demonstrated beyond doubt in the incarnate life, death, and resurrection of the eternal Son of God. In truth, God, above all, desires to be known, embraced, and worshiped as the supreme God of love—the very fountainhead of agape—he chose to reveal his true nature in the radiant splendor of his own boundless love, and he did so uniquely and decisively in Christ alone, the sole mediator and perfect manifestation of that love. To know the immeasurable height, unfathomable depth, limitless length, and all-encompassing width of God's redemptive love is nothing less than to know and personally experience God himself—in the fullness of his glory, majesty, and being (cf. Eph 3:17–19). Although across the centuries God has been revered and acknowledged as the God of serene peace, impartial justice, righteous vengeance, unyielding righteousness, tender mercy, and countless other dimensions of his multifaceted character, yet he is supremely and ultimately the God of love—the living personification, perfect embodiment, and very essence of agape itself. He longs with fervent desire to be known, adored, and proclaimed in the radiant light of this defining gospel truth. This same longing explains why Jesus, during his earthly ministry, frequently chose to refrain from preaching God's severe judgment and wrath against sin (see Luke 4:19 & Isaiah 61:2), focusing instead on the acceptable year of the Lord's favor.

Because humanity—in its spiritual poverty and limited vision—lacked accurate divine revelation and true knowledge of the Holy One, God's incarnate self-disclosure in human flesh became absolutely essential for our enlightenment and salvation. To know God today in any lesser or distorted light than the radiant brilliance of his self-revelation in his beloved Son is to mistake him for another deity or for someone he is not in his essential being. If you grasp every other aspect of him from partial glimpses or incomplete revelations yet fail to know his love or recognize him as the supreme God of love, then Scripture makes it clear: you have not yet come to know who he truly is in his deepest identity and heart. The inspired Scripture declares with unmistakable clarity: "*Dear friends, let us love one another; for love has its origin in God, and every one who loves has become a child of God and is beginning to know God. He who is destitute of love has never had any knowledge of God; because God is love. God's love for us has been manifested in that He has sent His only Son into the world so that we may have Life through Him. This is love indeed—we did not love God, but He loved us and sent His Son to be an atoning sacrifice for our sins*" (1 John 4:7–10 Weymouth). Love, the apostle stresses, originates in God—its source and very essence flow from the Divine Being himself—and therefore anyone lacking love has never truly known God, for "*God is love.*" This truth forms the bedrock of his identity. With equal force, John points out that God's love has been visibly manifested, historically unveiled, and experientially demonstrated to mankind solely in the sending of his Son into the world. There is no other proof, no clearer demonstration, of God's love and care for humanity in its plight until we fix our eyes on the Cross of his beloved Son, where love poured out its lifeblood for the life of the world.

In the preceding chapter of the same epistle, John writes with striking power: "*We know what real love is because Jesus gave up his life for us . . .*" (1 John 3:16 NLT). Until you come to know God as the God of love in his Son, you have not truly known him in His essential character. For the entirety of Jesus' ministry—every word, every deed, every breath—was ultimately about revealing and embodying God's love for man; he is the sacrificial, propitiatory Gift of that love to a lost humanity. God has chosen to be known nowhere else but in the Man through whom and in whom his love has been poured out like a libation upon all people without distinction. Among the many scattered and partial glimpses of divine revelation in human experience and spiritual seeking, the only one God has sealed with his stamp of approval, authenticity, and finality is the revelation of his love in Jesus Christ alone. Because he longs to be known for who he truly is: Love incarnate. This is precisely why the religions of the world remain beside themselves—deprived of the ultimate revelation of Deity to humanity—the revelation of God's love in his Son Jesus Christ. They have not yet encountered God in his true form, nor come to know him in his fullness, and they will continue to miss him until they turn to and embrace the historical, resurrected Jesus of Nazareth. To this day, scarcely any living religion can claim to possess an accurate, undistorted divine revelation of who the one true God really is in his multidimensional glory. The reason for this spiritual impoverishment is straightforward: God, in his infinite wisdom and sovereign counsel, has chosen to reveal himself nowhere else and in no one else but his Beloved Son—whose incarnate life was wholly devoted to demonstrating, embodying, and proclaiming his Father's unconditional love for sinful, undeserving, and lost humanity. Muslims, for example, can only offer a narrow, one-dimensional portrait of him as a stern God of judgment, enthroned in heaven on his moral high horse, awaiting the summons of all to the dreaded *Yawm ad-Din*—the Day of Judgment—a vision that largely overshadows the full spectrum of divine mercy and love.

RELIGION BEREFT OF LOVE: DO YOU TRULY NOT MIND IF WE DROWN?

This valid question remains unresolved: when love is absent, what remains of religion as the waves rise and the desperate cry for rescue echoes unanswered? The above title confronts us with unflinching honesty—when religion lacks the living heartbeat of love, does it abandon us to drown beneath the flood of suffering and sin, with no compassion rising from heaven to intervene? In vivid contrast, the Christian gospel declares with historical certainty: "*God's love for us has been manifested in that He has sent His only Son into the world so that we may have Life through Him. This is love indeed—we did not love God, but He loved us and sent His Son to be an atoning sacrifice for our sins*" (1 John 4:9–10 Weymouth). Christ himself proclaims: "*I have come as a light into the world, that whoever believes in Me should not abide in darkness. And if anyone hears My words and does not believe, I do not judge him; for I did not come to judge the world but to save the world*" (John 12:46–47 NKJV). His mission was anchored in love—salvation for the world, not judgement against it. Jesus forever stands as the divine portrait of God's love for humanity, painted with flawless precision on the canvas of history by God himself—to be remembered and recounted through all generations as the enduring testament of love. In Christ, we are able to perceive and prove with historical certainty that God cares deeply about us—so much that he became one of us in the incarnation, in order to die a vicarious death for every one of us in sacrifice. He gave up his life to break sin's curse, remove death's sting, and fill separation's void. Therefore, any religionist who has not yet come to know God in the light of his revealed love for humanity in his Son is missing the definitive revelation of God to a waiting world.

Though he may have been portrayed in earlier eras—such as in certain aspects of Judaism—as a God of judgment, fire and brimstone, thunder and wrath, where his revelation shone dimly and partially, now he desires to be known in his Son for who he truly is: the God of love—love personified. As Paul proclaimed with solemn authority: "*God overlooked people's ignorance about these things in earlier times, but now he commands everyone everywhere to repent of their sins and turn to him*" (Acts 17:30 NLT). He obviously desires all people to come to the full knowledge of his saving grace and love—an open invitation extended to every soul. Above all, in Jesus, God came down for the first time since creation to a level where we could truly relate to him and he to us in genuine intimacy. It matters not what tribe, tongue, or former religion we belong to—he welcomes each one with the open arms of his unconditional love, a welcome that transcends every border and barrier. Yet outside of Jesus, before God descended in incarnate solidarity, such two-way fellowship between Deity and humanity was never possible, and it remains impossible within the framework of mere religion—a chasm no human effort can bridge. That the Almighty Creator of the vast universe cares enough to desire intimate knowledge of us and to be known by us in reciprocal communion speaks volumes of his love—a love that defies every cosmic scale. This is the heart of the Cross, the core of the Christian Gospel—the Gospel of God's unmerited, transforming love for sinful humanity, a love that redefines existence itself.

One fateful day, the disciples of Jesus found themselves sailing at sea in a modest ship with their Master aboard, having rowed far out into the treacherous open ocean—caught midway between land and nowhere, adrift in solitude's grip. Suddenly, a fierce windstorm erupted, fierce gusts whipping across the water as towering waves crashed violently against their fragile vessel, threatening to engulf it completely. Tossed and battered by the tempest, they were plunged into terror and despair, their sails torn and useless in the gale, every hope seemingly swept away. And almost immediately, they all start screaming for help like frightened children who had encountered a horror, all for the fear of drowning at sea in what seemed like an imminent shipwreck. Sadly, no rescue boats were hastening to bring them lifejackets, as they were grimly convinced, as for where they expected the help to spring from, your guess is as good as mine—a cry into the void. In a last resort, however, someone managed to seize a moment's grip of himself, enough to speak calm into the others amid the storm and chaos, bolstering courage in his comrades, encouraging them to get busy bailing seawater out of their sinking ship, if they intended to live to tell the tale. All of this effort is not so much for saving the ship per se, but because he understood that saving the ship meant saving themselves—the vessel's loss meant their own lives were forfeited to the deep.

But having done all they could in desperate toil, all to no avail, as the waves swamped higher. Then suddenly, someone remembered that they had their Master, the miracle worker and Lord of the storm, aboard ship with them, and over there he is, reclining peacefully at the stern—deeply asleep in profound quietude—unperturbed by the pandemonium around him. And turning to him with apprehension and panic written on their fear-stricken faces, they implored: "*Teacher, do You not care that we are perishing?*" (Mark 4:38 NKJV)—a cry that echoes through the ages. As you can imagine, it was as though they were chorusing a litany, with their voices competing in desperation, searching the Master's eyes for answers to their peril, peering into him for assurance pertaining to their salvation from a shipwreck that looked inevitable. But more to the point, the question they posed to Jesus is one that I find eye-opening and pertinent to the case I am making today. Had the Second Epistle of Peter been penned at the time of that desperate question, one would have referred them to Chapter 3 and verse 9 where God has engraved the fact that He is "*. . . not willing that any should perish but that all should come to repentance*" (NKJV). Moreover, the very truth that God wills for none of us to perish eternally is the precise reason the eternal Son came into the world: to become salvation incarnate for every human soul ever born into this vale of tears and travail. Needless to say, the Master cared so deeply that none of his disciples should perish in that storm-tossed moment—yet his compassion reaches infinitely further: he cares that none of us should perish forever under the dominion of sin. For the divine will is resolute—God would have no man or woman die in the hopeless anguish of unpardoned sin; instead, he has given his only Son to bear our judgment, that whosoever believes in him should not perish but have eternal life.

Indeed, Christ stands as the sole lifeboat thrust into the storm-tossed sea for every sinner drowning beneath the weight of their own sin—the only saving grace extended to those who, in frantic desperation, strive against the relentless currents of their ungodliness and rebellion. Yet the deliverance of his disciples from literal shipwreck belongs to a different, immediate peril; still, the anguished cry they raised to their Master amid the raging tempest—"*Teacher, do You not care that we are perishing?*"—echoes with piercing validity when directed toward every founder of religion and every deity they proclaim today: "Do You not care that sinful humanity is perishing eternally in the clutches of sin?" From the sober testimony of historical scrutiny and spiritual discernment, the only answer that returns is a vast, resounding silence. If, for the sake of argument alone, we were to place Jesus Christ alongside all others and divide them into two companies—those who truly care that humanity faces eternal ruin in sin arrayed to the right, and those who remain indifferent or unmoved to the left—one figure alone would be left standing on the right: Jesus Christ. All others would drift inexorably to the left in apathy. For he alone has proven that his heart beats with tender, unrelenting love and compassion for lost sinners, a love that poured itself out in crimson streams at Golgotha. Besides him, across all the centuries there is no other to whom we can confidently turn and say, "Behold the Savior." And lest it escape our notice, everything inherent in the posture, practices, and devotional life of the religionist—across every tradition—betrays a profound absence of genuine care or tender compassion for sinful, wounded, and perishing humanity in its hour of utmost desperation. Fundamentally, I find this lack of heartfelt compassion to be one of the clearest and most profound lines of demarcation that separates biblical Christianity from every other world religion in all their diverse expressions. Where others offer moral frameworks, mystical techniques, karmic laws, or ceremonial observances, Christianity alone flows from a heart that is moved with divine pity and active love toward the lost, the broken, and the dying—ultimately embodied in the incarnate Son who wept over Jerusalem, touched lepers, ate with sinners, and poured out his lifeblood to rescue those who could not rescue themselves.

THE GOOD SAMARITAN INCARNATE: THE ONLY GOOD TO HAVE EMERGED FROM THE NAZARETH OF MAN'S RELIGION

In the unfolding of our biblical journey thus far, behold the heart of God's redemption laid bare with piercing clarity: through the incarnate ministry of the Son, his atoning death upon Golgotha, the victorious resurrection, and his exaltation to the right hand of the Majesty on high—a heart bent low in humble, unrelenting compassion toward the suffering human family. This is the living embodiment of the compassionate Good Samaritan: the divine Physician descending from the heavenly realms, who will not pass by with the indifferent procession of priests and Levites, but halts his eternal journey on the desolate, blood-soaked road where hope lies stripped, wounded, and bleeding; he steps down from the chariot of his throne, anoints the dying traveler with the healing balm of restoration, and binds him with bands of unbreakable assurance and grace. In this sacred pause, grant me grace to unfold and exalt yet further the theological treasures embedded in this truth, layer upon layer, with reverent precision. It may profit us greatly to set side by side the redemptive posture of Christ toward sinful, wounded, hurting, and spiritually perishing humanity on the one hand, and the posture of religionists and their institutional religions on the other—so that the unbridgeable chasm that separates these two realms of spiritual endeavor may stand exposed before our eyes. I believe with deep conviction that such a comparison would not only broaden your understanding and sharpen your intellectual grasp of the cumulative case I have been carefully building like a mosaic of truth, but also deepen your appreciation and gratitude for the finished work of the Cross of Jesus Christ—the decisive turning point of eternity where love ultimately triumphed over law.

A devout and thoughtful Jew named Nathanael once asked his fellow countryman and newly called disciple Philip with skeptical candour, "*Can anything good come out of Nazareth?*" (John 1:46 NKJV)—a question born of regional prejudice and low expectations of his time. If we were to turn that same probing question upon the "Nazareth" of all human religion today—that humble, seemingly unpromising village symbolizing all human spiritual striving—the answer would be a resounding, unqualified: No. Not one good thing has ever truly emerged, taken root, or borne lasting fruit from the collective history and practice of the religions of the world combined. Historically speaking, the only authentic good to have ever emerged—even partially—from the "Nazareth" of all human religion, namely the cradle of Judaism with its covenantal promises and preparatory ordinances, is the long-awaited Seed of the woman: Jesus of Nazareth, the eternal Son of God incarnate, the sovereign Savior of the world, the hidden treasure providentially unearthed in the otherwise barren field of mankind's spiritual striving. Apart from him, the Nazareth of man-made religion has remained throughout the ages a spiritually sterile wasteland—barren, desolate, and utterly devoid of any genuine, life-giving goodness: a vast graveyard littered with the ruins of shattered aspirations, forsaken hopes, and perpetually unfulfilled longings for true deliverance from the wretched bondage of sin, moral corruption, and the post-Fall misery that enfolds every human soul.

Peter, privileged to walk in closest fellowship with Jesus as one of the inner three, and thus intimately familiar with the sole priceless good—the one authentic and life-giving good news—to have historically emerged from the "Nazareth" of his own heritage religion (Judaism)—was filled to overflowing with inexpressible joy as he proclaimed to the Gentile world of how that: " . . . *God anointed Jesus of Nazareth with the Holy Spirit and with power, who went about doing good and healing all who were oppressed by the devil, for God was with Him*" (Acts 10:38 NKJV). That is to say, Jesus essentially went about the business of dispensing God's redemptive goodness to the sons and daughters of men in need. This jubilant apostolic testimony forms the bedrock of my unwavering conviction: Jesus of Nazareth stands alone as the only genuine good news that has ever broken forth from the Nazareth of all human religion across the centuries—God's one, exclusive, and all-sufficient gospel for a fallen, weary, and desperate humanity in its darkest hour of need. It requires no elaborate proof to see that, whereas every form of religion has offered no true gospel, no tidings of great joy to the children of Adam since the crushing pronouncement of original sin and the catastrophic rupture of the Fall beneath Eden's shadow, God alone possessed—and has now graciously declared—one singular, all-embracing good news in the person and work of his Son. And that singular, all-sufficient gospel is inseparably bound to the staggering truth that God " . . . *so [greatly] loved and dearly prized the world, that He [even] gave His [One and] only begotten Son, so that whoever believes and trusts in Him [as Savior] shall not perish, but have eternal life*" (John 3:16 AMP). This declaration stands utterly remarkable—indeed, it is the crowning miracle of revelation—especially when we consider that every human heart, by its very creation and deepest instinct, knows and understands the universal language of love; that love alone can heal, sustain, and make whole a fractured soul.

Yet across the long history of human religion, no such love has ever been offered—no genuine compassion, no tender empathy extended toward sinful humanity in the raw anguish of its guilt, brokenness, and suffering. Only in the gospel of Jesus Christ does the Father's infinite, electing love break forth to meet that universal cry, pouring itself out in the gift of the Son so that perishing sinners might live forever. Religion has never yet saved a single soul from the precipice of eternal ruin—not one. It has proven powerless even to heal the sting of a fly, much less to restore fallen humanity to the wholeness of spirit, soul and body. Across the centuries, there is scarcely any credible evidence that religion has genuinely improved the flourishing of its adherents in any lasting way—let alone wrought true, inward transformation of moral character. If anything, religion has too frequently had the opposite effect: it has degraded those under its dominion, shaping them into diminished, hardened, or more hypocritical versions of themselves than they were before they submitted to its sway. Jesus Christ, having grown up within the framework of Judaism with perfect Nazarene humility and faithful observance, was fully acquainted with the long, dismal record of religion's impotence—its complete inability to subdue rebellious hearts or renew depraved natures. Far from endorsing it, he became its most unflinching and piercing critic, exposing its outward forms as barren of the life-giving power that only he himself could bring. So incisive was his critique that he was, on occasion, seen pronouncing searing woes upon his own kinsmen—above all upon the hypocritical religious elite and scribes who cloaked themselves in ostentatious pharisaism—declaring with divine authority: "*Woe to you, scribes and Pharisees, hypocrites, because you travel over sea and land to make a single proselyte, and when he becomes a convert, you make him twice as much a son of hell as you are*" (Matt 23:15 AMP). This piercing rebuke lays bare the utter futility at the heart of all religion apart from Christ: the highest achievement of the religionist is not salvation, but multiplication of condemnation—they take sinners already bound for hell and, through their zealous proselytizing and burdensome legalism, render them twice the sons of hell, all under the pious veneer of religious devotion.

In this solemn indictment, Jesus exposes what human religion can never escape: it cannot deliver life; it can only deepen death. And in the very next breath, the Lord brands these religious leaders "*blind guides*" (Matt 23:16 NKJV)—spiritual shepherds so entangled in the rigid webs of their own dogma that they cannot discern the true path forward. At best, they wander in tragic misdirection; at worst, they deliberately mislead souls into ruin. Knowing full well that these authorities wore the blinders of harnessed beasts, and that any soul who followed their religious leadership was being led headlong toward eternal peril, Jesus issued a clear and urgent warning to the multitudes: "*Leave them alone; they are blind guides. If a blind man leads a blind man, both will fall into a pit*" (Matt 15:14 AMP). The meaning is unmistakable: Christ did not come to religionize humanity, to convert people into Judaism or any other system of world religion—for he saw with piercing clarity that religion, in the realm of eternity, is utterly worthless and offers next to nothing for the salvation of the soul. He understood with perfect certainty that the supreme and most pressing need of every human being is deliverance from the downward plunge into sin and death—and it was precisely this crisis that he descended from heaven to confront, resolve, and forever overcome through his own life, death, and resurrection. In fact, religion has only deepened the human wound it claims to heal; religious "*conversion*" has never been the cure—true salvation from sin, the redemption of the soul, and the rebirth of the spirit have always been humanity's most fundamental needs in the divine economy since the Fall.

Someone might well be prompted to ask: Are you claiming that Jesus stood in opposition to Judaism in its institutional and religious form? Precisely so—he did not come to establish, perpetuate, or elevate Judaism as the universal religion of the world. Though born under the Mosaic covenant, circumcised on the eighth day, and living out a life of perfect fidelity as a Jew, he was never an adherent of its ceremonial and ritualistic superstructure. He stood sovereignly apart from every form of religion, a truth he made unmistakably plain through his teaching, his sermons, and his parables—each one relentlessly challenging the entrenched status quo of religious observance and authority. In truth, he came first to seek and to save the lost sheep of the house of Israel (Matt 15:24), including the urgent task of rescuing his own people from the very religious system that had come to enslave rather than liberate them. Then, through his death, resurrection, and ascension, he flung wide the gates of salvation to the Gentiles, making one new people from Jew and Gentile alike. At the heart of his mission lay the decisive solution to humanity's deepest afflictions—the tyrannical dominion of sin, the paralyzing terror of death, and the piercing ache of alienation from God—never to compound those miseries with fresh burdens of guilt, shame, legalistic scrupulosity, or the strife born of religious injustice and division. It remains one of the supreme marvels of the incarnation that, though raised in the same synagogue culture, nourished by the same feasts and fasts, and instructed in the same traditions as every other Jewish child of his day, the spirit of "religious indoctrination" exerted not the slightest influence upon him. No trace of it stained his immaculate character, no shadow dimmed the boundless compassion of his heart. As Renan aptly observed in his research: "*Happily for him, he was also ignorant of the strange scholasticism which was taught at Jerusalem, and which soon was to form the Talmud. If some Pharisees had already brought it into Galilee, Jesus did not associate with them, and when later he met this silly casuistry face to face, it only inspired him with disgust.*"[1] Obviously because he was on a revolutionary mission to forever transform the religious status quo from its foundations, uprooting weeds to plant grace, and no wonder the religious establishment hated him with intensity, doing everything to avoid him like a plague, because they loved their religion more than human souls in need.

1. Renan, *Life of Jesus*, 338.

That is precisely why they walked past the wounded, bleeding, and dying without a second thought—like the callous priest and Levite in the parable of the Good Samaritan—prioritizing ceremonial purity over human pity. For the same reason, they conspired to crucify Jesus, a Man guilty of no crime, who had done nothing but " . . . *go around doing good and healing all who were oppressed by the devil, for God was with him*" (Acts 10:38 NLT). They even rebuked him for healing a man afflicted for thirty-eight years on the Sabbath, valuing ritual above redemption. On another occasion, they demanded, *"Is it lawful to heal on the Sabbath?"*—hoping to trap him (Matt 12:10 NKJV). To this he replied with piercing logic: "*What man is there among you who has one sheep, and if it falls into a pit on the Sabbath, will not lay hold of it and lift it out? Of how much more value then is a man than a sheep? Therefore it is lawful to do good on the Sabbath*" (Matt 12:11–12 NKJV)—a response that left their sophistry speechless. And that is what it often took to silence the religionists of his day—his words and his works—his razor-sharp words and undeniable miraculous deeds, which bore the clear stamp of divine origin and authority. And if God commanded such mercy even toward animals—"*If you see the donkey of someone who hates you lying helpless under its load, don't walk off and leave it. Help it up*" (Exod 23:4–5 MSG)—a call to compassion for an enemy's burdened beast—then consider how infinitely more he treasures human life, crowned with eternal dignity. When Jesus declared that the soul of one sinner holds greater redemptive worth to God than the entire universe, we must take him at his word. No wonder he went out of his way to aid the helpless and marginalized—healing the sick, casting out demons, and delivering the oppressed even on the Sabbath, choosing love's higher law over the strict letter of the Law. And supremely, he laid down his sinless life as the substitutionary atonement for sinful humanity on Calvary. Because he grasped the Law's deeper essence and true telos, he understood it was given for man's ultimate good—to guide us toward flourishing under the gentle, liberating reign of grace.

For the most part, Jesus' resolute commitment to human dignity, suffering, and redemption stands in sharp opposition to the typical attitude of religionists toward sinful, alienated humanity in its collective desolation. One cannot help but wonder—with a mixture of perplexity and sorrow—whether the deities behind these man-made religions and the religionists who serve them with ritualistic zeal possess any heart at all, any genuine capacity to feel the soul-rending impulses of human anguish, suffering, and pain. From discerning observation and historical scrutiny, they appear as educated heads but empty hearts—minds overflowing with doctrines, theological treatises, and rigid formulas that reverberate in hollow chambers, while their hearts remain devoid of love and compassion in any practical response to the bleeding, crying human condition that desperately longs for relief. They are doctrinaires in their approach to religion—rigid devotees to creedal codes that stifle life rather than nurture it. That is why they are so seldom moved, touched, or deeply stirred by the struggles, sufferings, and heartbreaking agonies of humanity writhing across the globe. They need to be reminded with prophetic urgency that the Law was made for man to flourish under its guidance, not man for the Law to enslave or oppress—given by God for humanity's ultimate good, welfare, and blessing, never for harm or diminishment (cf. Mark 2:27). This also explains the clear, militant advocacy in the New Testament against enslavement to the rigid Mosaic Law—a liberating cry resounding from Paul's epistles to the Gospels. Consider it logically: if the commandment against murder exists not primarily to protect human life—the precious, innocent life of a person from a violent aggressor—then of what real value or purpose is it? Its very raison d'être is the preservation and flourishing of human life.

The empty-heartedness and lovelessness so often seen in religionists appears to explain why they are quick to pick up stones of condemnation and hurl them as weapons of punishment and retribution against their fellow humans in zealous judgment. A classic illustration of this tendency is the woman caught in adultery in John's Gospel—her only hope of deliverance that day was Grace Himself, Christ. He alone stood courageously against the seething mob of self-righteous accusers, invoking the higher law of God's boundless grace and forgiveness that transcends legalism, in opposition to the summary death sentence of stoning already pronounced. Yet in sharp contrast to such religious cruelty, Scripture declares of Christ: "*For we have not an high priest which cannot be touched with the feeling of our infirmities; but was in all points tempted like as we are, yet without sin*" (Heb 4:15 KJV). In other words, God in the incarnate humanity of his Son entered fully into human suffering and pain, facing temptation in every conceivable form, yet overcoming it all in perfect sinlessness for our sake. There is scarcely any tragic human experience we could ever recount to him that he does not already know deeply and intimately through firsthand participation and empathetic union. Thus, his disposition toward sinful humanity remains one of profound, heartfelt compassion and overflowing mercy that reaches down to raise the fallen. Indeed, so deeply was he moved by one of the most shattering afflictions that assail our mortal existence—death itself—that the sacred record attests for the first time, "*Jesus wept*" (John 11:35 NKJV)—a brief, powerful statement that carries oceans of sorrow. This outpouring of grief sprang from the loss of Lazarus of Bethany, whom he loved as a close confidant and dear friend. The moment carries immense weight, for it concerns the very Redeemer who shed no tear for his own sake amid the excruciating ordeal of his crucifixion or the brutal torments inflicted by Roman authorities in collusion with faithless Jewish leaders.

When resolute women among his followers began to wail and mourn for his sake as they witnessed the brutal flogging he endured in resolute silence, his reply was both compassionate and pointed: "*Daughters of Jerusalem, do not weep for Me, but weep for yourselves and for your children*" (Luke 23:28 NKJV)—a redirection that turns their sorrow toward the enduring realities of the age to come. Thus, beyond all doubt, he was never a distant, unmoved spectator far removed from human anguish; rather, he embodied boundless empathy, his compassion for the forsaken human condition reaching depths unmatched in all revelation. For instance, his love for Lazarus burned with such raw, visible intensity that the surrounding mourners could see it plainly written on his face—his countenance openly revealed it in unguarded passion. The emotion mounted to such a powerful surge within his spirit that the evangelist records how he was " . . . *deeply moved within [to the point of anger]* . . . " (John 11:38 AMP). That is no less than a profound stirring that wove together grief with righteous indignation against death's intrusion. And so powerfully moving was this scene that it immediately drew from the onlookers the spontaneous testimony: "*Look how deeply he loved him*" (John 11:36 MSG). In those simple words the bystanders bore witness to affection made visible, tangible, and utterly undeniable. Love, when it is genuine, can indeed be seen and felt—not merely declared in speech, but demonstrated in deed and in truth. Above all, this is supremely revealed in the agape of God poured out for sinful humanity upon the Cross of his Son. Yet the Lord Jesus did not leave his response to human anguish confined to tears of sorrow alone. Having wept so profoundly, so authentically—with the raw grief of a friend who still clung to resurrection hope—he was stirred by the irresistible love of God for mankind to act with sovereign decisiveness. He commanded life back into the decaying cadaver of Lazarus, raising him from the tomb after four days in the grave's icy hold and restoring the miraculous breath that death had stolen. In that instant, Lazarus's "*last breath*" was stripped of its finality; death and the grave were plundered of their boast, denied the right to gloat or claim mocking victory over the lifeless body of one whom Jesus loved.

Especially not in the very presence of the Son of God, who is himself the very embodiment of life—the Resurrection and the Life. With a few brief, sovereign words of command that thundered through the very foundations of Sheol—"*Lazarus, come forth!*" (John 11:43 NKJV)—he shattered the dominion of decay in a single, glorious instant, restoring the miracle of breath and heartbeat to his beloved friend. In that moment, Mary and Martha could embrace their brother once more, their sorrow turned to unspeakable joy, as though joining the triumphant chorus that echoes down the ages: " . . . *Death is swallowed up in victory. O death, where is thy sting? O grave, where is thy victory?*" (1 Cor 15:54–55 KJV). By this public, dramatic showdown at the tomb—and through the multitude of other episodes scattered like precious jewels across the Gospel narratives—Jesus irrefutably proved that death stands as God's declared enemy in its arrogant usurpation of life (cf. 1 Cor 15:26). Not because death held any power to endanger his unchanging divine nature or to limit his eternal sovereignty, but because it had revealed itself as the cruelest terror afflicting every human heart—a merciless foe that takes perverse delight in cutting short the days of those the Lord loves with fathomless affection. Thus, the depth of his love for mankind compelled him, by the very logic of divine affection, to become death's unyielding adversary—an enemy he would never permit to endure within the creation he so dearly cherishes. So great was this love that he bound himself to an unbreakable covenant promise for every person—especially those who embrace the gospel of eternal life—that death itself would finally be " . . . *thrown into the lake of fire* . . . " (Rev 20:14 NIV). This is the apocalyptic decree of death's own demise: it will be extinguished forever, silenced eternally in the triumph of sovereign love, banished utterly from the new heavens and the new earth, never again to cast its shadow or utter its threat.

In light of the cumulative testimony laid out so far, we discern a sobering pattern: across nearly every decisive crossroads and climactic turning point—threaded through the vast tapestry of human history in its grand epochs and pivotal turning points—religion, in its organized structures and ceremonial observances, has catastrophically and irreparably failed humanity precisely when the soul stood most exposed in existential anguish and desperate vulnerability. Time and again it has proffered only outward rites where inward mercy was urgently needed, rigid legal codes where tender compassion was demanded, distant hierarchies where humble, personal intercession was called for—yet never once has it supplied the living, saving presence capable of meeting the broken heart at its uttermost breaking point. At virtually every such critical juncture—where institutional religion has proven not merely impotent but actively treacherous, an insidious adversary to mankind, a recurring nightmare that torments the collective soul with illusory hopes and hollow assurances—God in Christ has stepped forth in triumphant counterpoint, revealing himself as humanity's truest and most steadfast Friend: the genuine Good Samaritan Neighbor who halts on the bloodied road, stoops to bind the wounds, and pours in healing oil where every other passerby has hurried past in indifference. This conviction rests on the same pattern seen in the parable: just as the haughty Priest, cloaked in ritual piety, passed by the wounded, bleeding, dying man without a flicker of moral compunction or compassion—offering no tender care, no soothing mercy that could have meant life instead of death—and the Levite followed with mirrored indifference and cloistered arrogance, so too have the founders, prophets, and supposed deities of the world's religions collectively passed by humanity in her helpless vulnerability—shrouded in spiritual darkness like an impenetrable fog and mired in moral squalor that clings to every step in guilt and despair. Accordingly, Luke 10:30–36 offers a gripping parabolic portrait of this very reality.

Repeatedly proving itself to be nothing less than a cunning, subversive adversary to mankind in its core intent and outworking—and a persistent, soul-haunting nightmare that entraps the collective human spirit with illusory hopes that fade like mist and shattered promises that leave enduring scars—God in Christ has conversely and triumphantly revealed himself as man's truest, most faithful Friend—humanity's unwavering Ally across every age—man's authentic Good Samaritan Neighbor indeed, the compassionate, deliberate Healer who kneels to bind wounds and ease suffering where all others avert their eyes and hurry past in cold detachment. I make this assertion with absolute, unqualified conviction rooted in both scriptural testimony and historical witness because it follows the exact same pattern as the parable: just as the proud, self-assured Priest in the timeless narrative of the Good Samaritan—that cloaked figure of ritual piety and ceremonial pride, arrayed in garments of form without power—felt no qualms, no moral hesitation, no stirring of conscience as he strode past the wounded, bleeding, dying man in his utterly helpless, prostrate condition of desperate need—of tender, restoring care that revives dignity, soothing compassion that heals the soul, and life-sustaining mercy that could have meant the difference between life and death—and just as the Levite followed in the same calculated indifference cloaked in self-protective arrogance, so too have the founders, prophets, visionaries, and self-proclaimed deities of the world's religions—across their shared, accumulated legacy and testimony through millennia—walked past humanity in her helpless, vulnerable condition: enveloped in spiritual darkness as thick and suffocating as an impenetrable fog that blinds the inner eye, and trapped in moral squalor that sinks every faltering step into the mire of guilt, shame, and despair that drains the spirit. Accordingly—in perfect harmony with this profound contrast—Luke 10:30–36 presents a vivid, unforgettable parabolic portrait of the entire reality, a narrative mirror reflecting the eternal truth with brilliant clarity.

SOLUS CHRISTUS: THE SOLE SAVIOR AMID THE FADING SHADOWS OF SPIRITUAL FOUNDERS

Surveying the expansive weave of spiritual history from the inception of religious traditions onward, we behold a long procession of religious luminaries and founders who have risen in prominence only to pass away—none advancing the cause of true salvation, none resolving the deepest existential questions that torment the human soul. Strikingly, every one of them—apart from Christ the Savior—was afflicted by the same universal malady of sin that burdens all mankind; each lived under its dominion, each died as a mere mortal, and none transcended the limits of finite existence to attain everlasting life. Name any religious figure you will, barring Christ the Savior as the singular exception: when humanity languished in soul-rending existential crises—when the storm of sin and suffering raged most fiercely—they all passed us by with the same detached indifference, their silence and inaction cloaking a profound apathy. None stretched out a hand of real, redemptive help; none could deliver us from the tempest that threatened to swallow us whole. Only Christ—the incarnate Son—remains the exception who did not merely pass by, but entered the storm, bore its full fury in our place, and emerged victorious to offer eternal life to every perishing soul. Thus came Muhammad—the herald of Islam whose suras proclaimed submission to Allah, yet offered no redemptive transaction capable of ransoming the soul from divine wrath; likewise Judah the Prince—the redactor of Rabbinic Judaism whose Mishnah codified layers of legal wisdom and halakhic precision, yet bestowed no transforming grace and left the human heart untouched by renewing mercy; Zhuang Zhou—the Taoist sage whose Zhuangzi spun parables of illusion and detachment, answering the soul's anguished cry with serene philosophical indifference rather than transcendent deliverance; Zoroaster—the ancient bard whose Gathas exalted moral dualism in poetic splendor, yet passed by wounded humanity without providing any pathway to salvation. So too went Gautama Buddha—the renunciant whose sutras unraveled the chain of dependent origination, yet withheld the key that unlocks the kingdom of life; Akhenaten—the Egyptian visionary whose Great Hymn exalted the Aten in monotheistic fervor, a partial glimpse soon overshadowed by the fuller unveiling of divine glory; Confucius—the revered mentor whose Analects refined social rites and harmony, yet left the deeper ache of sin unaddressed; Mozi—the universalist whose teachings championed impartial love and equity, yet imposed no light yoke or easy burden. Even Montanus—the ecstatic prophet whose oracles announced new dispensations and fresh outpourings, yet faded without ushering in true renewal; Guru Amar Das—the Sikh patriarch whose contributions to the Granth wove threads of equality and devotion, yet could not mend the fraying edge at eternity's boundary; Philipp Spener—the Pietist whose collegia kindled warm devotion and inward piety, yet unearthed no tree of life to heal the nations. All these—noble, earnest, influential—arose and passed away, their legacies rich in insight or aspiration yet barren of the one thing needful: the power to save a single soul from sin's dominion and death's final claim.

All these luminaries rose like fleeting stars across the firmament of spiritual history, only to fade into darkness—offering doctrines rich in intellectual architecture and ethical insight, yet consistently sidestepping the soul's most urgent plea for salvific deliverance, inward transformation, and abiding eternal significance. Their traditions, though laden with wisdom, ceremony, and moral aspiration, skirted the existential abyss that haunts every human heart, leaving the anguished cry for rescue unanswered; in time, they quietly dissolved into obscurity, never once taking root in the solid ground of genuine, undying hope. It is precisely against this vast, shadowed backdrop that Jesus the Messiah stands forth in the Four Gospels with sovereign clarity, declaring the decisive and unbridgeable chasm: he presents himself as the singular, exclusive Way—proclaiming with unbridled authority, "*I am the [only] Way [to God] and the [real] Truth and the [real] Life; no one comes to the Father but through Me*" (John 14:6 AMP). As vividly portrayed in the Parable of the Good Shepherd in John 10, Jesus draws a razor-sharp, irreconcilable line between himself—the true Good Shepherd who voluntarily lays down his life to secure the protection, safety, and abundant life of the sheep (humanity exposed and vulnerable to the devouring wolves of sin and death)—and the religious leaders of every age, who are likened to mere hired hands with no ownership, no personal stake, and no sacrificial love. When danger approaches, they abandon the flock and flee to preserve themselves, indifferent to the peril of those entrusted to their care. In his own piercing words: "*I am the Good Shepherd. A good shepherd lays down his very life for the sheep. The hired servant—one who is not a shepherd and does not own the sheep—no sooner sees the wolf coming than he leaves the sheep and runs away, and the wolf worries and scatters them. For he is only a hired servant and cares nothing for the sheep*" (John 10:11–13 Weymouth). This stark contrast unveils the hollow core of every religious posture grounded in self-preservation rather than self-giving love—revealing that only the Shepherd who dies for his own can truly save.

A much closer look at the Parable of the Good Shepherd yields a lesson strikingly parallel to that of the Good Samaritan: the religious leaders and their institutional frameworks possess no authentic heart for suffering humanity—still less a heart that pulses in unison with the Father's tender compassion for the lost and the least. Consequently, all their lofty platitudes, solemn declarations, and meticulously performed rituals stand exposed as empty, hollow shells—mere clanging cymbals (1 Cor 13:1), resounding noise devoid of spiritual vitality or life-giving power. They care nothing for us because they do not own us; they share no covenantal bond, no eternal stake in our well-being as the Shepherd owns and cherishes his sheep. Only Jesus Christ—the eternal Son of God—has demonstrated himself to be the true Owner of the flock, and therefore the genuine Good Shepherd who pours out his life in self-giving, sacrificial devotion. There is no profit in turning to any other and pleading, "What will you do for us in our hour of mortal peril?" Their religious posture toward sinful humanity stands in total antithesis to the posture revealed in the life, teaching, miracles, and ministry of Christ—whose divine disposition toward the fallen and dying was that of the proactive

Good Samaritan, stooping to bind wounds rather than passing by. As Paul proclaims with triumphant clarity: " . . . *God demonstrates His own love toward us, in that while we were still sinners, Christ died for us. Much more then, having now been justified by His blood, we shall be saved from the wrath of God through Him. For if while we were enemies we were reconciled to God through the death of His Son, much more, having been reconciled, we shall be saved by His life*" (Rom 5:8–10 NASB2020). In a world where six to ten thousand religions—countless in their variations—vie for allegiance, to draw any sinner into one of these systems without first confronting and addressing the root malady of sin in his heart and life is akin to the priest or Levite in the parable pausing only to proselytize the bleeding stranger to their creed—while callously ignoring the one thing he most desperately required: compassionate care, tender love, and urgent rescue to carry him through the blackest hour of the night.

It would seem altogether reasonable to expect that these towering religious figures—along with the deities they proclaim—being elevated to such heights of veneration, commanding fervent worship, absolute fidelity, and at times even the shedding of blood in their name, would place humanity's deliverance from its fallen, sinful state at the very summit of their concerns—making it a driving priority of their existence. Yet, strikingly and tellingly, however, this central crisis never attains that level of urgency; it proves insufficient to provoke any of them to undertake a tangible, historically decisive act of redemption for the sake of mankind. None steps forth to perform the one thing needful: a sovereign, substitutionary intervention that breaks the chains of sin, conquers death, and restores the lost to God. Blaise Pascal, with his piercing theological acuity, laid bare this very deficiency with unforgettable clarity—exposing the chasm between the pomp of religion and the powerlessness of its founders to deliver what humanity most desperately requires:

> "In order to make man happy, it must prove to him that there is a God; that we ought to love Him; that our true happiness is to be in Him, and our sole evil to be separated from Him; it must recognise that we are full of darkness which hinders us from knowing and loving Him; and that thus, as our duties compel us to love God, and our lusts turn us away from Him, we are full of unrighteousness. It must give us an explanation of our opposition to God and to our own good. It must teach us the remedies for these infirmities and the means of obtaining these remedies. Let us, therefore, examine all the religions of the world and see

if there be any other than the Christian which is sufficient for this purpose."[2]

Pascal's ancient challenge continues to resound across the centuries with undiminished force. When we examine the matter with unflinching honesty, as he insisted, it stands evident that no religion has ever unveiled the true nature of God's love with the piercing, unmistakable clarity that shone forth in the incarnate life of Jesus Christ—nor has any proven itself sufficiently equipped to conduct fallen, sinful humanity back into living, intimate, redemptive communion with the holy God. Yet if any man presumes—or is lifted by popular acclaim—to the exalted role of founder of a faith intended to lead wandering souls toward the thrice-holy Sovereign whose glory is unapproachable and whose moral purity burns with the intensity of the seraphim's flame, then that individual must himself embody the archetype in perfection. He must stand as the supreme envoy, the living paragon of righteousness and virtue, faithfully mirroring the very image of the Majesty he professes to declare.

What confidence can the world repose in a messenger whose own conduct contradicts the divine truth he proclaims? None. The authentic ambassador—the true *beau idéal* of the Invisible—must himself be a living epistle, inscribed in the indelible ink of unswerving integrity, lest the sacred message dissolve into the fog of hypocrisy and the road to holiness be trodden underfoot by those very guides who pledged to lead others upon it.

It is upon this unyielding anvil of impeccable moral character and uncompromised witness that we stand in solemn astonishment and behold how the Prophet Muhammad—despite his widely celebrated eminence and revered historical stature—fell short of the divine standard of exemplariness he professed to fulfill and represent. Far from mirroring the spotless holiness of the Sovereign he proclaimed through prophetic declaration, his life and legacy cast a faint yet distorting veil over the true countenance of the Divine, enshrouding the King of heaven in confusion and misrepresentation. In reality, he did not stand as a faultless herald of eternal verities, nor as a living embodiment of virtue worthy to bear the sacred banner of the Eternal in authentic human form; his testimony proved ultimately hollow, his mission marred by the frailties and shadows of fallen human nature. Now place this faltering silhouette in stark, unrelenting juxtaposition against the radiant archetype of Christ

2. Pascal, Pensées, 1966: Section VII: Morality and Doctrine.

Jesus—the only begotten Son of the Most High, who is the effulgence of the Father's glory and the exact representation of his divine personhood. In him the ineffable Godhead stooped to tangible incarnation, manifesting in full the celestial attributes and the consummate portrait of the holy temperament he proclaimed with sovereign passion and authority, as though the very heavens held their breath in reverent hush. Far more than a mere announcement of "*God with us*" in mortal frame—though that is its core mystery—he embodied the profound reality in its every dimension, unfolding the divine life amid the crucible of human weakness, temporal limitation, sweat, sorrow, and suffering, translating the language of deity into the idiom of our frail existence without the slightest blemish or compromise. No creed, no cult, no founder dares claim for itself the self-subsisting title of the Way, the Truth, and the Life—an autonomous, all-sufficient, self-authenticating path to the Father. Thus Blaise Pascal spoke with unswerving conviction, leaving no room for equivocation: no religion suffices "*for this purpose*"—the sacred labor of forging an abiding, intimate, covenantal communion with the unseen Sovereign of the cosmos, drawing redeemed souls into hallowed nearness with the living God.

The sacred Scriptures thunder this truth with unassailable clarity: "*Nor is there salvation in any other, for there is no other name under heaven given among men by which we must be saved*" (Acts 4:12). Here stands the singular, non-negotiable reality: in Christ alone the separating veil is torn asunder, and the seeking heart is drawn upward into direct communion with the Father's throne. This is precisely why the religionists could not contain their fierce hatred and burning enmity toward the Son of God—because he laid bare and directly assaulted the foundational pillars and structural supports of their religious system, the very edifice that sustained their authority, prestige, and institutional standing before the people. Perceiving him as an existential threat to the religion that constituted their entire identity and power, they responded with merciless cruelty, delivering him into the hands of the Roman occupiers to be crucified as a common felon. But God thundered an emphatic NO—a sovereign, resounding repudiation of all their religious machinations, their hypocrisy, their manipulative schemes, their cynical political alliances, and their naked grabs for control that sought to snuff out the true Light. In glorious vindication, God raised his Son from the dead on the third day following that unjust execution, inaugurating the irreversible dawn of resurrection life. Therefore, once more, let any who lack the true pathway to salvation or the redemptive provision humanity requires to face the eternal stakes step aside with humility from the arena of spiritual claims, withdrawing from the contest and yielding the field entirely to Jesus—the Savior of mankind who possesses both in inexhaustible fullness (see Colossians 1:19). he alone in all the world can place his hand upon his breast in triumphant certainty and proclaim without shadow of hesitation or doubt: "*I, yes I, am the LORD, and there is no other Savior. First I predicted your rescue, then I saved you and proclaimed it to the world. No foreign god has ever done this. You are witnesses that I am the only God," says the LORD*" (Isa 43:11–12 NLT). Fact check: this stands as verified historical reality—eyewitnessed, faithfully recorded, and attested across the centuries.

THE POISONED FRUITS OF RELIGION: INSTITUTIONALIZED IGNORANCE, HATRED, AND PERSECUTION

Furthermore, from the radiant wellspring of moral profundity that flows through yet another of our Lord's incomparable parables—recorded in Matthew 25:41–46—we may turn to these celebrated religionists and the dim, constructed deities of their contrived pantheons and apply the same piercing indictment he pronounced upon those on the left in that eschatological vision. Given their historical neglect, apathetic indifference, and lack of passionate response to sinful humanity across the ages, the charge rings true: humanity hungered for God in spiritual famine, yet you gave no bread of life or sustaining word; humanity thirsted for his righteousness and justice, yet you offered no living water or refreshing truth; humanity wandered as a stranger in alienation's wilderness, yet you extended no welcome or hospitality; naked in sin's shame and exposure, yet you clothed it not with garments of righteousness or grace; wounded by transgression's deep gashes, sick in the soul's infirmity, and dying in the decline of sinful existence, yet you visited not nor ministered with healing balm or redemptive touch. They could scarcely be roused, stirred, or compelled to act—plainly because their religion always took precedence over every consideration of mercy and humanity, establishing a hierarchy that inverts divine values: religion first, humanity last. In effect, religion has chiefly succeeded in institutionalizing ignorance of God's true identity as love incarnate, systematically misrepresenting his compassionate and forgiving nature, and misappropriating his self-sacrificial, redemptive character. Consequently, when we examine the lives and moral conduct of these religionists—both historically and in the present—we find little desire to be associated with the deity they profess, much less to embrace their religion under its oppressive yoke. Compounding this spiritual barrenness, it has fostered institutionalized bigotry that sows division, hatred that festers like an open wound, and persecution that spills innocent blood—often directed against those of other faiths in sectarian zeal that defies reason. And today we witness individuals who would hesitate little before beheading another solely for believing differently—the accusation of being an "*infidel*" or kafir in Islam branding dissent as damnation.

None of these approaches aligns with or reflects God in his essential nature. God is fundamentally about love—particularly his love for mankind, as graphically demonstrated through the compassionate acts and ultimate atoning sacrifice of his Son on the Cross, which seals the new covenant. The unconditionality of God's love is seen in his refusal to harbor malice, resentment, or withdrawal toward those who withhold belief, oppose his truths, or even blaspheme against him—the so-called infidels. He never reaches a point where he revokes his love from the unbeliever, the skeptic, or even the atheist who denies his existence, though that love may remain unreturned for a long season. Jesus unveiled the unchanging essence of God's love and his quintessential Good Samaritan disposition toward all humanity without distinction when he commanded: "*But I say to you, love your enemies, bless those who curse you, do good to those who hate you, and pray for those who spitefully use you and persecute you, that you may be sons of your Father in heaven; for He makes His sun rise on the evil and on the good, and sends rain on the just and on the unjust*" (Matt 5:44–45 NKJV). In truth, God's consistent and overarching manner of revealing his divine love for humankind has always been—and remains—one of gently illuminating pathways that invite the unbeliever to discover compelling reasons to embrace the proclamation of his love and the redemptive salvation he offers, never resorting to their destruction for unbelief or skepticism. This is the very source from which Paul drew his confident assurance: "*If we are faithless, He remains faithful; He cannot deny Himself*" (2 Tim 2:13 NKJV). Ultimately, this truth centers on the foundational reality that the God Incarnate "*. . . did not come to destroy men's lives but to save them . . .* " (Luke 9:56 NKJV). This makes evident that his Good Samaritan disposition toward humanity endures unchanging, impervious to shifting circumstances. While mortals pass through endless fluctuations in their earthly journey, God remains immutable in his constancy. His love for the sinner is not a fleeting whim; it is the deliberate, eternal resolve he embraced to lay down his life in atonement for their sins, even while they remained in sin and estranged from him.

Thus, Christianity stands in radical distinction from those legalistic religions steeped in judgment and condemnation; it boldly proclaims the boundless divine love and the salvific embrace extended to fallen, sinful humanity. Somehow, religion persistently leaves a bitter aftertaste in the mouths of so many—perhaps an indelible trademark of disillusionment that lingers long after the encounter. For countless seekers today, this very bitterness serves as a primary barrier to receiving Christ and the gift of salvation he offers because they mistakenly perceive him as merely another institutional religion burdened with rituals and rules. But emphatically—no—he is not. If anything, he presents the true Way out of religion itself, out of every sour, scarring experience endured under its binding yoke that stifles rather than sets free. Christianity is nothing less than being Christlike in character and conduct; it must therefore be viewed and understood through the eyes of Christ himself, not through the distorted lens of religious legalism and tradition. God desires that all people be seen through the lens of his love—through the magnifying glass of the cruciform demonstration of his love for humanity in his Son, which enlarges every detail of mercy and grace. Our individual and collective failure as a society to view humanity through the eyes of God's love lies at the root of every war and woe that ravages nations, every hatred and bigotry that poisons hearts, and every malice and murder that stains the earth in our world today. Yet until the love of God invades our hearts like conquering grace and spreads across our world like healing balm, true peace in the fullness of shalom may forever elude us. For Christ came to unlock the hearts of all people—great and small—to the Gospel of God's eternal love, revealing its profound depths that plunge into the abyss and its heights that soar to the heavens for all to see and savor. On the Cross, he proved God's love for humanity beyond all doubt, leaving no stone unturned in exhaustive evidence and no room for reasonable skepticism or lingering shadows. That marks the limit of our human story with religion—until God arrived in his Son to set all things right with irresistible grace and power.

REDEFINING WORSHIP – TRANSCENDING RITUALS: WHY THE PERFECT GOD SEEKS HEART-TRANSFORMED WORSHIPPERS

Although most—if not all—religions philosophically endorse the Perfect Being Theory of God as a foundational axiom of deity, the entity they devote themselves to often seems entirely at ease accepting—or at times actively soliciting, and occasionally coercively demanding—worship from sinful, morally flawed human beings in their broken state. This should be regarded as morally repugnant, for it stands in fundamental conflict with the holiness and sublime moral character that must define true deity. "*Our God is a holy God, who dwells in our holy land or sacred temple*," they may declare with confident assurance. Yet the Christian God poses the penetrating question with divine logic: "*Can two walk together, unless they are agreed?*" (Amos 3:3 NKJV)—a question that demands careful reflection, and the answer is clear: no, genuine fellowship cannot exist without agreement in holiness. Hence his clear call: "*but as He who called you is holy, you also be holy in all your conduct, because it is written, 'Be holy, for I am holy'*" (1 Pet 1:15–16 NKJV). Do not claim that the Christian God, as revealed in his Son, is not the single most inspiring figure in human history—he earnestly wants every one of his followers to grow into his likeness in holiness and love. If that is not the hallmark of a truly inspiring leader—one we can follow with confidence, look up to with reverence, and pattern our lives after in genuine aspiration—then who else could possibly hold such enduring, world-changing influence across the ages? In the Sermon on the Mount that forever reshaped ethical thought, Jesus spoke to his audience with unwavering expectation: "*Therefore you shall be perfect, just as your Father in heaven is perfect*" (Matt 5:48 NKJV). He is not merely engaging in religious rhetoric, repeating empty platitudes, or signaling virtue—he is inspiring us to reach for the best, most exalted version of ourselves by deliberately mirroring the divine image and likeness of God in our daily conduct. If you know of anyone more inspiring than him in depth of character and breadth of impact, let me know—I would be eager to meet the one who surpasses the Light of the World.

When we hear testimonies like that of Nabeel Qureshi—who, until his passing, was a devout Muslim before embarking on a sincere journey of truth that led him to Christianity—we must grasp the profound weight of what he expressed: *"I left Islam because I studied Muhammad's life. I accepted the Gospel because I studied Jesus' life."* He even chronicled this transformative odyssey in his best-selling book—*Seeking Allah, Finding Jesus.* This underscores why there is simply no basis for equating the exemplary, spotless life Jesus lived in unwavering integrity, the salvific power of his atoning death, and the triumphant resurrection that followed with the life or legacy of any other religious figure in history's long pageant. After all, one of the primary reasons God created mankind in his image and likeness was so that humanity could participate in his divine nature of righteousness and holiness through covenantal communion with him. We too must press the question with logical urgency: how could these pagan deities and their figureheads possibly be morally aligned with sinful humans in ethical harmony, walking together in fellowship with worshippers steeped in sinfulness—people with whom they ought to fundamentally disagree on the very grounds of holiness? All the while showing no concern or moral unease over the fallen condition that defiles the soul. Something simply does not add up in this equation; perhaps there is something concealed in the doctrinal fine print they refuse to disclose. Once again, none of them bears any resemblance to the Christian God, who—centuries earlier in his covenant relationship with the Jewish people during the Old Testament dispensation of promise and prophecy—made it unmistakably clear that sin was a fundamental, pervasive problem that demanded atonement through sacrificial rite.

He then instituted a provisional means of atonement for sins under the Mosaic Law—a temporary shadow pointing forward to the ultimate fulfillment—awaiting the arrival of his Son, the spotless Paschal Lamb of God, who would accomplish a permanent, once-for-all expiation for the sins of all mankind through the atoning sacrifice of his own sinless death on Calvary's tree. It is abundantly clear that none of these so-called deities from pagan mythology bears even the slightest resemblance to the true and living God of Scripture, nor to his eternal Son, the Lord Jesus Christ. Unlike the capricious idols of antiquity—who descended upon humanity to impose arbitrary ethical rules or ritual demands, or to compel coerced worship—Jesus Christ came with no such agenda. He did not arrive as a tyrannical ruler intent on extracting loyalty or enforcing oppressive legalism. Far from it. As the Apostle John records, when the crowds, in misguided zeal, tried to seize him and force him to become their earthly king, Jesus withdrew alone to the mountain, deliberately evading the very crown that lesser men would kill to seize or die to possess (see John 6:15). Consider the profound irony: the Creator of all things deliberately fleeing any attempt by human hands to deify him. The same humility was vividly displayed during his wilderness temptation, as Luke records. There, the adversary displayed before him every earthly kingdom in a single moment, offering absolute power and glory: "*And the devil said to Him, 'All this authority I will give You, and their glory; for this has been delivered to me, and I give it to whomever I wish. Therefore, if You will worship before me, all will be Yours*'" (Luke 4:5–7 NKJV). Yet the Son of God rebuked him with unwavering authority: "*Get behind Me, Satan! For it is written, 'You shall worship the Lord your God, and Him only you shall serve*'" (Luke 4:8 NKJV).

In that cosmic confrontation, we behold the true essence of this Man—Jesus of Nazareth, fully God veiled in humanity, the incarnate Word who would tolerate no compromise with the prince of darkness. One cannot help but pause in the midst of such revelation, drawing a deep breath of awe, and ask: *What kind of Man is this Jesus?* He stands utterly unique among all the sons of Adam—Emmanuel, God with us, the hypostatic union of full deity and true humanity. He articulated this very truth in his conversation with the Samaritan woman at Sychar's well: "*But the hour is coming, and now is, when the true worshipers will worship the Father in spirit and truth; for the Father is seeking such to worship Him. God is Spirit, and those who worship Him must worship in spirit and truth*" (John 4:23–24). The implication is profound: at the moment of his declaration, the Father had found no such genuine worshipers among fallen, unregenerate sinners, for none could rise to the holiness of his divine standard. Thus, the Lord's earthly sojourn was never merely a philosophical interlude or moral exhortation; it was a purposeful, atoning mission to shatter humanity's moral bankruptcy, redeem the lost, and elevate them into authentic sonship. Small wonder the religious elite of his day regarded him with venomous contempt—despising him with fury as their superficial piety was laid bare. In the sacred economy of heaven, the "worship" offered by carnal, unredeemed hearts registers not as true devotion but as profane abomination—an affront to the righteousness and spiritual discernment of the Father whom Jesus called his own. To that holy Sovereign, such rituals carry the stench of moral corruption, utterly unfit for the purity of his presence. Herein lies the testimony of Christ: from Bethlehem to Calvary, he never once bowed to the norms born of Eden's Fall.

No—he came to overturn them entirely, forging a new creation where worship springs from hearts quickened by grace alone. In Isaiah

1:11–18, we see the ethical posture that befits the morally perfect and righteous God, confronting the profane offerings of wayward worshipers steeped in iniquity. He speaks with piercing precision: "*Though your sins are like scarlet, They shall be as white as snow; Though they are red like crimson, they shall be as wool.*" These words reveal the deep reservoir of his paternal affection, disclosing his unchanging compass: the stain of transgression must be cleansed before the incense of mortal devotion can rise as sweet fragrance in the nostrils of the Holy One. Compelled by divine necessity, God established a means of expiation for human sin—not primarily for our sake, but for the sake of his own name and unchanging integrity. As the perfectly righteous and morally flawless One, he cannot be aligned with sinful humanity, not even under the thin veneer of religion. Thus he declares: "*I, even I, am He who blots out your transgressions for My own sake; And I will not remember your sins*" (Isa 43:25 NKJV). The emancipation of perishing souls from the bondage of reprobation, the complete erasure of guilt's stain—this was the supreme passion of the Son, whom he described as being about his Father's business (cf. Luke 2:49). Rejecting feigned allegiance, coerced worship, or servile drudgery, he descended not as a tyrant but as a bondslave: "*. . . to serve and give his life in exchange for the salvation of many*" (Matt 20:28 TPT). Clearly, he cared far more about saving you than about you serving him—far more about healing your moral condition than about courting your religious devotion. He is utterly unlike those self-proclaimed deities and religious founders who appear perfectly content to leave their followers in their morally fallen state.

Sadly, that pattern has been the modus operandi of virtually every religion throughout history, and it persists unchanged to this day. If religion were to be given a face, that is the face it wears—and it is an ugly one. No quantity of religious platitudes or face-saving maneuvers can redeem religion from its own nature or rehabilitate its deeply tarnished reputation. In the end, one may reasonably conclude that any religion or deity that shows no concern for humanity's sinful condition and displays no compassion toward the human predicament—as we saw so vividly manifested in Jesus—is fundamentally proven false, no matter how many laws it has promulgated or how vast its sacred texts may be. If any is to be deemed worthy of holding a special place in our hearts and lives, it must at least demonstrate genuine compassion and love toward us, proving that we truly matter to it. Yet as far as historical evidence and biblical testimony reveal, only Christ has conclusively demonstrated divine love for all humanity. The all-encompassing love of Christ toward us, coupled with his limitless compassion for our desperate plight, is what ultimately secured him the most cherished place in our hearts—not merely because he is God, but because, though he is God, he was moved by redemptive love to fully identify with our humanity, becoming one like us to offer himself as the perfect substitutionary sacrifice required for the redemption of our souls from eternal ruin. From the lowest depths to the final resolution of the human story, Christ alone—not religion—stands as the first and last stronghold of salvation for mankind, the single unwavering beacon of hope for the healing of our fallen world. For my part, I hold this to be the ultimate litmus test for what constitutes true religion.

CUI PRODEST: WHO STANDS TO BENEFIT IN RELIGION—GOD OR MAN?

Within the systematic framework of Christian theology—particularly in the doctrines of human nature (anthropology), redemption (soteriology), and the person and saving mission of the incarnate Word (Christology)—it is both appropriate and imperative to inquire whether Christianity presents Christ as the exclusive, ultimate, and irreplaceable panacea for the profound existential voids and needs woven into the very fabric of the human condition. As has been carefully demonstrated in Chapter 5, this assertion holds with unyielding certainty: in the christocentric vision of Scripture and doctrine, the Son of God is not offered as one option among competing solutions, but as the definitive, all-sufficient provision for every anthropological deficits that has long characterized fallen humanity. He stands as God's sovereign remedy to the full scope of our alienation from Him—encompassing every dimension of separation, guilt, corruption, and death—and as the comprehensive, once-for-all response to every salvific exigency the human race confronts in its desperate need. By sharp contrast, religion as a universal phenomenon consistently inverts the roles: trapped in a misguided reversal, human beings toil with fervent zeal to supply those very deficiencies they erroneously ascribe to God himself. However, this notion is abhorrent to sound reason and to the plain testimony of divine revelation alike—as though the diligent performance of ceremonies, the strenuous pursuit of moral excellence, or any form of creaturely exertion could ever bridge the infinite gulf that separates finite creature from infinite Creator, or placate a Deity falsely conceived as perpetually dissatisfied, exacting, and insatiable. This stark antithesis compels a question of the gravest consequence: what is the authentic role or purpose of religion within the grand narrative of human existence? The urgency of this inquiry is bound up with a more fundamental issue—*cui prodest*: to whom does religion ultimately profit? If humanity itself is not the true beneficiary of its religious entanglements in every form, then who stands to gain? God, perhaps? Yet this supposition crumbles under sober scrutiny, for the Almighty is revealed as infinitely transcendent, utterly self-dependent, self-sufficient, and self-existent—needing nothing from any created thing, possessing all fullness in Himself alone.

Why, then, do so many religious systems persistently portray God as an entity somehow burdened with needs, as though He stood in want of something that creaturely acts could supply? The answer must be unequivocal: God can in no way, shape or form be said to gain or receive anything from the religious observances of men, for any such assertion would insinuate a defect within the Divine Nature itself or introduce contingency and dependence upon the created order—as if the Almighty had brought humanity into being out of some inner necessity, lack, or privation in himself. This notion stands in irreconcilable opposition to the cardinal Doctrine of Divine Aseity, which confesses that God, in His very essence, is self-sufficient, self-existent, and utterly noncontingent (ens a se). He possesses no admixture of act and potency, no relation of dependence upon anything outside himself; he requires no fellowship beyond the perfect, eternal communion of the Blessed Trinity, and no good beyond the boundless plenitude of his own infinite perfection. Therefore, the true purpose of religion is never to remedy any supposed divine deficiency, but to ordain and direct man toward his eternal destiny—the beatific vision—wherein the creature, having been drawn into the uncreated Light, finds its ultimate rest, fulfillment, and joy in the Creator who stands in need of nothing from it whatsoever.

In essence, the Creator-God stands in need of nothing whatsoever—possessing no deficiencies, no lacks, no requirements of any kind. Yet even if, for the sake of argument, one were to imagine some exigency or want within his being, fallen mankind would remain utterly incapable and unqualified to supply it—being wholly contingent, radically dependent, and formed from the dust by the very One upon whom all existence hangs. This foundational truth rings forth with luminous clarity in the Apostle Paul's address to the Epicurean and Stoic philosophers on Mars

Hill in Athens: "*Men of Athens, I perceive that in every way you are very religious. For as I passed along and observed the objects of your worship, I found also an altar with this inscription: 'To an Unknown God.' What therefore you worship as unknown, this I proclaim to you. The God who made the world and everything in it, being Lord of heaven and earth, does not live in temples made by man, nor is he served by human hands, as though he needed anything, since he himself gives to all mankind life and breath and everything. And he made from one man every nation of mankind to live on all the face of the earth . . .* " (Acts 17:22–25 NLT, adapted for flow). Here the apostle dismantles every pagan notion of a needy deity, declaring that the true God is the self-sufficient Giver who sustains all things and stands in need of nothing from the creatures he has made. One can almost hear him echoing the principle he had earlier set before the church in Corinth: " . . . *What do you have that God hasn't given you? And if everything you have is from God, why boast as though it were not a gift?*" (1 Corinthians 4:7 NLT). Notwithstanding this truth, the prevailing pattern across nearly every religious tradition throughout history has been precisely this inversion: human beings laboring assiduously in service to God, as though their rituals, offerings, and structures could somehow supply a perceived lack or need within the Divine. They have busied themselves with erecting temples, shrines, and elaborate houses of worship—adorned with exquisite art, sacred vessels, and ceremonial splendor—thereby unwittingly reducing the transcendent, infinite Creator to the level of a dependent, needy creature.

Yet the Apostle Paul decisively dismantles this erroneous paradigm, constructing an irrefutable defense of Divine Aseity: God has no needs whatsoever; the works of human hands can never minister to Him in any meaningful way; and mortal creatures, being wholly contingent and dependent, are utterly unqualified—even in theory—to remedy any supposed divine deficiency. Certain translations bring this piercing clarity into even sharper focus: "*He supplies life and breath and all things to every living being. He doesn't lack a thing that we mortals could supply for him, for he has all things and everything he needs*" (Acts 17:25 TPT); and likewise, "*human hands can't minister to his needs—for he has no needs! He himself gives life and breath to everything and satisfies every need there is*" (Acts 17:25 TLB). These renderings settle the question once and for all: the true beneficiary of human religion, in any authentic expression, is unequivocally humanity itself. It has always been so, and it will forever remain so in every genuine encounter with the Divine—the self-sufficient

God who needs nothing from us yet graciously draws us into life-giving communion with Himself. This lies at the very heart of the Christian message: Jesus Christ, through the finished work of his Cross and the triumph of his resurrection, meets humanity at the deepest level of its need—offering divine provision, redemption, and life where we are most destitute. The entire gospel narrative revolves around God's sovereign, self-initiated act of supplying what we could never supply ourselves, in radical contrast to the persistent pattern of religious traditions that portray humanity laboring to satisfy imagined deficiencies or demands in God. Here the roles are decisively reversed: not man striving to appease or fulfill a needy Deity, but the self-sufficient God stooping in love to provide for the creature's every lack—forgiveness for guilt, righteousness for corruption, life for death, and communion for alienation—all accomplished once for all in the person and work of His Son.

This calls to mind a striking episode from the Book of Judges, during a dark season when Israel had grievously forsaken the LORD their God and turned to the alluring snare of idolatrous worship. Into this spiritual famine stepped a humble Israelite named Gideon, who received a transforming visitation from the angel of the LORD. Stirred to holy zeal, he obeyed the divine command to tear down the altar of Baal, burn the sacred Asherah pole, and demolish the pagan shrines his own countrymen had erected in devotion. When the deed was discovered and the investigation quickly traced it to Gideon, the people erupted in outrage. They assembled as an enraged mob, pronouncing swift condemnation upon the young eidoloclast and resolving to put him to death for his audacious assault on their cherished Baal. At this critical juncture the narrative turns on the piercing response of Gideon's father, Joash, who confronted the furious crowd poised to execute his son in defense of their god: "*But Joash retorted to the whole mob, 'Does Baal need help? What an insult to a god! You are the ones who should die for insulting Baal! If Baal is really a god, let him take care of himself and destroy the one who broke apart his altar!*'" (Judg 6:31 TLB). Joash's incisive words instantly quenched the mob's fury, draining their rage and sowing seeds of uncomfortable self-examination. From that day forward Gideon was known as Jerub-baal—"*Let Baal contend*"—because he had dared to dismantle the altar of Baal (Judg 6:32 NLT). Who, except those blinded by unchecked religious fanaticism, could fail to see the force of this observation? Any so-called deity that requires frail mortals to defend, protect, or avenge its honor is, by definition, either a lifeless fabrication or a pathetically impotent and incompetent entity. Indeed, one may argue with compelling conviction that the true order is precisely the reverse: if any gods exist, they ought to be the ones contending for humankind—shielding their worshipers from harm, delivering them from evil, and providing vigilant care in every hour of need—rather than inverting the divine economy to demand servile guardianship from the very creatures they supposedly created.

CONCLUSION

Thus modern religionists should be gently yet firmly reminded: religion began to die a thousand slow deaths the very day Jesus was born—the moment God made an unprecedented, incarnate self-disclosure in his Son. And when that same Son rose triumphantly from the grave, he sounded the final death knell over religion's coffin forever, leaving religion to take its place in the empty tomb he vacated. To speak with wry precision: the birth, death, burial, and resurrection of Jesus Christ spelled R.I.P. for every religion of the world—and rightly so. They merit no more than to be left in peace, for they have never offered any true salvific remedy to humanity; moreover, the God they have blindly sought through the ages has at last come down to us in the person of his Son. It is therefore far more fitting—and morally imperative—that we direct our worship exclusively toward the God who has revealed us as the supreme object of his divine love: not for the sake of religion as such, but for the sake of love itself—not chiefly our love for him, but his infinite, electing love for us as a race. As Pope Leo XIV so aptly expressed it, "*Bringing Christ to others means offering love, bearing witness to a charity that is ready for anything. Only love is worthy of faith.*"[3] This is exactly what we Christians experienced when we opened our hearts to Christ the King of love—or, more truly, when Christ the King, who is Love incarnate, drew us into the wholehearted embrace and acceptance of his love for us. In the apostle's words: "*We love Him because He first loved us*" (1 John 4:19 NKJV). For this reason we may confidently conclude: any religionist who sincerely believes that God requires them to hate, persecute, or harm neighbors who believe differently stands immediately exposed as acting under the influence of the devil and malign spirits, ensnared by false religion. This aligns precisely with what Jesus forewarned his disciples: "*For you will be excommunicated from the synagogues, and a time is coming when you*

3. Pope Leo XIV — Social media post on X, 10th June 2025.

will be put to death by misguided ones who will presume to be doing God a great service by putting you to death. And they will do these things because they don't know anything about the Father or me" (John 16:2–3 TPT). In contrast, the divine disposition in Christianity toward unbelieving Jews and Gentiles alike remains unwaveringly this: "*This is My commandment, that you love one another as I have loved you*" (John 15:12 NKJV). For no Christian has ever been authorized to pursue unbelieving neighbors with malice; every one has been divinely commissioned to pursue them in love—with the glad tidings of God's redeeming love for the whole human family.

Conclusion

The Never-Ending Love Story—God's Relentless Pursuit of a Familial Heart

It is beyond dispute that every true relationship must originate at some foundational point of contact, and the bond between God and humanity is no exception—its genesis is enshrined in the ancient covenants of the OT. Envision these covenants as solemn, formal alliances between sovereign parties or business associates: precisely delineated contractual agreements in which personal intimacy is not merely absent but regarded as an improper anomaly, strictly forbidden and wholly proscribed. The sole binding duty imposed upon each signatory is rigorous, literal adherence to the stipulated terms—nothing more, nothing less, and nothing else. Such was the essential character of God's relational posture toward mankind throughout the long centuries that preceded the advent of his Son, Jesus Christ. Yet these covenantal frameworks, for all their weighty solemnity and divine gravity, have always labored under severe inherent limitations; they have never been characterized by the tender, affectionate intimacy we now know in Christ (to borrow the familiar expression). The most intractable obstacle has always been this: man, created as a free moral agent yet fatally compromised in his moral constitution, has never once possessed the strength or fidelity to fulfill his side of the covenantal compact with his Maker. Despite these repeated, catastrophic breaches that have scarred the vertical bond between God and humanity across millennia, this relationship remains—by an immeasurable margin—the most enduring and resilient tie in all of human history, one that, against every rational expectation, has endured the fiercest tempests of time and persisted through every age. And what has held it fast through every rupture and rebellion? Nothing less than the unconditional, unconquerable love of God—that steadfast, resolute affection that has refused to forsake mankind, no matter what may come.

Amid the apparent tumult of biblical history, a sovereign, unchanging purpose has ever guided the divine romance between the Creator and his singular object of affection—mankind. The narrative commences with the primal covenant established with nascent humanity under the federal headship of the first Adam in Eden's verdant paradise—the Adamic Covenant—followed by the postdiluvian covenant under Noah's headship—the Noahic Covenant—then the epoch-defining Abrahamic Covenant, which sharpened God's unfolding relationship with humanity, and finally the rigorously exclusive Mosaic Covenant with Abraham's natural seed, the Hebrews, who constituted the nation of Israel. Each of these earlier covenants functioned as prophetic foreshadowings, relentlessly converging toward the establishment of the all-embracing, antitypical New Covenant enacted between God and the God-Man himself. For the first time since the dawn of Genesis, this climactic covenant inaugurated a truly filial and familial intimacy between the Almighty and humanity. Herein lies the seismic weight of Christ's sovereign declaration: "*I am the way, the truth, and the life. No one comes to the Father except through Me*" (John 14:6 NKJV). The phrase "*no one*" extends without exception to Jew and Gentile alike. The Old Covenants, though hallowed and divinely instituted, ultimately led only to religion (Judaism as their fullest and truest expression in their time); the New Covenant alone transformed religion into a living, personal relationship. It stands supreme because it uniquely accomplished what no prior covenant could: it was consummated between God and the sinless God-Man under his flawless federal headship, signed in his name alone and sealed by his own blood on behalf of all humanity. He alone—the sinless Man—possessed the moral perfection to fulfill the covenant's demands perfectly where fallen humanity had catastrophically failed. It would therefore be categorically mistaken for any believer to declare, "I have a covenant with God." No—you do not. Christ alone entered that covenant in your stead, for you could no more keep it than Adam, Israel, or any other. In him—the God-Man Jesus Christ—humanity now finds its sole conduit into the deepest communion with the Father, resting securely on the twin pillars of forgiving grace and unconditional love.

Before the advent of Christ, even the most devout worshiped a God known only from a distance, shrouded beneath the solemn shadow of covenantal religion yet deprived of true filial intimacy—unaware that from eternity past the Divine heart had yearned with unquenchable longing for nearness to his creatures as sons and daughters. Thus the Son emerges as both Mediator and Reconciler, the living bridge spanning the vast chasm of estrangement between Creator and creation. In him, for the first time since Eden with crystalline clarity, the full scope of divine-human relations is unveiled as a love story—not man's wavering, faltering love for God, but God's steadfast, unconquerable love for man. On Calvary that love was plunged into history's fiercest furnace and emerged resplendently genuine, undimmed, and eternally authentic. There God spoke to every human heart not with the thunder and trumpet of Sinai, but in the universal language of cruciform love—a tongue unbound by tribe, tongue, race, or nation; a voice that reaches the very marrow of every soul from the depths of self-giving sacrifice. The gospel proclamation—"*Jesus loves you*" and "*Christ died for your sins*"—falls upon the human heart as the sweetest tidings ever uttered, the most harmonious melody ever composed. No historical parallel exists for this cruciform revelation of divine affection. The Cross stands as the one universal language of the human heart, transcending every culture and dialect, the master key that unlocks every soul to the love of God. Every biblical narrative, every doctrine of divine love, flows inexorably toward Calvary as its telos and ground zero—the pilgrim's ultimate destination. The true lingua franca of Scripture is neither Hebrew, Koine Greek, nor Jacobean English, but the love-language of the Cross, inscribed by divine wisdom in the one dialect every heart understands, fluent alike to the scholar and the illiterate.

When the early disciples—unlettered Galilean fishermen—began to speak this language of love with astonishing eloquence, even the cultured Sanhedrin could only marvel: "*They realized that these men had been with Jesus*" (Acts 4:13). They had sat under the instruction of the Master who spoke love more fluently and authentically than any before or since, receiving the Father's unqualified endorsement from heaven: "*This is My beloved Son . . . Listen to Him!*" (Matt 17:5). The crowds clung to his words with rapt delight because love saturated every syllable and every deed, leaving even his adversaries mute with astonishment: "*No man ever spoke like this Man*!" (John 7:46). From Bethlehem's lowly manger to Golgotha's cruel cross, from the cross to the empty tomb, every step of Immanuel was a deliberate stride of redemptive love. Deity stepped forth from eternity into time, from invisibility into visibility, from immortality into mortality, from celestial glory into earthly shame—not merely to reveal himself, but to unite himself eternally with the objects of his affection. As Thomas Aquinas so persuasively reasoned, nothing manifests love more perfectly than the Lover's willingness to be personally united with the beloved; therefore the Incarnation was necessary that God might befriend man in terms of equality and draw us into the love of his invisible perfections. The unparalleled tenderness of this revelation—God becoming man—renders it historically compelling, existentially relatable, and universally receivable. By the Cross, God drew us out of sin's mire with cords of grace and bands of love; he descended into hell's deepest dungeon to liberate captive souls; he translated us into his kingdom of light; he demolished every dividing wall of hostility; and he crushed beneath his heel the serpent, sin, and death in a triumphant, everlasting victory.

Poems by Israel E. Nwachukwu

FALLEN MAN: AN EVER-FALLING RACE

*From the fateful fissure of the first Fall—that archetypal tumble in Eden's shadowed grove, where frail flesh faltered from Father's flawless form—fading fervently in Eden's emerald echo, resounding through timeless twilight; ah, man has never stopped falling ever since he fell at the Fall—he has never stopped falling short of everything else since he fell short of the glory of God's image and likeness in the Garden of Eden. Falling from grace and bound by sin's gravity ever since—fallen man is ever destined to keep on falling until he experiences the againrising and ascension of the Christ. For Christ, the heavenly Man, is the only Man who never fell—the last Man standing in the midst of all fallen men who fell at the Fall of Adam's disobedience into sin. For the primordial apple did not fall very far from the tree after Adam and Eve had allowed God's commandment to fall on deaf ears, eating off the tree of the knowledge of good and evil in the beginning of time, and leaving their descendants the bitter legacy of the fateful Fall that fractured Eden's sanctity, defiled human innocence and severed man's relationship with his Maker (Gen 3:1–7). Alack and alas, Adam, once a highflier, having dug a pit by his own transgression, now finds himself fallen headlong into it, utterly cast down, yea, downcast and doomed downward—grounded and grovelling in a warped world of woe, leaving his descendants doomed to drink down the dregs of his defiance. His kin, rooted in his sin, cannot uproot their cursed condition inflicted by the Fall, forever fallen from his former heights in Eden—**sinners encumbered by sin's heavy yoke—prodigal sons estranged yet ever-called homeward**. Only Christ, the unfallen and infallible Second Adam, graciously takes the fall for all fallen and fallible* *descendants of the First Adam—transplanting the fallen to grace—breaking the agelong vicious cycle of unending fall into moral degeneracy and spiritual darkness in the fractured lives of all fallen men—halting mankind's perpetual descent, and yes, decline into sin's existential void by the shed blood of His cross—raising an ever-falling race trapped in death's fathomless abyss to the empyrean height of everlasting life and glory's radiant light by His triumphant resurrection and ascension. Hark! Yet behold! Christ the Redeemer, in His gracious vigil, "***upholds all who fall, And raises up all who are bowed down***"—For though we all falter and fall—in our shared frailty, where faltering begets falter—falling spirals to fall, we yet shall not be utterly forsaken—for no utter desolation consumes us. For though our path be strewn with stumbles and twilight triumphs of defeat, yet, Christus Victor, in His merciful guardianship, shall cradle the stumbling soul and lift the crestfallen spirit from its lowly bend—upholding us with the right hand of His righteousness. And on the third day, He shall raise us up in His glory—On that radiant dawn, He hymns us heavenward, ever-skyward, haloed in holiness, That we may live in the glorious sight of His presence forever—Beholding, with unveiled faces, yea, face to face, the ever-increasing glory of His countenance—Basking beatified in the eternal splendor of the Beatific Vision—that felicitous facet of visio Dei. Alleluia!* (Ps 145:14, 37:24; Hos 6:2) — (Prose Poem Title: Fallen Man—an Ever-falling Race).

GOD'S MAN-CENTRED CREATION

Let the plants exploit and draw sustenance from the inanimate elements all they can, and let the animals take turns in feeding on the plants without care or limit, and let the flesh-eating predators in the wild feast on the flesh of the prey to the limits of their appetite, but at the end of the day, all roads lead to man's communal table—where flora and fauna are destined to end up in his stomach for a meal—there he consumes without fear or worry of ever being consumed. All the while, the abiotic forces preoccupy themselves with balancing out the ecosystem to make life ultimately conducive for him still—crafting a universe that bows to humanity's sacred dominion. In this Divine order, man is destined to be food for no other—for all are in one way or the other subservient to him who remains unchallenged as the pinnacle of God's handiwork—the supreme masterpiece of the Creator's craftsmanship.

THE RECKLESS HASTE OF HUMANITY'S FIRST REBELLION

For though the Immortal Creator had fashioned them His image-bearers in beginning of time—His immortal image majestically cast upon frail mortal clay—calling them "gods" and "sons of the Most High" God (Ps 82:6–7)—yet, through the grievous Fall, Adam and his descendants are destined to fall the fall of death—doomed to die the death of mere mortals. Their blessed semblance, once radiant with the sacred spark of divine essence, now dimmed by sin's sorrowful sting—their celestial crown of glory cast down to corruption's cruel conquest—their exalted origin humbled within mortality's unyielding grasp—their mortal frame, fated to crumble from dust to dust whence it came, yet ever yearning for redemption's eternal embrace. For by eating freely from the forbidden fruit, poisoned with the venom of rebellion, they fell headlong into sin—cast down from the radiant heights of divine communion into the shadowed valley of sin's dominion. For by defying the Commandment of the Righteous Lawgiver, they fell by the beguiling counsel of the crafty serpent. Sadly, falling into sin equally meant falling into death—for to turn from the eternal Source of Life is to embrace the stark privation of life. Alas, Adam barely even lived before he died—scarcely ever tasted the savoury sweetness of divine life before the wretchedness of death's grim shadow fell upon him. He barely even walked before he fell—hardly ever walked in God's beatific blessing of immortality—before stumbling headlong into the chilling embrace of the serpent's cruel curse of mortality. He had barely even mastered his strides before racing swiftly into sin's treacherous snare—his faltering feet, yet to find their steady pace in the paths of righteousness, were woefully quick to run amok into the perilous pitfall of unrighteousness—echoing the wisdom of the Wise Preacher: ***"A heart that devises wicked plans, feet that are swift in running to evil"*** *(Prov 6:18 NKJV). Adam's heart, way too tender to discern the good from the evil, and feet, way too frail and feeble to stand steadfast in innocence, sprinted toward nocence, as if drawn by some fatal allure to forsake Divine grace. Oh what a mournful misstep, venturing into vice's vile vortex! Revealing the reckless haste of humanity's first rebellion, mirroring the soul's perilous inclination to trade eternal glory for momentary guilt in a moment's reckless choice, ever prone to stray before we stand, ever* *eager to embrace our own unrighteousness before we fathom the heights of God's righteousness. Man, made brute, now a shadow of the man he once was, merely murmurs his Maker's memory. Oh, what a wretched man he became! Who will deliver him from this miserable life dominated by sin and death? Thank God! The answer is Jesus Christ—the resurrection and the life (cf. Rom 7:24–25; John 11:25). (Prose Poem: The Reckless Haste of Man's First Rebellion).*

Bibliography

Aquinas, Thomas. *Of God and His Creatures: An Annotated Translation (with Some Abridgements) of the Summa Contra Gentiles of Saint Thos Aquinas.* Translated by Joseph Rickaby. London: Burns & Oates, 1905.

Athanasius of Alexandria. *On the Incarnation.* Translated by John Behr. Popular Patristics Series 44A. Yonkers, NY: St. Vladimir's Seminary Press, 2011.

Augustine of Hippo. *The City of God.* Translated by Henry Bettenson. London: Penguin Classics, 2003.

Calvin, John. *Institutes of the Christian Religion.* Translated by Henry Beveridge. Peabody, MA: Hendrickson Publishers, 2008.

de Sales, Francis. *Treatise on the Love of God.* Translated by Henry Benedict Mackey. London: Burns & Oates, 1884.

Gibbon, Edward. *The History of the Decline and Fall of the Roman Empire.* London: Strahan and Cadell, 1776.

Kazantzakis, Nikos. *The Last Temptation of Christ.* Translated by P. A. Bien. New York: Simon & Schuster, 1960.

King, L. W. *A History of Babylon: From the Foundation of the Monarchy to the Persian Conquest.* London: Chatto & Windus, 1915.

Maxwell, John C. [@TheJohnCMaxwell]. "Success in life has nothing to do with what you gain or accomplish for yourself. It's what you do for others." X, April 16, 2025. https://x.com/TheJohnCMaxwell/status/1912640649137889433.

Morgan, Christopher W., and Robert A. Peterson, eds. *Heaven.* Theology in Community. Wheaton, IL: Crossway, 2014.

Norwich, John Julius. *A Short History of Byzantium.* New York: Alfred A. Knopf, 1997.

Pascal, Blaise. *Pensées.* Paris: Guillaume Desprez, 1670.

Pascal, Blaise. *Pensées.* Translated by A. J. Krailsheimer. Harmondsworth, UK: Penguin, 1966.

Renan, Ernest. *History of the Origins of Christianity. Book I. Life of Jesus.* Grand Rapids, MI: Christian Classics Ethereal Library, n.d. https://www.ccel.org/ccel/r/renan/lifeofjesus/cache/lifeofjesus.pdf.

Spurgeon, C. H. *All of Grace.* London: Passmore & Alabaster, 1886.

Spurgeon, C. H. *All of Grace.* Grand Rapids, MI: Christian Classics Ethereal Library, 2010. https://ccel.org/ccel/spurgeon/grace.

Spurgeon, C. H. *The Cheque Book of the Bank of Faith: Being Precious Promises Arranged for Daily Use.* London: Passmore & Alabaster, 1888.

Spurgeon, C. H. "The Great Birthday." In *The Metropolitan Tabernacle Pulpit: Sermons Preached and Revised by C. H. Spurgeon, during the Year 1876*, 22:709–16. London: Passmore & Alabaster, 1876.

Worthington, Ian. *By the Spear: Philip II, Alexander the Great, and the Rise and Fall of the Macedonian Empire*. Ancients in Action. Oxford: Oxford University Press, 2014.

Scripture Index

OLD TESTAMENT

Genesis

Mark

Luke

John

John (continued)

Acts

Romans

1 Corinthians

www.ingramcontent.com/pod-product-compliance
Lightning Source LLC
LaVergne TN
LVHW020527100826
845148LV00010B/1370

9798385269440